MW00623355

# The Price Is Wrong

# The Price Is Wrong

Why Capitalism Won't Save the Planet

Brett Christophers

VERSO

London • New York

First published by Verso 2024
© Brett Christophers 2024

1 3 5 7 9 10 8 6 4 2

**Verso**
UK: 6 Meard Street, London W1F 0EG
US: 388 Atlantic Avenue, Brooklyn, NY 11217
versobooks.com

Verso is the imprint of New Left Books

ISBN-13: 978-1-80429-230-3
ISBN-13: 978-1-80429-232-7 (UK EBK)
ISBN-13: 978-1-80429-233-4 (US EBK)

**British Library Cataloguing in Publication Data**
A catalogue record for this book is available from the British Library

**Library of Congress Cataloging-in-Publication Data**

Names: Christophers, Brett, 1971– author.
Title: The price is wrong : why capitalism won't save the planet / Brett
   Christophers.
Description: London ; New York : Verso, 2024. | Includes bibliographical
   references and index.
Identifiers: LCCN 2023037196 (print) | LCCN 2023037197 (ebook) | ISBN
   9781804292303 (hardback) | ISBN 9781804292303 (ebk)
Subjects: LCSH: Sustainability – Economic aspects.
Classification: LCC HC79.E5 C4975 2024 (print) | LCC HC79.E5 (ebook) |
   DDC 338.9/27 – dc23/eng/20231026
LC record available at https://lccn.loc.gov/2023037196
LC ebook record available at https://lccn.loc.gov/2023037197

Typeset in Minion by Hewer Text UK Ltd, Edinburgh
Printed and bound by CPI Group (UK) Ltd, Croydon CR0 4YY

# Contents

# Figures

# Introduction

This book aims to resolve a striking paradox – a puzzle that ultimately is not really a puzzle. That paradox consists of two seemingly contradictory beliefs or propositions existing side by side.

On the one hand, we have been told, the basic economic problem at the heart of the challenge of responding to climate change has effectively been solved. To prevent climate change getting much worse than we already know it will be, the most urgent imperative, it is said, is to eliminate the combustion of fossil fuels. Insofar as the largest share of such combustion occurs in electricity generation, our number-one global priority, it is further said, is to shift such generation from fossil fuel sources – principally coal and natural gas – to zero-carbon sources – principally solar and wind, the ascendant renewables – as rapidly and comprehensively as possible.

For a long time, this was seen as economically improbable, if not impossible, and for a simple reason: fossil-fuel-based electricity was cheaper to generate than renewable power – often much, much cheaper. This basic economic fact stood boulder-like in renewables' way, evidently indisputable and insuperable. But, from the mid- to late 2000s, things began to move fast. The price of renewable power fell dramatically as investment grew and technologies improved. By the mid-2010s, most estimates indicated that the prices of renewable and dirty electricity were rapidly converging; by the end of that decade, most estimates showed the former now being *cheaper* than the latter.

It was, we have been told, an historic reversal. The economic obstacle to the decarbonization of electricity had been swept away. 'Falling cost of renewable energy is leading the race to net zero,' trumpeted one typical headline in 2020.[1] 'Renewables increasingly beat even cheapest coal competitors on cost,' announced a second.[2] 'Plunging solar prices spell bright future for renewables,' gushed a third.[3] Anybody paying even the slightest attention to developments in the energy sector in recent years will have noticed this theme becoming a constant drumbeat of economic and policy discourse.

On the other hand, though, we have been told there *is* nonetheless a problem. One of the main reasons why significant investment in renewables has been occurring for the past decade and more is that governments around the world supported such investment with an array of subsidies and other support mechanisms. These gave the private sector the initial confidence to invest. But, as growing investment through the 2010s precipitated falling technology costs, governments increasingly were minded to reduce fiscal supports in the belief that their job of stimulus was done. Some began phasing down – even removing – subsidies before the decade was out.

Cue panic. No sooner had governments signalled their intention to scale back support for renewables than alarm bells began ringing. Any such scaling back, governments were warned, would be to the severe detriment of the future development and growth of solar and wind power.

The voices of gloom and doom could be heard particularly widely and loudly in the US in 2021 and the first half of 2022. The country's main form of economic support to renewable electricity developers, its tax credits, were scheduled to expire. Policymakers were told in no uncertain terms that, unless these credits were secured for the long term, the result would be a collapse in investment, and climate catastrophe. Notably, these warnings did not come just from renewable energy companies themselves, whose appeals were neither surprising nor

---

1   D. Broom, 'Race to Zero: This Graphic Shows the Rapidly Falling Cost of Renewable Energy', 10 November 2020, weforum.org.

2   International Renewable Energy Agency, 'Renewables Increasingly Beat Even Cheapest Coal Competitors on Cost', 2 June 2020, irena.org.

3   A. Niranjan, 'Plunging solar prices spell bright future for renewables', 28 May 2020, dw.com.

disinterested. Independent commentators also implored US lawmakers to renew meaningful financial support.

The paradox, then, is this. There has been a long-standing consensus that the economic key to renewables winning out is being cheaper than fossil-fuel-based electricity; renewables successfully crossed this apparent Rubicon in the late 2010s, prompting delight that the chief obstacle had been dislodged. And yet, at the same time, the position is also widely held that governments reducing or removing economic support to renewables in the 2020s would have a deeply negative impact on new investment.

Indeed, often the same – seemingly contradictory – beliefs are expressed by the selfsame commentator. In mid-2021, for example, Robinson Meyer, then of the *Atlantic* and an influential US-based commentator on all things climate, could be heard chiding those who claimed the US was failing to decarbonize. It was not failing, he said; it was broadly succeeding. What is more, 'most important of all' to this success had been the fall in renewables costs, which had created a 'positive feedback loop'. 'As technologies develop, they get cheaper,' Meyer enthusiastically explained. 'As they get cheaper, more companies adopt them.' And, Meyer reminded readers, the US had done all this 'without ever passing a [climate] bill'.[4]

Just six months later, however, the same Meyer was mired in self-professed 'despair' at the fact that policymakers had not yet renewed the US's soon-to-expire renewables tax credits. 'The United States', he intoned, 'is on the verge of a massive, history-rewriting failure' – a 'very American climate tragedy'. By blocking the bill that would enshrine the credits, Senator Joe Manchin, Meyer said, had 'virtually sealed the planet's fate'.[5]

But had not the fall in costs already sealed the planet's fate – or at least, the United States' own part in fashioning the planet's climate future – in the other direction, and all without legislation? Meyer, in short, embodied our paradox. That he did so is instructive not so much in pointing up an error or analytical lapse on his specific part. On the

---

4   R. Meyer, 'How the US Made Progress on Climate Change without Ever Passing a Bill', *Atlantic*, 16 June 2021.

5   R. Meyer, 'We're Heading toward a Very American Climate Tragedy', *Atlantic*, 22 December 2021.

contrary: there are few more informed and careful thinkers around on matters concerning the politics and economics of climate change. That Meyer, of all people, internalized our paradox is instructive precisely because it underlines just how widespread adherence has become to the two seemingly contradictory positions that constitute that paradox.

If price indeed drives energy technology adoption, and if renewables are now cheapest, why is government economic support for renewables still so important – or at least, still *seen to be* indispensable? If renewables are now cheaper, why, to make the real stakes clear, are we still in fact failing on electricity decarbonization? For failing, we shall see, we indubitably are, as Matt Egan underscored in the title of an article that, while it was published in 2019, remains no less accurate today: 'Renewable energy is booming. But it's not growing fast enough to fight climate change.'[6] If not to help with price (since that hurdle, it is said, has now long since been satisfactorily negotiated), why *are* the types of economic support for renewables that are provided by governments still required? These are the questions for this book.

I

The main answer, and argument, is this. Viewing the economics of the energy transition and the development of renewable energy through the prism of price results in contradictory perspectives such as those identified above because, economically, the matter is not in fact principally about price. Price is a misleading yardstick for assessing the current and future prospects of investment in renewable energy infrastructure.

This is the main message that the book's title is intended to convey. To be clear, the point here is not that the particular prevailing price of renewable power is wrong – in terms, that is, of precipitating a faster transition. It is that to look predominantly at price when thinking about what makes for a successful (or failed) transition is to look in the wrong place: as an analytical lens on climate and capitalism, price is a siren. Thus the book's argument with those (principally economists) who obsess about what the price of renewables – and indeed of carbon

---

6  M. Egan, 'Renewable energy Is Booming. But It's Not Growing Fast Enough to Fight Climate Change', 21 October 2019, cnn.com.

– 'needs' to be in order for clean power to usurp fossil-based power is not that their *answer* is incorrect. It is that their *question* is. Price is the very wrong category to prioritize analytically.

The better, more meaningful, yardstick is profit. This is what we should be focusing on. The main economic reason why the decarbonization of electricity is progressing so much slower than we need it to, I argue, is that most governments worldwide have effectively outsourced responsibility for developing, owning and operating solar and wind farms to profit-oriented private sector actors, and yet the profits that such actors expect to be able to earn from investment in these activities generally underwhelm. It is simply not a sufficiently attractive economic proposition.

In its third annual survey of the transition away from fossil-fuel-based energy sources, published in 2023, the consultancy Bain & Company asked executives in the global energy sector what principally was forestalling the transition. The concern that rose to the surface was not price. Neither was it the availability of capital – of capital, there was generally an abundance. No. The hurdle was profitability – the capacity to turn capital into more capital. Four out of five executives considered 'the ability to create acceptable returns on projects a main barrier to decarbonization of the energy system'.[7]

As we will see, this profitability constraint also helps to explain why, despite the dramatic falls in costs discussed earlier, renewable energy sectors dominated by private capital nevertheless remain stuck on economic support from the state everywhere one looks in the world. For such support in practice is less about effectively keeping prices down than it is about keeping profits up, and hence keeping the private sector correspondingly eager.

The specific price that looms so large in existing commentary on and understanding of the energy transition is that which economists call the 'cost price' – essentially, the price tag on electricity output at source, or the amount that it costs to produce a given amount of electrical power. This explains why it is referred to sometimes as 'price', other times as 'cost'. Needless to say, to argue that we should set aside the existing emphasis on cost price and narrow in instead on profit is not to suggest

---

7  G. Dougans, N. Phadke, A. Robbie and J. Scalise, 'State of the Transition 2023: Global Energy and Natural Resource Executive Perspectives', May 2023, bain.com, p. 4.

they exist independently of one another. After all, does not the cost price of electricity have a direct impact on the profits that are earned from generating the electricity? Indeed, is it not actually the case that a lower cost price necessarily entails a higher profit, and thus that we are, for practical purposes, talking about the same thing when we talk about the one or the other?

These are two very reasonable and important questions, to which the answers are, respectively: yes, of course; and no. Yes, of course, the amount it costs to generate electricity directly and strongly influences the profits earned from such generation. But, as I will show, there are all sorts of reasons why lower costs of generation do not automatically equate to higher profits. In a scenario associated with lower generating costs, for instance, other costs, which is to say those not related to generation, may simultaneously be higher; what is more, the revenue-generating potential may not be the same in this latter scenario as it is in a scenario of higher generating costs.

Perhaps, if this simplistic equation between generating costs and ultimate profits did actually hold, renewables being cheapest would mean renewables being sufficiently profitable to spur much greater investment in new clean generating capacity than has been and is the case – and might also mean that the cheaper energy source would ineluctably be taking over in the way that is commonly imagined in fact to be true. Perhaps. Under certain institutional arrangements for the production and delivery of electricity, that might just be the case. But those, demonstrably, are not the arrangements we happen to have. One of this book's key lessons is that, around the world, we have historically built, organized and transformed electricity systems in such a way that the substitution of cheaper and cleaner generation for dirty and relatively expensive generation is not guaranteed at all.

At any rate, we talk a great deal in these uncertain and unnerving times about fossil fuel companies making excess profits – and we do so for good reason. But we very rarely talk about renewables companies not being able to make enough.

## II

That we – the world – definitively are not by any reasonable measure 'succeeding' on the decarbonization of electricity is indisputable. It is essential that we clear away any potential misconceptions on this score right at the outset. For, while our ongoing failure on power decarbonization may strike some readers as obvious, others may yet need convincing. Are we not installing more renewable generating capacity around the world than ever before? Has not electricity generation from zero-carbon sources reached all-time highs? These are among the potential objections I can already foresee.

Much of the celebratory commentary that has appeared in mainstream media outlets in the past couple of years would seemingly have one believe that, after a long period of sustained failure to take climate mitigation seriously, we *are* now succeeding, at least where power sector emissions are concerned. 'Record clean-power growth in 2023 to spark "new era" of fossil fuel decline', one headline, for example, recently announced.[8] 'Global wind and solar growth on track to meet climate targets', another triumphant headline has claimed.[9]

But we are not on track. There are numerous different ways to make this basic point, and we shall have occasion to refer to certain others at various points in the book, but, for now, let us focus on a measure that typically serves as well as any other to hold people's attention: money.

In 2021, the International Energy Agency (IEA), the world's leading intergovernmental organization for the analysis of the energy sector, issued an influential 'road map' to achieving net zero greenhouse gas emissions in that sector by 2050. Following that road map, the IEA argued, would be 'consistent with efforts to limit the long-term increase in average global temperatures to 1.5 °C' above pre-industrial levels, as per the 2015 Paris Agreement.[10]

Now, there are all manner of reasons why the IEA's central proposition – that net zero by 2050 in the energy sector would align with 1.5 °C

---

8    J. Gabbatiss, 'Record Clean-Power Growth in 2023 to Spark "New Era" of Fossil Fuel Decline', 12 April 2023, carbonbrief.org.

9    Reuters, 'Global Wind and Solar Growth on Track to Meet Climate Targets', 31 March 2022, reuters.com.

10    IEA, 'Net Zero by 2050: A Roadmap for the Global Energy Sector', October 2021, iea.org, p. 3.

– itself could be, and has been, questioned. For one thing, it implicitly makes certain assumptions, which may or may not be tenable, about progress in reducing emissions in non-energy sectors such as land use change. Should those other sectors ultimately disappoint, progress in the energy sector that the IEA currently considers likely to be consistent with 1.5 °C may end up not being so.

Moreover, the very concept (and goal) of *net* zero is hotly disputed and contested. Net zero is not actual zero. It allows for continuing emissions of greenhouse gases, just so long as they are matched in scale by the capture and sequestering of greenhouse gases, either at the source of their emission or from the ambient air. All existing projections for achieving 'net zero', including the IEA's own for the energy sector, assume that a certain level of such capture is credible and will be achieved. Again, should it not be – and many scientists and engineers have grave doubts – then the IEA's road map for emissions reductions would not in fact be 1.5 °C–consistent.

Nonetheless we shall leave these vital issues aside for now. What did the IEA's road map say about what needs to happen specifically in terms of investment in electricity generation capacity? While there is considerable detail, the road map basically posited two requirements. The first was a more or less immediate cessation of investment in new fossil-fuel-fired generating capacity, unless 'abated' by attached technologies of carbon capture and storage. 'No new unabated coal plants approved for development' was the exact demand.[11] The second requirement was a rapid and sustained increase in investment in new renewable generating capacity. In financial terms? From an average of around $300 billion per annum between 2016 and 2020, global investment in new renewables capacity would need to jump to an annual average of around $1 trillion between 2021 and 2030, reaching $1.3 trillion by the latter year.[12]

How have we been doing so far? Evidently, not well. We failed on 'no new unabated coal plants' at the first time of asking. In 2022, China alone approved two new unabated coal-fired generating plants *per week*.[13] As for renewables, for all the triumphalism mentioned above,

11    Ibid., p. 20.
12    Ibid., pp. 153–5.
13    Centre for Research on Energy and Clean Air, 'China Permits Two New Coal Power Plants per Week in 2022', 27 February 2023, energyandcleanair.org.

the numbers remain bitterly disappointing and woefully inadequate. In the year when the IEA published its road map – 2021 – total global investment in new renewable capacity was just over $400 billion; in 2022, it was just under $500 billion, making for an average over the two years of approximately $450 billion.[14]

Already, in other words, we are far off the pace of investment in clean power that is required if we are going to have any reasonable prospect of making good on our historic failures. If the IEA was broadly right in its estimate that a total of $10 trillion needed to go towards new renewables capacity during the current decade, the simple arithmetic would seem to suggest that the annual average of $1 trillion that that total originally implied has already increased to around $1.15 trillion for 2023–30 as a result of 2021–2 investment falling so far short of its target. Every year of underinvestment increases the burden on later years, insofar as the absolute shortfall needs to be made good. Little wonder that, by October 2022, the IEA had quietly lifted its estimate for the required investment in renewables capacity in 2030 to remain on the path of net zero by 2050 from $1.3 trillion to over $1.5 trillion.[15]

And, in fact, even this simple arithmetic substantially understates the extent of our ongoing failure. Every year in which less than is required is invested in renewables increases the subsequent investment requirement, not only by dint of the absolute shortfall but also because of the delay that it represents. One tonne of $CO_2$ emissions mitigated starting from today is worth more in terms of the future moderation of warming than a tonne of mitigation starting from next year, because emissions are cumulative: the sooner we substitute clean for dirty power generation, the shorter the time period over which the latter is able to continue to do damage. Climate change mitigation is much like monetary inflation in that respect. In the case of each, a dollar today is worth more than a dollar tomorrow.

14    BloombergNEF, 'A Record $495 Billion Invested in Renewable Energy in 2022', 2 February 2023, bnef.com.

15    IEA, 'Annual Global Energy Investment Benchmarked against the Needs in 2030 in IEA Scenarios, 2015–2030', 26 October 2022, iea.org.

## III

Before going any further, it is also necessary to say a few words about the book's scope, both in terms of what it does and does not examine, and, indeed, in terms of what it does and does not argue.

First and foremost, this is a book about climate change and electricity, and only electricity. It does not examine the world's attempts to reduce emissions directly from sources of $CO_2$ other than electricity generation (such as cement production and other industrial processes), let alone emissions of other greenhouse gases. This does, of course, potentially limit the purchase of its claims.

But it would be unwise to underestimate the significance of electricity. Not only is it the single biggest existing source of $CO_2$ emissions, but, equally importantly, the powers that be worldwide have evidently decided that the best way to decarbonize activities such as transport and heating is to electrify them while decarbonizing the electricity systems upon which they will increasingly come to rely. So, electricity – and the speed and comprehensiveness with which it is weaned off fossil fuels – is going to become even more important to climate than it already is. As the *Economist* put it in 2022, the world's current decarbonization strategy can effectively be captured in two words: 'Electrify everything.'[16] Electrification 'does not deliver everything that is needed', the magazine conceded. 'But it delivers a lot.' It would not be going too far to say that the world's mitigation strategy for climate change will effectively stand or fall on the basis of its electricity decarbonization efforts.

More specifically still, this is a book about the economics of particular forms of electricity, namely non-hydro renewables; that is, solar and wind power. It examines the economic drivers of the transition principally *to* solar and wind. It adopts this focus not out of any particular conviction on the part of its author regarding how electricity *should* physically be generated in the future, at least beyond the conviction that such generation should not use fossil fuels except where absolutely necessary (which, as soon as possible, should be never). Rather, it adopts this focus because just as the powers that be have seemingly decided that the way forward is electrification, so also,

---

16  'Electrifying Everything Does Not Solve the Climate Crisis, but It Is a Great Start', *Economist*, 23 June 2022.

in most parts of the world, they have seemingly decided that the way forward will be predominantly solar and wind, suitably backed up by a combination of electricity-storage mechanisms and one or more alternative zero-carbon fall-back generating sources – such as nuclear – for when the sun does not shine and the wind does not blow.

Just as important as these technical delimitations are scalar and commercial ones. This is a book about the development, ownership and operation of market-facing solar- and wind-based power-generating facilities, and the sale of the electricity that is produced. Two key points flow from this. First, the book is not about small-scale 'distributed' generation of renewable power for one's own use, by say community groups or individual households. Such generation has and will continue to play an important role in the energy transition, albeit to varying degrees in different countries. Drivers of the uptake of renewables are very different in that segment of the market; indeed, for the actors concerned, price may well be the key determinant of an investment decision. But our focus will be elsewhere: on the large, commercially oriented, 'utility-scale' renewables developments that, ultimately, will make or break most countries' attempts to decarbonize electricity.

Second, neither is the book about the business of designing, developing or manufacturing the technologies that renewable generating facilities use, such as solar cells and modules and wind turbines.[17] That is a very different business altogether, and one that has been much in the news in recent years, as it has increasingly become a primary locus of tension and even conflict among the world's major regional trading blocs.

That said, the business of such technology manufacture is necessarily a significant proximate presence throughout the book. How could it not be, given that the book is focused on the cost of electricity generation – which, in the case of renewable electricity, is indeed largely the cost of equipment sourcing and installation – and on the profits that ultimately arise?

In fact, one of the most important features of the economics of renewable energy is the close, iterative relationship between profitability in technology production and electricity production respectively. Will

---

17   On which, see especially J. Nahm, *Collaborative Advantage: Forging Green Industries in the New Global Economy* (New York: Oxford University Press, 2021).

Mathis and colleagues recently wrote an excellent, illuminating article about this for *Bloomberg*.[18] Governments' selective scaling back of subsidies to renewables generators in the second half of the 2010s, they noted, put pressure on generators' profits that those generators were partly able to pass upstream to their technology suppliers through reductions in equipment prices. The resulting squeeze on manufacturers' profits, compounded by the rise in costs of raw materials such as iron and silicon as the world reeled from the coronavirus pandemic, eventually saw the manufacturers respond. Vestas, one of the world's largest turbine makers, for example, raised the price of its turbines by on average more than 20 per cent in 2021. The effect? A squeezing of *generators'* profits.

Meanwhile, the book's argument that such squeezed profits represent a clear and present threat to ongoing investment in new renewable generating capacity should not be interpreted as a refutation of the significance of other obstacles to the decarbonization of electricity. Scholars and other commentators have persuasively documented any number of other factors that, to one degree or another, clearly also stand in the way of the shift away from fossil fuels in electricity generation. These range from the success of fossil fuel industry interests and their allies in capturing politicians and regulators, and thus in stymieing the introduction of more effective policy, to the legion bureaucratic barriers relating, for instance, to permitting and grid connection that continue widely to frustrate the speedy development of new solar and wind farms. That it can take as long as ten years to secure the necessary permissions for a new renewables plant has been a more or less constant critical refrain from developers in multiple jurisdictions for as long as solar and wind have been commercial propositions.

No, then. The book's argument is not that these other factors are not material impediments. They plainly can be. Its quarrel rather is with the widespread conviction that such other impediments are the *only* important ones now that the cost of renewable electricity has fallen to parity with (or below) conventional generation – which is to say, the conviction that the economics of renewables are no longer a problem. This conviction is increasingly the mainstream common sense. Implicitly or explicitly, it posits that, if only we can take care of the 'non-economic'

---

18   W. Mathis, R. Beene and J. Saul, 'Wind Power's "Colossal Market Failure" Threatens Climate Fight', 25 April 2022, bloomberg.com.

obstacles – those in the realms of politics and planning – and let markets and profit-seeking firms do their thing, then the transition will proceed smoothly and with alacrity simply because renewables are now cheapest. That common sense, however, is wrong. Economics itself *is* still a significant obstacle, and it is the one explored in this book. More than adequately analysed elsewhere, the role of vested interests, planning sclerosis and so on are here set to one side.

Finally, if the specific lens through which we should *not* be analysing the transition to renewable electricity is relative cost price (that is, the cost of generating renewable power relative to the cost of conventional generation, which is the comparison that is typically made), then what is the right specific lens? It is *expected* profit: the profit that an entity that is planning commercial investment in new solar or wind capacity expects to be able to earn by virtue of that investment. Note here that, while expected profit is, of course, related to actual profitability in renewable electricity generation at the time of such planning, it is not the same thing. After all, the expectation might be for profitability to go up or down.

In other words, the book's argument is not that fossil-fuel-fired generating plants are necessarily more profitable than renewable generation – they may be, but, equally well, they may not be, and, indeed, in large parts of the world during the period of writing this book (principally 2022), they generally have not been. When a commercial entity makes a decision about a potential investment in, say, new wind power capacity, the choice is almost always between wind farm and no wind farm, not wind farm and gas-fired plant, and thus the relevant profitability benchmark is the rate of return that the investor considers acceptable rather than the rate of return on dirty generating assets. However cheap renewables now are, it turns out that that profitability assessment – is the return going to be sufficient? – very often returns a negative conclusion.

Why is that? There is an abundance of reasons. A crucial one, as we will see, is competition: the business of electricity generation, and especially renewable electricity generation, is typically very competitive, which tends to depress profits. Relatedly, such competition tends also to limit the capacity of generating companies to capture the upside of any cost reductions delivered by, to take a non-random example, a shift to cheaper generating technologies, with other contributory factors serving further to constrain their capacity to do so.

But just as important to our story as pressure on profits is their predictability – or rather, the lack thereof. Particularly in countries with liberalized electricity markets, the price at which generators can sell their output is notoriously volatile. This renders investment decision making extraordinarily dicey. How much will it be possible to sell renewable power for? Often, it can be hard to predict a week ahead, let alone a year or more. Expected profitability represents a potential barrier to renewables development, in other words, not just in the sense of sometimes being unacceptably low, but also in terms of frequently being substantially unknowable. Hence one of this book's core insights: that the government financial support we continue to see worldwide for renewables is often as much about making profit visible as about making it viable.

## IV

In developing these lines of argument, this book departs quite significantly from most other accounts on the left of the relationship between capitalism and the climate crisis. Typically, although certainly not always, such accounts assert that capitalism is the problem because capitalism is inherently dirty – that is, destructive of the environment, climate included, by its very nature. 'The social metabolic order of capitalism is inherently anti-ecological', Brett Clark and Richard York, emblematically, wrote in 2008, 'since it systematically subordinates nature in its pursuit of endless accumulation and production on ever larger scales.'[19] Insofar as it is inherently anti-ecological, this argument has it, capitalism not only cannot save the planet but is, endemically, the principal source of its despoliation.

The argument elaborated in this book is different. It, too, suggests that capitalism will not save the planet, but for a different reason. Distilled to its essence, the argument runs as follows. The only things that are inherent to capitalism are the profit imperative and private ownership of the means of production. Renewable power is typically an uncertain proposition in profitability terms, and this means that capitalism – being profit-oriented by its nature – is ill-equipped to deliver it.

---

19  B. Clark and R. York, 'Rifts and Shifts: Getting to the Root of Environmental Crises', *Monthly Review* 60: 6 (2008), pp. 13–14.

Let us suppose, chief economics commentator of the *Financial Times* Martin Wolf recently wrote, 'that it was more profitable to use solar, wind or other renewable sources of energy than fossil fuels. Market forces', Wolf went on, 'would then drive the transformation of economies in a climate-protecting direction on their own.'[20] Wolf's basic proposition? That, whether the outcome is planet-saving or anything else, under capitalism, 'if something is profitable, it will be done'.

This core proposition is surely right. If greening business were more profitable than business as usual, then, certainly, capitalism would comprehensively be going green. As commentators on capitalism as varied as Karl Marx – a leading chronicler of capitalism in its nineteenth-century industrial form – and Matt Levine – a leading chronicler of capitalism in its twenty-first-century financial form – have argued, the substance, or colour – green or brown – of commodity production is ultimately immaterial to capital.

Marx made this case in theoretical terms.[21] A capitalist firm, he said, is, in reality, neutral about 'the nature of its product'. What the product substantively is and is used for – Marx used the term 'use value' to signify this – did not much interest the capitalist: the product could, Marx said, 'be of the most futile kind', just so long as its production and sale generated profit; a true capitalist was 'little concerned' either way. We in society, of course, laud meaningful use values, such as the warmth provided by a blanket or the motion by a bicycle, specifically for what they are; and so did Marx. But not a capitalist: a worker who 'produces for [the capitalist] a mere use value' – a product with a 'mere' use, but not a profit – is worthy of nothing but contempt. Greenness is a use value in Marx's terms. For the capitalist, it is, at best, a secondary consideration.

Levine often makes the same case but in a very different way. In 2013, for example, he wrote about a company that, at the time, was producing both vast profits and vast greenhouse gas emissions, specifically by generating electricity using old steam boiler power plants in California. As Levine described it, the company was, in Marxian terms, capitalist red in tooth and claw. Use values – in this case, electricity – were

20   M. Wolf, 'The Market Can Deliver the Green Transition – Just Not Fast Enough', *Financial Times*, 22 November 2022.

21   K. Marx, 'Theories of Surplus Value', in *Karl Marx and Friedrich Engels: Collected Works, Volume 31: Marx 1861–63* (London: Lawrence & Wishart, 1989), pp. 12–16.

produced only because they had to be; they were not the company's raison d'être. In Levine's words, actually producing electrical power was 'a frankly incidental component' of the business of producing profit; 'if [the company] could have done the whole thing synthetically they probably would have . . . they didn't have any particular interest in doing anything in the real world'.[22] Still less did they care if that real thing was environmentally friendly or not.

Levine's example is instructive for alerting us to an important potential counterpoint to our argument. If what it physically does and produces is not material to a capitalist, what has been physically done in the past *is* material, is it not? All capitalists operate within a landscape of existing physical assets (their own and others'), which, it could be argued, influences the extent to which they can ever be truly neutral vis-à-vis the actual product they elect to produce. After all, what already exists clearly shapes what it can be profitable to do today, and what is done today in turn shapes the economic value of existing, 'sunk' investments. One reason why capitalists continue to invest in brown assets, surely, is that the existing energy landscape is itself predominantly brown – it is littered with steam boiler power plants like the ones discussed by Levine – and this predisposes capital to remain brown, both so that new investments can leverage what is already there and so that what is there can continue to be valorized.

All this is certainly true. Yet the colour remains strictly secondary nonetheless. Capitalism's existing brownness encourages further brownness only to the degree that that is the most profitable path. Indeed, capitalism's oft-invoked 'path dependence' is itself fundamentally a phenomenon of profit palimpsests. The history of all hitherto existing capitalist societies, one might say, is the history of layers of exchange values, not 'mere' use values – as mediated, needless to say, by class struggle.

The point is this. The environmental impact of capitalism is contingent, not fundamental. If it is true that contemporary capitalism unavoidably destroys the environment, then it is true only in an indirect sense: which is to say, because the underlying search for profit – capital's true animus – and thus for growth itself happens to be environmentally destructive.

---

22  M. Levine, 'Electricity Market Rules Did Not Provide a Worthy Opponent for JPMorgan's Brainpower', 30 July 2013, dealbreaker.com.

The likes of Exxon and Chevron continue predominantly to drill for hydrocarbons instead of investing in renewables not because they and their executives especially love oil, but because they love money, and, indeed, at the time of this writing in early 2023, such companies are drowning in hydrocarbon profits courtesy of inflated oil prices.[23] The commodity – with its particular use value – in this case is but a means to a more fundamental end, namely making profit. That is true of all capitalist commodities, including, of course, the commodity that is money itself.

Not only, moreover, does the left often err in its explanation of why actually existing capitalism has proven so damaging to the environment in general and climate in particular, but, equally, it also often errs in its explanation of what little greening of capitalism has occurred thus far. 'The advent of green capitalism', Jake Bittle, for instance, claimed in mid-2022, 'is the result of a single overwhelming fact: clean energy is good business.'[24] Yet this is simply not true. As we shall see, clean energy – or at least, the capitalist production of clean electricity – is ordinarily not a very good business at all.

The advent of 'green capitalism' (such as it is), rather, is the result principally of government support helping to make clean energy a business that is just about sufficiently profitable to attract investment, combined with a certain willingness in some capitalist quarters to accept lower returns, either in the expectation that green profits will eventually be substantially forthcoming, and thus that there is long-term economic value in establishing first-mover advantage and market leadership, or – whisper it – in the service of delivering the use value of greenness.

Investment in renewable energy capacity around the world has, it turns out, always danced disproportionately to the tune of state subsidy. In the US, for example, as Ross McCracken and Housley Carr observed in 2016, 'the rate of new build for solar and wind has historically been heavily influenced by [tax] credits – booming when certainty exists and stalling when it does not'.[25] Little wonder that the most immediate

---

23    J. Jacobs, 'Exxon and Chevron Share $100bn in Profit after Surge in Oil Prices', *Financial Times*, 1 January 2023.

24    J. Bittle, 'Everything Has Changed: Green Capitalism and the Climate Left', 14 June 2022, thedriftmag.com.

25    R. McCracken and H. Carr, 'Wind Blows Ill for Natural Gas in Texas', *Platts Energy Economist*, 1 February 2016. Their observation built upon academic research

consequence when US policymakers did finally renew the country's renewables tax credits in the summer of 2022, through the passage of the Inflation Reduction Act (IRA), was a sharp jump in the share prices of clean energy companies.

And it is important to emphasize that there is, in all of this, a notable and enormously enlightening and suggestive historical symmetry, or, rather, mirror image. Capitalism originally turned *to* fossil fuels – specifically, coal – in early nineteenth-century England principally because they helped to make the main commercial, energy-intensive activity of the day, which was cotton production, more profitable.[26] Today, in turn, the world's most greenhouse-gas-emissions-intensive commercial activity is electricity generation, and, in electricity generation, capitalism is failing to turn *away* from fossil fuels sufficiently fast because clean alternatives for that activity are not proving profitable enough.

## V

Among the major shareholders particularly enthused by the US's 2022 IRA in view of its expected impact on clean energy profits was the world's largest asset manager, BlackRock, and its chief executive, Larry Fink.

Like many other major investment firms, BlackRock in recent years has been fighting fires on two simultaneous fronts. On the one hand, it has tried to persuade one group of sceptics – those who highlight the continued presence in its portfolio of vast holdings of fossil-fuel-based assets – that it is, in fact, committed to investment in green enterprise. On the other hand, it has sought to reassure a whole other type of sceptic that its putative commitment to supporting green enterprise is not coming at the cost of financial returns – that is, that it remains a pure financial capitalist and is not in fact (to use Fink's word) 'woke'.

---

substantiating exactly this relationship. See, for example, M. J. Barradale, 'Impact of Public Policy Uncertainty on Renewable Energy Investment: Wind Power and the Production Tax Credit', *Energy Policy* 38 (2010), pp. 7698–709.

26   A. Malm, *Fossil Capital: The Rise of Steam Power and the Roots of Global Warming* (London: Verso, 2015).

The IRA, as Fink saw it, presented a rare opportunity for BlackRock to satisfy both camps. If, during the coming decade over which policymakers have extended the US's renewables tax credits, BlackRock were to invest heavily in renewables enterprises, it would not only please those who *want* the firm to be 'woke', and to put the planet before profit; it would also please – or at any rate, not risk alienating – those who insist, by contrast, that BlackRock's only duty is to maximize investor returns. Because now, bolstered by the US government's support, generating renewable power would become much more profitable, and so also, by extension, would be the business of investing in companies in that sector. 'Those types of subsidies that are coming from the government to invest in decarbonization,' Fink said in December 2022, 'it's going to produce 12, 13, 14 percent returns very easily.'[27] Returns of such a magnitude, as we will see, are comfortably higher than those traditionally available in renewables.

The financial sector, including firms like BlackRock, looms especially large in the story that this book tells, and it is important to explain, at the outset, precisely why that is. Inasmuch as this is a book above all about investment, of course financial institutions and markets would play an important part, whatever the industry sector was: whether it is planes or pianos, marshmallows or microchips, investment always means money, and money is the financial sector's stock-in-trade. But the finance sector turns out to be disproportionately significant in the world of renewable electricity. Why?

While there are, as we shall see, numerous reasons, the most important is that, unlike many companies in other industry sectors, renewables operators generally do not have the luxury of funding major new capital expenditure out of operating cash flow. Perhaps the best and most striking comparison here is with oil and gas companies such as Exxon and Chevron, which enjoy exactly that luxury. In recent decades, the hydrocarbon 'majors' have been able to fund the lion's share of new exploration and development using profits from existing operations, relying only minimally on external financing. Indeed, increasingly, they have more money than they know what to do with. Under growing

---

27  Cited in K. Aronoff, 'BlackRock's Larry Fink Shows Just How Ridiculous GOP Fearmongering about Sustainable Investing Really Is', 2 December 2022, newrepublic. com.

pressure not to invest where, on profitability grounds, they would like (that is, in new oil and gas fields), and disinclined, on the selfsame profitability grounds, to invest where others want them to (namely in clean energy), Exxon and its peers have instead been returning profits en masse to shareholders via dividends and stock buybacks. They have, in short, been giving the finance sector far more cash than they take from it.[28]

Companies in the business of renewable electricity generation generally find themselves in very different financial circumstances. It is very rare for them, in contrast, to have at hand anything like the amount of capital needed to build a new solar or wind farm. This is partly because they are, on average, much younger than, say, oil and gas companies, and, therefore, have not had comparable time and opportunity to build up cash reserves. But it is also partly because of the very economic fact that this book centrally substantiates, which is that renewable electricity generation, unlike oil and gas production, tends not to be a very profitable business. To try to make profit, firms that are not themselves profitable must invest others' capital – usually supplied by financial institutions.

Hence this book is as much about the finance sector as it is about the energy sector. More specifically, it is about the profitability-related concerns, calculations, expectations and requirements of financial institutions as much as about those of electricity businesses themselves. This stands to reason. If a renewable energy developer needs capital from a financial institution of some kind in order to be able to proceed with a new power plant, then it is, ultimately, finance capital that decides whether the development will go ahead or not, and thus it is finance capital's motivations and machinations to which we must principally attend.

As excitement about 'ESG' (environmental, social and governance) investing has mounted over the past decade, there has been growing discussion about the volume of ethically minded capital ostensibly standing ready to support green investment opportunities as and when they arise. In 2021, for example, the UK's then Chancellor Rishi Sunak conjured the image of a 'historic wall of capital for the net-zero transition'. The following year, Mark Carney, previously governor of the Bank

---

28   B. Christophers, 'The End of Carbon Capitalism (as We Knew It)', *Critical Historical Studies* 8 (2021), pp. 239–69.

of England and chair of the international Financial Stability Board (FSB), but since 2020 taking the finance sector's coin in his role as head of ESG investing at Brookfield Asset Management, similarly invoked a 'wall of opportunity in just rolling out clean energy at scale'.[29]

But, as Carney's one-time colleague at the FSB, Dietrich Domanski, reminded people in early 2023, the small matter of profit remains something of a thorn in ESG's side. Yes, Domanski told the *Financial Times*, there is a significant amount of investment capital interested in the possibility of supporting decarbonization and other green developments. But, he added, without 'profits or profit expectations, there is a limit to what one can expect'.[30] His principal message regarding banks and asset managers? 'In the end we are talking about profit-orientated institutions.' It is an obvious point, perhaps, but one that is sometimes forgotten nonetheless.

The reality, then, is this. To be sure, there are plenty of financial institutions, with plenty of capital at their disposal, who are indeed very keen to invest in assets, projects and companies with genuine environmental bona fides, including wind and solar operators. Any meaningful dialogue with the institutions concerned serves to substantiate this fact, and stands as a corrective against blanket accusations of 'greenwashing'. Equally, and just as importantly, in most countries there is, in the renewables space at least, no shortage of proposed developments whose sponsors are attempting – sometimes desperately – to tap such investment capital.

The issue is in bringing the two together. The developments that renewables project sponsors propose to capital-rich financial institutions all too frequently are not considered suitable, investible or – to use the word favoured by the finance sector – 'bankable'. And, invariably, the primary reason is exactly the one alluded to by Domanski: 'bankable' essentially means 'expected to be profitable'. Hence a different metaphor is in fact needed to capture the nature to date of the all-important relationship between finance capital on the one hand and renewable energy on the other. Alastair Marsh has provided that better

---

29   Both cited in A. Marsh, 'A Dam Is Holding Back Net Zero's "Wall of Capital"', 22 November 2022, bloomberg.com.

30   Cited in L. Noonan, 'Banks Need Financial Prod to Tackle Climate Change, Warns Chief Supervisor', *Financial Times*, 1 January 2023.

metaphor. 'The "wall of capital" that was supposedly coming to finance the global energy transition', Marsh succinctly put it, 'has proven to be more of a dam.'[31]

## VI

Does any of this matter? And if so, how, and why? Before ending this introduction and beginning the book proper, it is worth briefly addressing this question. What might the reader hope to take away from the book in terms of key implications? What are the stakes?

The book's findings and arguments are relevant principally for two sets of significant issues. First, they clearly bear on understandings of and claims about the economics and drivers of the energy transition. An enormous amount has been, is being and will continue to be said and written about the main forces shaping the nature, speed and scope of humanity's stuttering response to the climate crisis. This book says something a bit different. If its content has any substantive credibility, then that matters.

Second, the book is also potentially significant for how the energy transition is being and will be governed and organized in practice; in other words, for the political economy of climate. If the economics of the shift away from fossil fuels and into renewables in electricity generation are not in fact what we thought they were – if, that is, it is not simply a question of keeping renewables at or below cost parity with conventional methods of generation – then perhaps the institutional arrangements within which that shift is occurring, and which are, presumably, designed to hasten that shift, are suboptimal and need to be reconsidered.

Let us take the two matters in turn, although, of course, they are in reality closely interconnected, for how energy economics is written and talked about indelibly colours energy's governance.

First, the point of contesting the prevailing dominance of the relative-prices thesis – which is to say, the conviction that it is relative cheapness that decides which energy sources win out – is emphatically not to suggest that the newfound relative cheapness of solar and wind

---

31    Marsh, 'A Dam Is Holding Back Net Zero's "Wall of Capital" '.

power is not a good thing; nor is it to suggest that renewables are not in fact now cheap. They generally are cheap, and that is, indeed, a wonderful thing. As many have argued, not only should cheap and abundant energy for all be the aim, but, given the rapid historical progress in technology development referred to earlier, such a utopia is increasingly within our grasp.[32] Rather, the point of this book is to accentuate the mistake of presuming that simply *because* renewable power is relatively cheap, it will be built. For good or ill, that is not the way capitalism works.

Just as importantly, to argue that the relative-prices thesis is wrong is not to gainsay its undoubted positive rhetorical significance in the climate debate to this point. As we will see, opposition to renewable energy around the world has, in many places, been deep and obdurate, and well-funded to boot. For many years, one of the main arguments against renewable electricity levelled by its opponents concerned precisely its cost: it cost more – sometimes much more – to generate power from wind and solar than, say, from coal, the argument went, and the subsidies that governments therefore used to make renewables competitive, it was further argued, violated principles of economic efficiency while placing an undue burden on consumers, taxpayers or both.

As the price of renewables has fallen, however, this oppositional argument has lost much of its potency. Even if it is not true that being cheaper will necessarily lead to victory for renewables, the fact that they are (generally) cheaper has helped to defang the cost-based critique, and the more that commentators and politicians have publicly highlighted this cheapness, the weaker the logical ground under the denialists has become.

Yet even as the argument around renewables' cheapness has been and still is somewhat useful rhetorically, it is nonetheless flawed analytically. This means two things. The first is that the thesis is certainly invalid as a guide to what is happening and to what is likely to happen by way of the rollout of new renewable capacity. The second is considerably more important. We are living at a time when governments around the world are widely endeavouring to withdraw economic support for renewables, and, correspondingly, are moving towards increasingly marketized

---

32   See, for instance, E. Klein, 'The Dystopia We Fear Is Keeping Us from the Utopia We Deserve', *New York Times*, 8 January 2023.

systems for electricity generation and delivery – and when they are doing both of these things, moreover, *explicitly because they believe that the relative-prices thesis is right*. In such a context, it is positively dangerous to assume – wrongly – that capital and the price mechanism will save the day.

This brings us then to the potential implications of the book's arguments specifically for the political economy of the energy transition. If the argument that cheapness wins out is erroneous, it is also, perforce, misleading in terms of informing people's views about what, politically and institutionally, needs to be done.

Renewable electricity generation is a business perennially plagued by investor doubts about expected profits, and this is the reason why economic support from the public sector, as we will see, remains integral to sustaining the appetite for investment in new solar and wind capacity more or less everywhere in the world. In a nutshell, these are the book's main findings.

But, of course, very different conclusions about advisable political-economic action can be drawn from these findings. One conclusion would be, and indeed widely is, to say the following: insofar as expected profits are, and are likely to remain, a problem, it is essential that governments continue to provide the same fulsome support that they historically have. That way, we can be confident that markets and private capital will ultimately deliver.

A very different conclusion, however, would be this. Insofar as capital and markets still seemingly cannot do without government subsidy, despite the historic fall in costs that was widely expected to remove the need for such support, we clearly should not in fact be relying on markets and the private sector to deliver the energy transition in the first place. They have been given the opportunity and found wanting. In short, it is the wrong model.

At this point, no more on the matter will be said; it is enough to identify and foreground the stakes. In any event, readers hoping to come away from the book with a judiciously argued five-point action plan as to how electricity systems and the decarbonization of electricity *should* be politically and economically organized will be disappointed. This is a book not about what *will* save the planet, but rather about what will not, and why. It is quite long enough as it is, and formulating a coherent and informed set of proposals for the reorganization of our energy systems would likely require at least as many pages again, not to mention that it is beyond the ken of this author.

Nevertheless, between the two alternative stylized responses outlined above to the maladaptive nature of our existing arrangements, it will be clear enough, by the book's final chapters, where my inclinations lie. My hope is that the book's arguments are sufficiently strong and compelling to enable the reader to better navigate debates around the economics and politics of climate crisis and energy transition, which are heated and complex enough as it is, and which are bound to become even more so as the temperature inexorably rises in the years ahead.

# 1

# Electric Dreams

Led by a man named Stephen Gaskin, in 1970 a group of disaffected residents of San Francisco headed east in search of cheap land and a different lifestyle. They settled in the hill country of Tennessee, establishing what became known simply as 'the Farm' – a commune striving for self-sufficiency, whose members initially lived in converted school buses and surplus army tents, which in the winter were heated by wood stoves. The commune rapidly developed into something altogether more modern, however. By the later part of the decade, with some 1,200 members now living mainly in cottages and chalets supplied by electricity and hot and cold running water, the Farm had begun to attract national media attention.

Visiting in 1979, the *Washington Post*'s Alice Alex learned that the specific foundations of the commune's successful operating model were 'soybeans and solar power'.[1] It harvested large quantities of both. And its members' ambitions for this model extended far beyond the commune's borders. 'You've heard what they say here,' one recent arrival told Alex. '"We're out to save the world." There's nothing wrong with that, now is there? For all I know, they might even do it.'

---

1  A. Alex, 'A Commune's Last Stand in the Tennessee Hill Country', *Washington Post*, 20 May 1979.

I

Fast-forward half a century from the 1970s, and the idea that developing clean-electricity-generating solar and wind capacity is essential to 'saving the world' from impending climate catastrophe is both widely voiced and widely accepted. It is not the be-all and end-all of cutting harmful emissions of greenhouse gases, by any means. But it plainly *is* paramount. 'Carbon-free electricity is the key to our efforts to achieve zero net emissions overall,' observed Australia's Ross Gittins in 2020, for example.[2] 'It's all about clean electricity,' concurred Bill McKibben, the influential US environmentalist, on Twitter the same year.[3]

Each commentator was articulating an axiom long espoused by the world's leading intergovernmental organizations both of climate science and of energy policy. In all credible 'mitigation scenarios with deep cuts of greenhouse-gas emissions', the Intergovernmental Panel on Climate Change (IPCC) has recognized, the electricity sector indeed plays a 'major role'.[4] Or, as the International Energy Agency (IEA), more pithily, has put it, 'The electricity sector is key to tackling climate change.'[5]

What is much less frequently articulated, however, is exactly *why* the electricity sector in general – and the build-out of solar and wind power capacity in particular – are so central to humanity's flailing attempts to mitigate climate change. It turns out that the explanation is multifaceted, and bears elaborating carefully, in steps. That is the primary goal of this chapter.

Nor, meanwhile, is it adequately recognized very often quite how formidably difficult the necessary transformation of the electricity sector actually is. The obstacles to that transformation are legion and come in various forms. Some have already received substantive attention from academics and other experts. Foremost among these are the technological obstacles – effectively decarbonizing immensely complex networked

---

2   R. Gittins, 'Zero Net Carbon Choice: Do We Want to Be Losers or Winners?', *Sydney Morning Herald*, 29 January 2020.

3   B. McKibben, 5 March 2020, twitter.com/billmckibben.

4   IPCC, *Climate Change 2014: Mitigation of Climate Change. Contribution of Working Group III to the Fifth Assessment Report of the Intergovernmental Panel on Climate Change* (Cambridge: Cambridge University Press, 2014), p. 559.

5   International Energy Agency (IEA), 'Secure and Efficient Electricity Supply during the Transition to Low-Carbon Power Systems', 2013, oecd-ilibrary.org, p. 1.

infrastructures is a daunting proposition in purely technical terms – and political obstacles – not least in the shape of concerted resistance to decarbonization on the part of vested interests in and around the fossil fuel industrial complex. While we will necessarily touch on such technological and political obstacles in later chapters, the principal focus of those chapters is on impediments in a domain that has been much less studied, and indeed which is typically (and increasingly) held to pose no significant difficulties at all. That, of course, is the economic domain.

First, though, in the present chapter, we adumbrate the sheer scale of the challenge. How much clean, carbon-free power-generating capacity is the world likely to need (and where), if we are to come anywhere close to remaining within temperature bands considered existentially bearable? How far 'behind the curve' do we currently stand in this regard? And to what extent are we catching up – or, rather, falling further behind?

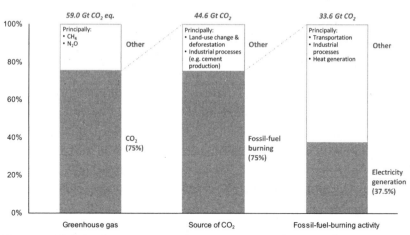

**Figure 1.1** Global anthropogenic greenhouse-gas emissions by type and source, 2019
*Source*: IEA, IPCC

At this stage of history, it is, perhaps, to state the blindingly obvious, but contemporary climate change – global warming – is caused by the emission of greenhouse gases from human activities (so-called 'anthropogenic' emissions) (Figure 1.1). The gas whose emission causes the most damage is carbon dioxide ($CO_2$). In turn, the bulk of anthropogenic $CO_2$ emissions derive from the burning of fossil fuels – coal, oil and natural gas. And the single activity responsible for the burning of most fossil fuels is electricity generation. This, then, more than anything, explains why the electricity sector is so pivotal to the project of climate change mitigation. We need, above all else, to wean the world off fossil fuels, and decarbonizing electricity generation is necessarily the lynchpin of that enterprise.

What, as things stand, is electricity primarily used for? While new uses for electricity are being developed all the time (a trend we shall have cause to explore in detail later in the chapter), the reality is that electricity is used ('consumed') today for much the same things, and by much the same end users, as it was half a century ago. The biggest consumer is the industrial sector, which uses electricity to operate anything from motors to computers and to enable the lighting, heating, cooling and ventilation of industrial facilities. The next-largest end user sector is households, which use electricity for heating, cooling and light-ing, and to power various domestic appliances. The third and final main consuming sector comprises what the IEA labels 'commercial and public services', for which the heating, cooling and lighting of office buildings and the operating of information and communication technologies are the main uses.

Together, these three sectors account today for approximately 90 per cent of electricity use worldwide; the other approximately 10 per cent is consumed mainly in transport, agriculture and fishing. That headline figure has barely changed in recent decades: in the mid-1970s, the three main user sectors consumed 92 per cent of electricity globally. The only significant change has been in the distribution of consumption between the three. The share of overall global electricity used in industry has fallen (from over 50 per cent to approximately 40 per cent), while proportionate consumption has increased in the residential sector (from roughly 23 to 27 per cent) and especially in the commercial and public services sector (from roughly 15 to 21 per cent).[6]

The burning of fossil fuels to generate electricity is incredibly emissions-intensive. In all plants powered by fossil fuels, the basic

---

6   IEA, 'World Electricity Final Consumption by Sector, 1974–2019', 26 October 2022, iea.org.

mechanism for producing electricity is creating pressure that causes turbines to spin; the turbines are connected to generators, which convert the mechanical energy of turbine rotation into electrical energy. Coal- and oil-fired plants use steam turbines: the fuel in question is burnt to heat water and thus produce pressurized steam. Some gas plants also use steam engines, while others use gas turbines. Here, the gas combusts in the presence of air, and the expansion of the heated air causes the turbine to rotate.

In being burnt to produce electricity, the different fossil fuels create varying amounts of residual $CO_2$. This pollution is typically quantified in terms of mass of emissions per kilowatt-hour of electricity generated. One kilowatt (kW) is a thousand watts, a watt being the basic unit of measurement of the amount of electricity produced by a generator; and one kilowatt-hour (kWh) represents the generation – or, from the side of the user, the consumption – of one kW over the course of one hour. The dirtiest fossil fuels, leading to the greatest amount of harmful emissions, are coal and oil. For every kWh of electricity generated from the burning of coal or oil in the US in 2021, for example, more than two pounds of $CO_2$ were emitted. Considerably less polluting, but nonetheless still a fossil fuel and still very much a source of greenhouse gas emissions, is natural gas. Its 2021 US emission factor was approximately one pound of $CO_2$ per kWh.[7]

These data begin to help us explain the colossal $CO_2$ emissions of the global electricity sector, for one of the dirtier fossil fuels – coal – also happens to be the one that is most widely used to produce electric power. In 2022, coal accounted for 36 per cent of all electricity production globally, and 59 per cent of electricity generated through the burning of fossil fuels; the equivalent figures were 22 per cent and 36 per cent respectively for natural gas, and 3 per cent and 5 per cent respectively for oil.[8] Combine coal's majority share of fossil-fuel-based electricity generation with its greater emissions intensity and you end up with stark figures for its share of emissions. Of the estimated 12.3 gigatonnes (Gt) of $CO_2$ emitted through global electricity generation in 2020, as

7  US Energy Information Administration, 'How Much Carbon Dioxide Is Produced per Kilowatthour of US Electricity Generation?', 25 November 2022, eia.gov.

8  See ourworldindata.org/electricity-mix. Unless explicitly noted otherwise, in this chapter all cited data pertaining to electricity supply and demand globally or for different world regions or individual countries are taken from this source.

much as three-quarters (9.1 Gt) was from coal-fired generation, versus 2.7 Gt from gas-fired plants and 0.6 Gt from oil-fired facilities.[9]

Two aspects of the mix of fossil fuels used in electricity generation warrant particular attention, the first geographical and the second historical. Both are integral to the wider arc of the argument developed in this book. The former concerns significant regional differences around the world in how electricity is produced. Consider coal's varying use, in particular. Where I live, in Sweden, coal no longer plays any significant part in electricity production. In Italy, meanwhile, coal presently (in 2022) stands for around 8 per cent of production. The figure is much higher in the US (19 per cent) and higher still in Germany (31 per cent). But even these figures are below the above-mentioned global average. The latter is explained by coal's dominance in a handful of crucial, highly populous territories. In South Africa, for instance, around 85 per cent of electricity comes from coal-fired plants. But the two really pivotal countries are China and India – the two largest electricity markets in the Asia-Pacific region, where, in 2022, coal generated around 61 and 74 per cent of electricity respectively.

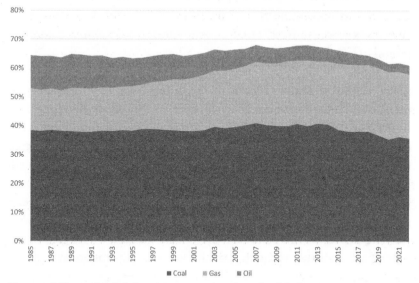

**Figure 1.2** Share of global electricity generation from fossil fuels, 1985–2022
*Source*: Our World in Data

---

9   IEA, 'Net Zero by 2050: A Roadmap for the Global Energy Sector', October 2021, iea.org, p. 114.

The important historical aspect of the use of fossil fuels in electricity generation is connected to this geographical aspect. It is a deeply sobering fact that, as Figure 1.2 shows, the share of global electricity that is produced from fossil fuels is almost exactly the same today as it was four decades ago. In 1985, fossil-fuel-fired plants generated 64 per cent of electricity globally; in 2022, they generated 61 per cent. One reason – to which we will return – is the relative decline of nuclear power since its heyday in the 1980s and 1990s. At its peak, in 1996, nuclear reactors generated around 18 per cent of global electricity; by 2021, that share had sunk to below 10 per cent for the first time since 1981.[10] Thus, even as the share of global electricity generation attributable to renewables (principally hydro, solar and wind) has grown, the share from *all* low-carbon sources – renewables and nuclear combined – essentially has not.

Without support from nuclear, renewables simply have not been able to keep pace with relentless absolute growth in global electricity demand, which almost doubled between 2000 (approximately 15,000 terawatt-hours [TWh] per annum) and 2022 (nearly 30,000). Thus, instead of substantively eating into the share of global electricity output attributable to fossil-based power, low-carbon sources collectively have only just succeeded in preventing that share from rising. And, like generation from low-carbon sources, *absolute* generation from fossil fuel sources has, of course, continued to rise: that is what a steady share of a growing pot means.

But the historical story is clearly not just about nuclear. It is also, inter alia, about the aforementioned geography. Electricity consumption in recent decades has been growing fastest precisely in those countries where electricity generation is most carbon-intensive, while growing slowly, if at all, in countries where generation is less reliant on fossil fuels. Between 2000 and 2021, consumption actually fell by 3 per cent in Sweden and 4 per cent in Germany; meanwhile, it increased by 4 per cent in Italy and 10 per cent in the US; but it increased by a jaw-dropping 196 per cent in India and 527 per cent in China. Fossil fuels have maintained their share of global electricity generation because they are the dominant sources of power output in those regions where such output is growing fastest.

---

10   For years prior to 1985, data are available at: IEA, 'World Electricity Generation Mix by Fuel, 1971–2019', 26 October 2022, iea.org.

Not only, moreover, is the electricity sector the effective epicentre of the global greenhouse gas emissions problem, but, because of the obduracy of fossil fuels, its emissions are also still growing. The 12.6 Gt of emitted $CO_2$ from electricity generation in 2019 increased by 5 per cent to 13.2 Gt (an all-time peak) in 2022, with emissions dipping temporarily in 2020 as a result of COVID-19.[11] Perhaps 5 per cent does not sound all that significant. But even holding electricity sector emissions steady would represent categorical failure at a moment in history when emissions need to be coming sharply down. And we are not even doing that. Indeed, of the fourteen different areas of human activity identified by the IPCC as being primarily responsible for greenhouse gas emissions, only one – land use change and forestry – saw greater absolute growth in such emissions between 2010 and 2019 than the power (electricity and heat) subsector.[12]

Hence it is impossible to disagree with the IPCC's own blunt conclusion, spelled out especially starkly in its 2022 report on climate change mitigation.[13] If we hope for the planet to remain habitable, the IPCC has concluded, then the dramatic reduction of emissions from electricity generation is a sine qua non. Needless to say, there are only two ways in which this could be achieved. One is to massively reduce global electricity consumption, which, short of a contraction forced by more or less apocalyptic global developments, simply is not going to happen, for all degrowthers' imploring. The other, of course, is to replace existing fossil-fuel-based means of electricity production with generation technologies that emit few or no greenhouse gases.

Meanwhile, in the same report, the IPCC made a further, particularly noteworthy, observation in the form of a striking juxtaposition of status quo and radical-mitigation global climate scenarios. On the one hand, it said, the electricity sector is, as we have seen, at the core of the climate problem as presently constituted, and will remain central to it if the world fails to substantially retire existing fossil-fuel-fired power installations and to cancel new such installations: 'most future $CO_2$ emissions from existing and currently planned fossil fuel infrastructure,'

---

11   IEA, 'Electricity Market Report 2023', February 2023, iea.org, p. 105.

12   IPCC, *Climate Change 2022: Mitigation of Climate Change. Contribution of Working Group III to the Sixth Assessment Report of the Intergovernmental Panel on Climate Change* (Cambridge: Cambridge University Press, 2022), p. 238.

13   Ibid. See especially Chapter 2.

the IPCC acknowledged, 'are situated in the power sector'. But on the other hand, it pointed out, in any imaginable future scenario in which the world achieves a broad measure of success in containing the climate problem, electricity generation will actually have ceased to be a meaningful climate concern. Thus 'most remaining fossil fuel $CO_2$ emissions in pathways that limit likely warming to 2 °C and below are from non-electric energy – most importantly from the industry and transportation sectors'.[14]

In other words, the electricity sector is where the IPCC believes the most radical transformation can and must take place. Electricity can and must go from being the very nub of the emissions problem today to ultimately not being a substantive part of the problem at all, and insofar as the IPCC believes that pathways that limit likely warming to 2 °C and below are credible, such a radical transformation in the electricity sector's role is what the IPCC thinks not just can and must happen, but *will* happen. This, one might say, is quite a burden of expectation.

Perhaps 'burden' is the wrong word, however. A better word might be 'hope'. For, if the electricity sector is where the world's scientific community is expecting radical change to occur, then the electricity sector is surely where the scientific community thinks – or hopes – that such change is indeed feasible. Such hope brings us to the second explanation for the centrality of electricity to the climate mitigation cause.

## III

If the transformation of technologies of electricity generation is essential to cutting greenhouse gas emissions associated with the electricity sector as it exists today, then such transformation is also essential to cutting emissions that currently have nothing to do with electricity.

To understand this apparent paradox, consider the best – and most readily appreciable – example, which is road transport, and especially passenger vehicles. As Figure 1.1 indicated, transport is, after electricity production, one of the other main sectors in which the burning of fossil

14   Ibid., p. 219.

fuels currently occurs, accounting for somewhere in the region of a quarter of direct emissions from fuel combustion.

How can road transport be decarbonized? Broadly speaking, there are two strategic and technical alternatives. One is to continue to use a fuel of some kind to directly power vehicle engines, but to use a fuel whose combustion does not cause harmful greenhouse gas emissions. Alternative fuels that have been or are being explored – and, in some cases, used commercially on a small scale – include ammonia, dimethyl ether, ethanol, hydrogen and vegetable oils.

The second alternative is, instead of fuel-based engines, to use electric motors powered by energy stored in on-board batteries. These batteries are charged electrically. If the electricity used to charge the battery has been generated without using fossil fuels, then the operation of the vehicle does not have an emissions footprint.[15]

Not just for passenger vehicle transport but across a range of other sectors, too, the decision has seemingly been made that the world's best hope for decarbonization is the latter approach. That is to say, instead of decarbonizing various significant greenhouse-gas-emitting activities *directly* – by substituting clean fuels for dirty fossil fuels in powering vehicles, firing industrial processes and generating heat – these activities are predominantly to be decarbonized *indirectly* – by shifting them to electrical sources of energy while simultaneously decarbonizing the electricity thereby consumed.

There are immediately two things to note about this. The first is the logic itself, such as it is, which is that electrification – that is, moving sectors from non-electric to electric forms of power – is the most expeditious means of rapid, affordable and large-scale decarbonization. It is the combination of cost, speed and scale that is seen to work uniquely in electricity's favour.

The second is that this logic is not necessarily ironclad in all cases – and it is certainly not a proposition of this book that it is. Perhaps the decarbonization of passenger vehicle transport, for example, could be

---

15   There are, of course, hybrids of these two broad alternatives. The most familiar are vehicles that have both traditional internal combustion engines (running on oil) and battery-powered electric motors. Another type of hybrid is a fuel cell vehicle, which, like 'proper' electric vehicles, has only an electric motor, but in which the motor is powered not by a battery but by a cell that generally uses compressed hydrogen (the 'fuel') and oxygen.

better achieved through transitioning not to electric vehicles but to hydrogen internal combustion engine vehicles? No view one way or another is taken in this book vis-à-vis such questions. The point to be made, rather, is that it essentially *has been decided* that electrification should predominantly be the way forward. Together, the various relevant communities of scientific experts, government policymakers, corporate strategists and financial investors have taken decisions that ultimately have led to the enshrinement of electrification in global climate planning. Right or wrong, good or bad, electrification largely *is* what is happening, and what will continue to happen.

From the side of science, for example, already in its 2014 report on mitigation options, the IPCC set out its stall, insisting that electrification was the master key insofar as 'the decarbonization of the electricity sector may be achieved at a much higher pace than in the rest of the energy system'.[16] By the time of its follow-up 2022 report, the scientific consensus had evidently further hardened. 'Stringent emissions reductions at the level required for 2 °C or lower', the IPCC said, 'are achieved through increased direct electrification of buildings, transport, and industry'.[17] 'The overarching solution', wrote the environmental scientist Simon Lewis in glossing the nearly 3,000-page report for the *Guardian*, 'is to electrify everything we can, from heating buildings to transport, and power everything using clean [energy].'[18]

By that stage, in any event, electrification had been increasingly institutionalized by (and in) government policy as the pre-eminent broadly based strategy for decarbonization. The UK, for example, is explicitly relying principally on electrification to reduce emissions not just in road transport but also in the buildings sector. The majority of its buildings currently use natural gas for heating: according to government figures, 86 per cent of British homes are connected to the gas grid and around 63 per cent of UK non-domestic floor area is heated by gas. And, while the government policy for buildings decarbonization announced in 2021 allowed some role for non-electric approaches such as district heating systems, electrification was to the fore.[19] This would be principally in the

---

16   IPCC, *Climate Change 2014: Mitigation of Climate Change*, p. 559.

17   IPCC, *Climate Change 2022: Mitigation of Climate Change*, p. 299.

18   S. Lewis, 'Scientists Have Just Told Us How to Solve the Climate Crisis – Will the World Listen?', *Guardian*, 6 April 2022.

19   HM Government, 'Heat and Buildings Strategy', October 2021, gov.uk.

shape of hydronic (air-to-water or ground-to-water) heat pumps: the stated ambition was to install at least 600,000 such pumps per annum by 2028. But the government also emphasized the potential scope to substitute hydrogen for natural gas, using electricity to produce the former through electrolysis. Either way, the government expects that, by the mid-2030s, the number of gas-fired boilers being replaced each year will be in the region of 1.5 million to 2 million.

Thus, read any recent informed prognosis of how, in decades to come, transport globally *will* be powered, how homes and offices *will* be heated and how industrial processes *will* be galvanized, and a greater role for electricity across all these domains will inevitably be assumed. The only variance tends to be in the degree of electrification: optimistic scenarios assume deep and broadly based electrification, combined with considerable success in decarbonizing electricity generation itself; less optimistic scenarios assume that electrification achieves lower levels of penetration.

As an illuminating example, consider the IEA's influential 'Net Zero by 2050' (NZE) scenario, which it published to considerable fanfare in 2021. Reaching net zero emissions globally by 2050, at least as the IEA sees it, is utterly contingent on electrification across the board. 'All end-uses today dominated by fossil fuels', it explained, 'are increasingly electrified in the NZE.'[20]

Rising from just 1.5 per cent in 2020, for example, electricity will account in NZE for around 45 per cent of energy consumption in the transport sector globally by 2050. This particular expected shift principally involves road transport (with electricity providing 60 per cent of energy use by that date), and, specifically, passenger vehicles; electrification is assumed to be slower and more limited for trucks, and even more so in shipping and aviation. Meanwhile, electricity is forecast to account for two-thirds of energy consumption in the buildings sector by the same juncture. Furthermore, the use of electricity for hydrogen production is also assumed to grow substantially.[21] All told, electricity

20   IEA, 'Net Zero by 2050', p. 142.
21   The growing importance of hydrogen production as a source of demand for electricity is particularly notable in BloombergNEF's own more recent modelling of a net-zero-by-2050 scenario. It projects that, by 2050, the production of hydrogen, especially to substitute for fuels in high-emitting industrial processes, will in fact be the leading single source of demand for electricity globally – above direct consumption in

will provide around half of energy use in final consumption across all sectors in 2050 in the IEA's NZE (up from 20 per cent in 2020), and electricity will rise from about 35 per cent to 90 per cent of household energy bills. Such, in short, are the electric dreams of the world's leading body in energy policy.

The second part of our explanation for the centrality of electricity to the mitigation of climate change, then, can be simply stated as follows: we need urgently to decarbonize electricity generation, not just because today's electricity sector emits so much $CO_2$, but because, in future – *and precisely in the cause of mitigation* – electricity will also be substantially used across a swathe of activities in which it presently plays only a marginal role. In other words, the electricity sector is set fair to get a lot bigger, and unless it is rapidly rid of its endemic carbon, so too, by extension, will its greenhouse gas emissions footprint. As the IPCC has explicitly acknowledged, the increased direct electrification of buildings, transport and industry will result 'in increased electricity generation in all pathways . . . limiting warming to 2°C or lower'.[22]

There is, therefore, an extraordinary double wager, and thus double risk, embedded in the world's chosen mitigation strategy, namely that transport and so on *can* be adequately electrified and that electricity production itself *can* be adequately decarbonized.[23] For now, we will park the crucial question of how *much* bigger the electricity sector is set to become, and what demands this expansion will place on the development of the world's non-fossil-fuel-based generating infrastructure. That question will be picked up again in the last substantive section of the chapter. First, we must address the question of what types of low-carbon electricity-generating technology are being prioritized, and why.

---

industry, buildings or transport. See N. Bullard, 'Net Zero Will Radically Change How We Use and Generate Electricity', 8 December 2022, bloomberg.com.

22   IPCC, *Climate Change 2022: Mitigation of Climate Change*, p. 299.

23   An excellent summary discussion of the challenges involved in electrifying the industrial, transport and building sectors is provided by M. Cembalest, 'Growing Pains: The Renewable Transition in Adolescence', March 2023, privatebank.jpmorgan.com, pp. 6–9.

## IV

At the time of this writing in the early 2020s, electricity production globally continues, as we have seen, to be dominated by fossil fuels, which accounted for 61 per cent of such production in 2022. Still, seen from a more positive angle, this does mean that nearly 40 per cent of annual production already derives from sources other than fossil fuels, which comprise nuclear and various types of renewables. In what relative proportions do these alternatives contribute? In 2022, the leading non-fossil-fuel-based source was hydropower, which generated 15 per cent of global electricity. This was followed in order of size by nuclear (9 per cent), wind (7.5 per cent), solar (4.5 per cent) and finally other renewables such as bioenergy (3 per cent).

This segmentation of the world of non-fossil-fuel-based electricity production, however, does not accurately reflect recent developments or, relatedly, likely future developments. In proportional terms (which is to say, in terms of their share of global production), neither hydro nor nuclear are growing technologies. Nuclear's share, as we have already noted, has halved since its peak in the mid-1990s, and absolute levels of output from nuclear have remained essentially flat – hovering between 2,500 and 3,000 TWh per annum – since that time. Absolute output from hydropower, meanwhile, continues to grow, but only very slowly in recent years; and hydro's share of global electricity production has consistently fallen since the mid-1980s, when it was around the 20 per cent mark.

If not hydro and nuclear, then, which non-fossil-fuel-based generation technologies, if any, *have* been growing in relative importance? The answer, of course, is principally wind and solar. Figure 1.3 illustrates this development emphatically. The share of wind and solar combined in global electricity production did not exceed 1 per cent until 2008; by 2022, it had reached 12 per cent, with more than sixty countries generating at least 10 per cent of their electricity from these two sources.[24] Or consider another common measure: net capacity growth. 'Capacity', in the electricity world, denotes the maximum amount of power that a generator (or combination of generators) can produce; 'net' growth denotes gross additions less any loss of capacity due, for example, to

---

24   Ember, 'Global Electricity Review 2023', April 2023, ember-climate.org, p. 10.

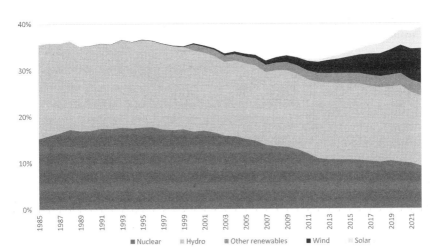

**Figure 1.3** Share of global electricity generation from non-fossil-fuel sources, 1985–2022
*Source*: Our World in Data

decommissioning. Of the 470 net GW of renewable generating capacity added globally across 2019 and 2020, some 416 GW, or nearly 90 per cent of the total, represented solar and wind capacity.[25]

The figures for absolute levels of output are perhaps even more striking. Combined global solar- and wind-based annual electricity production was a paltry 32 TWh (of which 97 per cent were wind-based) in the year 2000, but it had expanded to exceed 100 TWh by 2005 and 1,000 TWh by 2015, reaching 3,435 TWh (of which approximately three-fifths were wind and two-fifths solar) in 2022, representing a compound annual growth rate across those two decades of nearly 25 per cent. Seen in isolation – that is, not in relation to the world's continuing levels of output of dirty electricity, and not in relation therefore to the world's actual *needs* for clean electricity production – it has, indisputably, been a remarkable success story for the renewables industry. Solar, in particular, has expanded at a dizzying rate in recent years, with output increasing fivefold from 2011–16 and then threefold from 2016–21.

In any event, a fact of pivotal importance to this book is that the above pattern of recent development in the mix of non-fossil-fuel-based electricity generation is widely expected also to be broadly the pattern of development going forward. In other words, just as the installers and producers of low-carbon electricity have disproportionately and increasingly prioritized solar and wind over the past decade, so they are expected to maintain largely the same prioritization in the short- and medium-term future.

Such prioritization can be witnessed in any number of government pronouncements, in the Global South and North alike. It is evident too in the IPCC's relatively sober prognoses: as of 2022, for instance, the IPCC judged it 'likely that wind and solar will dominate low-carbon generation and capacity growth over the next couple of decades'.[26] And prioritization of wind and solar is likewise writ large in the IEA's scenario modelling. Indeed, having long been – or, at least, been perceived to be – a shill for the fossil fuel sector, the IEA has performed a dramatic volte-face in recent years to become an unabashed (and excitable) cheerleader for renewables in general and solar in particular. Its 2020 World Energy Outlook proclaimed solar power 'set for massive expansion', on course to become 'the new king of electricity supply'.[27] Its electric dreams are in fact oddly reminiscent now of Stephen Gaskin's, with which we opened this chapter.

Thus, just like the electrification of buildings, industry and transport, the prioritization of wind and solar development above other sources of low- or zero-emissions electricity production is now deeply embedded in global climate and energy policy. Indeed, when, in its most recent report, the IPCC estimated the potential contribution to future emissions reduction of around forty different mitigation options, solar and wind power ranked first and third – only the reduced conversion of forests and other ecosystems, which ranked second, was estimated to have comparable potential.[28] In other words, whether one's frame of reference is the energy sector specifically or the full range of human activities in general, solar and wind power are where the main possibilities for deep mitigation are seen to exist. To the extent, then, that non-fossil-fuel-based electricity

---

26   IPCC, *Climate Change 2022: Mitigation of Climate Change*, p. 689.
27   IEA, 'Outlook for Electricity', October 2020, iea.org.
28   IPCC, *Climate Change 2022: Mitigation of Climate Change*, p. 38.

production continues to grow, it is a safe bet that it will be predominantly wind and solar production.

The question is, why? Why has the recent past of non-fossil-fuel-based electricity expansion been principally a matter of wind and solar, and why is this expected to continue? This is a large question, the full answer to which has many components. But it is possible to provide a brief answer that is adequate for our present purposes. Essentially, the explanation ultimately lies in equal parts in the relative net advantages of wind and solar power *and* in the relative net disadvantages of the main alternatives. We will start with the latter, beginning with hydropower.

The benefits of hydroelectricity are well known and have been widely extolled since investment in large-scale production facilities began in earnest in North America in the late nineteenth century. As a source of electricity, hydro is, in many respects, hard to beat. Given sufficient financial resources and an accommodating physical milieu, it can be installed on a massive scale: China's Three Gorges Dam, for example, operating since 2012 and with a gigantic capacity of 22.5 GW, is the world's largest power station of any kind. Engineers and economists marvel not just at such sheer magnitude but also at hydro's relative productivity (the efficiency with which it converts inputs into output rivals that of any other technology) and flexibility (as energy demands fluctuate over time, the power output can be adjusted relatively quickly and cheaply). Furthermore, dams provide certain ancillary benefits, not least irrigation and water storage. In their heyday, massive hydroelectric projects were hailed by political leaders as great symbols of modernization, representing not so much humanity's taming of nature as its corralling of nature to meet society's demands. And then there is the apparent environmental benefit: no $CO_2$ emissions from power generation.

But the tide began turning against hydropower in the 1980s, and while – like most matters energy-related – hydro still divides opinion, the consensus has continued to sour, including during the more recent period of rapidly growing concern about climate change.

The early criticisms related to the patent social and environmental disbenefits. Large dam projects have frequently led to massive displacement of local populations; the Three Gorges project alone saw more than a million people displaced, for example. Meanwhile, water quality has typically declined and biodiversity shrunk. By the 1990s, major international investors in the private and public sector alike backed away from hydropower projects accordingly. The fact that many large dams failed to recoup the cost of construction clearly also played a part in this policy shift.

More recently, an additional set of concerns has been raised about hydroelectricity, specifically in relation to its potential to facilitate the rapid shift out of fossil-fuel-based electricity that is necessitated by the climate crisis. Such concerns are mainly fourfold. First, there is the simple question of time. Large dams take many years, and sometimes decades, to build, and while there is clearly a place for long-term capital projects in the panoply of measures to be taken against the emissions crisis – global electricity generation is not going to be decarbonized in a heartbeat in any credible scenario – the emphasis is and must be on building out non-fossil-fuel capacity *fast*. Hydro falls short on this score. That many governments have announced interim targets for emissions cuts (say, halving emissions from electricity by 2030) only adds to the incentive to prioritize faster means of decarbonization.

Second, there is a question of scope. Although significant hydropower potential clearly remains in many parts of the world, and especially sub-Saharan Africa, several countries, especially wealthy countries in the Global North, have already built out much of their suitable hydro capacity. Physical scope for expansion is constrained.

Third, there are growing worries that hydro, conventionally regarded as a highly reliable energy source, is becoming and will continue to become less reliable precisely as a result of climate change itself. Among the various extreme weather conditions whose growing frequency and intensity is held to be a consequence of climate change is drought. As Camilla Palladino recently reported, 2022 was a 'very poor' year for hydro generation in Europe because it was one of the driest years on record.[29] It would be foolhardy to turn to hydro to temper climate change if climate change is all the while tempering hydro.

Last but not least, scientists have learned that hydroelectricity is not so friendly to the climate after all. Submerged vegetation in hydropower reservoirs, particularly in tropical regions, is, it transpires, a large

---

29    C. Palladino, 'Hydropower: It Never Rains but It Pours', *Financial Times*, 24 May 2023.

contributor of emitted methane, a greenhouse gas that is much more potent than $CO_2$.

None of this is to say that relevant bodies see no role for hydropower in future fossil-fuel-free energy mixes. On the contrary. Hydropower will continue to generate large amounts of electricity, its share of overall output globally remaining broadly flat in the IEA's NZE scenario, for example, which would make it the third-largest energy source – after solar and wind – at mid-century. But it is not expected to enjoy anything like the growth – relative and absolute – projected for wind and solar. If hydro is part of the answer to our electricity–climate challenge, it is only a very small part.

The same can be said for nuclear power, which, in some respects, has enjoyed a similar trajectory to hydropower – considerable enthusiasm and robust capacity growth followed by a period of relative decline, which in nuclear's case has been longer and steeper. Nuclear reaction (principally fission) is a highly reliable and, statistically speaking, very safe source of electrical power. It came to prominence in the 1960s, during which decade more than ten countries built nuclear reactors.

No sooner had nuclear power established a foothold, however, than concerns mounted and began to take a toll. In the Cold War 1970s, with the proliferation of nuclear weapons casting an increasingly long shadow, governments came under pressure to curb investment in nuclear energy from environmental groups alarmed by the risk of reactor meltdown. Some countries ploughed ahead regardless, most notably France, where, by the early 1980s, nuclear became the leading source of electricity generation (which it comfortably remains today); Belgium, Sweden and a clutch of Central and Eastern European nations also became committed nuclear power standard-bearers. But other early adopters began to back off. Governments introduced new safety regulations that constrained investment by raising its cost and requiring an expanding package of subsidies to investment where such investment continued.

Then, of course, in 1986, came Chernobyl, where a steam explosion precipitated the unleashing of vast quantities of radioactive gas and debris by blowing open one of the plant's reactors. Ever since, nuclear power has been intimately associated with potential disaster by much of the public, notwithstanding the extreme rarity of actual meltdowns. Further blows to its reputation have come with growing concerns around the storage of nuclear waste, anxiety – especially after 9/11 – that nuclear plants could be the targets of terrorist attack (or indeed of outright military attack), and, of course, the meltdown at Fukushima twenty-five years after Chernobyl. These were, in reality, body blows.

In the US, which has the world's largest nuclear generating fleet, thirteen reactors were closed between 2013 and 2022, leaving around 100 in operation (out of a global total of between 400 and 500).[30] As for new plants, cost ($10 billion at a bare minimum) and length of construction (typically seven to twelve years) tend to militate against investment in much the same way, and for the same reasons, as they do large-scale hydroelectricity installations.

The only thing that has arrested the decline somewhat has been the heightening of the climate crisis in the past few years. Growing awareness of the need to decarbonize electricity generation has moderately changed the calculus around nuclear for the simple reason that it generates no $CO_2$ emissions. The global energy crisis beginning in 2021 gave nuclear a further fillip, principally by improving its cost-effectiveness and perceived dependability relative to conventional generating sources, which, in many places, saw huge increases in fuel prices alongside – and partly as a result of – supply constraints rooted in geopolitical conflicts.

Sensing a weakening of resistance to its favoured energy source, France persuaded ten other EU countries to join a 'nuclear alliance' that called on Brussels to provide more support to the technology.[31] On the other side of the Atlantic, encouraged by beneficial new legislation – President Biden's 2021 Infrastructure Investment and Jobs Act allocated funds to help keep existing reactors open, and 2022's Inflation Reduction Act included nuclear among the technologies eligible for tax credits – the head of the American Nuclear Society went so far as to describe 2022 as a 'positive inflection point' for the industry.[32] Others have wondered aloud whether 2022 might have kick-started a 'nuclear renaissance'.[33] Plants that had been due to shut down were in many cases saved, including in the US, while countries such as Japan and the UK

---

30   M. McCormick, 'US Nuclear Enjoys Revival as Public and Private Funding Pours In', *Financial Times*, 1 January 2023.

31   S. White, L. Abboud, A. Hancock and G. Chazan, 'France Mounts Battle for Nuclear Energy in Europe', *Financial Times*, 1 March 2023.

32   Cited in McCormick, 'US Nuclear Enjoys Revival'.

33   Ember, 'Global Electricity Review 2023', p. 37.

that seemingly had long cooled on nuclear power now proposed a raft of new reactors.

But, for all the fact that, with a relenting of opposition in some quarters, nuclear is here and there enjoying something of a new lease on life, it is still widely seen as beyond the pale. Germany is the best-known antagonist: it shut down its last three reactors in 2023. Certainly, no governments regard nuclear as the main tool for the ongoing decarbonization of electricity generation, and thus nobody is expecting the energy transition unfolding in response to the climate crisis to herald a new golden era of nuclear power. Most forecasters anticipate that, globally, nuclear will, at best, hold its share of global electricity production steady at around 10 per cent. The IEA, for its part, anticipates a very slight fall in share.[34] Like hydropower, and (one hopes) unlike unabated fossil fuels, nuclear will assuredly survive the energy transition. But it is not and will not be the driver and pivot thereof.

## V

Instead, wind and solar power have gradually but ineluctably emerged as the putative answer to society's electric dreams in the age of climate crisis. Again, the full explanation for this is dense and multifaceted, but perhaps the best entry point to that explanation is to say that wind and solar do not substantively suffer from the main perceived drawbacks that bedevil hydro and nuclear power.

For one thing, they are much quicker to develop. Once the necessary planning has been done and permits have been received, it takes many, many years, as we have seen, to build nuclear or hydroelectric plants. Wind or solar farms can, typically, be constructed in a fraction of that time. Relatively small onshore wind farms can be up and running in a matter of months. At the other extreme, large offshore wind farms – technically and logistically the most demanding of all wind or solar installations – may take three or four years to build. But that is still a considerably shorter time frame than usually applies to hydro or nuclear.

Furthermore, the environmental and social impact of wind and solar power is generally low. To begin with, it goes without saying that the

---

34    IEA, 'Net Zero by 2050', p. 115.

actual generation of power creates no greenhouse gas emissions –
although, given existing manufacturing and construction technologies,
it remains the case that getting a facility to the point of being able to
generate power (for example, making the steel used in wind turbines)
usually entails the production of some $CO_2$.

Indeed, it would clearly be erroneous to say that there is *no* detrimental
environmental or social impact. It is well known that wind power represents a collision risk for birds and bats, resulting in increased levels of
mortality if poorly located. Objections to solar and (especially) wind power
on aesthetic grounds are also relatively common and widely reported. And,
if not a cause of mass displacement, *à la* hydropower, the construction of
large onshore solar or wind installations can certainly interfere with existing ways of using and relating to the land. Sámi reindeer herders in northern Norway and Sweden, for example, have long protested the disruption
of seasonal grazing patterns caused by the huge wind farms in those
regions, and the associated threat to their livelihoods.

Yet, overall, all this has been – and continues for the most part to be
– considered a price worth paying, at least by those in society with the
power to weigh overall benefits against costs and to make decisions
accordingly. *No* technology, advocates of wind and solar power insist, is
perfect. There will always be costs, or at least perceived costs. But the
costs of *not* investing in a future of solar and wind power are, they say,
immeasurably higher.

In addition, wind and, in particular, solar have the advantage of being
able to be installed and deployed at a range of scales. To be sure, if these
technologies are going to have anything like the long-term transformative
impact on overall planetary health that is increasingly expected of them,
then large-scale facilities feeding large amounts of electricity into the
grid – and with the capacity to cleanly power large numbers of
households, businesses and buildings – are clearly the priority. But, in
any sensible and flexible energy future, there is, and must be, a place for
so-called 'distributed generation', meaning the smaller-scale generation
of electricity for use largely or exclusively *in situ*, at the local level.
Household rooftop solar panels are one (perhaps the classic) example;
another would be community-owned wind turbines. Needless to say,
household or community-owned nuclear reactors are not on the cards.

The two major concerns about solar and wind power have been – and
to one extent or another, continue to be – those of cost and reliability. In

the early days of wind and solar power in the 1970s and 1980s, turbine and panel technologies were immature and very expensive. As such, it was very challenging for enough money to be earned from selling solar- or wind-generated electricity to recoup the costs of developing solar or wind farms. Profit was a stumbling block from the start. But, as we will see in Chapter 4, governments increasingly stepped in, providing vari- ous forms of financial support to these fledgling technologies in order to help improve their commercial viability. In fact, and as we will see in Chapter 9, governments still widely provide assorted forms of financial support today, notwithstanding the fact that the underlying technology costs have declined dramatically in recent years. Why they do so is one of this book's central concerns.

The other significant worry about wind and solar power has been reliability. This worry is very simply stated: the wind does not always blow and the sun does not always shine. Wind and solar are, to use the technical lexicon, *non-dispatchable* technologies. A dispatchable tech- nology is one which can be actively calibrated to generate a specific quantity of energy; examples include gas turbines, coal-fired generating plants and large dam-based hydroelectric facilities. Non-dispatchable technologies are inherently more capricious: energy is generated using the underlying resource (such as the wind) when and to the extent that the resource is available; it is not possible to extract on demand (that is, 'dispatch') a specified quantum of power.

As we will see, in the economics of generating, selling and buying electricity, there are crucial differences between dispatchable and non-dispatchable technologies – not least, different risks, both to the seller and to the buyer. But the more mundane question concerns the extent to which solar and wind can be relied upon, given the inevitability of peri- ods that are windless, dark or both. This problem is compounded by the fact that, given existing technology, it is neither easy nor cheap to store, until such a time as it is required, any surplus energy generated by wind or solar facilities when physical conditions *are* conducive. At any rate, the IPCC, expressing a broad consensus, judges that for these reasons it would, as things stand, be extremely 'challenging to supply the entire energy system [solely] with renewable energy'.[35] Unsurprisingly, incum- bent fossil fuel interests have made much of this issue, citing the

---

35   IPCC, *Climate Change 2022: Mitigation of Climate Change*, p. 28.

intermittency of solar and wind power to fearmonger about impending electricity blackouts if the push to renewables is accelerated.

The expectation among experts, however, is that, in the medium and long term, advanced energy systems will be able to handle the intermittency of solar and wind power relatively comfortably. Part of the answer will be what is commonly called 'demand response', which essentially means motivating electricity users to adjust their consumption patterns to better fit the vagaries of renewables supply – for example, charging their electric vehicles when it is windy and sunny and electricity, being plentiful, is relatively cheap. But the bigger part of the answer will come on the supply side, taking two main forms.

The first entails the development of improved storage technologies, allowing renewable power generated when it is not needed to be held in reserve until it is. Considerable investment is currently flowing into this space, generically termed long-duration energy storage (LDES). For now, the main such technology is found in the hydro sector. Pumped-storage hydropower involves pumping water up into an elevated reservoir when electricity is cheap and abundant, and allowing that water to run back down to a lower level, where it rotates a turbine and thereby generates new electricity, when electricity is expensive and scarce.

This and other technologies of mechanical energy storage are expected increasingly to be complemented by storage technologies of various other kinds.[36] Lithium ion and other battery-based solutions are examples of electrochemical storage technologies. Thermal solutions, meanwhile, involve storing electricity in substantive physical solids – such as battery bricks or blocks of carbon – for subsequent release. Finally, chemical solutions effectively store energy in chemical form for later use in a generator or engine, such as with the production of hydrogen through electrolysis mentioned earlier.

Some experts believe that storage technologies will eventually be sufficient in themselves to enable large electricity networks to convert to a mixture solely of wind and solar power. Godart van Gendt of the consultancy McKinsey, for instance, told the *Economist* that LDES 'allows you to

---

36   See the excellent discussion in 'Decarbonisation of Electric Grids Reliant on Renewables Requires Long-Duration Energy Storage', *Economist*, 23 June 2022. See also M. Angwin, *Shorting the Grid: The Hidden Fragility of Our Electric Grid* (Wilder, VT: Carnot Communications, 2020), pp. 213–20.

go from 60–70% renewables on the grid to 100%'.[37] But most experts believe that storage will only resolve solar and wind's intermittency problems in conjunction with a second, complementary supply-side solution, which is one that we have already indirectly encountered.

As we have seen, in parts of the world with nuclear power facilities, policymakers bent on fossil-free-electricity futures generally do not plan to phase out such nuclear capacity. Rather, it will remain a crucial part of the electricity supply mix, albeit to varying degrees in different world regions. Partly this is on account of its own relative virtues, but it is also because it can provide security of supply when solar and wind 'fail'. Indeed, in such countries, as solar and wind expand and fossil-based sources are retired, nuclear stations will likely be called upon to operate more often than they presently do, their output today often proving economically uncompetitive versus that of conventional generators. Nuclear utilization rates (or 'load factors') are expected to increase to around 90 per cent by 2030, from an average of approximately 80 per cent today.[38]

In other words, part of the answer to solar and wind intermittency can be to have on hand one or more other generating source that can reliably be called upon – so-called baseload or 'firm power'. Until and unless vastly improved and affordable large-scale energy storage technologies are available, no country is likely to transition fully to renewable power generation. The only exceptions might be countries in which hydroelectric capacity is both abundant and highly reliable (and can thus serve as a renewable form of firm power, which it is not generally considered to be), or which are willing to rely on cross-border electricity imports in times of need – a strategy whose relative merits have been thrown into considerable doubt during the ongoing global energy crisis, and its evident impetus to energy protectionism.[39] Instead, as they build out their stocks both of intermittent solar and wind capacity and of functional storage facilities, most countries will rely on other, baseload-generating technologies to ensure security of supply.

Today, the main sources of such firm power are coal, natural gas and

---

37   Cited in 'Decarbonisation of Electric Grids Reliant on Renewables Requires Long-Duration Energy Storage'.

38   Bullard, 'Net Zero Will Radically Change How We Use and Generate Electricity'.

39   See M. Z. Jacobson, *No Miracles Needed: How Today's Technology Can Save Our Climate and Clean Our Air* (Cambridge: Cambridge University Press, 2023).

nuclear – in that order of magnitude. But the mix will, of course, change as fossil fuels are progressively phased out. BloombergNEF, an influential provider of research on energy markets, expects that, by mid-century, the provision of firm power globally will be almost entirely rid of fossil-fuel-fired plants that do not incorporate technological fixes to capture $CO_2$ at source and either sequester or recycle it, although a small rump of such unabated plants running on natural gas may remain. Instead, the three main constituents of baseload power – undergirding a wider electricity system comprising principally solar and wind – will, BloombergNEF thinks, be gas (with carbon capture), nuclear and hydrogen.[40] Germany, for example, regards the burning of hydrogen that is itself produced by solar and wind facilities as perhaps the most attractive and viable form of backup to renewables in the long term.[41]

Insofar as issues of cost and reliability are deemed surmountable, therefore, solar and wind power are overwhelmingly expected to be the main electricity-generating technologies of the future – *the* core mechanisms of weaning electricity production, and hence modern society more widely, off fossil fuels. In essentially any credible scenario for a future low- or zero-carbon global electricity-production infrastructure, solar and wind are the dominant sources of supply.

As we have done earlier in the chapter, let us take the IEA's influential 'Net Zero by 2050' (NZE) case as illustrative. From around just 12 per cent today, the successful realization of NZE would see solar and wind's combined share of total global electricity production jumping to 40 per cent already by 2030, and to fully 68 per cent by 2050.[42] Where is the remaining 32 per cent of electricity production at mid-century expected to come from? Mainly from other renewables (hydropower and bioenergy), contributing 20 per cent, and nuclear, with 8 per cent. The final 4 per cent of production in NZE at 2050 would be contributed by

---

40   Bullard, 'Net Zero Will Radically Change How We Use and Generate Electricity'. Note that hydrogen is effectively both a source of baseload power that can serve as back-up to intermittent renewables and, as we have already seen, a means precisely of storing the power originally generated by those renewable energy technologies.

41   'Electrifying Everything Does Not Solve the Climate Crisis, but It Is a Great Start'.

42   IEA, 'Net Zero by 2050', p. 117.

power plants fired either by hydrogen-based fuels or by fossil fuels, but which, in the latter case, would be equipped with mechanisms of $CO_2$ capture.

Of course, NZE and comparable projections imply a future global investment tableau with incredibly arresting characteristics. *Almost all financial investment in power production capacity must be in solar and wind farms.* Inasmuch as nuclear power and renewables other than solar and wind are expected merely to maintain their share of electricity production, investment in these alternative technologies only need be modest. And inasmuch as fossil-fuel-fired plants are expected to disappear almost entirely, the singular priority in their regard is *dis*investment – decommissioning – rather than investment, allied to modest retrofitting for carbon capture or hydrogen firing. The IEA has said that to achieve NZE, all unabated coal- and oil-fired plants must be phased out by 2040.

Indeed, it will be recalled from the Introduction that the IEA has stipulated more immediate requirements, too, most conspicuously that *no* new unabated coal-fired plants should be approved – none, ever. This was in 2021. Cue 2022, and, in just the first six weeks of the year, five new such plants with a total capacity of 7.3 GW were approved for construction in China alone.[43] Across 2022 as a whole, China approved the construction of a mammoth 106 GW of coal-fired capacity, the highest amount since 2015.[44]

Why would China do that? The answer, as Nathaniel Bullard has pointed out, is to ensure reliability of electricity supply; that is, to provide the security – firm power – that solar and wind cannot.[45] Bullard further noted that the particular need to which China's new commissioning of coal plants represented a response was for supply reliability only 'in special circumstances' – specifically, at times of exceptional power demand. The summer of 2022 saw peak demand in the country reach a level 20 per cent higher than ever before.

If it is only special circumstances that are calling forth new dirty

43   D. Stanway, 'China Starts Building 33 GW of Coal Power in 2021, Most since 2016', 24 February 2022, reuters.com.

44   'China Approves Biggest Expansion in New Coal Power Plants since 2015, Report Finds', *Guardian*, 27 February 2023.

45   N. Bullard, 'China's Coal Power Boom Is More Complex than It Seems', 2 March 2023, bloomberg.com.

power capacity on this scale, perhaps we have no need to worry? That would be entirely the wrong conclusion, for, as Bullard explained, the pertinent special circumstances not only are becoming less special (that is, more ordinary), but are doing so – in an irony of dreadful ironies – *because of climate change*. In China, climate change is causing both more intense and frequent heatwaves – which lift usage of air conditioning and thus electricity – and deeper drought – which, as already noted, inhibits hydropower generation and therefore increases the need for other reliable energy sources. Such was the combination of factors in play in the summer of 2022.

The more general point is that climate change requires us to transform the way we produce electricity not just to mitigate its intensification, but also, because that intensification both compromises and exceeds existing generating infrastructures, to adapt to it.

## VI

On the face of it, the shift to a decarbonized global infrastructure of electricity generation is simple to get our heads around, albeit – as we shall see – maddeningly difficult to achieve in practice. Shut down fossil-fuel-based plants, do not build any new ones, and instead build lots and lots of solar and wind farms. And, even if we, collectively, are failing, for now at least, on the count of not building new fossil plants, we seem, at least, to be progressing relatively well on the renewables front. In 2022, global production of electricity from solar and wind *increased* year on year by over 500 TWh, which was roughly the *total* annual output from solar and wind just a decade earlier. True, annual power output from fossil fuels still stands at over 17,000 TWh (in 2022), but, if the rate of growth of renewables output continues to increase dramatically – as it has been doing in recent years – would it not be fair to assume that substituting clean for dirty power production within a reasonable time frame is achievable?

Unfortunately, however, two significant factors make the picture much more complex and challenging than the simple aforementioned arithmetic might suggest. First, the target for renewables build-out is a constantly moving one. That annual global electricity demand is today around 28,500 TWh per annum (the figure for 2022) does not mean that increasing solar- and wind-based production to 28,500 TWh per annum would fully satisfy global demand (even leaving aside the issues relating to intermittency discussed above), because, by the time such an increase were achieved, demand would inevitably have increased. More and more electricity is being consumed globally every year.

Some of this ongoing growth in electricity consumption is by default, coming with the territory, so to speak, of industrialization, urbanization and population growth, all three of which tend today to be concentrated in world regions other than the historical hotspots of carbon emission intensity in the Global North. But we should not forget that much of the growth in electricity consumption – today, and even more so looking ahead – is by design: the electrification of buildings, transport and industry is, as we have seen, consciously planned, and will drive electricity demand ever higher.

And here is the terrifying thing. For all the recent uptick in the rate of growth of renewables output, we – globally – nonetheless have been falling ever further behind the curve in terms of the amount of renewables capacity that still needs to be installed. This is the case because global electricity consumption is growing faster than the supply of electricity from solar and wind, meaning that the gap to be 'filled' is getting bigger, not smaller, each year.

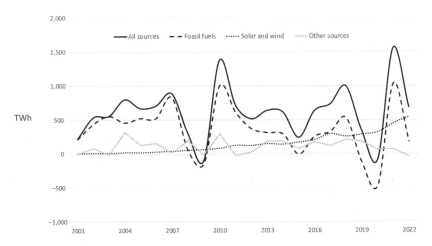

**Figure 1.4** Year-on-year growth in global electricity output, by source of generation, 2001–22
*Source*: Our World in Data

Figure 1.4, which is perhaps the single most important chart in this book, illustrates this dynamic in action: the solid black line (growth in all electricity) remains above the dotted line (growth in solar and wind). Equally important, the portion of incremental annual electricity supply that wind and solar are *not* providing – that is, the gap between the dotted and solid black lines – is being provided principally by fossil fuels (as represented by the dashed line), rather than by nuclear and hydro. This is why power sector emissions continue, as we saw earlier, to rise. Coal alone supplied more than half of the annual increase in global electricity output in 2021.[46] If we are being honest with ourselves, it would be difficult to argue that we are in any meaningful sense 'succeeding' in the face of the electricity decarbonization challenge until such a time as the level of output from fossil fuels is consistently decreasing, not – as it still is today – consistently increasing.

This, therefore, raises a crucial question. Given ongoing industrialization, urbanization and population growth, and given the world's evolving electrification plans, by how much might we expect global electricity demand to grow, and what does this mean for the burden being placed on the presumed growth of solar and wind capacity?

Let us return once more to the IEA's NZE scenario, which, it will be recalled, incorporated ambitious electrification targets. This particular scenario envisages global electricity consumption approximately doubling, to 60,000 TWh per annum, by 2050.[47] Given that, by that date, 68 per cent of supply is expected to come from wind and solar, the NZE projection for combined annual output from those two sources in 2050 lands at around 48,000 TWh – up from around 3,400 TWh in 2022. As the IEA concedes, this will require colossal investment. Indeed, its figures in this regard are nothing short of mind-boggling: a twentyfold increase in solar capacity and an elevenfold increase in wind capacity. This equates, according to IEA calculations, to the addition each year

---

46    IEA, 'Electricity Market Report: January 2022', iea.org, p. 6.

47    IEA, 'Net Zero by 2050', p. 113. It is important to recognize that this *is* just a prediction. As a wealth of research carried out in the past few decades has demonstrated, energy forecasting is substantially unreliable and highly contingent, being shaped by forces that are ideological, economic and political as much as 'scientific'; this is as true of the IEA's forecasts as anyone else's. The classic scholarly reference is T. Baumgartner and A. Midttun, eds, *The Politics of Energy Forecasting: A Comparative Study of Energy Forecasting in Western Europe and North America* (Oxford: Clarendon Press, 1987).

between 2030 and 2050 of an average of more than 600 GW of solar capacity and 340 GW of wind capacity.[48] To provide some context, the world's largest existing solar farm, India's Bhadla, covering approximately fifty square kilometres, has a capacity of around 2 GW.

And there is more. The IEA's projections for growth in global electricity demand are very much on the optimistic side – which is to say the low side. The inflationary impact of increasing electrification is explicitly expected to be countered by the deflationary impact of energy efficiency measures such as 'improving building envelopes and ensuring that all new appliances brought to market are the most efficient models available'.[49] Such hopes border on the Pollyannaish. Without achievement of the great strides in energy efficiency assumed by the IEA in its base-case NZE scenario, even more electricity will be needed – an extra 10,000 TWh per annum in 2050 in the buildings sector alone, according to the IEA's estimates. Little wonder that other forecasters think that the IEA is being altogether too conservative in its consumption projections. In BloombergNEF's own net-zero-by-2050 scenario, for example, total global electricity demand is projected to increase more than threefold compared to 2020 by mid-century.[50] Needless to say, such forecasts, to the degree that they are borne out, make targets for the build-out of solar and wind capacity even more daunting.

Meanwhile, the second factor that renders our simplistic starting picture of global electricity decarbonization requirements both more complicated and more challenging is regionality. Electricity production needs to be decarbonized globally, certainly, but different world regions have reached vastly different stages of such decarbonization, will experience vastly different rates of future growth in electricity demand, and will hence face challenges on vastly different scales. Some regions are already a considerable way along the path of successfully decarbonizing; some have barely begun.

To contextualize what follows in the remainder of this book, it is therefore helpful to foreground the question of where different regions broadly are 'at' in this regard. For selected regions, Figure 1.5 shows both the current mix of sources of electricity and the amount of

---

48    IEA, 'Net Zero by 2050', pp. 117–18.
49    Ibid., p. 62.
50    Bullard, 'Net Zero Will Radically Change How We Use and Generate Electricity'.

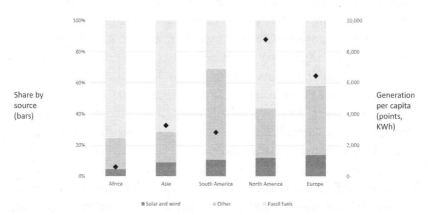

**Figure 1.5** Electricity generation per capita and share from different sources, selected regions, 2021
*Source*: Our World in Data

electricity generated per head of population. As the chart shows, both vary substantially. In Europe, fossil fuels now generate 'only' around 40 per cent of electricity, but electricity consumption levels are relatively high. Interestingly, although Europe has progressed furthest among the selected regions in terms of the proportion of electricity derived from solar and wind, it does not have the lowest dependence on fossil fuels. That honour goes to South America: dominated by hydropower, which supplies over half of its electricity, less than a third of South American electricity today comes from fossil fuels (mainly natural gas).

At the other extreme, Africa and Asia remain heavily reliant on fossil fuels for electricity. They also have low (in some cases, very low) levels of electricity production per capita, suggesting that it is in these regions that future growth in electricity output is likely to be disproportionately concentrated. Indeed, the IEA's NZE scenario sees some three-quarters of all global growth in electricity demand up to 2050 occurring in what it calls 'emerging market and developing economies'.[51]

The pace and scale of investment required to decarbonize electricity generation within a reasonable time frame can appear overwhelmingly

---

51   IEA, 'Net Zero by 2050', p. 113.

difficult even in countries that are already some way there and in which demand is relatively flat. Most recently updated in early 2023, Germany's transition plan, for instance, requires the installation of solar panels covering the equivalent of forty-three soccer fields every day, and thirty-one new wind farms (including four offshore) every week.[52] Certainly, power demand is growing in Germany, but not rapidly: it is expected to be about a third higher in 2030 than in 2022.[53]

That investment challenge is as nothing compared to that which looms elsewhere, however. Take Africa. Home today to around 1.4 billion people, almost half of those people still lack access to electricity.[54] African governments are widely committed both to universalizing access and to lifting consumption to closer to global average levels. That the continent is believed to harbour around 40 per cent of global renewable energy potential is thus a source of some comfort to environmentalists.[55] Long-term ambitions for Nigeria's electricity sector – as outlined in 2022 by the country's vice president, Yemi Osinbajo, for example – cast a sharp light on just how dramatic a transformation it and other African nations are envisaging. 'We should aim', Osinbajo said in an essay intended for consumption in the Global North as much as in Nigeria itself, 'to generate a national average power output of at least 1,000 kilowatt-hours per person which, combined with population growth, means that by 2050 we will need to generate 15 times more electricity than we do today.'[56]

Or, in the Asian context, consider briefly the case of India, and as just one indication of how fast electricity demand is growing and will grow there, consider that in 2018 alone an estimated 100 million people in India gained access to household electricity for the first time.[57] Commentators often mention India and China in the same breath when it comes to electricity and climate, but in terms of consumption they are poles apart: per capita output in India is still only around a fifth of what

52   P. Sorge and J. Fokuhl, 'Germany Faces $1 Trillion Challenge to Plug Massive Power Gap', 25 February 2023, bloomberg.com.

53   Ibid.

54   T. Wilson, 'Eni Calls for South–North Energy Axis between Europe and Africa', *Financial Times*, 6 January 2023.

55   As estimated by energy think tank RMI, and reported in ibid.

56   'Yemi Osinbajo on the Hypocrisy of Rich Countries' Climate Policies', *Economist*, 14 May 2022.

57   IEA, 'Renewables Integration in India', June 2021, iea.org, p. 12.

it is in China. Conservative projections foresee a quadrupling of total Indian electricity capacity by as soon as 2040.[58] If that vast new capacity remains anything like as carbon-intensive as the country's existing electricity infrastructure, it spells disaster.

## VII

As the climate crisis has escalated and as experts and policymakers have increasingly focused their attention on energy production and consumption as the kernel of the climate problem, it has become increasingly common to hear talk of 'the energy transition'. But there is not one global energy transition, even within a single sector such as electricity generation. If the electricity sectors of different world regions and the different countries within them are characterized by different supply mixes and different demand patterns and expectations, then clearly what is unfolding and will unfold is a series of geographically disparate local transitions – connected to one another in various ways, to be sure, but nevertheless each unique.

Of course, politics – not least the dreams and decisions of leaders like Nigeria's Yemi Osinbajo – will profoundly shape these local transitions and thus the variegated global transition to which they ultimately sum. But so too will economics. Solar and wind farms are being built into existing landscapes of electricity generation and delivery that in different parts of the world feature often markedly different institutional and commercial arrangements, incentives and possibilities. It is to those particular varying arrangements, incentives and possibilities – to, that is, the heterogeneous *business* of electrical power – that we now turn.

---

58  S. Ahluwalia, 'National Electricity Policy 2021: Making India's Power Sector Future-Ready', June 2021, orfonline.org, p. 9.

# 2
# The Business of Power

Fifty years after Stephen Gaskin and friends departed from San Francisco in search of an alternative place to establish their utopian, solar-powered commune, California was a place where people and institutions interested in developing solar power more commonly headed *towards*. By the end of 2021, the Golden State boasted 35 GW of solar generating capacity – the highest of any state in the country.[1] Solar by now provided around a quarter of the state's electricity, or enough to power an estimated 10 million homes. No fewer than around 900 companies were reported to be active in the state in the development and operation of solar power–generating facilities.

One of those companies was Clearway Energy – headquartered, ironically, in San Francisco. At the time of this writing, Clearway owns and operates electricity-generating plants across the US with a combined capacity of nearly 8 GW, of which about 5 GW represents wind and solar capacity. Developing, owning and operating electricity-generating facilities is what Clearway does. One of its most recent projects in its home state is the so-called Red Bluff Complex in Riverside County. Granted approval by the Bureau of Land Management in December 2021 (the project will be built on publicly owned desert land), Red Bluff is expected to cost nearly $700 million and to generate enough electricity to power

---

1  Solar Energy Industries Association, 'State Solar Spotlight: California', 2021 factsheet, seia.org.

approximately 130,000 homes. Among the companies to sign up-front contracts with Clearway to purchase electricity generated at Red Bluff was the food and beverage corporation PepsiCo. 'Sourcing renewable energy is a critical part of our journey to net-zero,' PepsiCo's vice president of sustainability said.[2]

I

When any new technology comes along and proves economically viable, the commercial world into which it is incorporated always changes to one extent or another as a result. This was as true for VHS video as for broadband Internet, for the personal computer as for crypto-currency. It has also always been true for new technologies of energy provision in general and electricity production in particular, from the Faraday disc to hydrogen fuel cells and from coal-fired power stations to solar farms. New technologies disrupt established ways of doing things economically as well as technically. We will see plenty of evidence of this in this book: the growth of solar and wind power is bit by bit reshaping what this chapter calls 'the business of power'.

Nevertheless, the reality remains that, to a much more significant extent, solar and wind power and the developers thereof are having to *conform to* the existing business of power. If the relationship between old and new, extant and incursive, is 'dialectical' (and it is), then the influence is considerably stronger in one direction than in the other. Developers of wind and solar power are not able to simply rip up the rules of the actually existing electricity industry; at best, they can chip around its edges. They must observe and understand the existing rules and tailor their business models accordingly. All of which is to say the following: the structure of the electricity industry as it is fashions (without ever quite determining) the conditions of possibility of new entrants and additions to that industry. The development of that industry, even – and perhaps especially – in times of technological disruption, is, if you like, path-dependent.

The example of Clearway Energy in California is usefully illustrative

---

2  'Clearway Completes Additional Long-Term Solar + Energy Storage Contracts for Riverside, CA, clearwayenergygroup.com.

because the generation of electricity around the world today increasingly occurs in commercial contexts characterized by four key features, all of which are evident in the Clearway case. Those features certainly do not apply everywhere, or necessarily always in full: sometimes only, say, two or three of them pertain, and only partially; and sometimes none do. But they – and, more importantly, their combination – are, more and more, the norm.

The four features can be simply stated. The first is institutional specialization – specifically the separation of electricity generation from the other main activities that make up the electricity industry, such as electricity transmission. Where this model of separability applies, institutional participants in the wider electricity industry typically specialize in just one activity or another. Electricity generation (developing and operating generating assets) is, for instance, what Clearway does – exclusively.

The second key feature is private ownership, which is to say the control of the activity of electricity generation by private, profit-seeking corporate actors – again, such as Clearway.

The third feature is competition in electricity generation. Generation is carried out by multiple actors who compete to sell the electricity they produce. In California, as we have seen, there are hundreds of producers of solar power besides Clearway, not to mention any number of owners of generating facilities of other kinds, whether fossil-fuel-based or 'clean'.

The fourth and final key feature is the market. Thus, markets of various kinds, rather than, say, governments or industry regulators, establish the terms of industry trade. Of course, whatever the industry, capitalist markets are often actively fashioned by government hands, and this is certainly true of electricity. In fact, it would be difficult to think of a sector in which markets are *more* deeply structured and shaped by state and regulatory design: electricity markets are in significant measure government constructs. As Mark Christie, a commissioner of the US Federal Energy Regulatory Commission, has recently put it, the advanced electricity 'markets' we increasingly see around the world today, 'despite the label [. . .] never have been true markets, but rather administrative constructs with some market characteristics'.[3]

---

3  M. C. Christie, 'It's Time to Reconsider Single-Clearing Price Mechanisms in US Energy Markets', *Energy Law Journal* 44: 1 (2023), p. 4.

Still, the point is that it is increasingly the case that, to the extent that they influence how electricity is produced and distributed, by whom and at what prices, governments do so indirectly and at one remove – that is, by establishing 'free' electricity 'markets', in which they strive not to intervene except in exceptional circumstances such as times of crisis (see Chapter 10). The premise, at least, is that buyers and sellers should be broadly free to trade on terms of their own choosing, either directly with one another or indirectly via organized market exchanges, and that investment in generating capacity should be guided by market-based price signals. This, once more, is the context in which Clearway operates in modern-day California.

These, then, are the four key features of the commercial milieu for electricity generation that increasingly represents the global norm. Yet things looked very different when, around a decade after Stephen Gaskin left California, that state enjoyed its – and indeed the world's – first bona fide non-hydro renewables boom. On that occasion, the technology in question was not solar but wind. In the first half of the 1980s, some $2 billion was ploughed into installing in the state more than 10,000 wind turbines with a combined capacity in the region of 1 GW, which at the time represented the vast bulk of installed wind-power capacity not just nationally but globally.[4]

Then, *none* of the aforementioned four key features of today's business of electricity generation substantially applied – not in California, and typically not anywhere else either. The commercial context in which electricity generation occurred usually looked very, very different. 'In most countries', Michael Davidson and colleagues have observed, the electricity sector was dominated by 'large-scale electricity companies' that were 'vertically integrated', meaning that they 'owned and controlled all [industry activities] under a single roof'.[5] Generation was not separated, in other words. Nor, generally, were these companies private. 'Governments', Davidson and his co-authors continued, 'typically opted for public ownership and operation.' Furthermore, these vertically

4   S. Knuth, 'Rentiers of the Low-Carbon Economy? Renewable Energy's Extractive Fiscal Geographies', *Environment and Planning A: Economy and Space*.

5   M. R. Davidson, F. Kahrl and V. J. Karplus, 'Towards a Political Economy Framework for Wind Power: Does China Break the Mould?', in D. Arent, C. Arndt, M. Miller, F. Tarp and O. Zinaman, eds, *The Political Economy of Clean Energy Transitions* (New York: Oxford University Press, 2017), p. 255.

integrated companies did not have to compete: they usually enjoyed what scholars (including Davidson) call 'natural monopolies', either at the national scale or sub-nationally.[6] Last but not least, markets played a limited role, if any. The companies in question were instructed where and in what to invest, and were required 'to serve all customers at cost-based prices in exchange for a guaranteed rate of return on invested capital, a model known as "cost-of-service"'.

What has happened, then? How and why did the historic norm for the 1980s described by Davidson and colleagues become the strikingly different contemporary norm described above and exemplified by California and Clearway? Explaining what has happened is the objective of this chapter. With necessarily broad brush strokes, we rehearse the various key forms of restructuring that have convulsed the electricity industry worldwide over the past four decades. We do so not out of dry historical interest, but because the convulsions are ongoing, and because understanding both the economics of solar and wind power and the prospects for these renewable technologies to make further inroads into the landscape of electricity generation *requires* us to know how the broader business of power has changed, and continues to change.

The approach taken is to consider, in turn, developments with regard to each of the four key organizational dimensions identified above. First, therefore, we examine the *unbundling* of national electricity sectors – that is, the tendency for generation and other core industry activities increasingly to be separated from one another, and for the 'vertically integrated' entities referred to by Davidson and his co-authors thereby to be dis-integrated. This is followed by discussions of growing *de-monopolization*, *privatization* and *marketization*. As subsequent chapters will make clear, each of these four trends is proving to be highly significant in fashioning the form, pace and pattern of the ongoing roll-out of solar and wind power.

Of course, the four processes, in reality, have been intimately bound up with one another. It is impossible to understand, say, the increase of

---

6  In economics, a 'natural' monopoly is said to exist if a single company can serve a particular market at lower cost than any combination of two or more competitors. Why 'natural'? Because a one-company industry is (considered to be) the most efficient industry configuration and is thus the configuration that one would expect to arise under 'natural' – that is, free market – conditions.

competition within the electricity sector without also attending to the parallel *and connected* processes of unbundling, privatization and marketization; indeed, the latter three have in part been pursued precisely to facilitate the former. But the electricity business is fiendishly complex and hard to understand at the best of times. The aim in what follows is to illuminate and simplify (albeit without dumbing down), and, to that end, analytical disentangling is a necessity.

Before proceeding, a quick word concerning the forces shaping the processes of industry restructuring of recent decades. Although much of what has occurred has been specific to the electricity sector, the refashioning of that sector has clearly been part and parcel of a much broader and deeper refashioning of regional, national and international political economies at large. Competition, privatization and marketization: these, after all, are the very watchwords of what we have come to know as neoliberalism.

The point of mentioning this is that, in zooming in over the next few pages on the details of what has actually happened around the world to the business of electricity since the 1980s, it is important to keep in mind the question of broadly why it has happened. We shall certainly have occasion to discuss particular aspects of this question in certain specific contexts. But the basic story of electricity is the basic story of 'neoliberalization' – the amalgam of processes whereby neoliberalism has effectively been engineered on the ground – more widely, as rehearsed in what is now a vast historical literature.

Thus what ensues is a story, for the most part, of reforms that were rooted in ideology and driven by state and quasi-state institutions, which have redounded to the benefit principally of capital and its particular class interests, with that capital–class constellation, needless to say, having played a consistently crucial role in lobbying for the enactment of the reforms in question. Perhaps most pointedly, it is a story with markedly different shades in rich and poorer countries. In the former, restructuring has typically been relatively endogenous – determined, designed and driven largely internally. In poorer countries, by contrast, much of the impetus for restructuring has been exogenous to national borders, although not, of course, to the global capitalist system.

As has been fulsomely documented, far-reaching neoliberal reforms were widely foisted upon countries across the Global South in the 1990s and 2000s as the price to be paid for much-needed fiscal support from bodies such as the World Bank and the International Monetary Fund (IMF). Restructuring of domestic electricity sectors along precisely the lines recounted in what follows – sometimes with local political elites serving as willing accomplices, sometimes much less willingly – was invariably a centrepiece of such reformism.[7] Given that both the World Bank and the IMF have latterly shed some of their reformist enthusiasm, it can be easy to forget, from the vantage point of the 2020s, quite how zealous those institutions were, and indeed quite how outspoken they were about their intentions. But it should not be forgotten. Perhaps the best jog to our collective memory is provided by the World Bank's 1993 policy paper setting out its understanding of its own role in the electricity sector. Five 'guiding principles' for World Bank action – essentially, five sets of pre-conditions for World Bank lending – were established. The third was particularly unequivocal and forceful. 'The Bank', the paper promised, 'will aggressively pursue the commercialization and corporatization of, and private sector participation in, developing-country power sectors.'[8] There, in a nutshell, was the blueprint for what was to come.

## II

The electricity industry produces electricity for sale to households, businesses and other users: that is its raison d'être. There are several reasons why in most countries an immensely complicated set of commercial arrangements exists to fulfil this seemingly straightforward function, of which arguably the key one – and thus the one with which we start – is geographical. Electricity is generated in one set of places, but consumed in others, of much greater number. Take the United States. As of 2015, there were around 7,000 generating plants scattered across the country,

---

7  Numerous studies of particular national cases amply testify to this. A prime example is a fascinating study of post-1980s transformations in the political economy of India's electricity sector, deployed as a lens on the wider transformation of India itself: E. Chatterjee, 'Underpowered: Electricity Policy and the State in India, 1991–2014', unpublished PhD dissertation, University of Oxford, 2015, ox.ac.uk.

8  World Bank, 'The World Bank's Role in the Electric Power Sector: Policies for Effective Institutional, Regulatory, and Financial Reform', February 2013, worldbank.org, p. 69.

producing power ultimately consumed by around 160 million different end customers.[9] How to get the power from the former to the latter, and to do so when, where and in the volume it is actually needed?

In strictly technical terms, the answer to this question is: by using an electricity grid, which is an interconnected network for the delivery of electrical power. Delivery of electricity through the grid usually occurs in two 'stages', or at two 'levels'. First, the *transmission* network takes power from sites of generation to electric substations, which are usually strategically located close to areas of concentrated demand. Such transmission occurs at high voltages (for maximum efficiency) and often over very long distances; if the electricity grid is compared to a country's road system, the transmission lines would represent its freeways. But most customers cannot safely receive power at such high voltages. Thus substations lower ('step down') the voltage and then transfer the electricity to end users via the *distribution* network – that is, the system's arterial roads.[10]

Needless to say, in its totality, the grid is a complex beast, requiring constant, careful oversight and upkeep. Alexandra Klass writes,

> Managing the reliability and security of the electric grid is a herculean task. At the present time, energy storage options for electricity are limited, which means that there must be enough, but not too much, electricity flowing through the grid at every moment, maintained at an appropriate voltage, that can be dispatched to customers on demand. If these conditions are not met, blackouts or brownouts can occur and the grid does not serve its function of providing safe and reliable electricity.[11]

---

9   A. B. Klass, 'Expanding the US Electric Transmission and Distribution Grid to Meet Deep Decarbonization Goals', *Environmental Law Reporter News and Analysis* 47 (2017), p. 10749.

10   As indicated, there are not always two levels. Sweden's grid, for example, has three levels – the middle tier comprises *regional transmission networks* that transfer electricity from the national, high-voltage transmission network to local distribution networks (and sometimes direct to large electricity consumers such as industrial facilities).

11   Klass, 'Expanding the US Electric Transmission and Distribution Grid', p. 10750. Whereas a blackout is a complete shutdown of power in a given area, a brownout is a partial outage, usually in the form of a temporary reduction in system voltage or system capacity.

In the aforementioned case of the US, the 7,000 generating plants and approximately 160 million customers are connected to one another by around a million kilometres of transmission lines – making up three major regional grids, which are only minimally interconnected with one another – and 10 million kilometres of lower-voltage distribution lines.

As indicated earlier, it was commonly the case around the middle of the second half of the twentieth century that everything involved in getting electrical power to customers was aggregated commercially under one roof. In other words, a single, 'vertically integrated' entity controlled the entire supply chain, from generation through to distribution, and it charged customers a sufficient amount to cover all of the various costs involved.

But it had definitely not always been that way. In fact, in its early decades the electricity industry in most countries was a phenomenally fragmented, 'bitty' thing, organizationally as much as spatially. It generally came into being as a patchwork of largely independent local systems, and only ever gradually and incrementally over time did it consolidate technologically – principally via the mechanism of centrally coordinated, long-distance transmission networks – and commercially.

The first, highly localized systems emerged in Europe and the US in the 1880s and 1890s. Sometimes, the protagonists were private companies. Industrial firms, for example, originally built electric plants for lighting and to drive motors. Other times, it was municipalities, for which lighting (of streets) was again a key motivating factor. As the nascent 'industry' developed, private electric companies tended to focus their efforts on denser, more populated, and hence more profitable urban areas, leaving publicly owned entities to serve less urban areas. By 1910, there were, for instance, as many as 1,500 state-owned and state-operated electric companies in the US, although that number rapidly diminished in the following decades as private companies took increasing control of the industry.[12]

Whatever the public–private mix, the electricity industry in most countries remained markedly fragmented until at least mid-century. At the end of the Second World War, for example, there were still more

---

12 R. D. Pomp, 'A Brief History of the Electric Utility Industry', in P. Burling, ed., *Impacts of Electric Utility Deregulation on Property Taxation* (Cambridge, MA: Lincoln Institute of Land Policy, 2000), p. 20.

than 570 entities (public and private) actively involved in the generation
and distribution of electricity in Britain, and more than double that
number – at least 200 in generation and 1,150 in distribution – in
France.[13]

If aggregation and consolidation of the electricity supply chain within
single vertically integrated enterprises was not a feature of the industry's
early history, however, this was increasingly what transpired, in a process
that was often – but not always – led and legislated by the state. For this
there were many reasons, the details of which need not detain us here.
Essentially, the growing consensus as the industry matured during the
first half of the twentieth century was that continuing fragmentation
militated against security and efficiency of supply. As one long-time
participant in the UK electricity sector, for example, later put it, the
sector in the pre-war era was blighted by 'heterogeneity' of, among other
things, 'voltages, systems, standards of safety and reliability, and prices'.[14] Were the system being created from scratch, this was clearly not
how it would be designed. What was needed, in short, was one or more
larger, standardized and more efficient undertakings.

In the event, the ensuing consolidation and vertical integration of the
electricity industry occurred at varying geographical scales, and to varying degrees, in different territories. Consider, by way of example, the
three countries whose emergent electricity sectors we have touched
upon in the preceding paragraphs: France, the UK and the US.

In France and the UK, vertical integration occurred at the national
level, and specifically under public ownership. In the former territory,
such integration would prove to be more or less total. Under legislation
introduced in 1946, *all* electricity enterprises active across the entire
supply chain, other than a small number of local distribution companies, were consolidated within a new state-owned entity, Électricité de
France (EDF). Meanwhile, the consolidation and integration of generation and transmission would be equally comprehensive in the UK,
where the Electricity Act of 1947 established the Central Electricity
Generating Board (CEGB), with monopoly rights over both activities

---

13   M. Heddenhausen, 'Privatisations in Europe's Liberalised Electricity Markets –
The Cases of the United Kingdom, Sweden, Germany, and France', December 2007,
swp-berlin.org, pp. 8, 17.

14   C. T. Melling, 'Nationalisation of Electricity Supply 1947: Reasons and Problems',
*Engineering Science and Education Journal* 7: 1 (1998), p. 12.

across all of England and Wales.[15] Where England and Wales differed materially from France was with regard to local distribution, which in England and Wales was exempted from vertical integration (but not from nationalization). The 1947 Act created twelve new publicly owned regional electricity boards, which purchased electricity from the CEGB and distributed and sold it to local customers.

In the US, vertical integration typically encompassed the entire supply chain (as in France), but it was very much a sub-national phenomenon. There were many hundreds of vertically integrated operators, mostly referred to as 'utilities', each of which enjoyed a monopoly on generation, transmission and distribution assets within a designated geographic service area. When necessary, they could purchase from one another (both within states and, increasingly, across state borders) both electricity per se and the transmission services necessary to move it. The largest were privately owned, but there were also significant numbers of smaller municipally or communally owned enterprises. The private entities operated under the oversight of state public utility commissions, which regulated investments and prices, allowing the companies to recover their operating costs and earn a return on investment. To take one illustrative example, Florida was, in all the aforementioned respects, broadly typical. As recently as the late 1980s, five private, vertically integrated utilities – Florida Power & Light, Florida Power, Florida Public Utilities Company, Gulf Power, and Tampa Electric – controlled about four-fifths of the market; they were complemented by around fifty municipal utilities and rural cooperatives.[16]

Crystallizing in the middle decades of the twentieth century in most relatively mature electricity markets, this vertical-integration model 'held' as the dominant way of structuring the industry until relatively late in the century.[17] It was generally not until the 1990s, and in many

---

15  Separate vertically integrated companies enjoyed industry monopolies in Northern Ireland and Scotland – one (the Electricity Board for Northern Ireland) in the former and two (the South of Scotland Electricity Board and the North of Scotland Hydro-Electric Board) in the latter.

16  Another country that featured sub-national vertically integrated monopolies was Germany, where, through the 1990s, nine such regional giants dominated the electricity industry. See S. G. Gross, *Energy and Power: Germany in the Age of Oil, Atoms, and Climate Change* (Oxford: Oxford University Press, 2023), pp. 273–4.

17  It was also a feature of many less mature markets: India, for example, in the 1950s and 1960s, established 'state electricity boards' as vertically integrated regional monopolies

places later still, that meaningful moves to substantively restructure national electricity sectors began to gather steam. When they did, unbundling – that is, the commercial separation from one another of the different parts of the supply chain – was almost always integral to the wider restructuring process.

Again, the exact extent and manner of unbundling have varied greatly from place to place, just as the manner and extent of vertical integration itself had in the first place. Notably, dis-integration has frequently seeded not three but four separate commercial activities. Alongside enterprises specializing in generation, transmission and distribution, fully unbundled electricity sectors – of which the UK's would be a prototypical example – also feature electricity retailers, often also referred to simply as 'suppliers'. These entities are not involved in the physical delivery of power. Instead, they intermediate strictly financially between end customers on the one hand and, on the other, the various entities that are involved in electricity generation and transport. Like grocery retailers, they pay one price for the product (here, power), and charge another. In effect, they are risk managers.

There are three particularly important observations to make about the landscape of unbundling; each is absolutely pivotal to the arguments developed later in this book. First, of all the four trends discussed in the present chapter – unbundling, de-monopolization, privatization and marketization – unbundling has probably progressed furthest, and in the most places.[18] Even countries where little has changed on the other three dimensions have often substantially unbundled their electricity sectors vertically. China might be the best (and most significant) example of this.

Second, of all the different stages or elements of the electricity supply chain, it is generation that has been most substantially and widely unbundled. In other words, even where two or more of transmission, distribution and retail remain largely integrated with one another, generation typically now stands materially apart. In India, for example, regional DISCOMs (distribution companies) still combine and control all distribution and retail, whereas, subsequent to reforms undertaken

---

fully controlling generation, transmission and distribution. See S. S. Kale, *Electrifying India: Regional Political Economies of Development* (Stanford: Stanford University Press, 2014).

18    See for example, V. Foster, S. Witte, S. G. Banerjee and A. Moreno, 'Charting the Diffusion of Power Sector Reforms across the Developing World', World Bank Policy Research Working Paper 8235, November 2017, worldbank.org.

in the 1990s, generation assets are owned and operated separately.[19] Much the same is true in China. There, separate retailers did begin to appear after the latest round of reforms, from 2015, but they remain thin on the ground and essentially immaterial.[20] By contrast, two significant earlier rounds of restructuring, in the 1980s and then around the turn of millennium, succeeded in carving out a largely separate generation sector, which is dominated today by the 'Big 5' producers – Huaneng Group, Huadian Group, China Energy, State Power Investment Corporation and Datang Group. As subsequent chapters will demonstrate, it is, in the context of energy transition and renewable technologies, impossible to overstate the importance of this widespread international trend towards unbundled electricity generation.

Lastly, and no less crucially for our purposes, such unbundling tends to be more pronounced for some types of electricity-generating capacity than for others, and solar and wind capacity is usually the most unbundled (that is, most likely to be separately owned) of all. This stands to reason. In countries where the unbundling of generation from what were previously vertically integrated electricity sectors has been only partial, the bits of generating capacity that remain integrated with the rest of the supply chain tend disproportionately to be the bits that always were so integrated – that is, the conventional fossil-fuel-based assets.

Consider the US case, which is an exemplar. There, the degree of unbundling of electricity-generating capacity has varied considerably from state to state (as indeed has the degree of industry restructuring more widely). At the aggregate national level, the share of electricity generated by independent (non-integrated) power producers (IPPs) increased from less than 2 per cent as recently as 1997 to 42 per cent by 2020. But the share of generation specifically from non-hydro renewables that is controlled by these independents is much, much higher – reaching 80 per cent in 2020.[21] And, to one degree or another, what is true of the

---

19   Only large customers (not ordinary households) can buy other than from DISCOMs, in which case not from retailers but directly from generators – but even they rarely do so.

20   H. Guo, M. R. Davidson, Q. Chen, D. Zhang, N. Jiang, Q. Xia, C. Kang and X. Zhang, 'Power Market Reform in China: Motivations, Progress, and Recommendations', *Energy Policy* 145 (2020), 111717.

21   See Tables 3.1.A and 3.3.A at eia.gov/electricity/annual/.

US is also true elsewhere. *Wind- and solar-based electricity generation is in large measure a discrete, standalone business.*

We have failed thus far, however, at least beyond some preliminary remarks of more general pertinence, to ask what is perhaps the most interesting question. Why? Why, that is, did countries around the world begin in the 1990s to unbundle what were ordinarily vertically integrated electricity sectors? Why do they continue to do so today? And why was the activity of generation a particular focus of these efforts? To provide answers, we need to connect unbundling to questions of competition.

## III

During the post-war era, the view was long held that, even if it were desirable (and many felt it was not), competition was simply not possible in the electricity sector. The sector was characterized by (vertically integrated) monopoly because monopoly was, effectively, inherent to it. Such monopoly was, to use the word used by economists, 'natural', meaning the lowest-cost – and hence most efficient – solution to meeting market demand. It is not hard to understand this view that conditions of natural monopoly indeed apply in the case of electricity, or at least in certain parts of the supply chain. Why have two or more networks of long-distance transmission lines, for example, when one technically suffices?

From the 1980s onwards, however, this long-held view was increasingly challenged by certain reformist economists and private sector actors. Competition, they argued, *was* possible. Not only that, they said, but many of the problems seemingly afflicting electricity sectors in that period in rich and poorer countries alike – underinvestment in the grid, power blackouts, high consumer prices – were attributable precisely to the absence of competition. If not quite a magic pill, competition was, it was claimed, the most important medicine in treating the ailing patient, and in rendering the operation of the sector (to use the favoured word) more 'efficient'.

But there was a catch, or proviso. The champions of competition emphasized that competition would only be possible and practicable in some parts of the supply chain, and not all. And it was exactly for this reason that vertical unbundling was considered necessary – that is, to facilitate competition. This argument had two components.

The first part of the argument ventured that companies could not be expected to compete effectively in one business area if lumbered with another, especially if the latter activity was not itself amenable to competition. Second, it was pointed out that conflicts of interest plainly could arise if governments were to try to engender competition without having first unbundled. For instance, competition in genera-tion might be hampered if a generator also possessing transmission or distribution assets discriminated against other generators needing to use those assets to deliver their output. In short, it was seen as neces-sary to unbundle the supply chain to enable companies to compete in those parts of the chain where competition was possible – and in those parts alone.

The parts in question, it was concluded, were the non-transport elements of the supply chain. Being 'naturally' monopolistic, electricity transport activities – long-distance transmission and shorter-distance distribution – were expected to remain monopoly businesses, albeit regulated ones (the question of regulation being one we return to below). But the other parts of the sector, argued the advocates of reform, could and should where necessary be de-monopolized. There were two such parts, which we will deal with in turn: retail and generation.

Progress since the 1980s in opening up electricity retail to meaning-ful competition has been mixed, at best. Some countries have experi-enced a degree of success. Even so, they are few in number, and empha-sis should definitely be placed on the word 'degree'. Most of the countries where competition has to a certain extent materialized are in Europe. Here, studies generally indicate the greatest levels of retail competition as existing in Germany, the UK and the Nordic countries.[22]

The UK case is well illustrative of why celebration of increased competition tends to be muted: the combined market share of the five remaining legacy (incumbent monopoly) suppliers – British Gas, E.ON, OVO, EDF and Scottish Power – was still above 70 per cent at the end of

---

22   For example, R. Poudineh, 'Liberalized Retail Electricity Markets: What We Have Learned after Two Decades of Experience?', OIES paper, EL 38, December 2019, oxfordenergy.org; ACER/CEER, 'Annual Report on the Results of Monitoring the Internal Electricity and Natural Gas Markets in 2020: Energy Retail Markets and Consumer Protection Volume', November 2021, acer.europa.eu.

2021, with consolidation among suppliers having contributed to this enduring industry concentration.[23] Beyond Europe, industry observers typically identify only two other countries as having had genuine success in de-monopolizing electricity retail: New Zealand and the US. And, in the latter, such success has been strictly regionally circumscribed. Over thirty states (albeit relatively less populous ones) still have no retail electricity choice at all. Comfortably the most competitive US retail market is in Texas, which is home to over 100 different electricity retailers. Most of the other US states with competitive retail sectors are located in the north-east of the country.[24]

Elsewhere in the world, competition in electricity retail is either negligible or non-existent, with supply to consumers continuing to be controlled by the monopoly providers of physical distribution. In some cases, this is because retail remains legally bundled with distribution, either in full – in which case the very concept of electricity 'retail' is effectively meaningless – or for the majority of customers. Examples of the latter scenario include Argentina and India. In both, customers whose consumption of electricity falls below certain stipulated loads – which includes all ordinary households together with most smaller commercial and industrial consumers – have no choice but to buy their electricity from the local distribution company. Larger 'open access' consumers, by contrast, have the option to contract directly with generators, although in practice relatively few actually do so.

In other cases, however, it is not legal restrictions that constrain retail competition. There are several countries in which legal provisions for retail choice have existed for some time, but competition remains trivial nonetheless.[25] Generally speaking, the degree of actual competition depends upon the ease of industry entry for would-be retailers, and the propensity to switch suppliers among electricity consumers. Where there exist substantial barriers to entry, to switching or to both, the result tends to be inertia, with consumer engagement – or rather a lack thereof – proving a particular impediment. As Rahmatallah Poudineh

---

23  'Retail Market Indicators', ofgem.gov.uk. Note that OVO has been considered a legacy supplier since its acquisition of SSE in 2020.

24  See 21st Century Power Partnership, 'An Introduction to Retail Electricity Choice in the United States', August 2017, nrel.gov; also, Angwin, *Shorting the Grid*, pp. 40–1.

25  Poudineh, 'Liberalized Retail Electricity Markets', pp. 6–7.

has remarked, retail electricity markets have been premised on 'the assumption that consumers will behave in the retail electricity market as they do in other offer markets', whereas the reality is that consumers have been dissuaded from switching by factors such as 'complexity of the retail market and electricity tariffs, transaction costs, uncertainty about the service quality of new suppliers, perceived barriers, and behavioural biases'.[26]

Meanwhile, progress internationally in opening up electricity generation to competition has been much more substantial. There are many more countries with competitive generating sectors, and with greater levels of actual competition. Some of the countries in which generation has been substantively de-monopolized include those mentioned above in relation to positive retail competition. The UK, for example, has a highly competitive generating landscape. The number of UK companies whose prime purpose is the generation of electricity – termed 'major power producers' (MPPs) – had increased from just six in 1989 to fifty-five by 2021.[27] As new generators entered the market, the number holding more than 5 per cent each of total generating capacity steadily increased, reaching nine by 2008, while, at the same time, the average market share of those leading players has fallen: the combined share of generating capacity controlled by the top nine in the market decreased from 82 per cent in 2012 to just 68 per cent in 2021. The US has also seen rapidly growing competition in generation, though again, as with retail, only in certain geographic markets: if the share of total electricity generated by IPPs now exceeds 95 per cent in states such as Connecticut and Illinois, it remains below 5 per cent in the likes of Florida and Kentucky.[28]

More significantly, electricity generation has also been de-monopolized relatively successfully in many countries in which there remains negligible or zero retail competition. This includes countries ranging from Argentina to China. In the former, an electricity sector historically controlled by three dominant vertically integrated utilities was restructured beginning in the early 1990s, and while retail – as we have seen – remained wedded to monopolistic control of physical delivery,

26   Ibid., p. 4.

27   S. Ashcroft and A. Annut, 'Competition in UK Electricity Markets', September 2016, gov.uk; 'Digest of UK Energy Statistics (DUKES): Electricity', gov.uk, Table 5.11.

28   'Net Generation by State by Type of Producer by Energy Source (EIA-906, EIA-920, and EIA-923)', eia.gov.

generation did not: already by the year 2000, there were forty-three generating companies owning ninety-six plants.[29] In China, de-monopolization of generation was the first significant vector of restructuring of the wider electricity industry, precipitated by crippling energy shortages in the early 1980s, and from the outset including investment by foreign as well as domestic firms.[30] Competition in generation has remained a consistent fulcrum of Chinese electricity sector policy ever since.

That competition has developed more fully and widely in generation than in retail is readily explicable. Competition in electricity, as we noted earlier, essentially requires unbundling, and across the breadth of the supply chain, generation – as we have also noted – is where unbundling has been most pronounced. Furthermore, policymakers have generally made more concerted efforts to remove obstacles facing new entrants to the generation space than those facing new retail entrants. Such efforts have been primarily twofold. First, companies that control transmission and distribution networks have widely been required to carry power produced by independent (and sometimes rival) generators on non-discriminatory terms. The 1992 Energy Policy Act, for example, gave the US Federal Energy Regulatory Commission the power to impose such terms on network owners. Second, policymakers have expanded the range of markets within which generators are able to sell their output, while often also augmenting the facility with which they can do so. We will pick up on this latter point in our discussion of marketization in the last part of the chapter.

Still, for all the evident international expansion of competition in electricity generation, certain countertendencies exist, and are important to recognize. Three are perhaps most significant. One relates to the aforementioned point about access to networks of physical power delivery. Even where access is supposed to be non-discriminatory and regulators supposedly police said provision, network operators sometimes still find ways to discriminate against certain independent generators. The particular importance of this in the context of this book

29   PwC, 'Introducing Competition in Retail Electricity Supply in India', July 2013, forumofregulators.gov.in, p. 17.

30   M. R. Davidson, 'Creating Markets for Wind Electricity in China', unpublished PhD dissertation, Massachusetts Institute of Technology, 2018, mit.edu, p. 20.

is that it tends to be renewables generators that are disproportionately discriminated against. In several countries, the entity or entities that control the grid in many cases also possess proprietary fossil fuel interests and have consistently erected impediments to equality of grid access for renewables generators, thus limiting the extent of competition provided by those generators. The US is one such country. South Africa is another.[31]

The second countertendency is one that is recognizable from all sorts of other industry sectors within which the free play of competition also theoretically prevails. As Marx once famously observed, competition creates monopoly. What he meant by that was that it is precisely through competing with one another and pushing down prices and profits that capitalist firms come to experience the strongest incentives to merge with one another and build market power. So it has been in 'de-monopolized' electricity sectors around the world. After an initial burst of new entrants, one country after another has witnessed substantial consolidation among generation firms as profits have been squeezed. In Argentina, for instance, there are fewer generating companies now (forty at the time of writing) than there were two decades ago.[32] In China, the leading national power producers, in the shape of the above-mentioned 'Big 5' and four smaller generation companies, have emerged in large part through a process of consolidation of provincial generators starting in the mid-2000s.[33] And so it goes on.

Finally, there are places where policymakers have long been *rhetorically* committed to the de-monopolization of electricity generation but where, in reality, efforts to stimulate competition have proven rather half-hearted. In countries ranging from France to India, South Africa and Sweden, incumbent generators – that is, those that dominated prior to industry reform – continue to enjoy positions of relative dominance. Eskom, for example, continues to control upwards of 90 per cent of

---

31   S. Welton, 'Rethinking Grid Governance for the Climate Change Era', *California Law Review* 109 (2021), pp. 209–75; K. Hochstetler, *Political Economies of Energy Transition: Wind and Solar Power in Brazil and South Africa* (Cambridge: Cambridge University Press, 2020).

32   'Listado Generadores, Comercializadores y Distribuidores', cammesaweb.cam mesa.com.

33   Davidson, 'Creating Markets', p. 280; I. Yin and E. Yep, 'China's Big 5 Power Producers Face Uphill Battle in Meeting Peak Emissions Targets', 7 June 2021, spglobal.com.

electricity generation in South Africa. In France, EDF still produces around three-quarters of all domestically generated electricity (418 of 549 TWh in 2021). In Sweden, Vattenfall's share of overall domestic electricity production remains around half (79 of 171 TWh in 2021).[34]

Besides market power, what EDF, Eskom and Vattenfall notably share, of course, is a particular type of ownership – public ownership. All three are owned by the state. State-owned generators also still control over half of electricity production capacity in India, although there the market power of such actors generally applies at the provincial rather than the national scale, which is also true in parts of the US: publicly owned generation entities, largely operating hydro facilities, dominate power output in the Pacific Northwest, for instance.

It would be difficult to prove that it is *because* they own leading electricity generation enterprises that governments in some countries have been reluctant to be more forceful in encouraging competition among generators – even if the suspicion must be that such is, at least, part of the explanation. At any rate, the key point is that few countries have achieved meaningful competition within the electricity sector without also effecting substantial privatization. It is thus to privatization, the penultimate crucial vector of industry restructuring, that we now turn.

## IV

To talk about privatization is to presume that something is or was owned publicly in the first place, and the first thing to say, therefore, is that where electricity is concerned, not everywhere by any means has this been the case. Earlier in the chapter, we discussed the fact that, in the middle decades of the twentieth century, in the face of fragmented and creaking infrastructure, there were widespread moves towards vertical integration of the electricity supply chain specifically under public ownership. France and the UK, implementing such a model in the 1940s, were exemplars. But some countries ploughed their own, very different furrow. The US, for example, rejected nationalization. For the last century, across the supply chain, US electricity assets have – with

---

34   EDF, '2021 Facts and Figures', April 2022, edf.fr, p. 63; Vattenfall, 'Annual and Sustainability Report 2021', group.vattenfall.com, p. 184.

isolated regional exceptions we have already encountered – always been mainly privately owned.

Elsewhere, however, it was mostly the case that electricity *was* overwhelmingly a publicly owned set of operations when, in the 1980s, calls for restructuring began to gain political support. Indeed, in many countries (though not everywhere), it was in large measure *because* electricity was in public ownership that reform was believed to be necessary; hence privatization was ordinarily a central pillar of restructuring proposals. This was very much neoliberal orthodoxy in action: proponents of reform were convinced that it was right and proper that the state should own as little as possible, the premise being that profit-maximizing private enterprises would always be leaner, more competitive and more efficient, and would generate better outcomes for consumers. Whether it was electricity, water or telephony did not much matter.

Of course, this was pure ideology: there never was any persuasive evidence that private sector enterprises were inherently more efficient than their state counterparts; and, generally speaking, the argument in favour of privatization conveniently elided the question of whether private enterprises would in practice share any efficiency gains with consumers, or whether they would simply pocket them.

Nevertheless, it was impactful and effective ideology. Neoliberal orthodoxy roundly won the day and electricity assets around the world were increasingly transferred to private, corporate ownership.

In some cases, this was true even of infrastructure of physical delivery (that is, transmission and distribution networks), despite the fact that it was explicitly recognized that competition was not possible in these parts of the supply chain. Why deny consumers the advantages of private sector efficiency, the argument went, just because a business was monopolistic? Advocates of network privatization insisted that good regulation by expert oversight bodies could effectively 'stand in' for competition, ensuring that private monopolies kept prices reasonable and continued to carry out the necessary infrastructure investment. Persuaded by this logic, governments in countries ranging from Argentina to the UK proceeded to comprehensively privatize transmission and distribution assets.

But this has often ended in failure. Much more than has been the case with state-led initiatives for either the unbundling or de-monopolization of the electricity sector, privatization initiatives have frequently ended up being reversed, and this has been particularly true of the privatization of delivery infrastructure. Vivien Foster and colleagues have identified dozens of cases of renationalization, mainly in distribution, and precipitated for instance by 'a dispute with the private operator, some kind of shock affecting the financial equilibrium of the private operator, or a change of government'.[35] Their research focused on the Global South – wherein most reversals have taken place in Latin America, South Asia and sub-Saharan Africa – but the Global North has not been immune. Having wholly privatized the ownership and operation of its electricity grid in the 1990s, for instance, the UK – for so long a standard-bearer for privatization – announced in 2022 that it would be renationalizing the operation of the country's transmission system.

For the most part, however, privatization, much like unbundling and de-monopolization, has principally involved infrastructure of electricity generation, not delivery. Today, the proportion of countries with private sector participation in generation is much higher than in short-distance distribution and much, much higher than in long-distance transmission.[36] And in the generation space too, there have been far fewer instances of renationalization.[37] Instead, what we have seen is, over more than three decades, an ongoing and seemingly irreversible transfer of power generation assets from public to private hands. The period of most substantial such privatization was the 1990s, and by the turn of the millennium the proportion of national generating capacity owned privately had already reached an average of 48 per cent in OECD and G20 countries. By 2014, the average privately owned share in those countries had increased to 55 per cent.[38]

Generation has been the primary locus of electricity sector privatization across the Global South, too. When the World Bank and the IMF set about trying to increase private sector participation in the electricity industries of debtor nations in the 1990s, they found generation to be the easiest nut to crack. Host country governments could be persuaded

---

35  Foster et al., 'Charting the Diffusion of Power Sector Reforms', p. 39.
36  Ibid., p. 30.
37  Ibid., p. 40.
38  A. Prag, D. Röttgers and I. Scherrer, 'State-Owned Enterprises and the Low-Carbon Transition', OECD Working Paper No. 129, April 2018, oecd-ilibrary.org, p. 29.

to relinquish ownership of generating assets, and private capital – especially Western private capital – could be persuaded to invest in such assets, especially when, as was often the case, the investment was protected by generous long-term power purchase contracts with state-owned utilities.[39] Even today, when pressure to privatize from institutions such as the World Bank has substantially diminished, there are non-Western countries that continue to welcome foreign capital to their power generation sectors with open arms, Vietnam being a prime example.[40] In terms of privatization of transmission and distribution, by contrast, the World Bank and its accomplices never had as much success: governments were much more reluctant to cede control, and capital, doubtless alive to the political risk, remained more reluctant to invest.

If there has been growing privatization of electricity generation assets worldwide since the 1980s, it is, for our purposes in this book, crucial to disaggregate that headline trend in two ways. The first is geographical: while the general tendency has indeed been towards greater private ownership of electricity generation assets, there are nonetheless enormous differences between countries. At one extreme there is a cluster of countries in which 80 per cent or more of generating capacity is now privately held, including several countries we have previously discussed (such as Argentina, New Zealand, the UK and the US), but also several we have not (such as Chile, Japan, Portugal and Spain).[41] At the other extreme, however, is a cluster of countries where less than 30 per cent of generating capacity is privately held, ranging from Croatia to Israel and from Indonesia to Mexico.

As previously noted, countries with low levels of private sector participation in electricity generation tend also to be those with low levels of competition among generators, with governments effectively protecting their proprietary assets. France is plainly one example of this. South Africa is another: wholly owned by the state, its national energy utility Eskom essentially controls the entire electricity supply chain.

Second, just as we saw earlier that solar- and wind-based generation tends to be more commercially unbundled from the rest of the supply

39   S. Pirani, *Burning Up: A Global History of Fossil Fuel Consumption* (London: Pluto Press, 2018), p. 146.

40   N. L. Dan, 'Vietnam's Renewable Energy Policies and Opportunities for the Private Sector', May 2022, nbr.org, pp. 3–4.

41   Prag et al., 'State-Owned Enterprises and the Low-Carbon Transition', p. 30.

chain than fossil-fuel-based generation, so too the former tends to be characterized by higher levels of private ownership. Again, this makes intuitive sense: state-owned enterprises are typically the legacy actors in electricity generation, thus disproportionately owning legacy (that is, fossil fuel) assets; meanwhile, the lion's share of investment in wind and solar power has occurred during a period (the past two decades) in which private ownership of generation assets has increasingly been the norm.

The data attesting to differential public sector and private sector levels of ownership of generating assets of different types are genuinely striking.[42] In what the IEA terms 'developing' economies, 59 per cent of fossil-fuel-based assets are publicly owned, compared to only 28 per cent of renewables assets. In 'advanced' economies, the public sector owns 21 per cent of fossil-fuel-generating assets. And its share of renewables assets? A measly 4 per cent. In both the Global South and especially the Global North, the green energy world to which we are gradually transitioning is, as things stand, overwhelmingly a privately owned one. The significance of this, economically as much as politically, simply cannot be overstated: insofar as the private sector is ruled by the profit imperative, profitability – its determinants, availability and scale – utterly dominates renewable energy's conditions of both possibility and performance.

Meanwhile, just as important to our collective ecological future as the coupling of renewable power with private ownership is, one suspects, the coupling of dirty power with public ownership. Particularly in the Global South, the governments to which the world is looking to increase the scale and pace of decarbonization remain directly and disproportionately invested economically in the business of continuing to burn fossil fuels to keep the lights on.

# V

Neoliberal wisdom says that, as well as staying out of the ownership of economic assets, the state should also stay out of control of the economy. This is, perhaps, the best-known neoliberal axiom of all: to maximize

---

42   IEA, 'World Energy Investment 2020', July 2020, iea.org, p. 18.

efficiency and to ensure the most productive allocation of resources, economic decisions pertaining to investment, production and price should be steered by the impersonal forces of supply and demand (to which economic actors rationally respond), not by government diktat or other forms of centralized authority. This is only possible, it is said, in the context of free and voluntary exchange – that is, in a free *market* context.

Thus, in the neoliberal milieu of the past few decades, the fourth and final fundamental vector of the restructuring of the electricity sector – and of, of course, much else besides – has been marketization: the turning over of sectoral transactions of all sorts to theoretically unfettered exchange between market actors.

Yet, immediately, we have a seeming paradox. For, while the direction of travel in the sector has indeed generally been strongly away from direct state intervention and towards markets, the principal exception to this rule is the very one with which this book is concerned: solar and wind power. From the outset, government 'interference' (as neoliberals would see it) in markets and pricing has been stitched into the fabric of the solar and wind power economy. It remains so today. In fact, the book's argument is that it *has* to be: markets cannot, and will not, do the job by themselves, that job of course being rapid and comprehensive electricity decarbonization. Markets, and the vaunted price mechanism, are failing. We will not be saying much more specifically about renewables in the next few paragraphs, but the book's thesis should nonetheless be borne in mind by the reader: precisely in the marketization processes that we now discuss lie the seeds of the main economic obstacles to decarbonization.

In any event, note, to begin with, that marketization does not necessarily require privatization: state-owned enterprises can and do operate widely in economic markets, both in the electricity sector and more generally. Strictly speaking, marketization does not require competition either: markets can be, and frequently are, monopolized. Nonetheless, believers in the powers of markets to generate efficient and productive outcomes typically hold that markets without competition are fundamentally impoverished: if they are to 'work', markets require competition; it is perhaps their most powerful ingredient. And what the marketization of electricity clearly does require, meanwhile, is unbundling. After all, if electricity provision is controlled from beginning to end by a

single, vertically integrated operator, then, by definition, a market –
exchange between *actors*, plural – is not possible.

Two important points flow from this. First, where the electricity
sector has not been unbundled, marketization has not occurred. Take,
for example, regions such as the south-eastern US, across most of which
vertically integrated utilities continue to enjoy private monopolies.
Aside from small amounts of electricity that some such utilities source
from third-party generators, prices are not set by markets. In particular,
the amount paid by electricity users is tightly regulated, being set by
state-level public utility commissions on the basis of operator costs.

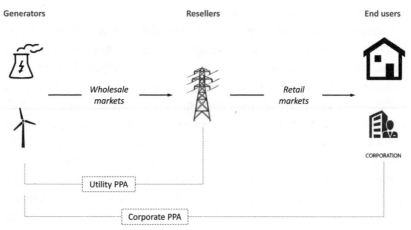

**Figure 2.1** Electricity markets
*Source*: Author

Second, insofar as it is (it will be recalled) in generation that unbundling has proceeded furthest, the closer one gets to the generation end of
the electricity supply chain, the more marketization has typically occurred.
This really matters. To visualize the point, consider Figure 2.1. Where it
has taken place, marketization of the electricity sector has spawned two
main types of markets: *wholesale* markets, in which generators sell electricity to suppliers (essentially, resellers) of various kinds; and *retail*
markets, in which such suppliers (re)sell that electricity. *Most electricity
sector marketization has been in wholesale.* The reason for emphasizing
this is that the proliferation and deepening of wholesale markets as the
main locus of trade in the power output of a generation sector that is now
largely unbundled is at the heart of the wider story of this book.

In the retail space, marketization has been more limited. 'Real' retail markets, providing electricity users with choice of supplier (and price), remain relatively rare at the global scale. Furthermore, the reality is that even in countries with 'free' electricity retail markets, and even before the energy crisis of 2021–2 raised widespread concerns about electricity affordability for ordinary consumers and thus prompted governments to act, elements of top-down price control have been surprisingly common all along – including in what we often think of as the most 'marketized' electricity sectors of all. For all the fact that Europe is very much the home of retail electricity markets, for instance, over half of EU member states still had some form of state intervention in retail prices as of 2020.[43] Some such intervention applied to non-household users, but, more commonly, it covered rates paid by households. In the case of the latter, the regulation either applied across the board – in the shape, for example, of a general price cap – or it was targeted at particular groups of 'vulnerable' energy consumer.

Price intervention in the wholesale space is considerably less common. Deregulated electricity wholesale markets are today very widespread, very large, very important, highly varied – and extraordinarily complicated. This is not the place to provide a detailed analysis of such markets in all their variety and complexity. Such details as are germane to arguments developed later in the book are discussed as and when needed. But a few basic features are important to highlight and foreground here.

First, what is sold in these markets? The obvious answer is 'electricity', in kilowatt- or megawatt-hours, but things are not that simple. The most material question concerns when the electricity that is traded will be delivered. It is possible to trade electricity to be supplied a certain number of weeks or months in the future, under forward or futures contracts. But the most important part of the wholesale market by far is the 'spot' market.

In financial markets, a spot market is one in which assets are traded for immediate delivery. In electricity, however, that is not the case. Rather, electricity for next-day delivery is traded on the spot market, typically in hourly or half-hourly chunks. Ahead of a cut-off point (usually midday), generators bid the amount of electricity they expect to

---

43    ACER/CEER, 'Annual Report', p. 12.

be able to supply for each day-ahead time period – for instance, the hour beginning at 4:00 a.m. Expected supply and demand determine the market-clearing spot price.[44] Prices in electricity spot markets are notoriously volatile, with, as we will see, hugely significant implications.

Of course, such a market design poses particular difficulties for solar and wind generators, who are only able to predict their likely supply of power up to thirty-six hours ahead of time to a certain extent. Thus there needs to be one or more mechanisms to enable reconciliation on the day of settlement between the amount of power bid in advance to (and cleared by) the spot market, the amount of power physically delivered when the time comes, and actual demand for electricity at that time. The main such mechanism is an intraday or 'real time' market, usually referred to (for obvious reasons) as the 'balancing' or 'regulating' market.[45]

Second, at what geographical scale do wholesale markets operate? The answer is: at a range of geographical scales. Some markets are nationally circumscribed. But others are sub-national: significant regional wholesale markets in the US, for instance, include the Mid-Atlantic (PJM West) and New England markets. Others still, meanwhile, are transnational, although that does not mean that prices are harmonized across borders. Among the best-known is the Nord Pool power exchange, which upon its launch in 1996 encompassed Norway and Sweden, but which has since expanded to take in more and more countries and today is pan-European. Note here, however, that

---

44   As we will see in Chapter 6, this placeholder statement is a gross simplification of the price-setting mechanism. On the history of electricity spot pricing, see especially D. Breslau, 'Redistributing Agency: The Control Roots of Spot Pricing of Electricity', *History of Political Economy* 52: S1 (2020), pp. 221–44.

45   Sometimes 'spot market' is taken to encompass both the day-ahead *and* intraday markets, sometimes just the former – we shall follow the latter convention. On the relation between day-ahead and real-time markets, Angwin, *Shorting the Grid*, pp. 148–51, is helpful. Note that those market participants who cause any system-wide imbalance to arise must shoulder the costs of balance being re-established. If, for example, there ends up being an overall deficit of power in a certain time period, and the grid operator calls upon a gas-fired plant to 'regulate up' its output to restore balance, any generators whose physical delivery is lower than they bid are penalized, receiving a lower price for their production than the spot price. Here, see the useful discussion in P. E. Morthorst and T. Ackermann, 'Economic Aspects of Wind Power in Power Systems', in T. Ackermann, ed., *Wind Power in Power Systems*, 2nd edn (Chichester: Wiley & Sons, 2012), pp. 511–15.

Nord Pool is not the only wholesale electricity market in Europe: several others exist: just as companies compete with one another *in* these markets, the markets *themselves* also compete with one another to attract trade.

Needless to say, the scalar expansion of wholesale electricity markets such as has occurred in Europe has been dependent upon commensurate infrastructural developments. Territories whose electricity grids were previously self-contained have increasingly been linked through the construction of interconnectors. Today, somewhere around 15 per cent of Europe's electricity is typically traded between countries in any given year. The likes of France and Norway have conventionally been the biggest net exporters, producing more power than they consume. But patterns shift. In 2022, both became net importers – France for the first time in more than two decades – as a result principally of nuclear outages in France and drought and low reservoir levels in Norway. One of the main territories these two countries imported from in 2022 was the UK, which, on an annual basis, became a net exporter for the first time ever.

And, third, who participates in wholesale electricity markets? We have already identified the two most obvious sets of participants: generators, who sell power, and electricity suppliers, who buy it for resale to users. But there are other important actors, too. Like all modern commodity markets, wholesale electricity markets attract pure, speculative traders, who purchase electricity – including from resellers who have over-ordered – for resale *in* the wholesale market. Meanwhile, no less important than those who trade in wholesale markets are those who operate market exchanges – in Nord Pool's case, Euronext N.V., a Dutch company. These entities have real power and influence. Insofar as they create the eligibility and trading rules for wholesale markets, they directly fashion the commercial viability of would-be market participants, not least (from our perspective) renewables generators.[46]

But organized wholesale exchanges such as Nord Pool or PJM West typically do not represent the only possible sales outlets for unbundled electricity generation companies. In many countries, they are also able to sell electricity directly, under long-term power purchase agreements (PPAs), either to electricity suppliers/resellers (via so-called 'utility

---

46   A case particularly well made by Shelley Welton with regard to the operators of US wholesale electricity market exchanges. See Welton, 'Rethinking Grid Governance'.

PPAs') or to end users with large electricity consumption requirements such as industrial firms or tech companies (so-called 'corporate PPAs', as in the case of Clearway and PepsiCo at the beginning of this chapter). Such PPAs, in particular corporate PPAs, occupy an important place in the renewables story, and thus in this book (Chapter 8).

As Figure 2.1 illustrates, PPAs enable electricity generation companies to circumvent organized wholesale – and, in the case of corporate PPAs, also retail – markets. Nevertheless, they should still be understood as a form of marketization, not as an alternative *to* marketization. Although PPA contracts occasionally attract a degree of price regulation, they are fundamentally a market phenomenon, only representing a different type of market – not a formal, organized, exchange-based, multi-sided market, but rather an informal, 'over-the-counter', bilateral market.

Indeed, the introduction of corporate PPAs sometimes represents a country's first tentative step towards marketization of the electricity sector more generally, especially in non-Western territories. Marketization was the front on which the reform of non-Western electricity sectors generally progressed the least far in the 1990s. Surveying the 'developing' world in the mid-2000s, David Victor and Thomas Heller found that 'market forces operate only on the margins of [most] electric power systems'.[47] Rather, throughout the supply chain, how power was sold, to whom and at what price usually all remained closely controlled. In China, for example, provincial governments would set the prices that grid companies paid to generators and central government would establish the tariffs at which the grid companies in turn sold power to consumers.

Allowing generators to contract directly with large industrial and commercial users preceded other forms of marketization in China's electricity sector. Next came retail and wholesale forward markets. By 2018, some 30 per cent of electricity nationally was being traded through the latter, albeit with the proportion varying significantly from region to region.[48] Spot markets were the final piece of the puzzle. Even so, one should not overstate the extent of marketization of China's electricity

---

47   D. G. Victor and T. C. Heller, 'Introduction and Overview', in Victor and Heller, eds., *The Political Economy of Power Sector Reform: The Experiences of Five Major Developing Countries* (Cambridge: Cambridge University Press, 2006), p. 11.

48   Guo et al., 'Power Market Reform in China', p. 2.

sector. Retail prices paid by ordinary household users, for instance, are still tightly regulated, with only limited departure from benchmark tariffs being permitted. And spot markets are still in a trial phase, consisting only of pilot programmes in selected provinces.[49]

Corporate PPAs likewise represented an important preliminary step in the direction of Western-style electricity markets in India, which, alongside China, by dint of its sheer scale, will arguably shape not just Asian but also global electrical (and hence ecological) futures more profoundly than any other nation. But, in India, too, electricity marketization, at least as that phenomenon is understood in the West, remains patchy. As in China, regulators continue to set retail tariffs. Also as in China, most output is not traded on formal wholesale exchanges – still only about 10 per cent, even as India has had such exchanges for longer than China has.[50] Instead, generators sell the bulk of their output via long-term utility PPAs with the country's DISCOMs.[51]

Holding local distribution and retail monopolies, India's DISCOMs, which are predominantly state-owned, are obligated to meet all local user demand. Insofar as they have no generating assets of their own, they rely upon the aforementioned bilateral PPAs with generators to ensure resource adequacy in the long term. Thus, as and when they project a future need for more output, DISCOMs sign PPAs for new, incremental generating capacity. In turn, these contracts enable their developer counterparties to raise construction finance: banks lend to them to develop and build, safe in the knowledge that the output of the new plant is guaranteed to be bought, and the loans repaid. 'The purpose of these long-term contracts', as the IEA has noted, 'is to ensure that new generation capacity will be built.'[52]

Why highlight these particular contracts in this more general introductory discussion of marketization? Partly because they point to

49   M. Sun, J. Zhang, Y. Pei and L. Gao, 'The Energy Regulation and Markets Review: China', June 2022, thelawreviews.co.uk.

50   A. Kumar Shukla, D. V. Thangzason Sonna and V. Kumar Srivastava, 'Renewable Energy – The Silent Revolution', *RBI Bulletin*, October 2021, rbi.org.in, p. 215.

51   Some of these contracts are awarded through competitive bidding in provincial and central auctions, some non-competitively; with regulated, cost-plus tariffs, the latter effectively set a 'glass ceiling' for the prices of the former. See S. Ahluwalia, 'National Electricity Policy 2021: Making India's Power Sector Future-Ready', June 2021, orfonline. org.

52   IEA, 'Renewables Integration in India', June 2021, iea.org, p. 74.

what will be one of this book's core themes – namely the extent to which planned installations of new generating capacity are considered 'bankable', which is to say, are able to secure financing. But partly also because they point to another important aspect of the electricity industry to which marketization increasingly often applies, and which therefore needs examining briefly here. That aspect is resource adequacy.

It will be remembered from Chapter 1 that, as countries decarbonize their electricity sectors, they need, given constraints in energy storage capabilities, to consider where electricity will come from when solar and wind facilities fail to produce. It will also be remembered that, for now at least, fossil-fuel-based plants are the largest producers of such 'baseload', always-available power.

As many have pointed out, however, there is a risk here. If governments – as we shall see that they are – are encouraging solar and wind to grow and to displace conventional generating facilities, does there not come a point when the business of conventional generation becomes unviable? Let us say that a gas-fired plant is profitable when operating, and earning revenue, at least 70 per cent of the time, and that, in the past, its utilization rate has on average exceeded this. But then solar and wind enter the picture and meet a growing share of the demand that the gas plant historically supplied. The plant's utilization rate falls – eventually to below 70 per cent. At that point, not only may it (and other such operational plants) get shut down by its owner, but no new potential sources of baseload power may get developed either – the economics cannot be made to work. Suddenly, the government's plans for long-term security of power supply are in tatters.

In India, where solar and wind provide less than 10 per cent of electricity, such concerns remain some way down the road. For now, at any rate, the government is happy to leave it to the regional DISCOMs to manage resource adequacy through PPAs. The assumption is that those entities contracted by the DISCOMs to provide future power will be able collectively to provide enough power, and at all times.

But, where solar and wind have advanced further, policymakers have often proven less sanguine, and have developed mechanisms designed to ensure that there will always be the necessary resources to meet peak electricity demand. The preferred such mechanism is a 'capacity market' – in other words, a market solution. In capacity markets, generators bid not to sell electricity but to be *available* in the future to generate electricity when called upon at short notice.

Thus a plant that is active in the capacity market will typically enjoy two income streams, one for being available to generate – say, $1 million per month if it is a 100 MW (100,000 kW) plant and its monthly capacity payment is $10 per kW – and one for the power it actually generates. The underlying principle is that if the latter income stream alone is not sufficient to encourage investment in new baseload generating capacity or for existing such capacity to remain open, then the two income streams combined will be.

Energy economists and regulators are divided on the question of the actual need for capacity markets. Thus, in Europe, for example, some countries, including France and the UK, have them, but others, like Germany, do not. Similarly in the US: capacity markets are used by grid operators in, for instance, New England and the PJM region, but not in Texas. Where capacity markets are not used, there is said to be an 'energy-only' electricity market.

One final observation is in order before we leave, for now, the complex but crucial realm of marketization. While, in theory, capacity markets are technology-neutral, in practice the proviso that generators must be able to demonstrate sufficient technical performance to contribute to security of supply effectively excludes one notable category of generator – renewables.[53] So how, if not through capacity markets, do policymakers try to incentivize investment in solar and wind power? That is a question for later chapters.

## VI

Carrying much of the burden of weaning the world off fossil fuels, solar and wind power are being developed into a long-standing but also constantly evolving commercial landscape of electricity generation and delivery. Unless we understand that landscape and its evolutionary dynamics, it is simply not possible to understand the opportunities

---

53    Angwin, *Shorting the Grid*, pp. 97–101, has a useful discussion of the relative contributions of energy and capacity payments for generators of different types in the US case.

available for future solar and wind power development, or the challenges that such development faces. What have we principally learned in this chapter about that landscape?

The key learning is that the generation of electricity is increasingly a separate business. While it used to be the case that generating electricity was typically one activity carried out by enterprises that also handled the other elements of the electricity supply chain, today generation is largely separate – wherever in the world one cares to look. It stands or falls on its own feet.

Then there are the three other crucial, connected, increasingly common characteristics. As well as usually being separate from the rest of the supply chain, electricity generation is usually competitive – much more so, indeed, than any of transmission, distribution or retail. The entities that compete in electricity generation, and especially renewables generation, are also typically private (rather than state-owned) corporations, existing to generate profit. And it is more and more the case that what types of generation capacity are installed, how much electricity is then produced, and how much the customers of generating companies pay for that electricity, are all determined by market mechanisms of various kinds, rather than by, say, direct, top-down government prescription.

Now that we have a handle on the commercial world into which solar and wind power are emerging, we can turn, in Chapter 3, to learn more about these sources of power themselves, and especially about their chief economic attributes.

# 3

# Free Gifts of Nature

Perched on a rocky outcrop of land overlooking the North Sea on Norway's blustery south-west coast, and situated roughly equidistant between Kristiansand and Stavanger, the Tellenes wind farm began generating electricity in September 2017. It was, at the time, the country's largest wind power facility, comprising fifty turbines each with a generating capacity of 3.2 MW and consisting of three fiberglass-reinforced epoxy blades.

We will be learning a fair amount about the Tellenes farm in this chapter, and, indeed, we will return to it periodically in later chapters, too. Not that there is anything particularly special about Tellenes: there is not. In fact, it is quite ordinary, one of tens of thousands of solar and wind farms around the world that today generate electricity principally or exclusively for sale. This ordinariness is the point. Using Tellenes as an example whose realness enables us to render concrete and tangible what might otherwise appear abstract or ungraspable, we can begin to unpack the contemporary realities of commercial wind and solar power.

Who actually develops and builds wind and solar farms? What technology do they use? What needs to be arranged and agreed – and with whom – to get a project to the point of being shovel-ready? How much electricity do solar and wind farms produce, and how reliably? How much does it cost to develop, build and operate a facility? And where does all the money to do so come from?

As would be true for all renewable power plants, the particular combination of answers to these various questions that applies in the case of Tellenes is, of course, unique. But the questions themselves have a universal importance, and Tellenes represents as good a lens as any other wind or solar farm to help us identify, illustrate and think through the key generic issues.

I

The place to start the discussion is with the basic facts about how a wind or solar power facility works. In Chapter 1, we briefly considered how electricity is generated from the burning of fossil fuels. Now, in a bit more detail, we consider how the sun and wind can be harnessed to produce electrical power.

Given that Tellenes is our example, we can begin with wind, the core technology of which is, of course, the turbine. Most turbines are so-called horizontal-axis models, meaning simply that the blades – of which there are typically three, as at Tellenes – rotate around an axis that is horizontal, or parallel with the ground. Standing atop a steel tower, the blades fit into a central hub, together with which they form the turbine's rotor. Usually, but not always, horizontal-axis models operate upwind, with the turbine pivoting at the top of the tower so that the blades face into the wind.

The way in which this contraption generates electricity is, in essence, straightforward. The flow of wind across the blade creates a difference in air pressure across the two sides of the blade which, in turn, causes the rotor to spin. A generator then converts this kinetic (mechanical) energy – or torque – into electrical energy.

Generally speaking, the longer the blades and the taller the tower – wind speed increases with height – the more electricity a turbine is able to generate. A very small 'micro-turbine' might have a capacity of just, say, 10 kW and stand only a few metres tall. The Tellenes turbines are relatively large, the towers standing around 100 metres tall and the blades measuring fifty-five metres in length, producing a total 'swept area' (through which the blades spin) of 10,000 square metres. Swept area is a critical metric, as the power output of a turbine is a direct function thereof. Each Tellenes turbine, as we have seen, has a capacity of 3.2

MW. But, while large, the Tellenes turbines are by no means the largest around. Huge models with blades more than 100 metres long and with a generating capacity of above 10 MW are now in operation.

By wind farm or 'plant', we simply mean aggregations of more than one turbine – Tellenes, for instance, comprises fifty, located over an area of about fifteen square kilometres. A term that is commonly used to refer to such consolidated groups of turbines producing electricity for sale is 'utility-scale'. 'Large-scale' works just as well, however. The key technical feature of utility-scale renewables plants – whether wind- or solar-based – is that they are connected to the transmission grid via a transformer substation. As noted in Chapter 1, such large-scale facilities, producing large amounts of renewable power for sale and consumption, are necessarily at the core of any truly transformative energy transition, and they are our main focus in this book. Anything above 1 MW is generally referred to as utility-scale capacity.

Below that approximate threshold, there are various 'distributed-energy' facilities. The key feature of these, other than their smaller size, is that they are strictly *local* resources. Either they are entirely off-grid, serving on-site energy demand (for instance, a 10 kW wind turbine at a detached family home or a 250 kW turbine at a university campus), or they are connected only at the distribution level of the electricity delivery system, supporting the operation of local distribution networks.

Utility-scale wind farms can be located either onshore or offshore. Tellenes, needless to say, is an example of the former. Most of the world's wind farms are located onshore, and at the time of this writing, onshore turbines accounted for around 90 per cent of all wind-generated electricity globally. For obvious reasons, offshore development involves all manner of technological and logistical challenges that do not arise on land. Equally, however, it allows for the generation of often prodigious amounts of power: higher wind speeds translate into more power for a given rotor size (in technical terms, offshore wind power has a greater *capacity factor* than onshore); and the fact that offshore facilities, especially those further from the coast, are largely out of sight means there are fewer objections on aesthetic grounds to giant turbines. Northern European nations, in particular, have increasingly favoured offshore in recent years, with the UK a leading example.

In turn, almost all existing offshore wind farms use turbines that are fixed to the seabed. But, as developers and policymakers increasingly explore opportunities to develop wind power in deeper waters, they are of necessity turning to the alternative, emerging technology of floating turbines. Limited to date to relatively small pilot projects off the coast of European countries including Norway and Portugal, much of the expansion of floating turbines over the next decade is expected to be concentrated in the deep waters of the Pacific off the US west coast; previous US offshore wind development has occurred largely in the shallower waters of the Atlantic, in the east.[1]

As to solar power, there are several different solar technologies, the principal one, accounting for more than 95 per cent of generating capacity globally, being solar photovoltaics (PV); solar thermal-electric systems are the main alternative to PV. The core PV component is the solar cell, which contains an internal electrical field across the junction between two layers or 'wafers' of semiconductor material (usually silicon), one positively charged and the other negatively charged. The incidence of sunlight upon that junction induces the generation of an electromotive force – in other words, it causes electricity to flow: that generative effect is what the term 'photovoltaic' refers to.

Individual cells, typically producing only about one or two watts of power, are connected together in chains to create larger units known as solar panels or modules. Even these have limited generating capacity, however, generally ranging from around 100 to 400 watts. Thus almost all solar power installations, including small residential ones, contain multiple modules – a standard residential system, for example, would have a capacity of around 10 kW. Utility-scale solar systems, needless to say, are orders of magnitude larger than this. The world's largest existing solar farm is Bhadla Park, a vast PV system comprising numerous subsystems owned and operated by different entities, and distributed across nearly sixty square kilometres in western India. Total generating capacity at Bhadla is over 2 GW. It houses more than 10 million panels.

We will, in due course, consider crucial questions about how, in practice, the life of a wind or solar farm commences, but this is a reasonable place to make an important observation about how and when such lives end. One of the things that is seldom mentioned about wind and solar power, but which is very significant, is that, despite rapid

1   N. Groom, 'California Offshore Wind Sale Ends First Day with $400 mln in High Bids', 6 December 2022, reuters.com.

improvements in the underlying technologies, they continue to have relatively limited operational lives. As the IEA has noted, 'many conventional hydropower, nuclear and coal plants operate far longer'.[2] Wind turbines typically last for anywhere from ten to twenty-five years; solar panels do somewhat better, but nonetheless almost never last beyond thirty years.

Of course, this finite lifespan does not mean that wind and solar farms simply cease operating after twenty-five to thirty years. Turbines and panels can be replaced with new models. But it does have major implications for the economics of the sector. As the IEA has further observed, in the 2030s, when some countries will still be grappling with installing solar and wind power on a substantial scale for the first time, others will increasingly be dealing already with replacing the first significant generation of installed capacity, at considerable capital cost. The issue of the costs of solar and wind power, in any event, is the one we turn to next.

## II

Building solar or wind farms is not a cheap business. We can begin to explore the costs by focusing first on the cost of construction itself. That is to say, excluding various ancillary expenses, some of which we will specifically look at as we proceed – for instance, the cost of connecting to the grid, or of the land needed to actually erect the plant on – how much does it cost to procure and install wind turbines or solar PV systems where none previously existed?

Needless to say, costs can vary a fair amount geographically, for instance in relation to the price of labour and materials, but we are interested, at this point, more in orders of magnitude than in exact numbers. We can use US data purely as an illustration, at least for onshore installations. The average construction cost for new utility-scale (1 MW-plus) US solar PV plants installed during 2020 was $1,655 per kW. This, note, was a capacity-weighted average: as we shall see shortly, the per-kW cost varies according to the size of the installation. The average

2  IEA, 'Net Zero by 2050: A Roadmap for the Global Energy Sector', October 2021, iea.org, p. 163, n. 6.

capacity-weighted construction cost for utility-scale US onshore wind installations in the same year, meanwhile, was $1,498 per kW – in other words, around 10 per cent lower.[3]

Unsurprisingly, offshore wind is much costlier to install. There are no equivalent data for the US – where, in the early 2020s, offshore wind still remains a relatively novel and little-used technology – but, here, we do have global data. The capacity-weighted average construction cost globally for offshore installations entering into operation in 2020 with capacities greater than 100 MW was $3,750 per kW. The cost ranged from a low of $2,050 per kW for the 730 MW Borssele III and IV farm in the Dutch North Sea, to a high of $4,530 per kW for the 200 MW Trianel farm near the German island of Borkum, also in the North Sea.[4]

At this preliminary stage in our analysis, two vital features pertaining to these various costs are important to highlight. First, economies of scale apply: generally speaking, the more capacity that is installed, the lower the cost per unit of capacity, which, of course, is another strong argument in favour of large-scale plants (over small-scale distributed-energy units) when it comes to the challenge of rapid decarbonization of global energy infrastructures. The aforementioned data for offshore installations hinted at this feature, but the relationship between scale and cost is more firmly established for solar and onshore wind, being the maturer technologies. The average construction cost for US onshore wind farms installed in 2020 was $5,059 per kW for generators with a capacity of 1 to 25 MW and just $1,393 for those with a capacity of above 200 MW – striking evidence of scale economies.[5] These US figures, incidentally, help put the construction cost of the Tellenes facility in Norway in context. With a total capacity of 168 MW, the plant, installed during 2016–17, cost around $250 million, or approximately $1,500 per kW.[6]

3  US Energy Information Administration (EIA), 'Construction Cost Data for Electric Generators Installed in 2020', 23 August 2022, eia.gov.

4  US Department of Energy, 'Offshore Wind Market Report: 2021 Edition', August 2021, energy.gov, pp. 75–6.

5  EIA, 'Construction Cost Data for Electric Generators Installed in 2020'.

6  S. Figved, I. Fredriksen and K. A. Kleppe, 'TV 2 avslører: Inntekter fra norsk vind sendes til en skattefri øy i Karibien', 24 November 2019, tv2.no. Based on an exchange rate of eight Norwegian kroner to one US dollar.

In turn, for US solar PV, the per-kW average construction costs in 2020 were $2,577 for generators with a capacity of 1 to 5 MW and $1,399 for those with a capacity of 100 to 250 MW.[7] In other words, for relatively small utility-scale plants, solar is much cheaper to install than onshore wind (let alone offshore), but, the bigger the plant, the more cost-competitive wind becomes. This substantially explains why the average capacity of utility-scale solar systems (which was 19 MW for systems installed in the US in 2020) is much lower than in the case of wind (178 MW, for onshore).[8]

Second, and of fundamental importance to the wider argument developed in this book, once these installation costs have been met, and until equipment replacement becomes necessary after, say, twenty-five years, that, at least in terms of significant expenses, is basically that, especially in the case of solar. Solar and wind energy are literally free gifts of nature: unlike oil or natural gas, nobody enjoys private property rights to them, and they do not need to be extracted – at considerable expense – from the Earth's crust. They are simply there, waiting to be harvested, by anybody who cares to do so. In short, if it costs a significant amount to *build* a large-scale solar or wind power facility, it costs very little to *operate* it. Most significantly of all, there are no fuel costs.

Economists use a measure called the LCOE (*levelized cost of electricity*, or *energy*) to help articulate analytically the cost structures of generating plants. LCOE expresses how much it costs a plant to generate electricity over its entire lifetime, averaged across the years and discounted to the present. Essentially, it is calculated by taking all the costs of all kinds incurred in developing, building and running the plant, and dividing this amount by the quantum of electricity generated over its lifetime. What is the overall, all-in cost per megawatt- or kilowatt-hour produced? As we will see in Chapter 4, commentators on renewable power, and especially on its prospects of widely substituting for fossil-fuel-based plants, invoke LCOE measures – comparing the costs of clean and dirty technologies – ad nauseam.

The key fact to be highlighted here, following the above observation about free gifts, is simply that the largest part of the LCOE for solar and wind plants is the upfront installation cost. In the case of wind, most

---

7   EIA, 'Construction Cost Data for Electric Generators Installed in 2020'.
8   Ibid.

estimates suggest that the upfront investment typically accounts for something in the order of 80 per cent of the LCOE; the remaining 20 per cent or so is accounted for by ongoing operations and maintenance costs. In the case of solar PV, the percentage accounted for by upfront installation is even higher: usually around 90 per cent.[9] That is to say, 90 per cent of the costs of a facility that can generate electricity for up to thirty years must be met before a single watt of power has been produced.

Renewables' cost structure, it will become clear, is terrifically important: it plays a hugely significant role in shaping investment decision making in the sector, in ways we shall explore closely in subsequent chapters. Consider, for instance, what happened when global supply chains buckled in 2021 as they failed to respond elastically to the resurgence in global economic activity associated with countries beginning to re-emerge from COVID-19 lockdowns. By the end of that year, the IEA reported, the prices of polysilicon, steel and aluminium – all materials that are indispensable for solar or wind technologies – had risen by approximately 200, 70 and 40 per cent respectively compared to the end of 2020.[10] Needless to say, turbine and panel manufacturers passed on as much of these cost increases to their customers in the generation business as they possibly could, resulting in price rises for such equipment of 10 to 20 per cent. Essentially, in view of their highly capital-intensive nature, solar and wind power had abruptly become 10 to 20 per cent more expensive on a lifetime basis.

And it is as important to understand renewables' distinctive cost structure in relative terms – specifically, relative to the cost structures of fossil-fuel-based alternatives – as in absolute terms. Indeed, part of the reason why crude comparisons between the costs of fossil-fuel-based and renewable electricity of the type we will encounter in Chapter 4 are so problematic is precisely that they ignore the different structural composition of the two sets of costs. The LCOE measure attempts to render technologies comparable by discounting all costs to the present (as a so-called 'overnight cost'), but, nonetheless, a plant where essentially all costs are incurred upfront is, in economic terms, nothing like a

9   See, for example, L. Hirth and J. C. Steckel, 'The Role of Capital Costs in Decarbonizing the Electricity Sector', *Environmental Research Letters* 11 (2016), 114010, p. 2; K. Dawson and P. Sabharwall, 'A Review of Light Water Reactor Costs and Cost Drivers', September 2017, inl.gov, p. 11.

10   IEA, 'World Energy Investment 2022', March 2022, iea.org, p. 39.

plant where costs are spread broadly equally over thirty years, even if both happen to have the exact same LCOE.

Whereas 80 to 90 per cent of the LCOE of wind and solar plants represents upfront investment, the equivalent proportion is only around 40 to 50 per cent in the case of coal-fired plants and it is lower still – as little as 20 per cent – in the case of natural gas, for which fuel costs (approximately 70 per cent) predominate.[11] Thus increases in the costs of key construction materials like steel and aluminium, such as occurred in 2021, are, as the IEA noted in its discussion of those particular increases, far less consequential for the price of these less capital-intensive fuel-based generating technologies.[12] The key point, then, cannot be overemphasized: understood as aggregations of expenses, fossil-fuel-based plants and renewable plants are entirely different economic phenomena.

## III

One oft-heard dictum about the electricity sector is that, while generating power renewably may be a very different business than using fossil fuels, both economically and in terms of side products (specifically, greenhouse gas emissions), there is no difference with regard to the core product. This product is identical in each case. An electron is an electron is an electron. 'All electricity is the same', one green electricity interest group concedes on its website, 'whether generated by coal, oil or the sun.'[13] 'The phrase "clean energy" is a little bit confusing', allows another such group. 'Once it enters the power lines, all electricity is the same.'[14]

11   Hirth and Steckel, 'The Role of Capital Costs in Decarbonizing the Electricity Sector', p. 2; Dawson and Sabharwall, 'Review of Light Water Reactor Costs and Cost Drivers', p. 11. It is worth noting that, while the cost structure of renewables is markedly different from that of fossil-fuel-based power-generating plants, it is actually quite similar to that which characterizes fossil fuel extraction. Much like the business of owning and operating solar and wind farms, the business of oil and gas extraction is highly capital-intensive and, usually, similarly long-term.

12   IEA, 'World Energy Investment 2022', p. 39.

13   'Maine has a Competitive Electricity Market', n.d., mainegreenpower.org.

14   G. Alexander, 'What You Need to Know about Electricity', 11 October 2022, earth911.com.

Yet the reality is that *not* all electricity is the same. To be sure, an electron *is* an electron is an electron. But the power produced by different types of power plants actually varies in several critical respects that are essential to understand when one is grappling with the complex political economy of the decarbonization of the electricity sector. All electrons are identical, certainly, but they come 'packaged' very differently.

The clearest axis of variance is quantity. Some facilities produce very small amounts of electricity, others produce very large amounts. This matters, not least (and most obviously) because renewables plants of different sizes can make varying contributions to the growing stock of cleanly generated electricity that the world requires.

To this first axis of variance we need to add two important others. One, already touched upon earlier, concerns *when* electricity is produced. Insofar as the sun does not always shine and the wind does not always blow, and insofar as, when they do, they shine and blow with varying and (beyond the very near term) unpredictable degrees of intensity, renewably generated electricity is temporally intermittent and volatile. Detractors – often with explicit interests in the fossil fuel industry – have made considerable play of this particular characteristic, indeed much too much play, invoking it opportunistically to scaremonger about blackouts and the like in the event of the closure of fossil fuel plants. Just because too much is made of it, however, does not mean that intermittency is imaginary or unimportant.

The main reason why renewables' inherent intermittency is important is, of course, that when they produce power might not match up with when power is actually needed by users. The stability and integrity of the electricity grid requires that supply and demand balance at all times. Maintaining such balance – the responsibility of the grid operator – implies all manner of technical and economic challenges, especially given that robust and affordable solutions are not presently available for large-scale storage of electricity generated when it is not needed.

Though we will have much more to say about this (and especially the economic aspects) in later chapters, what grid operators essentially do is call on generators to produce and 'place' on the grid the particular amount of electricity required to meet demand at any particular moment – no small task, as one can imagine. This is where the fact that power plants of different types produce power with different temporal profiles is critical. If wind and solar plants only produce electricity when it is windy or sunny, nuclear and fossil-fuel-based plants can produce it more continuously and predictably.

When and to what degree generators of different types deliver power to the grid depends, in practice, on a range of factors, including the speed with which they can actively ramp output up to meet shortfalls from other sources – gas-fired plants are the most responsive dispatchable technologies in this regard, while coal and nuclear plants are less flexible – together with their output capacity and operating costs. The upshot is that the generating sector at large is populated by a range of generators that effectively do different jobs for the grid operator and, ultimately, for electricity consumers.

Another way of expressing this is to say that different kinds of generator in fact produce different types of electrical power, meaning power output possessing different bundles of attributes in each case. As we have said, then: not all electricity is the same. Some types of generator, for example, are relied upon to supply the minimum load ('baseload') always required at all times of day or night; nuclear plants typically belong in this category. Others, such as single-cycle gas turbines, act mainly as 'peaking' units (or simply 'peakers'), helping to meet demand only when it is at its highest, for example in the early evening.

What 'type' of electricity do renewables plants provide? Generally, their output is included within the baseload category alongside the likes of nuclear; after all, renewables clearly lack the necessary response flexibility required of peaking plants. But, equally, this is not baseload output as conventionally understood, given that output will fall to zero when nature dictates. Essentially, solar and wind defy classificatory convention. Always 'on', they will sometimes fail to produce even baseload requirements, while at other times meeting baseload *and* peakload requirements with something to spare.

The second important axis of variance concerns *where* electricity is generated. Electricity produced in one location may be physically indistinguishable from electricity produced in another location, but the various infrastructures and actors involved in delivering electricity from where it is produced to where it is consumed are absolutely not indifferent to its geographic source.

As we saw earlier in the book, the existence of networks of electricity transmission and distribution reflects the fact that electricity generation and consumption are not spatially coterminous with one another, but rather display different geographic patterns. Indeed, the existence of such networks reinforces the spatial mismatch between production and consumption as well as being a product of that mismatch. Generators can commercially produce power in places where demand for that power is absent if – as will often be the case – infrastructure to deliver the power to consumers exists, although, as we will see, doing so may incur extra expenses.

The point here is that building, maintaining, upgrading and operating transmission and distribution networks costs money, and physically indistinguishable units of electricity generated in different places correspondingly entail often radically different burdens in terms of the effective network costs involved in delivering them to where they are consumed. Electricity, in short, has a materiality that is deeply economic–geographic, just like any other capitalist commodity.

And, again, wind and solar have highly peculiar characteristics in this regard, just as they do in terms of their temporal production profile. For all manner of reasons, not least relating to land's availability (they need large amounts) and cost, large, utility-scale solar and onshore wind facilities tend predominantly to be located in precisely those parts of countries where most electricity users are *not* located, and the same is true of offshore wind by very definition, of course. By contrast, fossil-fuel-based plants historically have generally been sited relatively close to major towns and cities.

Amid all the considerable huff and puff about intermittency, the geography of solar and wind power is sometimes obscured and drowned out by the noise. But, as we shall see, it is extremely important. The key issue is simply stated, yet technically and economically daunting, and thus anything but simply resolved. 'The expansion of renewable energy', as Shelley Welton has observed, will 'require construction of *a lot* more transmission infrastructure to connect remote solar and wind resources to population centers.'[15]

---

15   S. Welton, 'Rethinking Grid Governance for the Climate Change Era', *California Law Review* 109 (2021), p. 240 (emphasis in original).

# IV

It was in 2005, more than a decade before it began generating electricity, that plans for the wind farm at Tellenes in Norway were first formalized. The company originally behind the initiative was the giant Norsk Hydro, which at the time was active principally in aluminium production, oil and gas production, and hydroelectric power generation.

Before much progress could be made, however, the Tellenes project was overtaken by wider events. In 2007, Hydro sold its oil and gas business to the state-controlled Statoil, Norway's largest hydrocarbon producer, and, for one reason or another, the fledgling Tellenes project was included in the asset transfer. It then essentially got lost in the corporate mix. Three years later, it remained on the shelf, at which point Statoil decided to sell the project.

The buyer was a small Norwegian company called Zephyr AS. At last, Tellenes had an owner committed to the project and determined to see a plan transformed into reality. Nevertheless, it took a long time for this to happen. Construction did not begin until six years later, in 2016, by which time Zephyr had been joined by a partner in the project, in the shape of fellow Norwegian company Norsk Vind Energi AS. The same year, Zephyr and Norsk Vind sold their interests in the project to a new owner. That entity – an investment fund controlled by BlackRock, the world's largest asset manager – continues to own the Tellenes wind farm today.

An understanding of the types of commercial entities that are predominantly active in the business of developing and generating wind and solar power is indispensable to an understanding both of why that business has produced an existing global constellation of solar and wind farms that looks like it does, and, more importantly, of what we might expect that business to be able to produce by way of solar and wind facilities in future. The identity and nature of the particular entities involved in the history of the Tellenes wind farm provide us with a useful reference point around which we can map out a more general industry ecology.

At the risk of oversimplifying what, in reality, is a hugely complex commercial landscape, and one which varies significantly from country to country – unsurprisingly, given everything we learned in Chapter 2 about the intersecting vectors of transformation of the electricity industry in recent decades – we can say that there are, first, entities that *develop* wind or solar power facilities; second, entities that *generate* wind or solar power; and third, entities that substantially do both.

Zephyr and Norsk Vind are both examples of the first type: they are developers. By 'development', we refer here and indeed throughout the book to everything that occurs before construction can begin and a facility can begin generating power. Development is a complex and multifarious business, involving several crucial components, so much so that a separate section of this chapter – the one following this one – is given over to unpacking it.

Pure-play developers such as Zephyr and Norsk Vind in Norway *just* develop. They own and control projects up to (and sometimes including) the stage of construction, but they then sell out, their business done, before electricity generation itself actually commences. This is not necessarily to say that they never have anything to do with the activity of generation. Sometimes, developers stay on post-construction and handle the operations and maintenance of a facility on behalf of its new owner. Zephyr, for example, does this at several of the wind plants in Norway that it has itself developed and then sold, including the 200 MW Guleslettene facility (like Tellenes, controlled by BlackRock) and the 25 MW Mehuken farm (now co-owned by two Norwegian companies, Østfold Energi and Vardar). But a pure-play developer does not own the generating assets, nor, therefore, derive income directly from the generation and sale of power.

Who, then, does belong in our second category, that of owning wind or solar farms and capturing the revenue that electricity production generates? The range of entities active in the generation of wind or solar power while not also being active in developing plants in the first place is actually quite limited. Some, such as the aforementioned Vardar of Norway, are what we would typically refer to as 'energy companies' – that is, companies whose principal business is the production of energy. But the majority are in fact like the entity that owns the Tellenes wind park, namely BlackRock. That is to say, they are financial investment institutions. Usually acquiring assets from specialist pure-play developers like Zephyr, institutional investors – attracted by the green credentials furnished by investment in clean power – have become major owners of wind and solar farms in the past decade. Canada's Brookfield Asset Management, for instance, is one of the largest, controlling a vast portfolio of wind and solar facilities spread across four continents and with a collective generating capacity of nearly 8 GW.

Meanwhile, most energy companies with a significant presence in the wind and solar sectors belong in our third and final category, which is to say that they are both generators *and* developers. Whether they are renewables specialists, such as Denmark's Ørsted and China's GCL New Energy, or entities with both renewable and fossil fuel assets, such as Spain's Iberdrola and NextEra Energy of the US (the latter of which claims to be the world's largest producer of wind and solar power, with some 24 GW of net generating capacity), these companies generally retain ownership and control of – and hence earn revenue from the generation of electricity by – the wind and solar farms that they themselves have developed, sometimes adding to their portfolios of self-developed generating assets by acquiring assets developed by pure-play developers.

This, therefore, in essence, is what the commercial landscape of wind and solar power looks like, shorn down to its very basic bones. Developers develop plants, and the companies that subsequently sell the electricity that such plants produce are sometimes these same developers, sometimes not.

All that remains to briefly emphasize before we move on to the nitty-gritty of what development involves in practice is the fact that, as we saw in Chapter 2, most generators of solar and wind power are *not* vertically integrated into downstream parts of the electricity supply chain: they are not active in transmission, distribution or retail. There are, of course, exceptions, and important ones, including companies just mentioned such as Iberdrola and NextEra. But the generalization largely and increasingly holds.


## V


Developers of wind and solar farms cannot simply wake up one day, identify a piece of land, and instruct a contractor to begin installing turbines or modules on it. All sorts of preparatory work must be done to get a project to the point of being 'shovel-ready', by which is meant ready for construction to begin. Indeed, that multifarious preparatory work is precisely what the term 'development' refers to. What does it principally entail?

There are, generally speaking, four key pieces of the development puzzle, of which the first is territorial. In the case of solar and onshore wind, the developer must secure the land needed for the facility, through either acquisition or long-term lease. In the case of Tellenes, for example, property rights to the approximately fifteen square kilometres of land ultimately occupied by the wind farm were highly fragmented at the time when planning began in earnest, with control distributed among more than twenty owners of land parcels of varying size. Consolidating control of the necessary land was, therefore, a significant undertaking in itself. Such consolidation quite likely would not have been possible had the Norwegian Water Resources and Energy Directorate (NVE) not in 2012 granted the developers a permit to expropriate (with compensation) those landowners with whom purchase terms could not be agreed voluntarily.

An enormous amount of work often goes into securing leases or land-ownership. Not only is the necessary land, as at Tellenes, often held by multiple owners, but also such owners can have very different degrees of willingness to cooperate, and not all countries by any means are as open to granting developers expropriation powers as Norway has been. To be able to develop a 300 MW wind farm covering 34,000 acres of farmland in the US state of Illinois, for example, Apex Clean Energy had to negotiate leases with more than 150 local landowners. Not surprisingly, it took years. Even as some owners were acquiescent, others were strongly opposed, worrying, for instance, that the use of heavy equipment to prepare the ground for turbines would disrupt drainage patterns and that the presence of turbines would increase the cost of aerial seeding of crops.[16]

Neither, of course, is buying or leasing land for a solar or wind farm necessarily cheap. It is unclear how much it cost to purchase the land acquired for the Tellenes farm, but Apex told the *New York Times* that if its Illinois wind farm went ahead, Apex – or whomever it sold the project to – could expect to pay a total of around $210 million in lease payments over the project's anticipated thirty-year life.[17]

Such costs help to account for the paradoxical fact that certain US states in which climate denialism is most firmly entrenched nonetheless

---

16   D. Gelles, 'The US Will Need Thousands of Wind Farms: Will Small Towns Go Along?', *New York Times*, 30 December 2022.
17   Ibid.

are among those in which renewables have grown fastest and furthest. Texas is the prime example of this phenomenon. 'When someone says we are embracing green energy,' the head of Conservative Texans for Energy Innovation (CTEI) told a reporter in 2023, 'it's like shoving an ice pick through our ears.' Yet CTEI is pro-renewables. Why? Money. Recalling how an earlier generation of Texans had grown rich from the oil beneath their land, another Texan remarked: 'We struck wind.'[18] The lease payments made by developers such as Apex translate into land-owner returns often exceeding $100 per acre per annum, compared to below $10 for cattle rearing. In the end, in other words, 'support for wind comes down to economics.' 'It's not going to save the farm or allow me to retire,' said one farmer who had agreed to let Apex install one of its turbines on his 1,500-acre property, and who expected the corre-sponding annual lease payment to be about $50,000. 'But just having that steady income every year, you know what you're going to get.'[19]

Meanwhile, offshore wind development entails a somewhat unique territorial challenge. Developers cannot 'buy' the ocean floor (in the case of the more common fixed-foundation turbines) or its surface (in the case of floating wind turbines). Instead, they must lease territorial rights, which are awarded – increasingly through auction mechanisms – by governments. To take one example, in 2015 the US government, in the shape of the Bureau of Ocean Energy Management, auctioned the rights to a large area of the continental shelf off the southern coast of New Jersey for the development of offshore wind power. It did so in two leases, one of around 183,000 acres and the other of around 160,000 acres, both of which originally had terms – renewable upon negotiation – of thirty-one years. At the time of this writing, construction is yet to begin in either lease area, each of which is controlled by a partnership between major energy companies (France's EDF and the UK's Shell in one case, and in the other, Denmark's Ørsted and the Public Service Enterprise Group of the US).

Such vast offshore lease areas can generate windfalls to the beneficiary that dwarf those available onshore. Six shorter-term leases auctioned in 2021 for projects off the UK coast, for example, attracted bids that

---

18   Cited in 'Go to Texas to See the Anti-green Future of Clean Energy', *Economist*, 12 January 2023.
19   Gelles, 'The US Will Need Thousands of Wind Farms'.

translated into cumulative projected option fees of nearly £9 billion over ten years.[20]

As well as securing rights to the area required for installation of wind or solar power facilities, developers must also secure the right to use that territory for that particular purpose. Sometimes, as is generally the case with offshore seabed leases, the latter right comes bundled with the former, but typically it does not, and the developer must instead go through what can be a lengthy and convoluted process of gaining permissions from the pertinent regulatory and planning authorities. This is the second key piece of the development puzzle.

Again, Tellenes is instructive. In Norway, installing wind farms is contingent upon successfully securing a license from NVE. The first license application for the Tellenes project was submitted in 2006 by Norsk Hydro. As required by NVE, it contained assessments of the potential impact of the proposed facility under headings ranging from 'Biological diversity' to 'Noise' and from 'Social effects' to 'Aviation and defence interests'.[21] There was even a paragraph on the likely impact on television signals. ('In all probability' there would not be any.)

For obvious reasons, the implications for local birdlife are invariably high on the list of concerns when the relevant authorities review plans for wind development: a study published in 2013 concluded that US wind turbines kill over 140,000 birds each year.[22] Thus Norsk Hydro's 2006 license application duly considered the possible impact – and any appropriate remedial measures that needed to be taken – vis-à-vis six different local bird species, including the golden eagle, kestrel, kingfisher and peregrine falcon.

Meanwhile, the aforementioned 'social effects' of renewables development can, in principle, be either positive (for instance in the form of employment opportunities) or negative (ranging from the

20   In this case, the beneficiary was nominally the Crown Estate, which is essentially the real estate business of the UK monarchy and which owns the seabed out to twelve nautical miles. But the prospective windfall was surrendered to the Chancellor for the 'wider public good'. See W. Wallis, 'King Charles Hands Over Wind Farm Profits for "Wider Public Good"', *Financial Times*, 19 January 2023.

21   Norsk Vind Energy, 'Helleheia vindpark – Sokndal kommune: Konsesjons søknad – reguleringsplan – konsekvensutredninger', April 2006, nve.no.

22   S. R. Loss, T. Will and P. P. Marra, 'Estimates of Bird Collision Mortality at Wind Facilities in the Contiguous United States', *Biological Conservation* 168 (2013), pp. 201–9.

highly consequential, such as displacement of local residents, to the somewhat less consequential, such as interruption to hiking trails or public rights of way). In some cases, impacts on human and non-human populations have become inextricably entwined, resulting in highly emotive political-ecological and political-economic entanglements. A striking example is found at the other geographical extreme of Scandinavia, in the far north, where the development of wind farms has increasingly interfered with Sámi reindeer-herding grounds, threatening at once community livelihoods, ancestral traditions and wildlife itself. What, people are led to ask, takes precedence? The global climate fight? A (post)colonial nation's quest for energy security? Or the repeatedly violated rights of a minority people?

And who ultimately decides? In countries in which local authorities have long been used to an effective monopoly on local land use planning, the issue of renewable energy has increasingly seen moves by the centre to wrest back powers. In early 2022, for example, frustrated by wrangling over six proposed onshore wind farms in Italy, the country's highest executive body, the Council of Ministers, summarily stepped in to secure all necessary approvals.[23] At an even higher and wider level of authority, the European Commission has expressed concern that projects that can take only a matter of months to build can take up to a decade to receive all the permissions that are required. Even then, the permission is not necessarily watertight. Many fully permitted projects are subsequently contested in court. Around a fifth of permitted renewables projects in Germany come to face legal challenges, for example.[24]

Such matters, in the prickly realm of politics and planning, are not this book's explicit concern, but they are necessarily part and parcel of the wider energy debate. And, for reasons mentioned in the Introduction, they are certainly an implicit concern of the book and its thesis. Too rigid a focus on the bureaucratic obstacles that undoubtedly do sometimes hold up the development of new solar and wind farms can serve all too readily to give the impression that such obstacles are the most significant or indeed the only meaningful ones that remain today in the

---

23    A. Hancock, 'Slow Growth Knocks the Wind Out of EU Renewable Energy Targets', *Financial Times*, 20 September 2022.

24    C. Hodgson, 'Green Subsidies Lift Wind Industry's Longer Term Prospects', *Financial Times*, 27 February 2023.

way of more rapid decarbonization of electricity, not least now that the costs of renewable energy – for so long considered the principal stumbling block – have fallen to levels comparable to, or below, those of conventional generating sources. 'Waiting on permissions', Alice Hancock wrote, for instance, in the *Financial Times* in 2022, 'is the biggest hold up to [renewables] progress' – not just big, note, but 'the biggest'.[25] That this is in fact the case is today widely voiced common sense. But that does not necessarily make it true.

In any event, in the case of Tellenes, NVE was not persuaded by Norsk Hydro's initial 2006 license application, ordering updated impact assessments. As we know, the project was put on the back burner in 2007 when included in the assets transferred to Statoil, and did not get a new lease of life until 2010, when it was sold to Zephyr. The latter submitted a revised license application – accompanied by revised impact assessments – the following year, and in 2012 the license was granted. The Ministry of Petroleum and Energy ratified the grant in 2014.

But, even with both this license and 2012's land expropriation permit safely in hand, Zephyr remained some distance from the finishing line. Only two of four key pieces of the development puzzle were in place. The third would be to secure agreement to connect to the transmission grid, thus enabling actual delivery and commercial exploitation of the electricity that the plant would eventually be producing. A grid connection agreement typically specifies the conditions and timetable for connection, and any connection fees to be paid.

It might be thought that the question of grid connection is perfunctory, posing fewer challenges than securing rights to land and to the desired use thereof. But nothing could be further from the truth. Connecting new generators to the grid always raises questions of capacity limits, and, in the case of renewables, the stochastic nature of generation introduces additional technical concerns relating to frequency and voltage anomalies. Moreover, to accommodate new renewable generating facilities, it can be necessary to expand or upgrade existing transformer substations, or even build new ones, at costs running into millions of dollars. And then, as Gill Plimmer has recently noted, there is the incremental transmission load associated with the particular spatiality of renewables production, to which we referred earlier.

---

25   Hancock, 'Slow Growth'.

Significant system costs are incurred in upgrading grids 'designed to serve large coal-powered plants close to urban centres to [accommodate] more dispersed renewables development such as solar and wind farms'.[26]

How should all these incremental costs be apportioned between different stakeholders – the owners and operators of delivery networks, generators of different types and in different locations, and potentially also the government? Economists, regulators and policymakers around the world have struggled long and hard with these questions. 'Many of the conflicts between network owners or network operators and wind developers worldwide', as Poul Erik Morthorst and Thomas Ackermann observed around a decade ago, 'are often only indirectly related to technical issues. In fact, they are rather a question of what costs wind power entails and how those costs should be split.'[27]

Probably not coincidentally, those countries that elected essentially to socialize both the direct and indirect costs of renewables connection, for example by spreading the costs among all market participants, have tended to enjoy especially rapid renewables development. Denmark and Germany are examples.[28] Not only does this approach typically hasten the grid connection process, but it improves project viability for developers inasmuch as they are not required to shoulder all the costs themselves.

Elsewhere, the wait for approval of grid connection is usually measured in years, not months – 3.7 years on average for projects delivered between 2011 and 2021 in the US case, for example.[29] Meanwhile, the inclusion of, for example, all or most transformer and network upgrade costs in the connection fees charged to developers of new generating facilities can frequently make such fees prohibitive and stop a project in its tracks. It does not help that the logic of how connection fees for renewables plants are calculated sometimes appears obscure at best, the

26   G. Plimmer, 'Renewables Projects Face 10-Year Wait to Connect to Electricity Grid', *Financial Times*, 8 May 2022.

27   Morthorst and Ackermann, 'Economic Aspects of Wind Power in Power Systems', p. 489.

28   Ibid., pp. 490–2.

29   J. Hiller, 'Investors Plow into Renewables, but Projects Aren't Getting Built', *Wall Street Journal*, 22 January 2023.

UK's method for assigning such fees, for instance, being described by one consultant as a 'postcode lottery'.[30]

We will have more to say later in the book about the impact of grid connection costs on the profitability and thus viability of renewables projects. What merits emphasizing here is that these basic (but decisive) economic facts have often gotten lost in the mounting critical cacophony around grid operators ostensibly stalling the energy transition by failing in their job of connecting up proposed solar and wind projects sufficiently fast and on a sufficient scale.

In 2023, for example, researchers' discovery that less than 20 per cent of US renewables projects requesting connection to the grid between 2000 and 2017 were ever actually built elicited predictable howls of outrage about bureaucratic obstructionism. 'Red tape is slowing the shift to renewables' was one, typical, headline.[31] Of course, there were likely multiple reasons for this low percentage, and bureaucratic inefficiency, or indeed simple resource inadequacy, may well have been one of them; developers' failure to solve certain other pieces of the development puzzle – such as securing land rights or planning permissions – was almost certainly another.

But a crucial one, as the lead author of the aforementioned research told the journalist Attracta Mooney, was that developers often submit applications for grid connection more or less speculatively, without being aware, in particular, of what the costs of connection will actually be. 'Developers back away from projects when they find out their development triggers a huge bill for a grid upgrade or reinforcement,' Mooney observed. She cited a specific case of exactly this happening in the UK, where a project was scrapped when the developer realized it would face a grid upgrade charge of £19 million – 'more than the project was worth'.[32] Blame for such project 'failures' can scarcely be pinned on 'red tape'. If, in the US, only a fifth or so of all applications to connect

---

30   Cited in Plimmer, 'Renewables Projects Face 10-Year Wait'.

31   A. Hu, 'Red Tape Is Slowing the Shift to Renewables, but Biden's Permitting Reform Likely Won't Help', 8 June 2023, grist.org. The underlying research was J. Rand, R. Strauss, W. Gorman, J. Seel, J. M. Kemp, S. Jeong, D. Robson and R. Wiser, 'Queued Up: Characteristics of Power Plants Seeking Transmission Interconnection as of the End of 2022', April 2023, emp.lbl.gov.

32   A. Mooney, 'Gridlock: how a lack of power lines will delay the age of renewables', *Financial Times*, 11 June 2023.

renewables to the grid eventuate in operational plants, the proportion of informed and credible applications that succeed is clearly much higher.

Tellenes was relatively typical, then, in the sense that grid connection assuredly was not a perfunctory matter. It required both an upgrade to the nearest transformer substation, nine kilometres distant at Åna-Sira, and the installation of a new 132 kV power line to connect the plant to the substation. Not until early 2016 was the necessary grid connection agreement – for an undisclosed fee – in place.

Three of the four main pieces of the Tellenes development puzzle had now been assembled, therefore. The developer's job was nearly done, and the fifty turbines could soon be transported to the site and erected. Yet, in early 2016, one major challenge nonetheless still remained, and it was – in the context of the development of wind and solar facilities more generally – easily the biggest of all. How was the plant going to be paid for?

## VI

The temporal profile of the costs and revenues associated with a solar or wind farm puts special demands on the financing of that facility. Almost all the cost, it will be recalled, is incurred upfront; once a facility is operational and generating power, there are very few further expenses to be met, at least until it comes time for equipment replacement. Meanwhile, the revenues that these costs ultimately fund are spread over a period of twenty or more years. In practice, payback periods – the time it takes for revenue to earn out the original capital investment – of course vary, but anything much less than a decade is generally considered a success.

Except in cases involving large developers and relatively small solar or wind installations, construction is rarely funded using cash on hand. Rather, new funds need to be accessed, which raises the question of how exactly this should be done. Generally speaking, two options are available – to raise funds with equity or with debt – and in more or less all cases the eventual financing represents a combination of both.

Debt, needless to say, is loaned money, on which the borrower pays periodic interest before repaying the principal amount at maturity. Equity, by contrast, entails raising money by giving the capital provider an ownership interest. What exactly this interest is *in* in the case of wind or solar power developments is an important question, to which we shall return shortly.

The first key point to be made here about equity and debt financing is one that has profound significance for the rest of the book. This is that, whoever they are, and of whatever institutional type, private sector developers of wind and solar power have a strong preference for debt, and ordinarily try to maximize the proportion of construction finance that is raised with debt as opposed to equity.

There are numerous reasons for this preference for debt, of which the most important is simply that debt is usually cheaper than equity. Readers may have encountered a statement such as this previously – it is an oft-cited nostrum in the financial world – but what it means in practice is seldom explained. It is therefore worth briefly clarifying. Specifically, debt is cheaper (to the entity raising funds) in the sense that the creditor charges less for it. But, if the charge applicable to debt is self-evident – in the form of the interest rate – it is less so in the case of equity. What is the 'charge' on (or better, embedded in) equity? It is, essentially, the financial return that the fundraising entity forgoes by virtue of the fact that it has sold an ownership interest. The larger that equity stake, the greater the cost.

The higher the proportion that comprises debt, the more highly 'geared' or 'leveraged' funding is said to be. The funding of Tellenes, for its part, which finally occurred in mid-2016 and which – being the final piece of the development puzzle – enabled construction immediately to begin, was clearly very highly geared: reports indicated an equity investment of around $25 million, compared with loans exceeding $200 million.[33] The average debt-to-equity ratio in the financing of wind and solar power more generally is somewhat lower than that. In 2020, for instance, Guy Brindley reported that the proportion of debt in wind finance is typically in the 70 to 80 per cent range.[34] But the Nordics are renowned for above-average leveraging of renewables developments: a study of all wind farms built in Sweden in the years

---

33   Figved, Fredriksen and Kleppe, 'TV 2 avslører'; 'BlackRock/Tellenes Wind Farm: EKF Covered Loan', 29 June 2016, tagmydeals.com.

34   G. Brindley, 'Financing and Investment Trends: The European Wind Industry in 2019', April 2020, windeurope.org, p. 11.

2017–21 found that the average share of funds raised with debt was above 85 per cent.[35]

Whatever the exact extent of financial gearing, however, it is the wider implication of the preference for debt for the economic viability of new generating plants that matters to our account. Namely, if substantial debt financing cannot be successfully secured, then private sector renewables projects generally *do not reach completion*. The cost of equity is too prohibitive to enable the owner of the would-be generating facility to earn an acceptable return if no financial leverage is used, and hence the construction of such facilities usually does not proceed until and unless sufficient debt has been raised.

The implication can, in fact, be stated even more starkly and broadly. As the gatekeepers to capital, financial institutions ultimately determine the conditions of possibility of all major programmes of investment carried out by private sector actors – and indeed also by many public sector actors – in capitalist societies, and that is as true of investment in renewable power as in any other class of infrastructure. Of the four main types of preparatory work that must be undertaken before the installation of solar and wind plants and the generation of clean electricity can occur, financing represents the ultimate chokepoint – the point at which renewables development most often becomes permanently blocked. Much of this book is therefore given over to explaining precisely why this is so. As we shall see, it is a phenomenon that can only be properly explicated in the light of the fact that, as we saw in the previous chapter, the actually existing electricity industry within which renewables investment around the world occurs is increasingly one that is vertically dis-integrated and, at least where generation is concerned, also de-monopolized, privatized and marketized.

Needless to say, macroeconomic trends of the recent past have not lessened the challenge facing developers in this respect. Having enjoyed a low-interest-rate environment for a decade, developers in most countries saw interest rates rise sharply beginning in 2022 in response to the return of inflation. This was a genuine one–two punch to the gut of the sector. For one thing, commodity price inflation was, as noted earlier, especially pronounced in those materials used in solar and wind

35   C. Sandström, M. Staaf and C. Steinbeck, 'Vindkraft – en grön bubbla eller ett svart hål?', 23 May 2023, kvartal.se.

technologies. And then monetary authorities lifted interest rates, thereby increasing in turn the only other significant costs, alongside construction expenses, that developers face – debt servicing costs.' Growing one's renewables footprint', the *Financial Times* editorialized somewhat ominously in late 2022, 'requires a lot of investment, just when interest rates are rising.' 'An increase of 200 basis points in the cost of capital for solar PV and wind', the IEA, in its turn, cautioned, 'leads to a 20% increase in the final LCOE.'[36]

At a time of considerable headwind, therefore, it might not be overstating the case to say that financing is the challenge to which a solution simply must be readily and widely available in future if investment in solar and wind capacity on anything like the necessary scale and with anything like the necessary alacrity is to occur.

In any event, while some combination of relatively standard ('vanilla') debt and equity is the norm in the funding of private sector renewables development, there are some notable variants that warrant mention. One, particularly important given the territory in question, is the form of financing that has come to dominate renewables development in the US. This is so-called tax equity financing. We will have more to say about this later, especially in Chapters 4 and 9, because it connects intimately to a topic we will be dealing with principally in those chapters – government subsidies to solar and wind power. But a brief introduction is in order here.

In the US, developers of solar and wind facilities are eligible to receive tax credits of various kinds, which can be claimed on federal income tax returns. Under tax equity financing of such facilities, capital providers such as banks secure an ownership interest in the facility that entitles them, instead of the developer, to claim the credits and the associated right to reduce any tax owed: essentially, banks give developers cash, and the developers give the banks the tax credits. The funder may also negotiate a claim to a share of the plant's income, or of capital gains in the event of the plant being sold, or both, but it is the claim on the tax credit that the funder is mainly buying and the terms of which make or break the deal. Though labelled tax *equity* financing, it is more like a hybrid of equity and debt, and usually stands in for both.

---

36  'Orsted: Headwinds Buffet Renewables', *Financial Times*, 3 November 2022; IEA, 'World Energy Investment 2022', p. 39.

Meanwhile, one alternative financing approach that is relatively common in the early stages of development of a renewable facility – when developers are busy attempting to secure land, operating licenses and grid connections – is a so-called option or framework agreement. Under such agreements, large, well-capitalized actors such as energy companies provide pure-play developers with cash funding, in return for an option (and not, typically, an obligation) to take full or part ownership at a later juncture of one or more plants that those developers are developing. In 2020, for example, the major Spanish energy company Iberdrola signed such a deal with the Swedish specialist developer Svea Vind Offshore, giving the former the option subsequently to take majority stakes in eight offshore projects that the latter was developing in the Baltic Sea, and which were expected to begin operations from 2029 onwards.

To understand the financing of renewable power development, there is one final crucial consideration. This is the question of how – or perhaps more accurately, where – particular projects are held in legal–organizational terms. If the developer is a major energy company (say, Sweden's Vattenfall), a wind or solar farm is generally held like any other fixed asset: it appears on the company's balance sheet. In the case of specialist developers, however, this is rarely how it works. More commonly, an individual project is made into a 'company' in its own right, using a special-purpose vehicle (SPV) structure. In other words, the asset does not appear directly on the developer's balance sheet; it sits within the SPV, in which the developer, in turn, owns shares. Sometimes, in the case of especially large projects such as offshore wind developments, major energy companies also use off-balance-sheet structures, establishing SPVs that are often joint ventures in which more than one energy company holds shares.

At any rate, where an SPV structure is used, financing occurs at the project level, and hence the label that is used – project finance. Equity investors acquire shares *in* the project SPV, and banks lend *to* the project (not to the developer). If, by contrast, a solar or wind development is held on a company's own balance sheet, financing is not specific to the development itself, even if (as is often the case) funding of that particular development is the sole purpose for which new capital is raised and used. Whether it is equity or debt, fundraising occurs rather at the corporate level; and hence, once again, the term used – corporate finance. Lenders lend to the company as a whole; investors buy shares in the company as a whole.

Thus, although Zephyr, alongside Norsk Vind Energi, developed the assets that became today's wind farm at Tellenes in Norway, it did not directly own them. The assets sat, and still sit, within an SPV, named Tellenes Vindpark DA. In fact, it was this entity that was granted the all-important operating license, expropriation permit and grid connection. And it was this entity that was refinanced in mid-2016, enabling construction finally to go ahead. In assuming ownership and control, the BlackRock investment fund – BlackRock Global Renewable Power II – put equity capital into Tellenes Vindpark, and the debt providers, led by DekaBank of Germany and Rabobank of the Netherlands, lent to Tellenes Vindpark.

But what was it, from the perspective of DekaBank and Rabobank, that actually made Tellenes fundable? Why did *this* particular project not founder on the rocks of debt financing in the way that countless other prospective wind and solar farms have done and continue to do? More generally, what, to use the vernacular of the industry, distinguishes 'bankable' renewables projects from non-bankable ones, and allows the chokepoint of debt financing to be successfully navigated?

## VII

For many years, financial institutions balked at the very mention of solar or wind farms. As recently as just two decades ago, in 2004, total annual investment globally in new utility-scale renewable capacity of all kinds was less than $40 billion – a paltry sum.[37] Whether it was debt or equity was more or less beside the point. Investment capital was simply not being channelled into renewables infrastructure in anything more than isolated, bite-sized chunks.

Behind the reluctance to invest was a simple economic reality. The technology was expensive – much more expensive than it needed to be if a profit were ever to be made from buying it, installing it and selling the electricity that it served to generate. In the mid- to late

---

37    REN21, '10 Years of Renewable Energy Progress', November 2014, ren21.net, p. 8.

1990s, for instance, solar PV systems still cost about $8,000 per kW to install.[38]

Consider the economics that would-be solar power generators – and the financial institutions that might provide them with capital – faced in that period. One such was Detroit Edison, a vertically integrated electricity company based in Michigan. In 1995, it proposed to build its first solar PV facility, with a peak capacity of 28 kW. It was expected to cost around $250,000 and to be able to produce about 40 MWh of electricity annually.[39] But the problem was this: the average retail price of electricity was only around seven cents per kWh (including taxes).[40] The sale of 40 MWh of power per annum would therefore bring in less than $3,000 – and that figure was revenue, not profit. No commercial bank in the world would make a construction loan based on those numbers.

It was, in part, to address this form of fundamental economic impasse that governments around the world stepped in historically to help try to make the economics of renewables work. In the event, Detroit Edison did build that plant, and it did cost $250,000. But the US Department of Energy paid almost half of this amount – $116,000. And even that was not enough to balance the company's books. The approximately 200 residential customers who signed up for the company's SolarCurrents 'green rate' service agreed to pay an additional $6.59 per month on average for each 100 watts of service.[41]

At that time, therefore, private finance capital remained very much on the sidelines of the nascent renewables sector, in the US and globally. But rendering the generation of solar and wind power profitable – and thus bankable – was, it was already clear, the explicit goal for governments and the electricity industry alike.

38    'Detroit Edison Plans Solar Power Project', *PR Newswire*, 2 August 1995.
39    Ibid.
40    EIA, 'Table 8.10: Average Retail Prices of Electricity, 1960–2011', eia.gov.
41    'US Energy Department Honors Detroit Edison Solar Power Project', *PR Newswire*, 24 October 1996.

# 4

# The Price Is Right?

First appearing on US television screens in 1972, *The Price Is Right* is one of the longest-running television series of any kind and one of the most famous and successful game shows in history. Although the game itself involves numerous variations on a theme, the central concept is straightforward – hence, perhaps, the show's popularity and longevity. Contestants are shown a purchasable item – impasse that say a juicer, a kettle or a pair of sunglasses – and are asked to guess the retail price. The contestant whose guess is closest, but without going over the correct retail price, wins. And that, essentially, is that.

It is common to see the show as a metaphor of sorts for late capitalism. More than anything else, it comes across as a veritable orgy of consumerism, and has been interpreted as such by any number of cultural theorists. The contestants guess the price of certain consumer products. And the prizes taken home by winning contestants are also consumer products, mostly donated by consumer products companies in return for the 'free' advertising that placement on the show represents. Indeed, the show only really makes sense in a thoroughly consumer capitalist world. It stands to reason that its champion is precisely the man or woman who knows the price of everything. Contra Oscar Wilde (not to mention Marx), such a person is here more savant than cynic.

But the show is, in fact, a metaphor for capitalism – or, more specifically, for our understanding of capitalism – at a deeper and much more interesting level. Taken for what it is, it seems to say not just that *the* price (of a particular item) is right, but that price per se is right: the right thing to single out. In identifying and selecting price as its cardinal measure, the show is wholly in tune with an understanding of capitalism that regards price as the economy's impartial arbitrator and conductor.

Think of all those supply and demand curves in economics textbooks. They all convey the same essential message: that price contains meaningful and unambiguous signals to which companies and consumers, like automatons, respond, at least if in possession of transparent information. Price is the 'right' thing to seize upon analytically because it is both the one true representation of the relative balance of supply and demand and, in turn, the guiding force of all economic behaviours: too high, and new supply will be brought to bear or demand will sink; too low, and vice versa.

Like the game show, in short, modern economics tells us both that *price* is right – it is the economy's universal thermostat, objectively gauging, regulating and directing economic forces at large – and that if *the* price is right, then things will somehow fall into place, settling into an agreeable 'equilibrium' trajectory.

But what if price is not right?

I

That price was and is the key variable in shaping the fortunes of renewable electricity was stamped into the public consciousness from the get-go. To understand both how solar and wind power *were* faring and how they likely *would* fare in the future, the critical factor to consider, we have consistently been told, is the price paid for such power. More specifically, the crucial metric is said to be the relative (rather than absolute) price: if electricity can be generated more cheaply from renewable sources than from fossil fuels, then the former will (or at least, should) surge ahead; but if fossil-fuel-based power is cheaper to produce, then it, instead, will remain dominant.

From the earliest days of utility-scale solar and wind installations in the 1980s and 1990s, a dominant narrative thereby emerged and congealed about why renewables development was occurring so much more slowly than many people hoped. Renewable electricity, in short, was too expensive – more expensive, that is to say, than electricity from conventional sources.

A whole range of voices contributed to this emergent explanatory orthodoxy, providing a range of estimates for exactly how much dearer renewable power actually was, and thus how great an economic obstacle existed to its potential development. A particularly important stake was driven into the discursive ground in the UK at the beginning of the 1990s. In 1991, the UK government created the Renewable Energy Advisory Group to review national prospects for renewable energy in terms, inter alia, of economic viability. When the group published its report the following year, the reading was grim. Reportedly costing at least two to three times as much as existing sources of electricity, renewables, the authors concluded, faced a long, uphill battle to make inroads into the landscape of electricity generation.[1] The estimate of 'two to three times' subsequently stuck: fifteen years later, it remained common to read that, as electricity sources, renewables – and solar in particular – were more expensive than fossil fuels by precisely that multiple.[2]

By the early 2000s, a consensus preferred metric had emerged among industry experts for measuring and representing the relative prices of renewables and other sources of electricity generation – the 'levelized cost of electricity' (or energy), or LCOE for short, which we introduced briefly in the previous chapter. As we saw, LCOE expresses the average cost (in present-value terms) of each unit of electricity produced during the lifetime of a generating plant. By the early 2010s, even non-experts were conversant, or at least superficially so, with LCOE: it had become nothing less than a lingua franca for discussing the economics of the energy transition. For as long as solar and wind's LCOEs remained higher than those of fossil fuels, the argument went, the odds were stacked against them. So much explanatory baggage was attached to LCOE that it became – and remains – nothing less than a fetish. We will have more to say about that fetish later in the chapter.

---

1 B. Maddox, 'DTI Says Costs of Renewable Energy Are High', *Financial Times*, 18 December 1992.

2 For example, J. Graff, '*Observer* Writers Weigh Up the Merits of the Competing Technologies: Solar', *Observer*, 11 June 2006; T. McNichol and M. V. Copeland, 'Here Comes the Sun', *Business 2.0*, 1 November 2006.

In any event, a diverse and noteworthy epistemic community soon cohered around LCOE, positing it as *the* measure of relative energy prices and presenting evidence that renewables were indeed the costlier alternative. Undoubtedly the most significant and influential proponent of the position that price was pivotal and that renewables were pricey was the IEA. An intergovernmental organization, the IEA had its origins in hydrocarbons – it was created in 1974 to help Western industrial countries coordinate their response to the oil crisis – and was long seen by many as a mouthpiece for the fossil fuel sector. Its basic, long-standing stance on what drives transformations in the technological landscape of electricity generation is utterly unambiguous: 'The change in the mix of technologies used to produce electricity is driven mainly by their relative costs.'[3] There, in a nutshell, we have the very essence of the wider argument that 'the price must be right'.

And, year after year, the IEA faithfully churned out reports cataloguing fossil fuels' lower LCOE than renewables'. Its 2000 annual report on wind energy, for instance, read as follows: 'The primary constraint affecting [wind-power] market development is the comparatively low cost of conventional generation.' Note here that the IEA was not saying that other issues did not shape the evolution of the wind sector. When considering constraints on the wind market at that time, it highlighted land availability, grid limitations, and political and planning hurdles.[4] Its claim was (and is), rather, that price was the *primary* driver.

Alongside the IEA, other authoritative voices helped cement the hegemony both of the emphasis on relative price as the primary determinant of the energy transition, and of LCOE as *the* measure of relative price. Some, predictably, were within the finance sector. LCOE is anything but a straightforward metric – calculating it means making assumptions about a raft of factors ranging from capital costs to fuel costs, tax subsidies, capital structure and the costs of complying with environmental regulations – and the US bank Lazard rapidly positioned itself as, and came in turn to be regarded as, something of an arbiter of analytical rigour in the field. Among industry stakeholders, its annual analyses of the levelized cost of various forms of energy are awaited and consumed as eagerly as the IEA's own reports. Version 1.0 of Lazard's

---

3    IEA, 'World Energy Outlook 2011', iea.org, p. 178.
4    IEA, 'Wind Energy Annual Report 2000', May 2001, nrel.gov, pp. 34, 37–9.

LCOE analysis was published in 2008; the latest version (16.0) was published in April 2023.[5] Meanwhile, as so often is the case with such things, academics published articles and books that gave a scholarly imprimatur to the fetishization of LCOE. An early paper by the influential energy economist Anthony D. Owen, for example, published in 2004 and containing LCOE estimates by technology for 2002, showed coal and gas enjoying a clear cost advantage over renewables.[6]

Of course, what one made of the LCOE data depended, to some extent, on who they were. For journalists (among others), LCOE became an easy way to help explain to readers what was happening. Why were renewables not growing faster? Because they were too expensive. In 2015, for example, Reuters reporters explained that more than 500 coal-fired plants were under construction in Asia because coal-based generation remained cheaper not only than renewables, but also than natural gas.[7]

For the IEA, LCOE has long been a tool principally of prediction. The body's flagship publication is its annual *World Energy Outlook*, in which it makes medium- to long-term projections for national and international energy markets of all types, electricity markets prominent among them. It is, arguably, for its annual *Outlook* that the IEA is today best known, and LCOE explicitly underwrites the forecasts it contains. These forecasts circulate, and are reproduced, widely. In the aforementioned 2015 article, in which they explained what was then happening on the ground in Asia, for instance, Reuters' journalists also cited the IEA's forecast that, in view of its relative cheapness, coal's share of the South East Asian power market would grow from a third to a half by 2040.[8]

For supporters of renewable energy, the implication of LCOE estimates showing that renewables were at a cost disadvantage compared to fossil fuels was clear enough from the outset: economic support of some kind was required in order to offset that disadvantage. Otherwise, solar and wind would never make headway. In fact, this was another

---

5   Lazard, 'Levelized Cost of Energy+', April 2023, lazard.com.

6   A. D. Owen, 'Environmental Externalities, Market Distortions and the Economics of Renewable Energy Technologies', *Energy Journal* 25: 3 (2004), pp. 140–1.

7   F. Tan and H. Gloystein, 'Natural Gas Losing Its Shine as Asia Holds Faith in Coal Power', 3 November 2015, reuters.com.

8   Ibid.

significant stake in the ground planted by the UK's Renewable Energy Advisory Group in the early 1990s. Its 1992 report highlighting renewables' higher price insisted that the government could and should intervene in the market to help renewables become established. It also included recommendations for how this should be done and who ultimately should bear the cost.[9]

Such arguments built upon what were at the time increasingly influential currents of thought about the necessity for state–market collaboration in tackling environmental problems. Not least among these were the forceful propositions of the original 'ecological modernists' in 1980s Germany. The thinking of Udo Ernst Simonis and other ecological modernists shaped government policy vis-à-vis renewables as it emerged in the 1990s not just in Germany itself – the famous *Energiewende* – but internationally. That renewables' relative costliness militated against a market-only approach, and hence necessitated government intervention, was at the very core of such thinking. As Hans-Josef Fell, an arch proponent of ecological modernisation and co-author of Germany's pioneering Renewable Energy Sources Act of 2000, once put it, 'The market can do a lot, it can break up rigidities, ensure more economic efficiency, and give citizens new opportunities to influence the energy industry. But we cannot foster renewable energy through the market alone.'[10]

And, finally, for opponents of renewable electricity, the implication of studies suggesting that solar and wind were two to three (or more) times more expensive than alternatives was no less clear: namely that to pursue renewable power was evidently folly, imposing inexcusable economic costs on taxpayers, consumers or both. Consider, for example, the longtime climate sceptic Bjørn Lomborg. 'If we really care for people without electrical power,' the Dane wrote in 2008 in response to proposals to expand solar power in India, and referring to data indicating that solar in that country was fourteen times more expensive than diesel, 'shouldn't we use our resources so that 14 kids get power instead of just one?'[11] Or, in the words the same year of a critic of the UK government's then

---

9    Maddox, 'DTI Says Costs of Renewable Energy Are High'.

10    Cited in S. G. Gross, *Energy and Power: Germany in the Age of Oil, Atoms, and Climate Change* (Oxford: Oxford University Press, 2023), p. 291.

11    B. Lomborg, 'A Chilling View of Warming', *Wall Street Journal*, 13 September 2008.

commitment to produce 20 per cent of the country's energy renewably by 2020, expanding wind power in line with the government's plans would be 'economic madness as it has been calculated that the cheapest form of wind energy is two-and-a-half times more expensive than that generated from conventional power stations'.[12]

Without wanting to belabour such LCOE-fuelled critiques of renewables, two important points about them bear highlighting. The first is that, in the hands of policymakers, among others, LCOE has long served as a convenient camouflage or fig leaf of sorts. If the slow actual or expected rollout of renewables and the associated ongoing dominance of fossil-fuel-based energy could be safely ascribed to the innocent but indomitable variable of relative price, one did not need to discuss uncomfortable issues of power and vested interest. In 2011, for example, a spokesperson for Thailand's Energy Ministry said that even twenty to thirty years in the future, up to 80 per cent of the country's electricity would still be generated by fossil fuels, 'because they were still the cheapest and would ensure that the poor could afford electricity'.[13] Needless to say, no mention was made of the close links – widely acknowledged and reported on – between ministry officials and fossil fuel companies.[14]

Second, dogged opponents of renewables have continued to invoke renewables' ostensible costliness as a supposedly ineluctable barrier to faster renewables development long since LCOE data actually began to show that renewables had achieved cost parity – or better – with fossil fuels. We will come back to the specific numbers themselves later. Suffice it to note here that, around the middle of the 2010s, the data assembled by the likes of the IEA revealed a changing of places in the cost hierarchy among different generating technologies. Having hitherto consistently shown wind and solar to be more expensive technologies for electricity generation than coal or natural gas, the IEA reported in 2015 that 'the cost of renewable technologies – in particular solar photovoltaic – have declined significantly over the past five years, and . . . *are no longer cost*

12   F. A. Chapman, 'We Should Develop New Energy – But Refuse Wind Farms', *Sentinel*, 30 September 2008.

13   'Dismal Role Seen for Renewable Energy', *Nation*, 23 March 2011.

14   See, for example, S. Kunnuwong, W. W. Saelim and K. Thossaphonpaisan, 'Coal and Renewable Energy Reporting in Thailand', 2020, stanleycenter.org, p. 17.

*outliers*.[15] In other words, as the IEA saw it, the fundamental, long-standing, price-based obstacle to electricity decarbonization no longer obtained.

Yet, for opponents of renewables, this was seemingly no matter. The likes of Lomborg continued to rail against solar and wind power, continued to do so on the nominal grounds of relative price, and continued to invoke the IEA as a putatively reliable source.[16] And politicians continued to use their fig leaves. 'Liberals in green power standoff', the *Australian* newspaper splashed in 2018. Among the reported parliamentary critics of the Australian government's (modest) plans to grow renewable electricity were Michelle Landry and Craig Kelly. 'Coal is still the cheapest form of power', the former protested; Landry happened to be MP for Capricornia – one of Australia's main coal-producing regions. 'When I have constituents coming into my office and breaking down in tears in front of me because they can't pay their electricity bill', Kelly, in turn, lamented, 'it is very hard to go into parliament and vote for something that will make electricity prices higher than they would otherwise be.'[17] Kelly, for his part, is a serial climate change denier, and, notoriously, the founder, in 2019, of the group of Parliamentary Friends of Australian Coal Exports.

But, whoever it was – a journalist, the IEA, a renewables advocate or antagonist – and wherever in the world they happened to be considering the question of the energy transition, in the crucial period of the 1990s and 2000s during which dominant ways of understanding the drivers of that transition fell into place, essentially everyone agreed on one thing. Price ruled. Renewables' time would come only once they were the cheapest option.


## II


How can we account for this? Why did the view develop (and become the consensus) that price was the key barometer of renewables'

---

15   IEA, 'Projected Costs of Generating Electricity: 2015 Edition', September 2015, iea.org, p. 19 (emphasis added).

16   For example, B. Lomborg, 'World Bank Must Change Course', 11 April 2019, project-syndicate.org.

17   Both cited in B. Packham, 'Liberals in Green Power Standoff', *Australian*, 1 August 2018.

prospects? After all, not all purveyors of that argument by any means had, or have, vested interests in favour of the energy status quo – indeed, some of those who have argued most stridently about the singular importance of price have been among renewables' strongest supporters. Equally, there was nothing inevitable about implacable opponents of renewables adopting arguments about price as their preferred narrative fig leaf. What then explains the seemingly unassailable hegemony of the price logic?

The previous section hinted at part of the answer. Entities such as the IEA and Lazard are powerful and influential. If they thought the key issue was relative price, it was inevitable that many others would conclude likewise. But such influence only gets us so far, and, of course, it does not help explain why Lazard and the IEA themselves alighted upon price in the first place. In reality, we cannot understand the wider attractiveness and sheer hold of the claim that economics in general, and price in particular, was the key, without recognizing that it reflected and reproduced core elements of a prevailing intellectual zeitgeist. That is to say, the argument fitted an existing conceptual paradigm. This fit is an absolutely crucial part of our story.

There were two distinct parts to this paradigm, and the price-centred perspective on prospects for renewable electricity described above emerged in the 1980s and 1990s very much at the confluence of the two: it was, in this sense, intellectually and institutionally overdetermined. The first part concerned understandings of contemporary environmental problems, as embedded in Western environmental policymaking. The second concerned understandings of the drivers of historical energy transitions. Let us take them, relatively briefly, in turn.

In the early years of environmental policymaking in countries such as the US in the 1960s and 1970s, policy was informed overwhelmingly by ecological arguments, such as the idea, in Beth Popp Berman's words, 'that organisms and their environment depend on one another in complex, unpredictable ways'. Policies were designed as far as possible to respect 'the deep interdependence of the living and non-living elements in an ecological system', using relatively straightforward tools such as strict limits on levels of air and water pollution.[18]

---

18  E. P. Berman, *Thinking Like an Economist: How Efficiency Replaced Equality in US Public Policy* (Princeton, NJ: Princeton University Press, 2022), p .9.

In the 1980s, however, there was a sea change in understanding and, eventually and accordingly, also in policy design. What Berman calls the 'economic style of reasoning' took over. What she means by this is that environmental problems increasingly came to be seen *as* economic problems. More specifically still, they came to be seen as price problems. How so?

The basic argument of those who propounded the new orthodoxy, popularized for policymakers internationally in seminal texts such as 1989's *Blueprint for a Green Economy*, was that the world's growing environmental problems represented an endemic failure of capitalism's price mechanism.[19] Price is supposed to signal to consumers the full cost of producing a particular product, but, in the case of many of industrial societies' most important products (say, cement), it did not. To be sure, some inputs – labour, capital, technology – were priced. But, alongside these priced inputs, were resources or 'services' provided by the environment effectively free of charge. Producing cement, for example, 'uses' the atmosphere as a waste sink for carbon dioxide, and the market price of cement did not incorporate this particular cost.

This, then, was how environmental issues were now increasingly framed. Because environmental resources were (wrongly) priced at zero, there was, it was argued, an inherent tendency in capitalism to overconsume them, thus causing environmental degradation. And the answer therefore seemed obvious – namely to accurately cost the environmental resources consumed in production (so-called 'externalities'), and then to incorporate this estimated cost into the overall prices of goods such as cement, thus forestalling the tendency to overconsumption. The authors of the *Blueprint* described this approach as 'using the market, or establishing *market-based incentives*'.[20] As much as anything else, then, *Blueprint*, and serial other books like it, was in fact a blueprint for a specific mode of understanding and modulating the relationship between society and nature.

Berman calls this mode the 'economic style', and it quickly became dominant: by the 1990s, Berman says, it 'pervaded' Western environmental regulation, calling forth 'technologies of market design' in place

---

19    D. Pearce, A. Markandya and E. Barbier, *Blueprint for a Green Economy* (Abingdon: Earthscan, 1989).

20    Ibid., p. 155 (emphasis in original).

of 'technologies of pollution reduction'. The first major initiative constructed on this basis, according to Berman, was the US Acid Rain Program of 1990, which created a national 'cap-and-trade' market in pollution credits – earned by producers who emitted less sulphur dioxide than they were permitted – and which has since served as 'a model for cap-and-trade programs around the world'.[21] To be taken seriously today by the powers-that-be, those writing and talking about environmental problems and how to address them have no choice, Berman notes, but to frame those problems explicitly as pricing problems with pricing solutions. There is simply no alternative, and this includes in relation to the problem of climate change.

The implication for our own discussion of understandings of the transition from fossil fuels to renewables in electricity generation should, by now, be obvious. When, in the 1990s, people began to try to grapple conceptually with the drivers of that transition, they did so in an epistemic milieu in which it had become the norm, at least among those whose voices were heard in the corridors of power, to explain more or less everything about contemporary environmental issues in price terms. It is wholly unsurprising that, in such a milieu, price – relative price – also became the benchmark of technology-transition talk.

If climate change at large was fundamentally a failure to get price right, so also surely, the logic went, was society's attachment to fossil fuels specifically in electricity generation. We can return to the LCOE metric to see how the logic specifically played out. Those influenced by *Blueprint* and the like conceded that fossil fuels, indeed, had a superior – that is, lower – LCOE on paper. But only on paper. The electricity produced by, for instance, a coal-fired plant was 'cheap' for the same reason that cement was 'cheap' – that is, because, and only because, its environmental costs were unpriced. Its cheapness was, in a sense, artificial.

Economists who wrote about the lower cost of conventional electricity compared to renewable power, such as Anthony Owen, mentioned above, were generally careful to make this precise point. Often so were those policymakers who faced opposition from critics of renewables' relative costliness when seeking to introduce measures designed to make renewables more economically competitive. As

---

21  Berman, *Thinking Like an Economist*, pp. 8–9.

Stephen Gross has noted, the draft text of Germany's 2000 Renewable Energy Sources Act, for example, stated that 'the external cost of producing electricity from conventional energies is not reflected in the price, but is borne by the general public and future generations'.[22] This was *Blueprint* logic writ large. Indeed, Gross goes so far as to suggest that the 'entire justification' for the renewables subsidies introduced by the 2000 German legislation – the nature of which we shall turn to shortly – 'hinged on the theory of externalities, the bedrock of Ecological Modernization'.[23]

Meanwhile, if the prevailing emphasis on the price mechanism in understandings of environmental issues were not in itself enough to nudge thinking about the challenge of electricity decarbonization towards a price framework, superimposed on top of this orthodoxy was a second discourse that leant strongly in the same direction. This was concerned with how the drivers of past energy transitions were to be understood.

There is a vibrant and long-standing academic literature on historic energy transitions. In the past decade or so, as scholars have been motivated by today's energy and climate challenges to mine historical experiences for any possible clues about how such transitions might unfold now and in future, that historiographic tradition has blossomed still further. As one would expect, the literature points to the influence of all manner of different factors – political, cultural and technological, as well as economic – in shaping the pace and form of past transitions. Yet historians do not consider all such factors to have been equally important. The literature has long accorded pride of place to one particular factor – price.

In what manner, then, and to what extent, did price evidently influence the major energy transitions of the past? Roger Fouquet, a leading researcher in this field, has summed up the main conclusions of the literature in the following useful terms.[24] Essentially, Fouquet says, historians have found that for a 'full' energy transition from one energy form to another to take place, the price of the winning

---

22   In Gross, *Energy and Power*, p. 291 (Gross's translation).

23   Ibid.

24   R. Fouquet, 'Historical Energy Transitions: Speed, Prices and System Transformation', *Energy Research and Social Science* 22 (2016), pp. 7–12.

technology must be lower. This, he notes, is not to say that other factors play no part. Of course, they do – but only ever contingently. In other words, propitious political, cultural, geographical or other such factors can make such a full energy transition more or less likely and will fashion the substance of that transition in myriad ways, but only one factor – a lower price – is *necessary* for the transition to occur.

Just as this thesis does not gainsay the influence of non-price factors, nor, Fouquet adds, does it mean that energy technologies with higher prices have never progressed beyond the drawing board. Historically, limited markets for new technologies can and do successfully form even if their price is higher than that of incumbents, for instance if 'the new technology offers new characteristics of value to the consumer'.[25] Nevertheless, transitions are destined to remain stillborn or partial if the price does not fall sufficiently to become competitive.

A favourite example cited by Fouquet is kerosene lighting, which only ever succeeded in supplanting gas lighting in some regions. Fouquet explains the patchwork nature of that transition as follows:

Kerosene was used for lighting in the late 1800s largely by the poor and rural population that could not afford the investment in the infrastructure to supply gas to their homes. However, in urban areas, the price of kerosene lighting never dropped cheap enough to compete with gas lighting (once piping was installed) and, therefore, gas lighting remained the dominant source of lighting until the price of electric lighting dropped sufficiently.[26]

The lesson? For there to be a full transition such as the world today needs away from carbon-intensive energy forms, history suggests – at least according to the orthodox literature summarized by Fouquet – that 'the price of the energy service is crucial . . . If [in the past] the price of the service fell sufficiently (either because the energy efficiency improved or the price of energy declined), full transitions could occur'.[27]

---

25   Ibid., p. 7.
26   Ibid., pp. 8–9.
27   Ibid., p. 8.

The focus on price in explaining past energy transitions has been particularly striking in the historiography of the most important transition of them all, which of course was the specific transition that, today, the world is essentially endeavouring to undo – which is to say, the historic shift *into* fossil fuels. As Andreas Malm, among many others, has observed, Britain in the late eighteenth century and the early nineteenth was the 'incontestable birthplace' of the fossil economy, coming to account for as many as four-fifths of total global emissions of $CO_2$ from fossil fuel combustion by 1825.[28] It was in Britain in that era that the decisive technological shift from water and the waterwheel to steam and the steam engine – and thus to coal – took place, this shift occurring first and foremost in the cotton and cognate industries. For decades now, historians have been exploring that particular local industrial–technological transition, seeking to answer the pivotal question: why did it occur?

They have given a variety of answers, but the dominant narrative, as Malm has demonstrated, has long been centred on price, or more exactly on relative price: in short, and exactly in line with Fouquet's parsing of the historical literature more widely, 'shifting relative prices drive technological change'.[29] Malm describes this as the 'Ricardian–Malthusian' reading of technological transformation in the Industrial Revolution, and highlights the work of prominent proponents of the thesis such as the US historian Bob Allen. Coal and steam, the likes of Allen have concluded, were essentially the cheaper option; that, in a nutshell, is the theory they have presented.

Is it any wonder, therefore, that those contemplating the necessary transition away from fossil fuels today – not just in electricity generation, of course, but especially there – have long cleaved to precisely the price-based arguments we examined earlier in this chapter? On the one hand, they have been thinking and working in a world in which understandings of environmental problems such as greenhouse gas emissions are increasingly saturated by the logic of the price mechanism. On the other hand, they have had historians not just intimating, but effectively telling them, that, insofar (in Malm's words) as 'fossil fuels won the original race [during the Industrial Revolution] because they were

---

28   Malm, *Fossil Capital*, p. 13.
29   Ibid., p. 83.

cheapest', then 'the same advantage will now have to be secured for renewable alternatives if they shall have a chance'.[30] It would be hard to think of a more compelling intellectual pincer movement, allowing precious little space for the germination of alternative explanations either for why wind and solar have struggled to make much headway or for what must happen for them ultimately to supplant hydrocarbons. The apparent lesson of both environmental economics and economic history seems so clear. 'Capitalists slowly unrolling technologies with lower prices: this' – Malm again – is ostensibly 'the manual to follow'.[31]

## III

Increasingly persuaded through the 1980s and 1990s by the accumulating evidence that renewables were at a cost disadvantage to conventional sources of electricity generation and by the burgeoning argument that this represented a significant (indeed, the most significant) obstacle to a flourishing renewables sector, governments around the world widely acted. They did so, of course, with markedly varying degrees of haste and determination, and in a variety of different ways. In the following paragraphs, we will not be much concerned with the specific details of particular countries and the paths that their policymakers have taken in this regard. Such detail – where germane to our narrative – will feature at various points later in the book. Our interest here, rather, is in the broader pattern. How, in general, where minded to do so, did policymakers seek to intervene in the electricity sector to improve renewables' prospects?

As we shall see, while the approach taken in any particular country is certainly unique in its granular detail, policymakers have selected from a palette containing a relatively small number of core policy options. It is these few main policy types that we will consider, in terms of their basic forms and mechanisms. But, before doing so, it is important to make a

---

30  Ibid., p. 14. For an example of an essay in which such a conclusion has been drawn, see, for instance, R. C. Allen, 'Backward into the Future: The Shift to Coal and Implications for the Next Energy Transition', *Energy Policy* 50 (2012), pp. 17–23.

31  Malm, *Fossil Capital*, p. 14.

crucial, more overarching point, which is that, when confronted with the proposition that what was holding renewables back was their costliness relative to fossil-fuel-based electricity technologies, governments principally intervened vis-à-vis the former rather than the latter. That is to say, they generally did little to make conventional technologies less competitive, for example by introducing carbon taxes and therefore making those technologies more costly. Instead, they sought to make renewables more competitive. This was renewables carrots rather than fossil fuel sticks.

| Investment support | Financial support | Revenue support | | |
|---|---|---|---|---|
| | | *Demand stimulus* | *Incremental revenue stream* | *Price control* |
| **Nature of mechanism**<br>Subsidization of the cost of construction of solar, wind farms | Subsidization of the cost of financing construction | Expansion of clean power market through supplier procurement obligations | Creation of a separate market for 'cleanness' of renewable power, usually via a certificate programme | Use of instruments to regulate the electricity price received by renewables generators |
| **Selected examples**<br>• Investment Subsidy Scheme (Belgium)<br>• Investment Tax Credit (US) | • Carbon Emission Reduction Facility (China)<br>• Climate Response Financing Operation (Japan) | • Renewable Portfolio Standard (China)<br>• Renewable Purchase Obligation (India) | • Electricity Certificate System (Norway/ Sweden)<br>• Energy Certificate System (New Zealand) | • Feed-In Tariff (Japan)<br>• Contracts for Difference (UK) |

**Table 4.1** Renewables support mechanisms
*Source*: Author

The basic range of support mechanisms that have been introduced to bolster renewables is shown in Table 4.1. Some countries have consistently focused on one among these; others have used two or more, either in conjunction or successively. Again, these details are not presently our concern.

As the table indicates, one approach was to support investment – essentially, the construction cost. Any number of countries, from Japan to Norway and Spain, have, at various points, provided developers with investment grants or subsidies of different types. One of the better known, most impactful and certainly longest-standing programmes of investment support has been in the US, where tax credits for investment in renewable energy – already briefly mentioned in Chapter 3 – date as far back as the late 1970s. Adopted mainly for solar projects, the Investment Tax Credit (ITC) provides the developer with a credit against tax liability corresponding to a percentage of the capital sum invested in a project. At the time of this writing, the ITC rate is 30 per cent. In essence, the ITC and similar mechanisms that have been used in other countries make renewable electricity less costly specifically by reducing the cost of construction. Such mechanisms are generally implemented through the tax system.

The second column in the table refers to a form of support that could be considered a subset of investment support: namely, financial support. An important way in which policymakers have sometimes sought to improve the economic competitiveness of renewables generation has been to actively lower the cost of capital incurred by renewables companies. Insofar as most such companies rely heavily upon external financing to develop and operate projects, and insofar as the bulk of the financing requirement occurs at the initial investment stage, financial support *is*, effectively, investment support.

Such support has been and is especially important in non-Western markets. This stands to reason. In many such countries, the market cost of borrowing to develop renewables is punitive, and thus without a mechanism for lowering that cost, financing typically represents a major – frequently insurmountable – barrier to project realisation. Recent research found that in a sample of leading emerging economies (Brazil, India, Indonesia, Mexico and South Africa), the average cost of capital of a utility-sized solar farm is presently some 660 basis points higher than in the EU (10.6 versus 4.0 per cent).[32] Notably, this extra cost appears to relate not principally to the perceived risk of the solar facility itself, so much as to market perceptions, doubtless sometimes

---

32   A. Persaud, 'Unblocking the green transformation in developing countries with a partial foreign exchange guarantee', version 7.0, June 2023, climatepolicyinitiative.org, p. 5.

exaggerated, of macroeconomic (currency and default) risks.[33] Whatever the source of the risk premium, and whether exaggerated or not, the point is that there are large parts of the world where renewables investment is disproportionately costly specifically because finance is disproportionately costly.

Active subsidization of the cost of financing the construction of new renewables facilities can be effected in a variety of different ways. In the Global South, development finance institutions (DFIs) have played a prominent role. In this, they have been encouraged and directed by policymakers located in host countries, within governments in the Global North, and at multilateral governance institutions such as the World Bank. DFIs can help lower the cost of project finance either by lending directly, at below-market rates, to developers, or more indirectly by providing protections against project risks and thus lowering the risk premium demanded by private lenders.

Both such mechanisms were employed, for example, to facilitate the development of two solar plants in Senegal that began producing power in 2021. Under the World Bank's 'Scaling Solar' programme, which aims to promote private investment in renewable energy in low-income countries, three DFIs (the European Investment Bank, the International Finance Corporation, and France's Proparco) provided debt finance to the Kael and Kahone plants, while a fourth (the Multilateral Investment Guarantee Agency) issued around €7 million in guarantees to protect against non-commercial project risks.[34]

Meanwhile, in East Asia, specifically in China and Japan, central banks have played an increasingly important role in subsidizing the cost of 'green finance' in recent years. Both the Chinese and Japanese central banks launched the mechanisms of greatest relevance to domestic renewables projects – the Carbon Emission Reduction Facility (CERF) in the former case and the Climate Response Financing Operation in the latter – in 2021. Each such mechanism works not by direct lending to renewables companies, but through the refinancing of loans extended to those companies by commercial banks.

---

33   See ibid.
34   'Two PV Plants Bring Clean Energy to Senegal', *Renewable Energy Magazine*, 2 June 2021.

Take China's CERF. Where they lend to eligible sectors (which include but are not limited to renewables) and disclose the estimated emissions reduction impact of the projects that they finance, China's banks can apply to the PBOC (People's Bank of China) for refinancing of up to 60 per cent of the loan principal at a rate of 1.75 per cent – a level well below prevailing interest rates in the country's interbank and bond markets throughout the period since the CERF was launched. In turn, the PBOC stipulates that loans must be extended to qualifying recipients at rates at or near the prime lending benchmark. The first CERF refinancing occurred in December 2021. By the end of 2022, the PBOC had loaned commercial banks some 300 billion yuan (around $45 billion) under the scheme, supporting lending to qualifying projects totalling 600 billion yuan.[35]

Globally, over the course of the past few decades, policymakers' preference has, however, increasingly shifted towards mechanisms that apply to the revenue rather than the cost side of the business of renewable electricity generation.[36] As Table 4.1 shows, such mechanisms have been of three main types. Of course, supporting the revenues earned by renewables generators does not actually lower the LCOE of solar or wind power in the way that, say, the United States' ITC does. But it does effectively or implicitly lower the LCOE, inasmuch as costs matter to a firm – including a firm that generates electricity – less in absolute terms than relative to revenues. Reducing actual costs, in short, is not the only way to counteract a cost disadvantage such as renewables companies originally had; bolstering their revenues can have the same result in terms of economic viability and competitive position.

One of the three principal types of revenue support was indirect. It took the form of obligations on electricity suppliers (or, less often, users) to procure a minimum proportion of electricity from renewable sources. Such obligations support revenues for owners of renewables facilities by guaranteeing demand for their output. Again, many countries have introduced obligations of this kind at various points in recent decades.

---

35 'PBOC has lent banks $44 billion for "green projects" ', 31 March 2023, centralbanking.com.

36 Note that by no means all cost-based incentives have been focused on investment or financing costs. For example, some countries, among them China, have incentivized the generation of renewable power in part through reduced income or sales taxes.

One such country was the UK, where the Renewables Obligation (RO) – in place between 2002 and 2017 – required that a specific and annually increasing percentage of the electricity sold to users by electricity suppliers was derived from clean energy sources.

A key question to be asked of different support measures is always, who pays? In the case of measures such as the ITC that are implemented and funded through the tax system, taxpayers effectively pay. Minimum-purchase obligations such as the UK's RO are different in this respect. To the extent that sourcing renewable power has been more expensive for electricity suppliers so obliged than sourcing conventional power would have been, those suppliers themselves have paid. But, where government regulation and conditions of competitive intensity have allowed, suppliers have, of course, passed on to ratepayers as much of the increased cost as they possibly can.

A second (and sometimes linked) form of revenue support came in the shape of the fashioning of an incremental revenue stream explicitly for renewably generated electricity. In countries including Denmark, Italy, the Netherlands and Sweden, as well as the UK and the US, this has been an integral part of the government support package. Specifically, companies generating clean electricity have been able to sell not just the electricity itself but, separately, also its renewable quality. The mechanism has usually been a certificate scheme. Such schemes issue the generator with a certificate for each unit of renewable power that it generates. The generator can then sell the certificate in a secondary market. In Sweden, where a certificate scheme is the principal form of government-sponsored support for renewables generators, the sale of such certificates accounted for 15–25 per cent of wind operators' revenues in the years 2018–20.[37]

Who buys the certificates? Typically, the buyer is an electricity supplier: it can, in turn, use the certificate to market 'green' electricity tariffs, inasmuch as the certificate constitutes proof that a unit of renewable power has indeed been produced. However, because the markets for electricity and for such certificates are separate, the fact that a supplier offers a green tariff only means that it has bought certificates: it does not necessarily say anything about that supplier's own

---

37  C. Sandström, M. Staaf and C. Steinbeck, 'Vindkraft – en grön bubbla eller ett svart hål?', 23 May 2023, kvartal.se.

electricity-purchasing practices.[38] Said supplier could just as conceivably source all its supply from a coal-fired plant, under a long-term power-purchase agreement, as from a wind farm. The certificate merely certifies that renewable energy has been generated – not that the bearer itself procured such energy.

Third, and finally, policymakers introduced various forms of price control. Worldwide, this final form of renewables support from governments has been easily the most consequential of all the mechanisms surveyed here, which is to say it is the one that has had most influence in nurturing and buttressing the rollout of renewables installations. Not unrelatedly, it has been the mechanism most favoured both by actors within the renewables sector itself and, no less importantly, by their financiers – on which more in due course.

How does such support work in practice? There is a wide variety of approaches. Probably the most common type of such price-control mechanism for renewables has been the so-called 'feed-in tariff', which generally offers fixed prices per MWh produced, under long-term supply contracts that are either held with, or sponsored by, state-owned entities. Feed-in tariffs were first instituted to meaningful effect in Germany in the early 1990s. Though their initial form there differed from later norms – rather than being set at fixed levels, as they would be in Germany from 2000 onwards, the prices that suppliers paid German renewables generators were set at 90 per cent of the retail electricity price – the basic idea, namely that of controlling wholesale prices, would remain consistent. The pertinent inaugural policy framework, Germany's Feed-in Law of 1990, did not in the event do much to boost solar development: in solar's case, the technology remained too expensive, even with the support of price controls. But, as Stephen Gross has related, the 1990 law did successfully precipitate Europe's maiden wind boom, making it profitable for the first time – albeit 'just barely' – to develop the power source in Germany's windy north. By the end of the 1990s, the country had over 6,000 operating wind farms, providing ten times as much generating capacity as at the beginning of the decade.[39]

An alternative mechanism to feed-in tariffs sees the generator sell its output on the spot market as usual, at the spot price, but also entitles the

---

38  See for example, Angwin, *Shorting the Grid*, pp. 231–4.
39  Gross, *Energy and Power*, p. 276.

generator to a so-called 'feed-in premium'. This 'premium' is either a fixed amount per MWh (that is, on top of the market price), or a variable, 'sliding' amount that is itself linked in some specified way to the evolution of market prices, and which can under some schemes be negative – thus requiring the generator to make a payment *to* the government – if market prices are sufficiently high.

Whether we measure 'success' in rolling out solar and wind power in terms of absolute capacity installations, on which score China leads the way, or the amount of installed solar and wind capacity relative to conventional sources, which would lead us to highlight countries such as Denmark, or the combination of the two, in which regard Germany has enjoyed notable success, such price controls have, in all cases, been nothing less than a pivotal part of the policy toolkit. Needless to say, they will feature prominently later in the book.

## IV

Albeit from relatively trifling beginnings, the past two decades have seen enormous growth in investment in the design and manufacture of wind turbines and solar cells and modules. Manufacturers of wind turbines, for instance, earned total estimated revenues of just $7.5 billion globally in 2003. But, over the next decade, the wind turbine market grew at a compound annual rate of over 20 per cent, to reach nearly $60 billion in 2013.[40] Similarly strong growth has occurred in the solar module manufacturing market. In 2010, manufacturers globally shipped PV modules with a cumulative capacity of less than 20 GW. This figure had increased sixfold – to more than 120 GW – by 2019.[41]

What have been the causes and consequences of this surge in investment? Given the raft of measures introduced by governments to help make the generation of electricity from solar and wind plants more competitive with conventional generating technologies, it would be natural to assume that growing demand for equipment from generators

40   'Global Wind Power Equipment Manufacturing Market Size from 2000 to 2013', March 2014, statista.com.
41   IEA, 'Solar PV Module Shipments by Country of Origin, 2012–2019', October 2022, iea.org.

as a result precisely of such measures is what has driven the equipment-manufacturing industry's growth. Such an assumption would, in fact, be largely fair. Knowing that there is a market that is strongly supported by government incentives of various kinds clearly provides a manufacturer with much of the confidence required to invest capital in designing, making and improving products destined for that market.

Moreover, through the 2000s and especially the 2010s, as developers in possession of long-term feed-in tariff contracts, selling into electricity markets buoyed by renewables purchase obligations, placed larger and larger orders for turbines and modules, manufacturers responded with alacrity. Indeed, there is now a large body of academic research that has consistently found statistically significant positive effects of government support for renewable energy installation and generation on aggregate investment in renewable energy technologies, across multiple jurisdictions.[42]

But it would be wrong to imagine that the story of surging investment in the underlying technologies has been solely a 'pull' story. From the standpoint of manufacturers, there has also been an element of 'push', and especially in the territory that rapidly came to dominate the renewables equipment market globally – China. There, from early on, encouragement to manufacturers came not just in the form of actual or expected demand from subsidized developers of solar and wind farms, but also directly from the state.

Both national and local governments furnished an array of support mechanisms ranging from access to cheap credit to subsidies for research and development expenditure. Such support was integral to driving investment in solar and wind technologies among both publicly and privately owned Chinese manufacturers. The result of this direct support – and, certainly, also of growing demand from developers of proliferating renewable generating facilities both in China itself and overseas – was, ultimately, global industry dominance. By 2019, for example, Chinese firms were

---

42   For example, F. Polzin, M. Migendt, F. A. Täube and P. von Flotow, 'Public Policy Influence on Renewable Energy Investments: A Panel Data Study across OECD Countries', *Energy Policy* 80 (2015), pp. 98–111; G. Ang, D. Röttgers and P. Burli, 'The Empirics of Enabling Investment and Innovation in Renewable Energy', OECD Environment Working Paper No. 123, 2017, oecd-ilibrary.org; D. Azhgaliyeva, J. Beirne and R. Mishra, 'What Matters for Private Investment in Renewable Energy?', *Climate Policy* (2022), 71–87.

producing more than 60 per cent of all solar PV modules shipped globally. Even today, China's dominance of manufacturing of key pieces of equipment remains staggering: 96 per cent of wafers for solar panels, for instance, and 83 per cent of offshore wind blades are produced there.[43]

The Chinese case is also noteworthy for unsettling another assumption that is often made about renewables policymaking. This is the assumption – again, quite natural – that government support, whether for equipment manufacturers, plant developers or both, is principally, or even solely, about climate – that it is, essentially, environmental policy. Once again, this assumption is *largely* fair, at least when such support is considered at the global scale. Certainly, in, say, Europe, environmental concerns have indeed historically been the principal driver of renewables support.

But the same is not true, or at any rate *was* not true, of China. Its instruments of support for solar and wind technology manufacturers in many cases long pre-dated the meaningful integration of environmental considerations into Chinese state policymaking. Those instruments were, and to a lesser extent still are, a matter rather of energy policy – concerns around energy security here being paramount – and industrial policy – specifically, the objective of making China a leader in a hi-tech global growth industry, able to export equipment competitively to the lucrative European and US markets.

What has been interesting about the post-COVID-19 period has been the first signs of policymakers in the latter markets finally responding. Having seemingly been happy to see US-based developers rely substantially on Chinese equipment imports through the 2010s, the US government abruptly changed tack in 2022, using that year's Inflation Reduction Act to introduce a battery of incentives not only for developers of new renewables generating facilities – as discussed earlier in the book – but also for domestically based equipment manufacturers. In the new, post-COVID, 'post-globalization' era, industrial policy was evidently back on the agenda in the US, too.

Whatever the exact mix of causes, clearly the past twenty years or so have seen consistent and substantial growth in investment in the underlying technologies of solar and wind power, the consequences of which have been equally clear to see. What has occurred has been, in many respects,

---

43   D. Brower, A. Chu, M. McCormick and J. Jacobs, 'Inside America's Energy Revolution', *Financial Times*, 16 February 2023.

a prototypical story of successful large-scale industrial equipment manufacturing, a capitalist fairy tale straight out of the business school casebook – albeit one featuring a healthy dose of government intervention. Competition intensified as new players in new territories were attracted to the perceived honeypot. Experimentation with different raw materials and different production techniques served to deliver enhanced production efficiencies. And, last but not least, the size of the leading manufacturers increased dramatically through both organic growth and industry consolidation, leading to vastly expanded production volumes and concomitant economies of scale. All of this combined to generate a striking and singularly important outcome – tumbling technology costs. In the case of solar equipment, for example, where the cost reductions were most pronounced, the price of PV modules in the US dropped by some 85 per cent between 2010 and 2020.[44]

As we know from our discussion in Chapter 3, the fact that functioning solar and wind plants have zero fuel costs and only minimal operation and maintenance costs means that the bulk of their lifetime costs comprise upfront investment, of which, in turn, the generating equipment – the turbines or modular PV systems – accounts for the lion's share. Thus the decline in the cost of turbines and modules inevitably led to a more or less commensurate decline in the cost measure that analysts of electricity markets – and, especially, renewable electricity – most doggedly track: the LCOE. As it became cheaper and cheaper to produce solar and wind equipment, in other words, it became cheaper and cheaper to generate electricity using such equipment.

Any number of organizations – from Bloomberg to the IEA and from the International Renewable Energy Agency to the US Energy Information Administration – publish regularly updated analyses of prevailing, historic and projected LCOEs for different electricity-generating technologies. A simple Google search will yield a whole host. And, while the specific numbers vary – as noted earlier, a raft of assumptions must be made when comparing costs across different technology types – all analyses show the same key (and widely commented upon) underlying trend in terms of historic costs, namely declining costs for

44    D. Feldman, V. Ramasamy, R. Fu, A. Ramdas, J. Desai and R. Margolis, 'US Solar Photovoltaic System and Energy Storage Cost Benchmark: Q1 2020', 2021, nrel .gov, p. vi.

renewables, not just in absolute terms but, more importantly in the view of many commentators, also in relative terms. Having previously been more expensive than conventional sources (and much more expensive in the case of solar), renewables have for several years now been broadly cost-competitive, even if there has been an unexpected uptick in their costs since 2021.

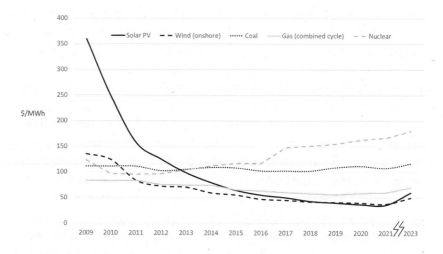

**Figure 4.1** Levelized cost of electricity by source of generation, 2009–23 (utility-scale, unsubsidized, mean value)
*Source*: Lazard

For illustrative purposes, Figure 4.1 reproduces the data published by Lazard, whose estimates, as noted earlier, are widely regarded as something of an industry gold standard. The numbers largely speak for themselves. Around 2010, solar PV and (onshore) wind remained the two most expensive of the five sources graphed – the other three being coal, gas and nuclear – although, in wind's case, the gap had already narrowed to a sliver. By 2016, however, and every year since, solar and wind have been the cheapest: cheaper than natural gas, and *much* cheaper than coal and nuclear. A new era in the economics of power generation, it seems, had dawned.

# V

It was in the early to mid-2010s that analysts of the energy scene began to take serious note of the falling costs of renewable electricity and, moreover, to leap directly from the observation of this trend to bold conclusions about the likely implications for the future of electricity generation. Among the first notable reports was one published by the US Energy Information Administration in 2013.[45] Although it attracted relatively little comment, its gist would become more or less ubiquitous over the next decade. Renewables' prices, it observed, were falling fast, and would continue to do so, and thus renewables, not fossil fuels, would be the fastest-growing source of energy in the future.

2015 saw the publication of a set of similar projections, which garnered, however, considerably greater attention – partly, one imagines, because the author was BloombergNEF, a much-followed source of research and analysis on transformations in the energy sector, and partly because of the hyperbole that surrounded the launch of the publication. The cost of renewables, solar in particular, BloombergNEF said, was (and would carry on) 'plunging'; this increasingly made solar 'first choice for consumers and the poorest nations', and hence renewables would attract the bulk of spending on new power plants, 'dwarfing' spending on fossil-fuel-based plants.[46] It was a striking picture indeed.

Yet what has been even more striking is the subsequent, essentially universal, acceptance of the logic. From political right and left, from Global South and North, everyone, seemingly, has gravitated to the view that, now that they are cheaper/cheapest, renewables are primed for an unprecedented golden growth era. And, in the process, everyone has become an LCOE expert and fetishist. If you want to know what the future of renewables looks like, we are repeatedly told, *just look at the relative costs.*

First to be persuaded were relatively predictable acolytes, from within the business community or – if they were academics – from within the

45    Energy Information Administration, '*AEO2014* Early Release Overview', November 2013, eia.gov, p. 14.

46    E. Goossens, 'Renewables to Beat Fossil Fuels with $3.7 Trillion Solar Boom', 23 June 2015, bloomberg.com.

mainstream. 'Renewable energy will replace fossil fuels because they [*sic*] will be less expensive, as reliable, and as convenient as fossil fuels,' insisted Steve Cohen, of Columbia University's Earth Institute, in 2017. 'The issue is not if, but when.'[47] Cohen was echoed by, among others, the sustainability entrepreneur James Ellsmoor, who, writing in *Forbes* in 2019, told the business magazine's readers that renewables' lower costs were indeed poised to propel their 'mass adoption'.[48]

In time, even those perhaps less inclined to accept the growing consensus were ultimately seduced. A notable – and enormously important – convert was the IEA. As we have seen, its LCOE numbers, like others', began in the mid-2010s to show renewables becoming cost-competitive. But, having long been notoriously cautious regarding renewables' prospects (to the ire of critics), it took some time for the IEA to actually believe what it was seeing. When it finally made its leap of logic (and perhaps also of faith), however, it jumped in two feet first. Its 2020 World Energy Outlook made for remarkable reading for long-time IEA watchers. Solar, the IEA noted, 'is consistently cheaper than new coal- or gas-fired power plants in most countries, and solar projects now offer some of the lowest cost electricity ever seen'. The view of its executive director, Fatih Birol, on what this meant? 'I see solar', Birol excitedly announced, 'becoming the new king of the world's electricity markets.'[49]

Among the last to move into line were holdouts on the left, environmental campaigners who, again and again, have seen their hopes for meaningful transformation of energy systems comprehensively dashed. Such past disappointments – and not wanting to get burned anew – perhaps explain why left environmentalists were relatively slow to join the hype around renewables' cheapness and that which it ostensibly portended. But, today, even grizzled veteran activists roundly and eagerly articulate the apparently unassailable price logic.

---

47   S. Cohen, 'Why Renewable Energy Will Replace Fossil Fuels', 17 July 2017, columbia.edu.

48   J. Ellsmoor, 'Renewable Energy Is Now the Cheapest Option – Even without Subsidies', 15 June 2019, forbes.com.

49   IEA, 'World Energy Outlook 2020 Shows How the Response to the Covid Crisis Can Reshape the Future of Energy', 13 October 2020, iea.org.

Consider, for instance, Bill McKibben, who in 2021 could be heard enthusing that renewable energy had become 'startlingly' cheap.[50] McKibben, it turned out, had been reading a new report by the think tank Carbon Tracker, and he could not hide his excitement. 'The numbers in the report' – LCOE numbers, needless to say, in this case those reported by BloombergNEF – 'are overwhelming,' McKibben gushed. Solar's newfound cheapness, McKibben explained, 'will keep pushing us to replace liquid fuels with electricity generated from the sun, and, eventually, no one will have a gas boiler in the basement or an internal-combustion engine in the car.' Perhaps, he allowed, the Bloomberg 'analysts are too optimistic', but, even if they were, 'we'll still be swimming in cheap solar energy'. Such, the consensus has it, is the irresistible motive force of relative price.

And the consensus has held, even in the face of what, at first blush, might have appeared countervailing real world developments. In 2022, for example, just a year after McKibben wrote his paean to cheap renewables, solar and wind costs suddenly went into reverse and, for the first time in more than a decade, rose, as inflation and supply-chain blockages bit. Was this a blow to the economics of renewables? Not in the round, BloombergNEF's analysts assured nervy readers. For, while solar and wind costs had indeed risen, the cost of the coal and gas used in conventional power plants had risen by even more, and therefore the all-important price gap between clean and dirty power 'has widened, not closed'. In fact, 'the gaps between wind and solar, and gas-fired power, have never been greater'.[51] A series of graphs showing updated relative LCOEs was duly presented as supporting evidence.

What has also increasingly been accepted, furthermore, is that the relative cheapness of renewables today is such that they can out-compete fossil fuels even without government support. Subsidies, some vouch, are no longer needed. Having stimulated competition and scale economies in production to the extent needed to drive costs down, government supports for renewables, the argument runs, can now be safely removed without jeopardizing future investment. Thus when, for

---

50   B. McKibben, 'Renewable Energy Is Suddenly Startlingly Cheap', *New Yorker*, 28 April 2021.

51   N. Bullard, 'Renewable Energy Provides Relief from Rising Power Prices', 14 July 2022, bloomberg.com.

example, campaigners worried that the UK government was being premature in 2016 in moving to reduce subsidies for solar and onshore wind, the renowned energy economist Dieter Helm retorted, 'Subsidies should be a temporary measure, not permanent. They did their job.'[52]

The view propounded by Helm soon spread. The title of James Ellsmoor's 2019 *Forbes* article on the economics of renewables, mentioned above, was, for instance, 'Renewable Energy Is Now the Cheapest Option', but it was bookended by three crucial additional words that would not have been included some years previously – 'Even without Subsidies.'[53] Meanwhile, the same year, over at Bloomberg, Mark Chediak and Brian Eckhouse waxed lyrical about renewables 'outgrowing' subsidies. 'On sun-drenched fields across Spain and Italy,' they wrote, 'developers are building solar farms without subsidies or tax-breaks.' 'The training wheels are off,' they reported a market analyst as saying. 'Prices have declined enough for both solar and wind that there's a path toward continued deployment in a post-subsidy world.'[54]

While the claim that renewables have outgrown the support mechanisms originally introduced to offset their lack of price-competitiveness can be heard from commentators of all persuasions, it is, unsurprisingly, the free market right that makes this particular case most fervently. Being at once convinced on principle by the rule of price and (also on principle, if not always in practice) staunchly anti-interventionist, free market disciples have poured scorn on governments that have chosen to retain support for solar and wind. Few individuals or organizations, for example, have called as consistently and vociferously for the termination of subsidies for price-competitive renewables as has the US Institute for Energy Research – an avowed free-market-supporting non-profit organization, but also one that is often described as a front for the fossil fuel industry.

Relatedly, and no less importantly, the same such groups often make a parallel argument. If renewables' underlying competitiveness means they no longer need government support, then, clearly, by the same token, governments also have no need to consider the other type of

---

52    Cited in J. Pickard and K. Stacey, 'Lords Will Try to Rescind Cuts in Solar Grants', *Financial Times*, 6 January 2016.

53    Ellsmoor, 'Renewable Energy Is Now the Cheapest Option'.

54    M. Chediak and B. Eckhouse, 'Solar and Wind Power So Cheap They're Outgrowing Subsidies', 19 September 2019, bloomberg.com.

intervention that could originally have been used to level things up between expensive renewables and cheap fossil fuels, but which, to date, policymakers have been much more reluctant to countenance – which is to say, taxes on carbon. *Take your hand off the lever of renewables subsidies*, governments, in short, are told, *and keep it off the lever of carbon taxes.*

## VI

The problem, of course, is that, a decade on from the first promises that their unprecedented cheapness would see renewables rapidly begin to supplant fossil fuels in electricity generation, and long since commentators on all sides of the climate–energy debate subscribed to the relative-prices explanatory orthodoxy, such wholesale technological substitution is not – yet – happening. As we saw in Chapter 1, renewables are not taking over. If anything, they are falling further behind. Moreover, and as we shall see in Chapter 9, governments are not finding themselves able to safely remove support mechanisms. On the contrary: they are having to retain and reinforce subsidies. In late 2022, notably, there was widespread relief not just in the US but around the world that US policymakers had found a way to agree on a long-term extension of the country's tax credits for wind and solar generating facilities.

So why is what we are told *ought* to be happening *not* happening? There are any number of different theories, but two are particularly prominent. The first theory is that the problem is bureaucracy: essentially, slow permitting, slow grid connection, or a combination of each. Which is the main alleged culprit depends on the territory. In the EU, for example, the planning system usually gets the blame.[55] In the UK, the finger is typically pointed at grid managers. A 2022 article in the *Financial Times* reported that renewables developers were then being told that there would be a wait of six to ten years to be connected to the UK grid. Interestingly, one developer cited in the article explicitly counterposed the negative power of red tape to the positive power of relative price: 'Solar and onshore wind are the cheapest forms of new electricity

---

55    See, for example, C. Hodgson, 'Europe's Wind Industry Flags Further Weakness in 2023 despite Energy Demand', *Financial Times*, 29 January 2023.

generation and yet projects are being delayed due to a lack of long-term planning and investment in electricity infrastructure.[56]

The second prominent theory is that there is something more nefarious afoot, namely that the capacity for the cost advantage of renewables to drive through transformative change is being frustrated by the vested interests of the fossil fuel industry.[57] Through their influence on policymakers, this argument has it, companies in and around the coal and natural gas sectors are succeeding in forestalling the decarbonization of electricity, against both ecological and economic logics.

Whatever the actual argument, however, the key point for our purposes is that the problem – the force retarding the transition to clean electricity – is deemed to be anything *but* economics. With renewables now so cheap, after all, how could it be economics that is standing in the way? It is not possible – in theory.

In fact, taken to its logical conclusion in the face of the seeming paradox of cheaper renewables coexisting with ongoing investment in fossil-fuel-fired power, the theory of relative prices calls into question the very validity of the empirical LCOE data. 'In a conventional model,' as J. W. Mason puts it, 'lower-carbon technologies must be more expensive than existing ones, since otherwise they would already have been adopted.'[58]

By this way of thinking, if the data are not in fact erroneous, then the problem *must* be located in the extra-economic domain of politics, or planning, or both – it simply cannot be otherwise. Indeed, so compelling is the relative-prices world view to those who adhere to it that it is not even necessary to find evidence of those countervailing political or bureaucratic forces. Deductively, they have to be there – stubbornly impeding the motive force of the price mechanism.

Consider the following quintessential example, taken from the 2021 Carbon Tracker report that so impressed Bill McKibben. 'We have

---

56   G. Plimmer, 'Renewables Projects Face 10-Year Wait to Connect to Electricity Grid', *Financial Times*, 8 May 2022.

57   Note that in some instances these two arguments overlap, not least in those parts of the US where fossil fuel interests continue to enjoy considerable control of grid management. See S. Welton, 'Rethinking Grid Governance for the Climate Change Era', *California Law Review* 109 (2021), pp. 209–75.

58   J. W. Mason, 'Climate Policy from a Keynesian Point of View', May 2021, jwmason.org, p. 12.

established', the report confidently asserted, 'that technical and economic barriers have been crossed by falling costs.' In other words, the economic (and technical) challenges to decarbonization have been met. The logical implication? It can only be something else that is standing in the way. '*It follows*', the authors comfortably concluded, 'that the main remaining barrier to change is the ability of incumbents to manipulate political forces to stop change.'[59] Any other explanation was literally inconceivable.

What are policymakers (and indeed the rest of us) expected to take from all of this? The conclusion is seemingly ineluctable. Sweep away the political and planning obstacles, and the price mechanism will do the rest.

The most inconceivable thing of all from the conventional perspective, meanwhile, is that the primary obstacle to decarbonization of electricity is not (or is no longer) price, but nonetheless is still economic. Yet that is the very argument we shall be making in the rest of the book.

---

59   K. Bond, H. Benham, E. Vaughan and S. Butler-Sloss, 'The Sky's the Limit', April 2021, carbontracker.org, p. 54 (emphasis added).

# 5

# The Price Is Wrong

In the early 2010s, plans were drawn up for the development of one of Europe's largest onshore wind farms on the Fosen peninsula in central-west Norway, directly across the Trondheim Fjord from the country's fourth-largest city, and around 600 kilometres north of the Tellenes wind farm (Chapter 3).

In 2014, despite strong objections from local Sámi reindeer-herding communities concerned about potential disruption to winter pastures, development of the project began in earnest. In March of that year, the four power companies behind the plans – Statkraft, Agder Energi, NTE and TrønderEnergi – created a formal corporate vehicle to control the project, called Fosen Vind AS, in which the state-owned Statkraft was the controlling shareholder with a 50.1 per cent stake. In the summer, a tender request for offers for turbines with a cumulative generating capacity of 600 MW was sent out.

But less than a year later, in June 2015, the development came to a grinding halt. Statkraft summarily announced that it would not be taking the project forward. 'Statkraft finds it regrettable that the projects cannot be realised,' said president and CEO Christian Rynning-Tønnesen.[1]

What had happened? Why had a project behind which four major power companies had enthusiastically rallied – and indeed which

---

1 'Statkraft Halts Wind Power Planning in Central Norway', 4 June 2015, statkraft.com.

Statkraft itself just the previous September had described as going 'full steam ahead' – hit what appeared to be an insurmountable roadblock?[2] Notably, the problem was not political or bureaucratic. In fact, upon announcing the halt, Rynning-Tønnesen was careful to acknowledge that any such obstacles had been actively cleared away: 'The authorities have contributed by facilitating wind power development,' he said.

In September 2014, Christian Stav, the head of NTE, had given a hint of what the problem would turn out to be. The joint owners would not make a final decision on whether to go ahead, Stav had explained, until two crucial – and presumably related – things had been achieved. One was to secure additional equity financing from an external investor. The second was to properly run the numbers in order to check (with as much certainty as was possible) that the project would make money. 'Before the owners can make an investment decision,' Stav had said, 'the profitability of the projects must be established.'[3]

It was specifically on this latter score that Fosen Vind fell short. Why did Statkraft halt proceedings in June 2015? Simple: the numbers could not be made to work. 'Updated analyses', Statkraft chief Rynning-Tønnesen told reporters, 'show that the projects in central Norway will not be profitable.'[4] So that, it seemed, was that.

Do the costs of generation – as gauged in metrics such as the LCOE and the like – play a part in determining the profitability of renewables operations such as that which was planned at Fosen? Of course they do. But, as we shall see, the costs, principally of those 600 MW of turbines, definitively were not Rynning-Tønnesen and Statkraft's concern – least of all, one might add, the relative costs of renewables versus fossil fuels.

|

To suggest that, in considering the economic drivers of the prospects for renewable electricity, we should be focusing on profit rather than price, might appear odd, even outlandish. After all, have the prophets of price not satisfactorily grounded their world view – that price rules all – both

2   'Fosen Vind AS etablert i dag', 17 September 2014, e24.no.
3   Ibid.
4   'Statkraft Halts Wind Power Planning in Central Norway'.

in theory and in history? Is it not the case that this world view accords with both the theoretical principles of mainstream environmental economics and the historical lessons that economic historians have typically drawn from the study of past energy transitions in general, and the transition to fossil fuels during the Industrial Revolution in particular? It is indeed. Yet it turns out that for all its consonance with theory and history, the conventional view is wrong. Why? Because it is the wrong theory and the wrong history.

Let us start with theory. The view that the relative prices of different sources of energy will determine the relative dominance of the two in the evolving energy mix is, as we have seen, very much a view from within the economics mainstream. This mainstream tradition is sometimes labelled 'orthodox', other times 'neoclassical'. It is also principally a form of 'supply-side' economics, so called because it rests on the premise that the supply of goods and services is the key determinant of levels of economic growth and prosperity.

Supply-side economics is frequently contrasted with what many regard as the main theoretical alternative, namely the 'demand-side' economics most closely associated with the English economist John Maynard Keynes. Where supply-siders say that the theoretical (and policy) focus should be on supply, and that demand takes care of itself – that, as per Say's law, in colloquial terms 'supply creates its own demand' – Keynesians say that the key is the level of demand for products and services. This, not supply, determines growth and employment prospects, and so policymakers should seek actively to stimulate demand, especially through government investment, if it is lacking.

For all their differences, however, both supply-side and demand-side theories are, ultimately, price-oriented theories. To be sure, in Keynes, relative prices do not have the overtly instrumental role of coordinating economic activity that they enjoy in neoclassicism. But any theory of supply and demand – whether it emphasizes the former or the latter – is at some level a theory of price, particularly so when, as in Keynes, the concern is with *effective* demand (or supply), which is nothing if not a price concept. Perhaps the most important technical difference between supply-sideism and Keynesian demand-sideism is that, in the latter, the processes through which prices respond to changes in supply and demand take time.

Though it is usually not presented with comparable formal (mathematical) elegance, a better theoretical account of how the economic world actually works in practice, especially at the level of the firm, is provided by a third tradition – in fact, the first of three, chronologically speaking. This is the political economy – often labelled 'classical economics' – most closely associated with Adam Smith, David Ricardo and Karl Marx.

As Anwar Shaikh, among others, has observed, political economy fundamentally turns not on price but on profit. Thus, unlike supply-side neoclassicism or demand-side Keynesianism, political economy is – to use Shaikh's felicitous turn of phrase – 'profit-side'. What does this actually mean? It means, as Shaikh says, that, for political economists, the production of goods or services 'is always initiated on the basis of prospective profit', just as was (or indeed, was not) the case with the production of wind power at Fosen in Norway in 2015. Does this profit-sideism negate the relevance of price and supply and demand? No. But it does imply (Shaikh again) that 'both effective supply and demand are regulated, through different channels, by expected profitability'.[5] Should they not foresee profitability, in short, capitalists do not invest. If there is one theoretical principle above all others that underlies the present book, this is it.

While certainly notable in both Smith and Ricardo, profit-sideism is most explicit in Marx. 'Production is organised and investment is undertaken by capitalists', Thomas Weisskopf has said of the Marxian theory, 'in order to make profits; a fall in the average rate of profit – and consequently in the expected profitability of new investment – is bound sooner or later to discourage such investment.'[6] This, accordingly, is the particular theoretical vantage point from which we shall proceed. Even if they are confident about demand conditions, firms will be reluctant to invest if they think the return on investment will be too low.

While this way of thinking brooks no space for orthodox economics (environmental or otherwise), it does not entirely obviate Keynesianism. Judiciously parsed, the Keynesian revolution added to classical

---

5   A. Shaikh, *Capitalism: Competition, Conflict, Crises* (New York: Oxford University Press, 2016), pp. 615–17.

6   T. Weisskopf, 'Marxian Crisis Theory and the Rate of Profit in the Postwar US Economy', *Cambridge Journal of Economics* 3 (1979), p. 341.

economics crucial insights that can make the latter stronger, not weaker. Two stand out. The first (with veiled echoes of Marx) pertains to questions of economic coordination, the limits of markets as coordinating mechanisms, and the attendant need for central planning. The second pertains to questions of uncertainty, and the degree to which the future for which capitalists and governments invest can – or as Keynes saw it, cannot – be accurately predicted. Both sets of insights feature in subsequent chapters.

What, in turn, of history, and the history of energy transitions such as the one that fuelled the Industrial Revolution? It will be recalled from Chapter 4 that the theory of relative prices has long been the dominant explanation for the victory of steam and coal over water power in early nineteenth-century England. In *Fossil Capital*, however, published in 2016, Andreas Malm shattered that received wisdom.[7] He did so in two ways.

First, Malm demonstrated that the existing orthodoxy is belied by the facts. It is simply not true that steam was cheaper. On the contrary: water was, and remained, cheaper, mainly because it required no human labour to call forth its powers, whereas coal could only be transformed into an energy source through massive inputs of costly human labour power.

Second, Malm assembled a series of compelling alternative claims. Steam was preferred partly because it was spatially advantageous. Unlike a waterwheel, a steam engine could be put up more or less anywhere, enabling the industrial capitalist to set up in the fast-growing northern towns where labour power (not to mention other sources of agglomeration economies) was concentrated, and many of the biggest of which happened to be located close to coal mines. Water power was, of course, considerably less spatially flexible; firms had to go to it, source workers from elsewhere and then invest in maintaining them – in the shape, most notably, of worker colonies, where capital, lacking the luxury of being able to readily replace workers, was much more vulnerable to strike action.

Steam was also temporally advantageous. Water's irregularity of supply became a significant problem for the burgeoning English cotton industry of the early nineteenth century specifically in the context of the

---

7   Malm, *Fossil Capital*.

increasing demands of export markets. Furthermore, the flexibilization of working conditions and the long working days that were required to compensate for such irregularity and associated work downtime were substantially fettered by the 1833 Factory Act and later the 1847 Ten Hours Act. As Malm put it, 'water followed its own clock – not that of the factory'.[8] Steam-based production was much less affected.

Last but not least, steam fitted much better in the brave new world of capitalist private property. Large-scale, reservoir-based water power schemes would perhaps have been preferable to steam for capital at large, but such inherently collective arrangements fell foul of opposition from individual capitalists who saw such schemes as a restraint on their independence and private property rights. Private property and water 'did not mix well'; the latter, invested in at scale, required 'complicated communal relationships'. Coal and steam did not suffer the same 'collective drawbacks'.[9]

For our purposes, in any event, the specific reasons for the victory of the steam engine and coal are less important than the more general implication of Malm's account. The investment decisions that drove the early nineteenth-century energy transition ultimately hinged not on price, but on profit. The spatial and temporal advantages of steam all consisted in one way or another in the fact that steam better enabled capital to secure a reliable and disciplined supply of labour power and accordingly represented 'a superior medium for extracting surplus wealth'.[10]

In sum, there is in fact support in neither history nor theory for the claim that relative cheapness is today the economic key for renewables in winning out against fossil fuels in electricity generation. If wind and solar power are to thrive, and ultimately dominate, then history and theory suggest that profit, not the right price, is the sine qua non.

## II

It is always comforting to be able to root one's explanatory approach in historical precedent and theoretical principles, as we indeed can with a

---

8    Ibid., p. 192.
9    Ibid., pp. 119–20.
10   Ibid., p. 124.

profit-oriented approach to energy transitions. But, arguably, it is not strictly necessary. A more pragmatic perspective on explanatory justification might be to say that, first and foremost, we should simply listen to those on the ground who make the investment decisions that actually make energy transitions happen – or not happen, as the case may be.

In the case of renewables, the principal decision makers are energy companies, other developers and – in particular – the financial institutions whose decisions about whether or not to advance investment capital, and at what cost, ultimately determine whether solar and wind farm projects proceed or not. What, we might therefore ask, is the overriding question in the minds of such financiers when presented with investment proposals by renewables developers? It is the following: will I get my money back, and with an acceptable level of financial return? The basic answer to this question is, of course: only, generally, if the project is profitable.

Now, intuitively, one might imagine that, for all their ultimate focus on profit rather than price, such financiers nonetheless would pore over historic and projected figures for the costs of different electricity-generating technologies, fixating – like seemingly everyone else – on the hallowed LCOE. After all, the relative-prices framing has a seductive logic to it; it 'feels' right, which is part of the reason why it enjoys such dominance. Lower costs – say, solar at $50 per MWh versus coal at $100 – surely *means* higher profit. The logic is ironclad, is it not?

Consider, by way of analogy, the hypothetical example of a company that makes and sells a particular type of smartphone that retails at $200. To do so, it uses an established mix of inputs – materials, labour and so on – and an established set of processes for combining those inputs to produce and distribute the phone in question. Those inputs and methods cost it $150 per phone, yielding a handsome per-unit profit of $50. But then, out of the blue, the company happens upon an entirely new constellation of inputs and production methods that allow it to produce the same phone for just $130 per phone, and thus to generate a $70 profit. Immediately, it switches. Relative costs have won the day.

Is electricity not equivalent? There too, does the price mechanism not prevail? Which is to say, is the cheapest productive constellation not chosen? Yes, but, crucially, only under certain conditions.

Some of these conditions we have already alluded to. There are, for example, political conditions; that is, is the institutional landscape free of vested interests that might serve as impediments to the smooth working-out of the aforementioned economic logic? Is it also free of bureaucratic impediments? As is all too clear, in the real world the answer is frequently 'no'.

But those conditions are not this book's concern. Its concern – its argument, in fact – is that there are also significant economic conditions. In other words, only under certain economic conditions are cost and profit necessarily aligned, meaning that the lowest-cost option maximizes profit. Three sets of such conditions are particularly important. Briefly, they are as follows.

First, there is a condition relating to industry structure. Is the company that sells the electricity (or smartphone) to the end user the same company that produces it? Or, to use the technical argot, is the industry vertically integrated? As we shall see, relative costs tend only to win out if it is.

Second, there is a condition – obvious, when one thinks about it – pertaining to the relationship between costs and revenues. To what extent are the latter independent of the former? The fact that our smartphone company was able to grow its per-unit profit from $50 to $70 by changing production inputs and methods depended upon it being able to hold the retail price of the phone constant at $200. But is this realistic in the world of electricity? If the industry switches from an energy source with one LCOE to an energy source with another LCOE, what happens to industry turnover, and to profitability?

And, third, there is a condition to do with the nature of the product. Specifically, do the two energy sources generate the exact same product with, accordingly, the exact same revenue potential? In our smartphone analogy, they did. But what about electricity? Is renewably generated electricity really the same as electricity generated through conventional means? And, if not, what does this mean for revenue and profit?

The rest of this chapter is given over to a closer consideration of these conditions, one by one (even if in practice they often bleed into one another). But, in point of fact, we already have a good sense from Chapters 2 and 3 of what will become apparent. For, as we have seen, today's electricity sector is typically *not* vertically integrated, even as historically it usually was. And, in various important respects, electricity is *not* just electricity: it makes a significant difference to the product and its sellability how exactly it is generated.

In short, in the actually existing world of electrical power, economic conditions that the conventional price-based framing implicitly presumes to apply universally actually apply only (and indeed increasingly) infrequently. This is why the price-based framing is wrong, and the profitability framing is right.

If the disciples of cheapness are unaware of all this, the bankers financing today's wind and solar farms – and, lest we forget, also the coal- and gas-fired plants that are still being built – certainly are not. They know perfectly well that it is profit that matters, and they also know what most influences it. The great irony, then, is that the constituency that matters most to the materialization of new renewable power capacity is in fact the one constituency among whom LCOE data are generally neither here nor there, are rarely looked at, and are almost never spoken about. In a recent savage critique of the fetishization of LCOE, JPMorgan's Michael Cembalest described the metric as a 'practical irrelevance'.[11] He was expressing a position widely held among his peers in the financial sector.

## III

Industry structure is the most straightforward to deal with among the three key sets of economic conditions to which we must attend. A useful way to approach this question is to take two ideal type models of decision-making entities. In model 1, there is a single energy company, vertically integrated across the whole supply chain, which produces electricity and also distributes and retails it to end users. In model 2, there is a company whose business consists of developing and operating renewable electricity-generating assets (in the US, it would be called an 'independent power producer'), but which is not involved in anything beyond generation. It sells wholesale. Now, let us compare and contrast these models.

All else being equal (which of course it almost never is – but we can ignore that for the time being for the sake of illustration), our vertically integrated company in model 1 will generate electricity renewably if the

---

11   M. Cembalest, 'Growing Pains: The Renewable Transition in Adolescence', March 2023, privatebank.jpmorgan.com, p. 14.

costs of doing so are lower than the costs of conventional generation. This stands to reason. Like all capitalist enterprises, it aims to maximize profits, and hence all it cares about when it comes to sourcing is the all-in cost of its sellable product. The LCOE rules.

Turning to model 2, before looking at matters through the eyes of our independent power producer, how might an electricity distributor without generating assets – say, Ambit Energy of the US, or one of India's regional DISCOMs – look at the economics? Just like the vertically integrated company in model 1, it too cares solely about cost, and therefore buys the cheapest electricity possible – renewable electricity, that is, if in fact renewable power happens to be cheapest.

But here is an important thing. Such a distributor does not hold all the cards. Who is to say that the distributor is able to find on the market renewable electricity at that cheap price and in the volume required? What, for instance, if some renewables generators are indeed producing at a lower LCOE than conventional generators, but, for whatever reason, are able to apply a substantially higher mark-up when selling wholesale? This is just one possible eventuality. The point, more generally, is that the distributor, unlike the vertically integrated energy company in model 1, does not have the option of itself generating the power renewably if the power is not for sale on the market at the right price. That is not its business.

As for the independent producer in model 2, whatever the LCOE that it will incur in developing and operating a wind or solar farm, unless it is guaranteed a long-term fixed price for its output in advance, it can have no certainty that it will be able to sell its electricity at future prices that will enable a profit to be earned. Or, to put things more generally, just because it can generate power at a certain cost, there is no certainty that it has the necessary incentive to do so.

Remember, here, that our independent producer's decision matrix looks very different from that of the vertically integrated energy company (in model 1) or the electricity distributor (in model 2). The latter two typically have delivery obligations, and thus need to procure supply, and the choice they face is between electricity from different sources – in our example, renewable or not. Weighing up the merits of a particular investment opportunity (or opportunities), the independent producer meanwhile does not *have* to develop the project, and a financial institution does not *have* to fund it. The choice is: develop/finance, or do not; and, if a comparison is made at all, therefore, it is typically not with coal- or gas-fired plants and their respective production costs, but rather with an acceptable ('hurdle') rate of financial return. Is the project under consideration expected to meet or exceed that hurdle rate?

Indeed, this, as we have seen, was exactly the decision matrix that Statkraft and its partners weighed up vis-à-vis Fosen in Norway in early 2015. The choice was just that: to develop the wind project, or not. In June of that year, they elected not to: the prospects of profitability appeared too slim. Short of the type of heavy-handed intervention that Norwegian governments of recent history would not remotely countenance, the developers in question could not be *made* to invest. As Martin Wolf of the *Financial Times* has put it, and precisely in the context of the political economy of the stuttering energy transition, 'while it is possible to prevent businesses from doing profitable things, it is impossible to make them do things they consider insufficiently profitable'.[12]

The conventional transition model against which the present book argues assumes an effortlessly smooth trade-off between fossil fuels and renewable electricity sources, just as stick-figure mainstream economics more widely assumes all manner of comparable smooth trade-offs, not least between present and future goods. But real world processes of production and consumption involving real world businesses do not come even close to approximating to such smooth trade-offs.

Were the real commercial world of electricity production and supply still aligned with the vertically integrated structure of model 1, then the price mechanism would perhaps see a cheaper source of electricity rapidly supplant a more expensive one – again, all other things would need to be equal, and, as we shall shortly see, they are not. But, as Chapter 2 showed, the business of electrical power has been moving, and continues substantially to move, away from such a model. Wind- and solar-based electricity generation, we saw in that chapter, is today in large measure a discrete, stand-alone business. Model 2, in short, is increasingly, often statutorily, the norm, and in model 2 the LCOE definitively does not decide.

---

12  M. Wolf, 'Dancing on the Edge of Climate Disaster', *Financial Times*, 23 November 2021.

## IV

Simple mathematics tells us that a reduction in the cost of producing electricity (or any other commodity) only increases industry profits if revenues do not decline by at least as much. In our smartphone analogy mentioned above, if switching to the cheaper production assemblage – costing $130 rather than $150 per unit – also saw revenues fall from $200 to $180 per unit, the per-unit profit would not have changed: each phone would still yield a profit of $50. Would the industry adopt the cheaper technology if this were the expected profitability outcome? It is an open question.

The principal determinant of the extent to which cost reductions are (or are not) accompanied by falls in revenue is the degree of price competition that exists in an industry. In a highly price-competitive industry, what Marx called the 'coercive law' of competition would compel companies to reduce retail prices in line with reduced costs in order to remain competitive. At the other extreme, in an industry characterized by perfect monopoly as opposed to perfect competition, there would be no incentive to pass on cost reductions to consumers. The monopolist could and would capture all of the cost upside itself. In reality, of course, real world industries exist somewhere between these two poles. The general point to take away is this: for capital to be able to realize the benefits of cost reductions, a degree of monopoly power is necessary.

An excellent illustrative example in this regard is the commercial banking sector. Its largest costs are interest (borrowing) costs; its largest source of income is interest (lending) income. What happens when its borrowing costs fall as a result of falling interest rates? The reality – infuriating to consumers and regulators alike – is that interest income never falls by as much, often only relatively little, and even then typically very slowly. In other words, the industry is able to capture the bulk of the cost benefits. And the main explanation is monopoly power: in country after country, including those such as the US and UK that are associated in the popular imagination with competitive financial sectors, commercial banking is in fact oligopolistic and features precious little price competition. Meanwhile, when banks' borrowing costs increase as a result of rising interest rates, those cost increases, needless to say, are generally passed on to consumers in full and with alacrity.

What, then, of electricity? Champions of the argument that a falling LCOE will see renewables displacing conventional means of generation are clearly expecting the electricity industry to pass on much, and perhaps even all, of the fall in industry costs that such a transition would, on the face of things, entail. When the likes of the environmental campaigner Bill McKibben wax enthusiastic about a future in which 'we'll be swimming in cheap solar energy' (Chapter 4), for example, it is quite clear who the 'we' is. It is us – all of us. Similarly, implicitly if not always explicitly, orthodox economists also discount the industry's ability to capture the value generated by the shift from a higher, dirty LCOE to a lower, clean one. That the successful, unencumbered functioning of the price mechanism leads to more 'efficient' – read, cheap – outcomes for consumers is, after all, nothing less than an article of faith for the economics mainstream, whether the product in question happens to be energy or eggs.

Such an expectation that any falling costs from cleaner generating sources would be passed on to consumers is paradoxical, however. For, if the industry actually is broadly competitive and cost reductions are passed on to consumers on account of the force of Marx's coercive law, then there is surely ample cause to question the industry's appetite to undertake the transition from fossil fuels to renewables in the first place. The question that nobody – not economists and not McKibben – ever asks, is, why, unless externally forced, would the electricity industry accept, let alone actively embrace, a highly disruptive transition that lowered production costs but saw little, if any, of the resulting efficiency gains accruing to industry actors?

Indeed, it would perhaps not be going too far to say that there is a fundamental contradiction to the argument that renewables will supplant fossil fuels in electricity generation – and can do so both without government subsidy and by dint purely of market forces – now that the cost of renewables generation is lower. On the one hand, protagonists insist that it will be energy consumers who thereby benefit. Yet the *industry* would have to stand substantially to benefit in order to want to make the switch.

At any rate, casting our minds back to the industry analysis elaborated in Chapter 2, we should recall here the following key pertinent facts about economic conditions in the global electricity sector. First, we know that, refashioned by the hands of policymakers over the past three decades or so, the sector has become significantly more competitive. Second, we know that, in an equally pivotal (and closely connected) vector of industry restructuring, policymakers have also pursued widespread marketization, whereby prices increasingly have come to be set via market mechanisms rather than by regulators or other centralized decision makers.

What is the cumulative upshot of these two trends? To varying degrees in different parts of the world, the electricity industry has become not just more competitive, but, more pointedly and precisely, more price-competitive. That is to say, its general direction of travel has been and is *away* from a model in which there exists substantial capacity for the industry to capture and profit from cost reductions.

There is, moreover, another vital observation to be taken from Chapter 2, and one which links our analysis here to the discussion about industry structure and vertical unbundling in the previous section of the present chapter. For what will also be recalled from Chapter 2 is that the increase in competitive intensity within the electricity industry in recent decades has been far from even across the (all the while disintegrating) supply chain. Some disaggregated parts of the supply chain have seen a significant increase in competition. Some have seen practically none.

As we saw, policymakers' efforts to introduce meaningful competition, and especially meaningful price competition, have generally progressed furthest in respect of generating companies, selling into wholesale markets. Competition typically remains much more limited among suppliers to end users, which is to say, in respect of retail price – as opposed to wholesale price. This matters a great deal.

Consider, in particular, the implications under the second ideal type model of industry structure described earlier, namely comprising independent producers and separate distribution companies. If the industry successfully reduces generating costs by switching to renewables, who in this model captures the upside? Generators? Distributors? Consumers? Or a combination – and in what relative proportions?

The inference from Chapter 2 is that generators would not stand to gain much, if at all, because that is where the coercive law of price competition operates with the fullest force, meaning that cost reductions are perforce passed on. Those reductions might not necessarily be passed all the way on to consumers: the lack of price competition among distribution companies would be expected to result in those companies capturing much of the upside. But the crucial point is clearly this: the particular industry constituency that the world is relying on to actually, physically, make the switch to renewables – that is, generating companies, those that produce our electricity and sometimes also, in the process, produce greenhouse gas emissions – is seemingly not the industry constituency that would stand most to gain economically from that switch.

And there is one more thing to consider before we move on to the question of the nature of the product (electricity) itself, and how this, in turn, might condition the relationship between profit and price. Specifically: what if, by dint of the industry structures peculiar to renewables-based electricity generation and delivery on the one hand, and the fossil-fuel-based electricity sector with which we are more familiar on the other, levels of price competition prove to be very different between the two? Certainly, we should not simply assume that competitive intensity – both across the industry as a whole and within the various key parts of the supply chain – remains constant as the process of technological displacement occurs and the universe of industry actors is transformed accordingly.

Might it in fact be the case, one ought at least to allow, that the world of electricity is becoming more competitive – with all that that implies for commercial incentives to switch or not to technologies with lower costs – not just as governments actively and deliberately remake it that way, but also as it decarbonizes and, indeed, *because* it is decarbonizing?

Readers should simply hold on to that question. The preceding discussion suffices for now to suggest that there is no good reason to think that the shift into renewables with their lower LCOE is necessarily good for profitability in the industry as a whole or for generating companies more particularly, and is thus something that one would expect to see such companies actively and roundly pursuing. Rather, whether it is good for profitability depends. In fact, as Chapters 6 and 7 will argue, there are good reasons to think that the shift into cheaper renewables is not good for profitability at all.

## V

One of the most obvious differences between fossil fuels on the one hand, and wind and solar energy on the other, is their relation to the Earth's surface. The former are located – and must be extracted from – beneath the ground. The latter are above-ground phenomena. While the avoidance of costly processes of subterranean exploration and mining is one more reason why the lifetime costs of solar and wind plants are today often relatively low, there is one category of cost that they cannot avoid – land (or, in the case of offshore wind, oceanic territory) costs. Space must be bought or leased in order for solar and wind plants to be established.

There is no simple answer to the question of how much space. This is especially true in the case of wind farms, where a host of factors relating principally to topography and wind patterns influence optimal spacing between turbines and hence land requirements. A square kilometre of land can be sufficient for anywhere from 2 to 10 MW of wind power generating capacity. Requirements for solar are lower, and tend to fall into a narrower range. The same square kilometre would likely be sufficient to install modules with a cumulative generating capacity of 25 to 50 MW.

The significance of renewables' land requirements to our discussion in this chapter is that the availability and cost of land vary enormously – and generally in an inverse relationship with one another – from place to place. Where available land is abundant, it tends to be cheap. Where it is hard to come by, it is much dearer. Take the US. One 2019 study reported that the average price of land per acre ranged from a low of just $1,558 in remote, predominantly rural, Wyoming to more than 100 times that amount – $196,410 – in heavily urban and densely populated New Jersey.[13]

All other things being equal, therefore, developers of wind and solar power have a very strong incentive to undertake development where land is cheapest. But, of course, as we already intimated in Chapter 3, one obvious problem with such a strategy is that such places tend to have very little demand for electricity. Again, consider the US case, and

---

13   T. C. Frohlich and M. B. Sauter, 'Here's How Much an Acre of Land Is Worth in Each of Contiguous 48 States in the US', 8 May 2019, usatoday.com.

the aforementioned land-price extremes of Wyoming and New Jersey. Total annual electricity consumption in Wyoming in 2020 was approximately 60 MWh per square kilometre; in New Jersey it was nearly 4,000 MWh per square kilometre.[14]

If the spatial mismatch between the cost of land supply and the demand for electricity availed of a frictionless solution, this mismatch would not matter: developers could simply locate new plants in the location with the lowest land prices. But the solution to getting electricity from where it is produced to where it is consumed is, in practice, far from frictionless. It requires a system of physical delivery – high-voltage transmission over long distances, lower-voltage distribution over shorter distances – and the construction, operation, maintenance and renewal of that system is highly complex and very costly.

What has this to do with our analysis in this chapter of the implications for profitability of switching from fossil fuels to lower-cost renewables in electricity generation? To help demonstrate the significance, recall once more our simple smartphone analogy. It will be remembered that a hypothetical manufacturer for which raw material and production costs were $150 per phone discovered a new production process that could reduce such costs to $130 per unit. Switching to this new production process appeared to be a no-brainer. But what if the manufacturer then discovers that, while the 'new' phone has the exact same functionality and quality, it can actually only be produced for $130 in a specific remote location, and distributing it to where consumer demand is located will on average cost an incremental $25 per unit? All of a sudden, the economics do not look so good.

This is more or less exactly the scenario to which solar and wind power give rise. Their LCOE indeed is now frequently lower than for a new fossil-fuel-fired power plant. But LCOE measures invariably exclude transport (that is, delivery) costs: they represent solely generation costs, not the all-in cost of bringing power to market.[15] Moreover,

---

14   'Electricity Consumption by State, 2020', ipsr.ku.edu.

15   As the influential Lazard LCOE analysis states in bold text on its first page, 'Other factors would also have a potentially significant effect on the results contained herein, but have not been examined in the scope of this current analysis. These additional factors, among others, could include . . . network upgrades, transmission, congestion or other integration-related costs'. See Lazard, 'Levelized Cost of Energy+', April 2023, lazard.com, p. 1.

exactly as in our smartphone analogy, getting the power produced by wind and solar farms to where demand is concentrated tends on average to cost more than it does for conventional generators, which are generally sited closer to demand centres. Indeed, the fact that renewables facilities are disproportionately located in relatively remote locations with relatively cheap land is one important reason *why* their LCOE – like the cost of the 'new' smartphone – is as low as it is. It is only in such locations that costs can be kept so low.

LCOE numbers are misleading, then, in the crucial sense that they do not compare like with like. Certainly, electricity is electricity – be it green or brown – but different forms of electricity enjoy different levels of marketability insofar as (albeit, not only because) they have different geographical origins.

Let us now generalize the issue at hand, before returning to consider the specific question of geography in more depth. From a profitability perspective, what we are specifically interested in once electricity has been generated at a given generating plant and at a given LCOE is its *net* revenue potential – that is, the income that can be earned from selling the electricity, minus any additional costs incurred in enabling that sale, and which are not incorporated in the LCOE. Whether the profit associated with a source of electricity with a lower LCOE will in fact be greater than for a more expensive source depends intimately on the respective net revenue potentials of those two sources. Products alike in subatomic form can, in reality, be metaphorical apples and oranges in respect of their ability to generate net revenue.

Transport costs are not the only costs that are usually excluded from LCOE figures, but which, nonetheless, potentially have a significant influence on the relative profitability of different electricity sources inasmuch as they can vary substantially between those sources. The same is true, for example, of the costs of network integration, including, but not limited to, grid connection. The IEA, for its part, is increasingly aware of what all this means for the interpretive value of the LCOE measure itself: because it ignores certain such costs, 'the LCOE does not provide a complete measure of competitiveness'.[16] Indeed not. In an attempt to

---

16 IEA, 'World Energy Investment 2022', p. 41. Nor does LCOE provide a useful measure of how the growth of renewables affects what are referred to as 'total system costs' – that is, the overall cost of an entire, integrated system of electricity generation and physical delivery. A key reason why renewables' LCOE is misleading in this regard

address these limitations, the IEA has provisionally developed an alternative measure, the value-adjusted LCOE (VALCOE), which seeks to provide 'a more complete metric of competitiveness', and which, interestingly, shows renewables in an inferior (and fossil fuel sources in a superior) light to the basic LCOE measure. But the VALCOE does not (yet) account for the costs of network integration, still less of power transport.

While geography, therefore, is certainly not the only factor that makes some types of electricity potentially less economically valuable than others in view of varying incremental costs above and beyond the costs of generation, it is particularly significant and thus warrants specific attention.

Long recognizing the significance of electricity transport costs, and increasingly alive to that significance with the growth of renewable generating sources for which land costs play an outsized role, actors involved in operating (and regulating the operation of) transmission grids attempt in various ways to make generators bear the consequences of their locational decisions. In other words, they try to ensure that, say, a wind farm developer that chooses the very cheapest land in the most remote location pays a price, literally, for doing so, inasmuch as the cost of its output being distributed to market will be disproportionately high, and, correspondingly, its LCOE 'artificially' low. The goal, essentially, is to reduce opportunities for geographical arbitrage, a situation in which the land-cost saving conferred on a generator by a particular locational decision exceeds any penalty related to associated transport costs.

The most common, straightforward and direct mechanism used in trying to reduce or even eliminate such arbitrage opportunities is varying transmission charges. All generators pay charges to grid operators to transmit output via their cables, and so it is possible to vary such charges in such a way that generators whose output necessitates costly transmission due to distance from demand centres pay higher charges than those whose output is more cheaply transported. As the UK's grid operator, National Grid ESO, for example, explains on its website, its

---

is that it does not take account of the need for (and cost of) back-up power, storage facilities or both, which arises from the problem of renewables' intermittency. See Cembalest, 'Growing Pains', pp. 14–17.

charging methodology – which is inordinately complex, comprising several separate components – 'produces tariffs that vary by location based on how close a generator is to demand . . . This', in theory at least, 'incentivises generators and demand to be close to each other reducing the need for investment in the transmission system.'[17]

But our 'in theory' caveat is important. It is universally recognized that this approach is rarely more than moderately successful. It is certainly not in the UK case, for instance. 'Despite multiple methodology revisions', the authors of a 2022 report by the consultancy Energy Systems Catapult observed of the UK approach to transmission charging, 'locational signals for investment are weak.'[18] What they meant by this is that those charges do not accurately or fully incorporate the actual variance in transmission costs associated with different generator locations. To use our smartphone analogy again, the equivalent would be our phone manufacturer only being required to pay some, not all, of the extra $25 per unit in transport expense created by the choice of a remote production location. The rest of that extra cost is absorbed by other market participants. Thus the 'signal' referred to by Energy Systems Catapult is considered 'weak' in the sense that (some) generators are not currently sufficiently incentivized by transmission charges to develop facilities closer to demand.

Somewhat more ambitiously, then, an increasing number of countries use location-based pricing. In other words, policymakers shape the net revenue – and hence profit – potential of generators in different geographical locations not (or not only) by regulating how much they have to pay to get their output physically to market, but by regulating how much the market pays them for that output. They do so by allowing prices in wholesale (and generally also retail) markets to vary by location, which, traditionally, has not been the norm – usually, generators enjoy the same revenue potential wherever they are based. The guiding principle in designing such systems of location-based pricing is that the closer a generator locates to demand centres, the higher the price it should expect to receive, as recompense for placing a lower

---

17   ESO, 'The Charges for Using Great Britain's Electricity System', nationalgrideso .com.

18   Energy Systems Catapult, 'Location, Location, Location: Reforming Wholesale Electricity Markets to Meet Net Zero', May 2022, es.catapult.org.uk, p. 6.

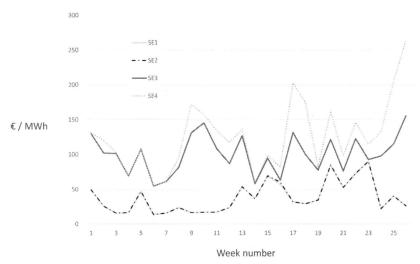

**Figure 5.1** Weekly average day-ahead wholesale electricity prices in Sweden's four bidding areas, H1 2022
*Source*: Nord Pool

burden on what, in many countries, is an increasingly strained transmission resource.[19]

One such country is Sweden, for which Figure 5.1 shows the – striking – outcome, specifically for wholesale prices.[20] The marketplace for the trading of electricity in Sweden (Nord Pool) is divided into four zones, namely SE1 to SE4, from north to south. Most of Sweden's considerable hydro power and wind power is generated in the north, where land is abundant and relatively cheap, but most of the demand for power

---

19   Note that this principle is also expected to apply in reverse from the electricity user's side; that is, the closer a user locates to centres of generation, the lower the price they should expect to pay. Note, too, that there is an equivalent theoretical mechanism of incentivization from the user's side in respect of transmission charges, which are levied on users as well as generators – namely lower such charges for users that locate close to centres of generation.

20   There is no particular significance to the period for which the chart shows the regional price differences: it was simply the most recent full calendar half-year when this chapter was first being drafted. The core pattern that the chart displays – higher prices in regions SE3 and SE4 – has been a consistent feature of the market for many years, even as the degree of price difference between regions has varied across time.

is concentrated in the south, where the vast bulk of the population lives. Hence the country's use of location-based pricing; and hence, in turn, the locational pricing differences displayed by the chart. The costs and constraints of transmission capacity explain why wholesale prices in SE1 and SE2 are lower than in SE3 and SE4.[21]

The model used by Sweden is, for obvious reasons, called a zonal-pricing model. Other countries to use such a model include Australia, Italy and two of Sweden's Nordic neighbours – Denmark and Norway. But it is not the only model available for location-based pricing. The main alternative is so-called nodal pricing, as used, for example, in New Zealand, Singapore and several US markets, where the network is divided into hundreds or even thousands of location-specific nodes, each with a unique wholesale price that theoretically represents the marginal cost of supply at that location.

The key point to take away for our purposes is that, in a country such as Sweden, wind power can be produced as cheaply as it is only because there are regions – the north in Sweden's case – where land is cheap. But the very factor that depresses costs also depresses revenue potential: the quid pro quo of low land costs for wind farms in the north of the country is a below-average local wholesale price. If wind developers in Sweden want to sell at the higher wholesale prices currently available in SE3 and SE4 – and of course part of the rationale for location-based pricing in the country has been precisely to incentivize development closer to centres of demand – they have to pay for the privilege in the form of higher land prices, and thus a higher LCOE. That, as the Swedish government sees it, is the market economy in action: there should be no such thing as a free lunch.

Whether free lunches have been entirely eliminated even in countries with location-based electricity pricing is, however, an open question. In Sweden, which has such pricing, wind farm developers continue predominantly to prefer the north and its cheap land, just as, in the UK, which does not have such pricing but is said to be considering introducing it, renewables developers also prefer the north (especially Scotland) and its own relatively cheap land.

---

21   At times of low demand, and thus of low burden on the transmission system, prices will often equalize between zones. It is when demand is higher and the interconnectors that join the zones are operating at full capacity that prices between regions diverge.

Indeed, we can be stronger still in our observation. For now, at least, the reality is that whether a country uses location-based pricing or not, there typically remains a significant geographical mismatch between the location of renewables plants, with their hunger for cheap land, and the location of demand. Notably, this includes countries whose future decarbonization trajectories will play disproportionately significant roles in shaping planetary outcomes. In China, for instance, solar and wind plants are heavily concentrated in Ningxia, Qinghai, Heilongjiang and across the north of the country more generally, whereas demand and demand growth are concentrated in the east and south-east.[22] In India, the clustering of renewables facilities in areas with cheap land and thin populations is, arguably, even more pronounced, with 'a mere six out of 30 states accounting for 90 percent of the registered solar and wind projects'.[23]

Meanwhile, if the LCOE reported for renewables is often misleading on the low side insofar as the geography of renewables generation can – and to a varying extent does – constrain net revenue potential, the LCOE reported for conventional generating sources can be misleading on the high side, at least in relative terms compared to renewables.

The key issue here is the relative maturity of different plant types. Recall that LCOE refers to the lifetime costs of generating electrical power; that is, the average cost incurred in generating a unit of power over the entire life of a generating facility. One of the problems with the basic LCOE comparisons that are often made, however, is that they are rendered in temporal as well as spatial abstraction. Just as observers pay little heed to where electricity is produced, and what this geography might mean for profitability, so also they pay little heed to when electricity is produced in relation specifically to a plant's overall life.

Is LCOE a 'fair' comparison? If we – as a society – were starting from scratch in building a global infrastructure for electricity production, perhaps it would be: the entire lifetime costs of generating plants, whether fossil-fuel-based or renewables-based, would stand to still be

22   W. Peng, Z. Mao and M. R. Davidson, 'Promoting Large-Scale Deployment and Integration of Renewable Electricity', in H. Lee, D. P. Schrag, M. Bunn, M. R. Davidson, W. Peng, W. Pu and M. Zhimin, eds, *Foundations for a Low-Carbon Energy System in China* (Cambridge: Cambridge University Press, 2021), pp. 42–7.

23   S. Ahluwalia, 'National Electricity Policy 2021: Making India's Power Sector Future-Ready', June 2021, orfonline.org, p. 5.

incurred. But, of course, we are not starting from scratch. The reality of the energy transition that we need to effect is that there exists a vast legacy infrastructure of conventional plants, much of the lifetime costs of which have already been incurred, and hence which are, in the terminology of economists, 'sunk' costs – gone, part of history, and no longer pertinent to ongoing investment decisions.

It is entirely possible for renewably generated power to appear cheap on paper relative to conventional sources when average costs over a plant's lifetime are compared, while nonetheless looking relatively expensive on a power output basis when only costs yet to be expensed are compared. And, as David Roberts has pointed out, the latter is commonly the more meaningful real world comparison. Often, 'renewables aren't competing with other new sources. They are competing with existing sources, power plants that have already been built and paid off. Those old, partially or completely amortized plants', which may very well have a high LCOE, are, in practice, at least if fuel costs are low, 'producing extremely cheap power'.[24]

This dynamic interacts in important ways with the effect of industry structure discussed earlier. As we saw, it should in theory be in the interest of a vertically integrated electricity supplier always to use cheaper sources of generation, inasmuch as cheaper generation means higher profits. But what if that supplier has an existing fleet of conventional generating plants of the type described by Roberts? Then the calculus potentially changes, as numerous recent cases involving such vertically integrated utilities in the US has made clear.

In 2022, for example, the Iowa-based MidAmerican Energy, which serves more than 1.6 million customers across four states, announced plans, labelled Wind Prime, to invest some $4 billion in new proprietary wind generation assets. But environmental campaigners nevertheless balked. Why? An alternative investment strategy, using mainly solar, would, they said, not just make electricity cheaper for MidAmerican's

---

24   D. Roberts, 'Two Remarkable Facts That Illustrate Solar Power's Declining Cost', 3 February 2017, vox.com. Needless to say, the economics on the fossil-fuel side of the comparison can change if technical goalposts are moved at some point *during* a plant's operating life. The requirement proposed by the US Environmental Protection Agency in May 2023 that existing coal-fired power plants be fitted with carbon-capture technology, for instance, would, if actioned, modify the temporal distribution of affected plants' capital costs: some such costs would prove to have not been sunk, after all.

ratepayers but also allow the company to retire its operational coal plants more rapidly. As consultants who modelled MidAmerican's revenues and profits under the two different scenarios intimated, however, *not* retiring those coal plants was, arguably, the very point. 'Wind Prime is not about decarbonization,' one consultant concluded. 'Wind Prime's purpose is to maximize revenues for MidAmerican.'[25]

Sunk costs, then, take us from questions of space to questions of time – to the matter not of where electricity is produced, but when. And time, it transpires, makes a difference to revenue and profitability potential in another crucial way, concerned in this case with the shorter run rather than the longer. Specifically, the temporal profile of production matters not just in the sense of when costs are incurred over a plant's lifetime, but as much, if not more, in the sense of when during a typical day or week electricity can be and is generated. We will conclude this chapter's substantive analysis with a consideration of how and why this is so. The crux of the issue is, once again, this: while identical in physical form, not all electricity is alike in its capacity for commercial exploitation.

As electricity sectors around the world have gravitated in their various ways towards market and market-like arrangements (Chapter 2), they have more and more become attuned to the fluctuating rhythms of supply and demand. When demand is high, prices tend to rise. They also tend to rise when supply is constrained or uncertain. Now, the relative movements of supply and demand shape pricing outcomes (though not in isolation, of course) whatever the market and pricing mechanism happens to be: as we shall see in Chapter 8, for example, even long-term power purchase contracts are priced in large part according to supply and demand experiences and expectations. But the influence of supply and demand is writ largest and clearest in the competitive wholesale spot markets into which generators around the world increasingly sell their output, and in which prices can and do vary markedly at a range of different timescales.

In terms of weekly (and monthly) price variation, consider, for example, Figure 5.1 above, which showed that the wholesale price of electricity in the first half of 2022 in Sweden was very different not just between north and south but also temporally, ranging, for instance in the

---

25  Cited in J. Tomich, 'Green Groups, Tech Companies Fight $4B Iowa Wind Project', 17 January 2023, eenews.net.

southernmost bidding region (SE4), from a weekly average of €55 per MWh in mid-February to some €265 in late June. In terms of hourly variation, meanwhile, consider Figure 5.2. For two wholesale markets at opposite ends of Europe geographically, it shows day-ahead prices for the day on which the chart was created – Thursday, 18 August 2022. Though hourly price variation was clearly considerably greater that day in the Nordic region (for which the benchmark 'system' price is shown) than in Spain, it was hardly immaterial in the latter: prices ranged from a low of €99 per MWh (between 4:00 p.m. and 5:00 p.m.) to a high of €189 (between 9:00 p.m. and 10:00 p.m.).

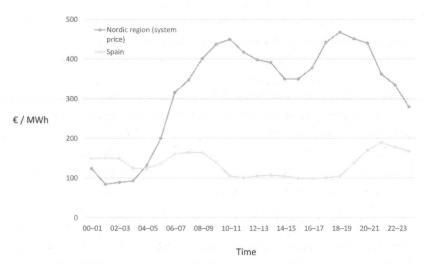

**Figure 5.2** Hourly day-ahead wholesale electricity prices, Nordic region and Spain, 18 August 2022
*Source*: Nord Pool, OMIE

The reason why these temporal variations in price are so significant to our examination of the dynamics of cost and profitability associated with different generating technologies, of course, is that these different technologies have notably different output profiles: when they can and do generate electricity, both hour to hour and day to day, as well as week to week and month to month, varies enormously. We discussed this briefly in Chapter 3: some types of generating plant can generate power predictably, constantly and consistently; others are more irregular, not to mention more unpredictable. Moreover, just because a plant can generate power at a particular time does not mean that it can necessarily dispatch it to the grid and thereby monetize it. Its ability to do so depends, inter alia, upon demand conditions and dispatch rules. We will learn how this usually works shortly, in Chapter 6.

The upshot, as we also saw in Chapter 3, is that the generating sector as a whole in any country is populated by a range of different generators that fulfil different roles within the overall system of provision, some, for example, supplying baseload requirements while others serve as 'peaking' units that help meet demand only when it is at its highest.

For our purposes, at this stage of our story, the crucial point is simply that two plants of different types, even if they can produce the exact same amount of electricity over the course of a year, month or indeed day – even, further, if they dispatch and sell the exact same amount of electricity during the period in question – are nonetheless highly unlikely to earn the same income from the sale of that electricity. One plant will almost inevitably produce and sell power at times of higher average prices than the other. That is to say, it will generate electricity that the market judges more valuable, even if it is physically identical. Time, like space, is money.

In fact, Figures 5.1 and 5.2 exhibit temporal (and in the case of the former, also spatial) variation in electricity pricing that is of such a magnitude as to raise the distinct possibility that relative LCOEs are essentially meaningless as a guide to the likely profitability of different types of generating plant.[26] A lifetime generating cost that is, for example, 10 per cent lower, is, after all, immaterial if, by virtue of its geographical location and temporal output profile, a wind or solar facility produces electricity possessing, say, a 30 or 40 per cent lower lifetime revenue potential than that produced by a conventional fossil fuel facility.

And all this, of course, is to limit our consideration of the net revenue potentials of different types of generating facility to the sale only of

---

26   See also P. L. Joskow, 'Comparing the Costs of Intermittent and Dispatchable Electricity Generating Technologies', *American Economic Review* 101: 3 (2011), pp. 238–41. Here is probably as good a place as any to note that LCOE was originally developed to compare the costs of plants specifically (and only) with similar generating attributes, namely dispatchable-baseload nuclear and coal plants. In that particular calculative context, LCOE *was* appropriate – the problem has been its widespread subsequent use outside the specific comparative milieu for which it was designed. See Cembalest, 'Growing Pains', p. 14.

electricity itself. As we saw earlier in the book, though, many countries feature markets for trade not only in electricity but also in generating capacity – that is, being *available* to generate when called upon at short notice. In the US, for example, where such capacity markets are common, capacity payments often represent a substantial portion of a generator's income.

The significance of this? Essentially, all generators active in capacity markets are conventional, fossil-fuel-fired plants, and thus, in terms of net revenue potential, renewable and conventional generators represent apples and oranges respectively in the further significant sense that they have different sets of revenue opportunities available to them. One study carried out in 2020 found that no less than around 18 GW of coal capacity in just one US electricity region (the PJM mid-Atlantic market) would be uneconomic were it not for the capacity payments accruing to that capacity.[27] Truly, LCOEs do not compare like with like.

No wonder, in short, that when companies set about developing wind and solar farms, and banks set about making decisions as to whether – and at what cost – to finance those developments, LCOE numbers are, in reality, among the very furthest things from their minds.

## VI

Let us now finally return to central-west Norway, and the decision by Statkraft and its developer partners in June 2015 to call a halt to development of the planned 600 MW Fosen wind farm. The explanation, as we saw at the outset of the chapter, was that updated analyses indicated that the project was not expected to be profitable.

But why exactly not? What was happening – or was expected to happen – that militated against the expectation of adequate financial returns? The narrative that has long dominated mainstream discussion and analysis of renewables' prospects – the narrative, that is, that we explored in Chapter 4 – would suggest that the problem, if economic in nature, must have been production price. Perhaps, in Norway, it was not (yet) cheaper to produce electricity renewably than conventionally.

27   M. Goggin, 'Capacity Markets: The Way of the Future or the Way of the Past?', 27 March 2020, esig.energy.

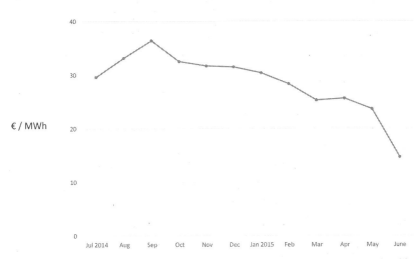

**Figure 5.3** Monthly average day-ahead wholesale electricity price, NO3 (Molde/Trondheim), July 2014–June 2015
*Source*: Nord Pool

But no. The problem was nothing of the sort. The problem was projected revenue. Look closely at what had happened to wholesale prices in the bidding region – NO3 – in which Fosen is situated, as charted in Figure 5.3. From around €30 per MWh in mid-2014, the monthly average price had risen to €36 by September 2014, which, not coincidentally, was the very month in which Statkraft said the project was proceeding 'full steam ahead'. Then, however, prices began to fall. By March 2015, they were at €25. In June, they collapsed to below €15 per MWh, their lowest level in three years. It was precisely then that Statkraft pulled the plug. In this depressed market environment, wind's favourable LCOE did not make the slightest bit of difference.

We know now, then, that a relatively low cost of generation does not necessarily translate into sufficient expected profit to precipitate investment in new renewables development, specifically for those actors predominantly active in the generation sector in any particular country, and specifically within the context of the industry structure – vertically integrated or not, competitive or not, and so forth – that prevails in that country. We know, that is, why the relative-prices explanatory orthodoxy is wrong.

But, in terms of understanding how profits are in fact determined, what factors shape profit expectations, and how in turn these impact renewables investment – in the past, today and likely in future – there is much we do not yet know. How, for example, are electricity prices actually set in practice, not least in the world's proliferating wholesale markets? How do changes in industry costs impact industry revenues? How accurately and how far ahead can developers and their financiers project renewables revenues and thus returns? What *is* the actual and expected profitability profile of solar and wind farms? And what does this mean for the prospects of ongoing private-capital-led decarbonization of the electricity sector? These are the crucial questions we turn to now.

# 6

# The Wild West

In 2018, something remarkable happened to the UK's onshore wind industry. Having grown to nearly 2.7 GW in 2017 from below 500 MW a decade earlier, annual installations of new capacity, in the words of the trade association RenewableUK, suddenly 'plummeted'.[1] Less than 600 MW of new capacity, comprising just 263 turbines distributed across fifty-four sites, were brought to market during the year, representing a year-on-year decline of approximately 80 per cent. It was the lowest level of annual installation of new onshore wind generating capacity that the country had seen since 2011.

What, then, had happened? What – or who – was to blame for this historic failure? The first possible culprit that might spring to mind is easy to rule out. As at Fosen in Norway three years earlier, this abrupt reversal in wind's fortunes had nothing to do with equipment costs. It had, for several years, been as cheap in the UK to produce electricity from onshore wind facilities as using any other generating technology, or cheaper, and wind's costs were continuing to decline.

Nor, second, was the UK wind market downturn of 2018 the fault of developers' seemingly perennial bureaucratic bugbear – namely permitting restrictions erected by planning authorities or environmental regulators. This is not to say that such restrictions did not exist. They certainly

---

1 L. Clark, 'New Onshore Wind Installations Plummet in 2018', 18 January 2019, renewableuk.com.

did, at least in England. Indeed, just three years earlier, in the face of pressure from over 100 of his Conservative Party colleagues, then prime minister David Cameron introduced new planning rules for England designed precisely to constrain the development of new, 'unsightly', onshore wind farms. The rules inhibited local authorities' power to grant licences to wind farms by giving local residents an effective veto on new projects. The impact of the new rules was an immediate fall in annual installations of incremental UK onshore capacity of nearly 50 per cent compared to 2014.

By 2018, however, the effect of the introduction of the new planning regime had washed through. Sustained in significant measure by developments in Scotland and Wales, which have separate planning laws, new UK onshore installations increased in 2016 and increased again – to 2017's 2.7 GW, an all-time high – the following year. The precipitous decline in investment that then occurred in 2018 had nothing to do with bureaucratic blockages or the like. In fact, a vast reserve of onshore wind with the potential to 'close the gap between the low carbon power we need and the amount Government policy is actually delivering' was, RenewableUK observed, literally 'ready to go': approximately 4.5 GW of UK onshore wind capacity, capable of generating over 12 TWh per annum, was 'shovel-ready', inasmuch as it had already gone through the relevant permitting processes.

Last but not least, it was not depressed or falling wholesale electricity prices that caused investment to collapse either. This, as we saw, was what had led Statkraft to call a halt to development at Fosen in 2015. But, in the UK in 2018, by contrast, wholesale prices were healthy and heading in the opposite direction. They began the year at around £50 per MWh; they would end the year at around £65 per MWh, having at one point risen to nearly £70.

Yet, wherever one looked, UK wind projects were failing to get off the ground. Across the length and breadth of the country, sites were waiting for foundations to be dug and turbines installed, but the shovels remained more or less everywhere inert.

I

To understand the fate of solar and wind power in any particular historical and geographical context, one must understand the local business of power – that is, the local political-economic conditions under which electricity is produced, distributed and consumed; this has been one of this book's core messages. Since the early 1990s, the UK electricity sector has gone through a fundamental and convulsive process of restructuring, encompassing all of the elements surveyed in Chapter 2, from unbundling to de-monopolization, privatization and marketization. The key to coming to grips with what happened to the country's onshore wind industry in 2018 is the last of these elements – marketization.

Today, the UK has one of the most marketized electricity sectors in the world. Moreover, in terms of its core elements, the particular marketized model exhibited by the UK happens to be the model on which the rest of the world has increasingly been converging. What has happened, and is happening, in the UK, therefore, has crucial lessons for future developments and possibilities elsewhere.

Our interest here is specifically in the UK's wholesale 'spot' market, and that portion of the electricity physically routed through the country's transmission and distribution system that is traded on this market for next-day delivery; even in the most liberalized of electricity sectors, such as the UK's, some of the electricity physically fed into the system is not traded on the spot market – it might, instead, be sold directly to electricity suppliers or end users under long-term power purchase contracts, for example. How does the spot market function?

We can best approach this question by addressing two crucial narrower questions. First, whose electricity gets traded? Imagine, for instance, that demand for electricity at a particular time on a particular day is very low, and that generating companies connected to the network are able and willing to provide much more power collectively than is required. Export – to a different physical transmission network, possibly overseas – is, of course, one possibility for siphoning off 'surplus' output, but we shall leave that possibility aside for now. Simplifying matters thus, if potential supply exceeds actual demand, and actual supply must balance with the latter (as it always must), then whose output is traded and physically dispatched, and whose is not?

Our second question is much easier to articulate. At what price, or prices, is electricity traded in the spot market? In other words, what do buyers of electricity in the spot market – principally electricity suppliers who resell that electricity to end users in retail markets – pay, and what do the generators that produce such electricity in turn receive?

In the UK, as in other countries using the same basic model, generators prepare bids for particular settlement periods of, say, half-hourly or hourly duration, specifying the quantity of electricity they expect to generate in that period and the price at which they are willing to sell it. These bids are submitted to the system operator – National Grid ESO in the UK's case – and it is the system operator that determines which bids will be accepted in order to match supply to demand, and hence which generators will generate and physically deliver power.

The way in which the system operator, using automated software, does this is by ordering, or *stacking*, the generators' bids, from least to most expensive. Inasmuch as its responsibility is to dispatch the mix of generators with the lowest overall cost – an approach known as 'economic dispatch' – the system operator accepts the bids of all generators from cheapest to dearest until the point at which cumulative pledged supply meets the expected demand. This sequence in which power plants with ascending-price bids contribute electricity to the market at any particular time is called the 'merit order'. All plants required to generate in order to satisfy demand are described as being 'in merit'; more expensive, non-generating plants are out of merit.

The first key thing to note about this model is how the electricity that is actually accepted and delivered is priced; it is not a case of in-merit generators simply being paid at the price that they bid. Rather, all electricity traded for a particular settlement period is priced equally, and this uniform price – variously referred to as the wholesale price, spot price or merchant price – represents the bid offered by the highest-bid generator among those dispatched, which is to say the most expensive producer in the merit order. This pricing mechanism is called the 'single-clearing price' mechanism.[2]

---

2  For a useful recent discussion of this mechanism and its history, with a US focus, see M. C. Christie, 'It's Time to Reconsider Single-Clearing Price Mechanisms in US Energy Markets', *Energy Law Journal* 44: 1 (2023), pp. 1–30.

Why does the most expensive generator set the price received by all? It is a good question, eliciting much head-scratching at the time of drafting of this chapter in late 2022, as electricity prices in Europe (including the UK) hit all-time highs – and it is a question to which we shall return. The standard explanation is that which the *Economist* recently offered its readers: 'Just like in any other market for a homogeneous good, the price of power is set by the most expensive supplier.'[3] In other words: generators are supplying the same thing, so should be paid the same as one another.

The second key thing to note about the model in question is what determines how much different generators bid – that is, how they price their bids. Conventional wisdom has it that bid pricing reflects generators' respective costs. As the UK's Energy and Climate Intelligence Unit, for example, puts it in an explanatory primer, generators 'submit bids that accurately reflect their costs, safe in the knowledge that they will have those costs covered if they are accepted and have to generate'. The primer continues, 'bidding higher risks not making the cut-off in the stack and hence not being able to make any income for that [settlement] period'.[4]

At this point, an alarm may have sounded in the mind of the reader, who will recall from the previous chapter a vital question concerning the relationship between generating costs and profits. Does a lower generating cost – such as is widely and enthusiastically ascribed to renewables – necessarily mean a commensurately higher profit, and thus an equivalently higher propensity to invest in new such generating capacity? This is commonly supposed to be the case. But our preliminary acquaintance with the merit order already raises the possibility of an alternative outcome. If bids reflect costs, then might not lower generating costs mean lower bids, lower wholesale prices and lower revenues?

In any case, the standard theory is that bidding into the merit order is based, more specifically, on generators' *marginal* costs, and thus represents an example of marginal pricing, the marginal cost of a product or

---

3  'Europe's Energy Market Was Not Built for This Crisis', *Economist*, 8 September 2022.

4  Energy and Climate Intelligence Unit, 'Paying Back: UK's Investment in Renewables Is Being Rewarded by Lower Bills', March 2022, eciu.net, p. 8.

service being the cost of providing one additional unit.[5] But, although this theory is widely invoked as being definitive and generalized, it does not and indeed cannot apply to renewables, even as it is routinely extended to them. The marginal costs of solar and wind plants are effectively zero, because there are no fuel costs. Thus, if such plants did bid according to marginal cost, their bid price would be zero. It is obviously not zero, however.[6] The costs that principally determine the bids placed by renewables operators are the costs of amortizing the upfront capital investment, typically in the form of payments to debt providers – and that is not a marginal cost.

The third and final key point to emphasize at this juncture, before we move on to see how this market model helps explain the sharp fall-off in UK onshore wind power installations in 2018, concerns the geographical extent of the model's application. As a basic rule of thumb, the more liberalized a country's electricity sector is, the more likely it is to feature a wholesale market that operates broadly in the way that the UK's spot market does, and the greater the likelihood that a substantial share of the electricity produced and consumed in that country is in fact traded on the spot market. As a way of organizing the exchange and pricing of electricity, however, the model used by the UK is certainly far from universal.

Thus there are any number of places where this model is, for now at least, absent or peripheral, including some of the world's most significant power markets. China and India represent prime examples. In both, pricing has been only partially marketized, with considerable price-setting authority remaining with statutory or regulatory entities, at both provincial and national levels. In both, criteria other than price are generally used to determine dispatch order. Moreover, in both, such marketization as has occurred typically involves long-term, bilateral contracts rather than formal multi-sided exchanges, and the latter – to the extent they exist – are focused predominantly on forward or futures

---

5   This, for example, is how the *Economist* explains bid pricing. See 'Europe's Energy Market Was Not Built for This Crisis'.

6   Not normally, at any rate. But there are instances in some countries in which renewables operators do place zero or even negative price bids, and are nonetheless profitable – specifically when they are the beneficiaries of government subsidies that mean the effective price that such operators receive for generating is positive even if the bid price and market-clearing price are at or below zero. We will revisit this point in Chapter 7.

contracts rather than spot trading. Last but not least, all of this, in both countries, is regionally variegated.

In this final respect, notably, China and India happen to be much like the US. Parts of the US, including Texas, New England and the mid-Atlantic region, do feature deep and competitive (but regional) spot markets just like the UK's, employing economic dispatch, a fully fledged merit order and single-clearing prices. But in other parts of the country, such as the south-east, there has been long-standing resistance to liberalization, and restructuring has been very limited. Still dominated by vertically integrated monopolists, these regions lack organized wholesale markets and pricing remains heavily regulated, albeit still linked – only in very different ways – to generating costs.

In short, together with the likes of Australia, New Zealand, selected other neoliberal stalwarts such as Chile, and parts of the US and Canada, Europe – including the UK – represents today the heartland of the prototypical electricity spot market as we have described it here.

## II

The signature characteristic of electricity spot markets based on merit order dispatch is price volatility, existing at all temporal scales from the very short term – from hour to hour – to the much longer term – month to month and even year to year. If one does not recognize and understand this volatility and its implications, one cannot understand the political economy of the decarbonization of power generation. It really is as simple as that.

We saw strong initial evidence of such volatility in the previous chapter. Figures 5.1, 5.2 and 5.3 all presented data attesting to highly volatile spot market prices. The shortest timescale over which such volatility was apparent was hourly: Figure 5.2 showed that prices vary markedly over the course of a normal day in the Nordic region and Spain, proving especially volatile in the former. The next-longest timescale at which we saw volatility was weekly, in the form of huge swings in average electricity prices from week to week in the four different regions of Sweden's wholesale electricity market (Figure 5.1). Finally, Figure 5.3 demonstrated volatility from month to month in spot prices in the Molde/Trondheim bidding region of Norway's electricity market.

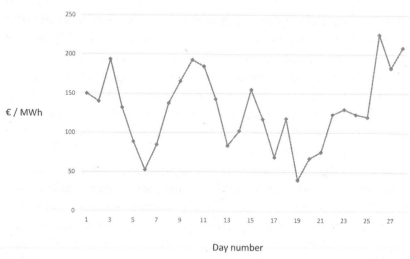

**Figure 6.1** Day-ahead wholesale electricity price in Germany, February 2022
*Source*: Nord Pool

We can usefully complement those three illustrations with a depiction of volatility at the one significant scale that they did not address, namely day-to-day volatility. Consider Figure 6.1, which charts average day-ahead wholesale prices in a European territory for which we have not yet provided any market data – Germany – and for a month selected at random from 2022 – February. As the figure plainly shows, volatility was extreme, with average daily prices ranging from a low of below €40 per MWh on 19 February to a high of €225 just one week later – a more than fivefold increase.

Partly, of course, swings in electricity spot market prices such as those depicted by Figure 6.1 and the three charts included in Chapter 5 are a function of simple, undifferentiated supply and demand dynamics, which is to say the supply and demand of electricity *in general*, independent of generating source. As I noted in Chapter 5, for example, variance in supply and – in particular – demand goes a considerable way to explaining the intra-day volatility demonstrated by Figure 5.2: prices tend to peak during the two parts of the day (early morning and evening) when demand peaks.

But undifferentiated supply and demand dynamics only get us so far as an explanatory variable – in fact, not very far, not least when considering price variance over longer timescales. Such variance is rooted, rather, in the nature of the specific market mechanisms elaborated in the previous section, and in particular the way in which they mediate the supply of electricity of different types. This has two critical, interlinked dimensions.

First, there is the question of which generating source provides the all-important 'last' unit of power necessary to balance overall supply and demand within any settlement period. Recall that the merit order stacks bidders by offer price. Insofar as different generating sources have different costs and cost profiles, and insofar as bids reflect these costs, it is generally the case that different generating technologies sit atop one another in the merit order 'stack'. In other words, the lowest-price bids usually all come from generators of one particular type, bids in the next-highest price band from generators of another type, and so on as one ascends the stack. At the time and place of this writing, for example, in northern Europe in 2022, renewables generators would typically bid lowest and were thus the first to be dispatched, followed – as and when necessary – respectively by nuclear, coal and finally gas.

As we have seen, the wholesale price received by all generators in a particular settlement period is the price offered by the highest-bid gener-ator among those in merit and dispatched. Hence, if renewables plants can satisfy all demand, then the wholesale price will be established by the bid price of renewables. But if, at the other extreme, electricity demand is high, the wind is not blowing and the sun is not shining, and nuclear and coal also do not suffice – perhaps because nuclear has been phased out on safety grounds and coal on environmental grounds – then the whole-sale price will be established by the bid price of gas.

Shifts of this nature – from the spot price being set by renewables to being set by gas – can occur frequently, unpredictably and over relatively short time frames. Of course, if the gap between the bid prices of renewables generators and of gas-based generators were small, there would be little impact on merchant wholesale prices as such shifts occurred. But, in periods when gas prices are high and gas-fired power plants have commensurately high marginal operating costs, the gap can in fact be a veritable gulf. Electricity prices can leap by orders of magni-tude within the space of twenty-four hours if, say, wind speeds suddenly drop and the system operator is required to dispatch gas-fired plants that had lain idle just the day before. This is volatility writ large.

Take, for instance, the region of Sweden where I live, Nord Pool's SE3 bid region. And take the specific period during which the first draft of this chapter was prepared, which was late August of 2022. Warm and windy conditions occasioning abundant solar and wind power gave way in notably short order to still and markedly chillier weather. Accordingly, the system operator – the state-owned Svenska kraftnät – was obliged in equally short order to reach considerably higher in the bid stack in order to source sufficient electricity output to meet demand. One day, all generators in merit were renewables plants; the next day, gas-fired plants were suddenly in merit, and were burning gas whose price, not least due to the ongoing war in Ukraine and the associated upheaval in gas markets, had soared to nosebleed-inducing levels.

How large was the concomitant day-on-day change in the SE3 electricity price? Nearly 1,000 per cent! On 21 August, the day-ahead price was €38 per MWh; on 22 August, it was €372. Can there be any other product, anywhere in the world, subject to such volatile price movements?

Even if there occurs no change in the identity of the generating source that sets the electricity spot price, however, considerable price volatility is nonetheless still possible, albeit usually at the scale of weeks and months rather than hours and days. This brings us to the second key dimension of electricity's extreme price volatility in spot markets. If the first related to shifts in the source of delivery of the last in-merit unit of power, the second relates to shifts in the costs – and hence bid prices – associated with particular sources.

As we have seen at various points in this book, the costs of generating power using solar or wind farms, or indeed nuclear plants, can go down as well as up over time. But the degree of variance in such costs over time-scales of weeks or months is as nothing compared to the variance one often finds with conventional generating plants. The reason for the latter cost variance is straightforward: commodity (that is, fuel) prices are themselves often highly volatile. For evidence, look no further than Europe in the early 2020s, where the price of the fuel that plays the largest role in firing conventional generating plants – namely natural gas – has been remarkably volatile. By way of example, Figure 6.2 shows monthly average day-ahead gas prices in the UK between mid-2021 and mid-2022, which ranged from below 100 pence per therm to above 300 pence.

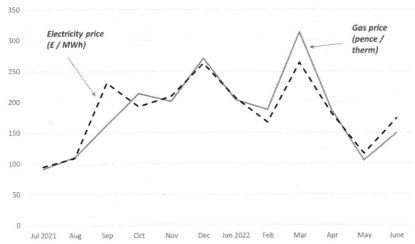

**Figure 6.2** UK monthly average day-ahead wholesale gas and electricity (baseload) prices, July 2021–June 2022
*Source*: Ofgem

As it happens, gas-fired plants generated the last unit of in-merit electricity traded in the UK electricity spot market more or less throughout that twelve-month period – more than 80 per cent of the time, despite the fact that such plants accounted for less than 40 per cent of the country's electricity supply over the same period.[7] There was, therefore, very little of the abrupt switching from electricity prices being set by renewables to being set by natural gas that we saw earlier in the Swedish (SE3) case. But UK electricity prices were nevertheless highly volatile, precisely because natural gas prices were so volatile.

Moreover – and exactly as one would expect – changes in the UK electricity wholesale price tracked changes in the gas wholesale price with almost mirror-like precision (see Figure 6.2). For, as the cost of gas went up and down, so, in turn, respectively and resultingly, did the cost of being able to generate electricity from gas, the price that gas-fired plants bid to generate, and lastly, more than 80 per cent of the time, the price received by all electricity generators irrespective of the source of generation.

Price volatility in liberalized electricity spot markets, therefore, is the result principally of the two factors we have examined here. Of course,

---

7   N. Thomas, 'UK Looks to Break Link between Soaring Gas and Power Prices', *Financial Times*, 1 October 2022.

these factors combine and connect in different ways in different times and places: electricity price volatility is the result sometimes primarily of fuel price volatility, sometimes primarily of changes in the identity of the provider of the last in-merit unit of power, and sometimes of both. In any event, the key learning is as follows. The two factors serve together to engender such pronounced price volatility that various commentators have taken to referring to these as 'wild west' wholesale spot markets. It is an apt moniker.

## III

The next step in our analysis is to consider the consequences of the volatility that characterizes electricity spot markets, in particular for investment in new generating capacity. Once we have done so, we will be in a position to explain properly the plunge in investment in new onshore wind capacity that occurred in the UK in 2018.

The main point to be developed here can be very simply stated. In the absence of overt mechanisms of price stabilization, spot market price volatility has – in places such as the UK – a profoundly chilling effect on renewables investment. There is, in short, a deep and impactful aversion to taking on so-called 'merchant risk' – that is, the risk associated with selling renewably generated electricity exclusively or predominantly at volatile merchant (wholesale) prices.

If the main point is simply stated, however, it nonetheless bears careful elucidation. Not all relevant actors by any means are fearful of merchant risk; furthermore, in terms of its influence on investment, some actors' aversion to such risk is more impactful than that of others. Where in the industry is aversion to price volatility, and especially aversion that actively inhibits investment, concentrated?

It is clearly evident, to some extent, within the heterogeneous community of developers of renewable power that we encountered in Chapter 3. Many such developers are indeed demonstrably averse to price (and hence revenue) risk. Even where they say they will accept such risk, their actions often speak louder than words. 'We are not afraid of merchant risk per se,' Vattenfall's CEO, for instance, boldly proclaimed in 2020 – even as the company had just recently withdrawn from possible participation in the Hollandse Kust Noord offshore wind project precisely in the light of price volatility.[8] The 'per se' was clearly an important caveat.

But the developer universe, as we saw in Chapter 3, is a motley group, and alongside a core of established – and often conservative and risk-averse – players, there is a large number of younger operators displaying notably different perspectives on risk. The word 'entrepreneurial' is overused in these neoliberal times, but it actually describes very well the risk orientation of many such smaller, emerging renewables developers. They are fledgling, often brash, and indeed often out to change the world, no less – in a word, adventuresome. Yes, such developers tend to say, *electricity prices can go down – but they can also go up, so let's focus on the upside and the corresponding profit potential.*

Thus, among the range of actors substantially involved in bringing new renewables projects to fruition, it is in fact not developers themselves who are typically the most averse to volatility risk, and it is certainly not developers' own such aversion that principally serves to chill investment. Instead, when renewables projects wither on the vine because of aversion to price volatility risk, the decisive aversion is usually that of another actor – namely the banker.

When potential lenders to such projects see price charts such as those we have been considering in the past few pages, they tend very quickly to get very cold feet. The provider of construction debt financing to aspiring generators has one, and only one, question in mind when weighing up whether to make that loan: will the recipient be able to meet its payment and repayment obligations? The business of large-scale debt financing is about as far from entrepreneurial as one can imagine: it is about cold, hard, calculative rationality. The banker wants to know how much income the loanee will be generating, and on what schedule, and hence what its capacity to service its debt will be. Insofar as it militates against the knowability of future income streams and of debt-servicing capacity, spot-market price volatility is pure anathema to the banker's calculus.

Indeed, bankers are nothing if not honest about such aversion. 'Merchant projects' – those renewables projects that sell all or the bulk of their output into the spot market, at merchant prices – 'are inherently

---

8    C. Naschert, 'With New Hands at the Wheel, Vattenfall Stays on Strategic Course', 24 September 2020, spglobal.com.

challenging for [lenders],' one financier observed in 2017.[9] Raymond Gifford (a US utilities lawyer) and colleagues noted in the same year that projects of this kind have tended to be tolerable 'for only the highest-risk investment capital'.[10] More recently, an executive of a major provider of loans to European renewables developers put it this way: 'Typically, we don't like merchant risk.' The same executive continued, 'For a time, we had a kind of blanket refusal to take merchant risk. That's not very practical in the current circumstances – but we still don't like it.'[11]

As these quotes suggest, banks are sometimes willing to finance merchant projects in the renewables space. But it tends to be only banks with a particularly high risk tolerance. More importantly, given the risk exposure, such lending inevitably comes at a cost to the borrower, which is to say the developer. The way that Gifford and his co-authors explained this logic was to say that 'investors rightly require higher expected returns, often in the mid to high teens, to compensate for the risk of investing in a highly cyclical industry'.[12]

How this works from the lender's perspective is further fleshed out in the following statement, made by another banker who, like the individual who referred to a blanket refusal to take merchant risk, also works at a European bank that is active in the renewables market. 'We don't like to absorb power price volatility,' this person explained. 'We'll take merchant price risk – right now we often don't have a choice – but we'll charge three times more for it.' What this means, the individual said when pressed, is that, instead of charging an interest rate of, say, 5 per cent, the bank will demand a rate of 15 per cent. Why? 'Low returns and volatility don't go. No bank in the world will take power price risk at low returns.'[13]

A – maybe *the* – key obstacle to a more rapid build-out of wind and solar power in territories with liberalized wholesale markets is, therefore, now coming into focus. It is essential to be as precise as possible about

---

9    Cohn Reznick, 'US Renewable Energy Brief: The Tax Equity Investment Landscape', 1 September 2017, ourenergypolicy.org, p. 5.

10    R. Gifford, M. Larson and R. Lunt, 'The Breakdown of the Merchant Generation Business Model', June 2017, wbklaw.com, p. 8.

11    Interview with author, 18 February 2021.

12    Gifford et al., 'The Breakdown of the Merchant Generation Business Model', p. 2.

13    Interview with author, 11 February 2021.

the exact nature of this obstacle. What it is not is a dearth of finance capital wanting to invest in renewables. Even the most cursory familiarity with the contemporary energy investment milieu is enough to demonstrate that capital is both abundant and eager.

The obstacle, rather, is the effect of price volatility on the perceived investibility of projects under development. Essentially, there are not enough projects characterized by a level of revenue risk that potential financiers deem to be acceptable – or, at least, projects in which financiers are prepared to invest at a cost of capital that developers, in their turn, are willing to pay. The word used in financial investment circles to denote the quality of a project in terms of its perceived investibility is 'bankability'. The International Renewable Energy Agency, for its part, was alive to the bankability problem as early as 2018. 'There is not a lack of investment finance,' it acknowledged. 'There is no lack of capital in the marketplace for good projects; there is, however, a lack of bankable projects to attract investment and fulfil today's appetite for renewable energy projects.'[14]

What is really, fundamentally, at stake here is the matter of uncertainty. As noted briefly in Chapter 5, it is in relation to questions of uncertainty that Keynesian economics offers some of its most powerful and helpful insights. A central theme of such economics, as J. W. Mason has written, is that 'economic processes are non-ergodic – that is, they take place in historical rather than logical time, and there is no rational basis for predicting many future developments in even probabilistic terms.'[15] As Keynes saw it, investors make a brittle peace with the unknowability of the future by assuming that people's expectations about the future are broadly reliable and that, partly as a result, the future will look much like the present.

But, if all investments are uncertain, as indeed they are, then investments in renewables suffer from a twofold incremental uncertainty. For one thing, the inherent price volatility we have been discussing serves to magnify uncertainty of the more generalized kind. Furthermore, the fact is that this – the shift to renewables – is an energy *transition*, and

---

14 International Renewable Energy Agency, 'Scaling Up Renewable Energy Investment in Emerging Markets: Challenges, Risks and Solutions', January 2018, irena .org, p. 3.

15 J. W. Mason, 'Climate Policy from a Keynesian Point of View', May 2021, jwmason.org, p. 15.

transition is a phenomenon not just characterized but *defined* by transformation and the uncertainty that goes with it.

Major economic transformations, such as that which the energy system is undergoing, pose, in Mason's words, 'fundamental' rather than contingent uncertainty, not least because neither of the assumptions that Keynes said investors habitually make is 'serviceable'.[16] One might add that all of this is before even raising the spectre of geopolitical strife rooted in energy supply and security, which requires that all quasi-certainties about future energy markets be ripped up.[17]

This being given, it is wholly unsurprising that, for all the confidence of assorted 'expert' energy economists in being able to predict future electricity prices, and thereby give investors a putative source of confidence with which to advance capital, the reality is that power price forecasts tend, in the words of Gifford and his colleagues, 'to be egregiously wrong' – not just wrong, but egregiously wrong.[18] And bankers know this better than anybody else. They, more than anyone, know, often from bitter personal and institutional experience, that, as the same authors went on to write, such 'inaccurate forecasting has resulted in repeated, dramatic losses for investors in competitive generation assets'.[19]

Do bankers foresee a more stable and predictable future for energy markets, one in which investments can be confidently made, more or less secure in the knowledge of what level of income merchant generators will be able to earn? On the contrary. Far from anticipating price volatility to decline any time soon, they widely expect it to persist, and perhaps even intensify.


## IV


Two key questions arise from the preceding discussion. The first relates to the matter of investment not in renewables but in conventional, fossil-fuel-based generating assets, such as coal- and gas-fired plants. In

---

16   Ibid., pp. 15–16.

17   H. Thompson, *Disorder: Hard Times in the Twenty-First Century* (Oxford: Oxford University Press, 2022).

18   Gifford et al., 'The Breakdown of the Merchant Generation Business Model', p. 3.

19   Ibid.

discussing the dampening effect of wholesale-price volatility on bankers' willingness to invest in electricity-generating assets, why, the reader may reasonably ask, has our focus been specifically, and only, on renewables? Inasmuch as conventional generating plants also sell power in the spot market, are they not also susceptible to its vagaries? And does this not mean that things more or less even out?

A part of the answer to this question involves taking a historical perspective. Investors have been financing coal- and gas-fired plants for decades; many of the plants still in operation today were financed well before the new millennium, some even in the 1950s or 1960s. Electricity spot markets, by contrast, are a relatively new phenomenon, almost non-existent – at least at any meaningful scale – before the 2000s. Indeed, the coevalness of large-scale renewables investment with large-scale spot markets is noteworthy, if accidental. In any event, the point here is that very many fossil-fuel-based electricity plants around the world in territories that today feature liberalized wholesale markets were financed without the price volatility characteristic of such markets having to be considered. The markets did not yet exist.

Meanwhile, the more significant part of the answer to our question is that there is, in fact, an important difference between prospective renewable and conventional generating facilities with regard to the impact of spot market price volatility on the bankability of such assets. Where conventional plants are developed today in countries in which, as in the UK, the bulk of electricity is sold through spot markets, the volatility of such markets does not imperil the financing of such plants to anything like the degree that it problematizes renewables financing. But why should that be the case?

Banks' concern with price volatility, needless to say, is on the downside. Their worry is that wholesale prices will, in future, be lower than is necessary for a generator to be able to service debt raised to finance construction. Yet this worry is much less acute in the case of, say, a new gas-fired generating plant than a new wind farm. Returning to Figure 6.2 demonstrates why.

When spot market electricity prices fall, so also, in countries such as the UK, do gas prices. In fact, as we saw, the former fall precisely *because* the latter fall. The significance of this is that gas – the fuel – is of course a gas-fired plant's principal operating cost. Accordingly, banks that finance gas-fired plants can afford to be much more relaxed about price volatility. To be sure, electricity prices, and thus the revenues earned by such a plant, could at some point fall, but, in all likelihood, so also, in such a scenario, would that plant's costs have fallen; from a profit perspective, therefore, it would be a wash.

Essentially, the use of merit order dispatch and the status of gas as the predominant source of the last unit of dispatched power combine in such a way as to afford a certain symmetry of revenue and cost dynamics for gas-fired generating plants. In the terminology of finance, there is an inherent *hedge*. This hedge – a mechanism whereby risks are offset or balanced – moderates the anxieties of plant developers and, more importantly, of their financiers vis-à-vis electricity price volatility.

Renewables plants enjoy no such inherent hedge, because, of course, there are no fuel costs. The principal cost of running a solar or wind farm in the years following its construction is the cost of servicing the debt raised to finance that construction, and that cost is generally fixed: it remains the same whether the electricity price is £20 per MWh or £200.

There is, therefore, more than one reason why gas-fired plants continue today to be built, even as the climate crisis escalates. In seeking to account for this phenomenon, commentators typically point to factors such as resource inadequacy (renewables are intermittent, it is said, and thus for as long as storage solutions are inadequate we cannot rely on them to deliver) or to the instrumental power of the fossil fuel sector (lobbying and other interest group machinations, it is said, continue to sway policymakers). Both such factors are clearly part of any satisfactory explanation. But the explanation, our analysis suggests, also has a simple economic element. In countries with advanced electricity wholesale markets, gas-fired plants remain in certain respects easier to finance than renewables facilities, even – and the subclause is crucial – if gas-generated electricity is more expensive than renewable power. Market designs help explain why.

Given that there is no inherent hedge against price risk for renewables, one would expect it to be the case that extrinsic hedging mechanisms have been explored and, to one extent or another, implemented. Furthermore, insofar as financiers' concern is specifically with price volatility, one would also expect it to be the case that any such mechanisms have been designed specifically to furnish a measure of price stability.

That price stability indeed is something that lenders explicitly covet in renewables investments is no less clear than their aversion to volatility. 'If there isn't a guaranteed revenue stream that would pay off a significant element of the debt,' one banker has observed of solar and wind investments, 'we wouldn't get involved.'[20] 'It is very clear,' Philip Bazin of Triodos Bank, in his turn, has explained, 'that without a market stability mechanism, the cost of capital [for renewables] is going to increase.'[21]

What is the most stable price possible? A fixed price, of course. For the more risk-averse actors in the renewables market, therefore, hedging mechanisms that allow for price fixing represent something of a holy grail, significantly enhancing the prospect of bankability, if not necessarily guaranteeing it. In turn, from the perspective of the developer, a fixed price, in the words of Jonathan Cole, head of offshore renewables at Iberdrola, unlocks access to capital that is 'much cheaper than if you have to add merchant risk into the other risk of the project.'[22]

Thus the second key question arising from the discussion in preceding sections of this chapter is as follows: What extrinsic hedging mechanisms have been, and are, available to provide renewables developers and their financial backers with price and revenue stability? Or, to phrase the question another way, what stability-oriented mechanisms have been introduced in order to render bankable otherwise uninvestible projects?

Three main categories of such mechanisms exist. The first entails effectively circumventing the spot market. Specifically, electricity can be sold by generators under bilateral power purchase agreements that, in many cases, allow for substantial insulation from price volatility, and often over long periods of time. These agreements represent a sufficiently substantive and significant phenomenon to merit a detailed treatment in their own right. They are the subject of Chapter 8.

The second mechanism entails actual – that is, financial – hedging. Let us say that a renewables developer proposes building a new solar farm that would sell power into the spot market. If it is unable to secure affordable financing because of investor concerns about the volatility of future power prices, one option available to it is to use one or more

---

20    Interview with author, 18 February 2021.

21    Cited in H. Evans, 'What Route for UK Renewables in a Post-subsidy World?', *European Daily Electricity Markets*, 9 May 2018.

22    Cited in ibid.

financial instruments that enable the volatility risk to be offset. This may serve to assuage the investor concerns.

There are various such financial instruments available. One of the most common is a futures contract, which is an agreement to buy or sell an asset at a predetermined future date and price. If the developer's concern is that prices in the electricity spot market might fall, it can hedge by taking the sell ('short') side on electricity futures contracts. If spot market prices do then fall, the negative outcome in terms of income earned in the spot market is compensated for by a gain in the futures market: the trading value of the contract enabling sale of electricity at a fixed future price typically rises as the variable spot price declines. Such futures contracts tend to be the instrument of choice for financial hedging among Europe-based electricity-generating companies.

In North America, swaps are more common. These are contracts through which two parties effectively exchange cash flows or liabilities. Swaps are basically substitutes for futures contracts, and have the same effect: a party averse to the risk of falling electricity prices can offset that risk by entering into a swap that pays out if prices do indeed decline.

Electricity swaps are especially common in Texas. Because most electricity generated in Texas is sold through its spot market, the demand for hedging mechanisms to ensure project bankability is commensurately large there. 'There are examples of wind farms in states such as Maine and New York using [swap] hedge contracts to cover some of the power they sell into markets run by the New York ISO and ISO New England Inc. But hedging wind', emphasized Michael Copley in 2015, 'is a Texas story.'[23] Among several examples cited by Copley was Pattern Energy's 283 MW Gulf Wind project, which used a ten-year swap with a Credit Suisse subsidiary to hedge about 60 per cent of the power it sold into the Texas wholesale market.

But effective hedging via financial markets requires considerable financial sophistication and expertise, which all but the largest energy companies ordinarily lack. It can also be expensive, not to mention extremely demanding on company cash flow. The exchanges on which futures contracts trade, for instance, require the counterparties to those contracts to post collateral to cover open positions. If the spot

---

23    M. Copley, 'Questions Grow about the Appetite for More Hedged Wind in Texas', *SNL Energy Finance Daily*, 20 May 2015.

market moves against those positions, more and more cash needs to be posted.

There is, moreover, a further considerable risk associated with the financial hedging of energy production. What if a renewables plant physically fails in future to produce the amount of actual power that it expected to produce when it entered the swap or futures contract, and which was assumed by the terms of that contract? Enormous problems can thereby arise, as we shall see later in the book. Hence, in part, the deep reluctance among many renewables generators to even countenance financial hedging.

That just leaves still to be considered the third and final category of mechanism designed to impart stability to an otherwise chaotic market milieu. This is, far and away, the most significant such mechanism in the history of the renewable electricity sector to date, and it is the one that finally enables us to solve the puzzle about the UK's onshore wind sector with which we opened the chapter. This mechanism, of course, is government intervention.

## V

As we saw in Chapter 4, governments around the world have used all manner of different instruments in their efforts to try to stimulate investment in wind and solar power. These instruments, in different combinations, have been used both in countries where electricity is sold in large part in wholesale spot markets, and in countries where either such markets do not exist or only marginal amounts of power are actually traded in them. Our focus in what follows is on the former. Our interest is specifically in how the instruments in question have – or alternatively have not – succeeded in mitigating the price volatility to which spot markets expose renewables generators.

Indeed, the fact that some instruments do not contribute to hedging price volatility risk is something that it is very important to recognize. Consider, for example, the certificate schemes that many countries – including many in Europe – historically have used to try to bolster the income earned by renewables generators and thereby offset the cost disadvantages from which such generators long suffered. Typically, these schemes simply provide a revenue premium for electricity that is renewably generated. For example, if 'normal' electricity earns €40 per MWh in a certain spot market, a wind farm might earn an additional €2 for the fact that its product is green. But that does nothing to help with volatility. If the spot price drops from €40 to €20, the wind farm's per-MWh revenue drops from €42 to €22.

Nor do instruments that provide support by subsidizing construction costs assist in any way with price volatility. The US's long-standing Investment Tax Credit (ITC), for instance, covers a percentage of the capital sum invested in a renewables project. Certainly, that can be enormously helpful to a developer, but, if the viability of the business plan, even with support for construction costs, requires long-term electricity prices consistently above, say, $40 per MWh, the ITC will not prevent the plant from making losses in the event that spot prices fall below $30 and stay there. What it does, rather, is lower the level of the break-even spot price, which perhaps would have been $50 per MWh if there were no tax credit.

By contrast, instruments of government support based on price controls *can* explicitly provide stability, even if not all do. Feed-in tariffs (FiTs) and comparable instruments are the exemplars here. It will be remembered from Chapter 4 that Germany was a FiT pioneer. It introduced such fixed-price tariffs in 2000 and, in doing so, furnished renewables developers and their financial backers with, in Stephen Gross's words, 'unbelievable stability', thereby eliminating 'nearly all the risk of putting capital into renewables'. There remained a slight question mark about the legality of this support mechanism in the context of the EU's political-economic governance framework, but when the European Court of Justice gave FiTs the thumbs-up in 2001, the risk of investing in German renewables, remarks Gross, 'evaporated entirely'. The tariffs payable in Germany to solar operators were especially generous. 'For the first time in history,' Gross has observed, 'it became profitable to sink capital into solar power on a mass scale.' It was, he says, 'now impossible not to make money investing in [German] solar.'[24]

The UK, in its turn, began paying fixed tariffs to renewables generators in 2010. Its FiT scheme was eventually phased out and replaced by so-called Contracts for Difference (CfDs), but the ultimate effect of a CfD, which is a form of sliding feed-in premium, is broadly equivalent

---

24  Gross, *Energy and Power*, pp. 290–1, 294.

to that of a FiT. The generator enters a long-term contract, essentially with the government, stipulating an agreed fixed 'strike price' for the contract's duration. It then sells its output on the spot market during the years when the contract applies. But, if the spot market price (the 'reference price') falls below the strike price, the generator is compensated for the difference, while, if the reference price is above the strike price, the generator must pay back into the scheme. In other words, the net price that the generator receives is always effectively the strike price.[25]

That the objective of its CfDs is explicitly to encourage financial investment, and that the mechanism by which they are designed to do so is the mitigation of price volatility, is something on which the UK government has never been less than clear: 'CfDs incentivise investment by giving greater certainty and stability of revenues to electricity generators by reducing their exposure to volatile wholesale prices.'[26] In other words, the use of CfDs (and FiTs) is as much about intervening in, and shaping, markets for finance as it is about shaping markets for electricity. Indeed, Gross, reflecting on the seminal German case, goes a step further, maintaining that the country's famous FiT scheme has served *less* as an electricity market device than as 'a device for raising capital'.[27]

And given that financial institutions' wariness of backing renewables projects that sell into spot markets is rooted specifically in the price volatility of such markets, it is exactly as one would expect that such institutions express a clear preference for instruments of government support that provide price stability over instruments that do not. Feed-in tariffs and the like 'give you revenue stabilization', one banker stated, 'and that's the key'.[28] They are thus the gold standard for investors in renewables.

Equally, one of the main reasons why financial hedging instruments like swaps and futures contracts are so significant in a place such as Texas is precisely because the US's own long-preferred forms of

25  The reason the net price received is only *effectively* the strike price, and not *actually* the strike price, is that the reference price is not exactly equivalent to the price that any individual generator receives for its output on the spot market, but rather a spot market price average of one kind or another (methods for its calculation being varied).

26  Department for Business, Energy and Industrial Strategy, 'Feed-In Tariffs and Contracts for Difference schemes and Guarantees of Origin', March 2022, gov.uk, p. 8.

27  Gross, *Energy and Power*, p. 291.

28  Interview with author, 11 February 2021.

government support for renewables – the ITC and the Production Tax Credit (PTC) – do not confer price stability. This is not to say that such government support has been misguided, still less immaterial. Far from it: it has been indispensable. But, in a place like Texas, where electricity is traded predominantly in the spot market and price volatility is therefore endemic, tax credits historically have been necessary *but typically not sufficient* to generate project bankability.

In short, for all the allure of government funding in the shape of reduced costs (the ITC) or extra revenue (the PTC), tax credits do not mitigate merchant risk, and this unnerves investors. 'The greatest shortage of tax equity for wind projects is in the Texas panhandle,' one market participant observed in 2017.[29] Indeed, whether the financing method is tax equity or something else, many banks are only willing to finance renewables projects that will be selling into US electricity spot markets such as are found in Texas 'if there is a hedge agreement in place that provides investors with some certainty on the project's cash flows'.[30] What feed-in tariffs and CfDs provide by way of stability in many countries around the world, other mechanisms must provide elsewhere.

In fact, banks have sometimes proven willing to finance renewables projects stabilized by feed-in tariffs (or comparable government measures) even if such tariffs do not necessarily subsidize the projects in question. For a variety of reasons, including the fact that renewables technologies clearly were relatively expensive historically and thus did need subsidizing, it has become customary for the various forms of government support for renewables to be grouped together under the generic label 'subsidization'. But, sometimes, this is not entirely accurate.

Consider, for instance, the UK government's award in 2019 of CfDs for new offshore wind farms with a cumulative capacity of 6 GW, to be delivered to market by between 2023 and 2025. These contracts were awarded via auction, and the average strike price that the winning bidders offered was £40 per MWh.[31] At the time, the wholesale electricity price in the UK was around £50 per MWh. In other words, the bidders – and their backers – knew that if spot prices were to remain

---

29    Cited in CohnReznick, 'US Renewable Energy Brief – Summer 2017: The Tax Equity Investment Landscape', September 2017, cohnreznickcapital.com, p. 5.

30    Ibid., p. 4.

31    'Contracts for Difference Allocation Round 3: Results', 20 September 2019, gov .uk.

above £40, they would consistently be paying *back* into the government scheme, rather than receiving subsidy.

Two brief points about this are important to make here. The first is that it helps us to sharpen our understanding of what exactly it is that government support actually does for renewables investment. As indicated, the habitual position among commentators has been that government support is there to subsidize. But, in territories or regions where electricity trades largely in spot markets, and where the main support mechanisms are FiTs or similar, this has never been the whole story, even when renewables were relatively dear and needed subsidy; government intervention was also designed to stabilize. Now that renewables are not relatively dear, government support – at least in territories or regions with the aforementioned market and regulatory features – is designed *primarily* to stabilize. We will return to this point in Chapter 9.

The second point is that, if we need a sharper understanding of what governments are actually doing when supporting renewables, we also need a sharper critique of that support, if critique is something we are inclined to provide. Just as support has been widely conflated with 'subsidy', so, in turn – and, indeed, as a result – such support has typically been denounced as a form of state largesse that those on the left should contest more or less as a matter of principle – charity, essentially, for those least deserving of it, which is to say private sector investors.[32]

But the de-risking of renewables does not necessarily represent government largesse. As we saw with the UK's CfDs, for example, schemes can pay *back*, not just out. Moreover, de-risking, to one extent or another, is widely necessary. As the case of Texas, among others, shows, if governments do not step in to provide revenue stability, other sources of stability must be found.

In any event, if it is to be expected that, when investing in renewables projects in marketized electricity sectors, financial institutions strongly favour government support mechanisms that mitigate price volatility, what also is to be expected is what happens to investment in instances when support of such a kind is withdrawn. Insofar as mechanisms such as feed-in tariffs provide a crucial protective blanket, one would imagine

---

32   See especially D. Gabor, 'The Wall Street Consensus', *Development and Change* 52: 3 (2021), 429–59.

that, should such a blanket be summarily removed, thereby exposing renewables developers and their financial backers to the cold winds of spot market volatility, there would be a distinctively chilling impact on investment appetite.

Do we have any good historic examples of this in fact happening in practice? We do, in the shape, inter alia, precisely of the collapse in investment with which we began this chapter. As we saw, annual installations of new onshore wind capacity in the UK, having previously been growing, suddenly collapsed in 2018, falling year-on-year by as much as 80 per cent. The cause of this collapse was not higher costs, or lower electricity prices, or stifling bureaucracy. No. The cause was a policy shift.

The one government support scheme for which new UK onshore wind projects were still eligible in 2017 – the Renewables Obligation scheme – was closed that year. Meanwhile, such projects were barred from competing in the new CfD scheme. Denied, thus, any kind of 'market stabilisation mechanism', onshore wind, as Henry Evans observed, was abruptly subjected to 'the volatility of the market'.[33]

The reaction of the relevant stakeholders was entirely predictable: they exited new development en masse. Keith Anderson, the then chief executive of Scottish Power, one of the UK's leading developers and operators to that point of onshore wind farms, expressed the private sector's standpoint best, speaking bluntly – but no less eloquently for that – for the industry and its backers as a whole. 'If you think I'm building a £2.5bn wind farm at merchant risk on wholesale power prices', Anderson said, 'then you're bonkers.'[34]

## VI

We have been focused in this chapter on barriers to investment in renewables associated with uncertainty around expected revenues and profits, and rooted specifically in market and price volatility. As such, we

---

33   H. Evans, 'UK MPs Call for Fixed Contracts to Halt Green Finance Decline', *European Daily Electricity Markets*, 16 May 2018.

34   Cited in S. Pfeifer, 'Subsidy-Free Renewable Projects on "Cusp of Breakthrough"', *Financial Times*, 28 March 2018.

have been geographically as well as thematically focused, inasmuch as only some parts of the world are home to electricity sectors in which market and price volatility of the kind we have been discussing substantially exists.

It is important to say a bit more about this geographical focus, not least because not doing so might leave the book open to a charge of Global North–centrism. Why, readers would be entitled to ask, focus on Europe, North America and other countries with significantly liberalized and marketized electricity systems, when both the weight of the world's population and anticipated future growth in electricity consumption are concentrated elsewhere?

Part of the answer to this question concerns current electricity usage. The countries with electricity sectors of the type considered in this chapter typically display per capita levels of electricity consumption, and often also of greenhouse gas emissions from power generation, far above global averages, and warrant close scrutiny on these grounds alone.

But the more important part of the answer concerns the direction in which the rest of the world is heading. That is, it is crucial to understand the economic impediments to investment in renewables in countries with highly liberalized and marketized electricity sectors because this is the structural model that other countries are increasingly adopting. What in the contemporary world is already a common approach to the organization of electricity generation and distribution, in other words, will, in all likelihood, be an even more common approach in future – redoubling the importance of coming to grips with it. The world, in short, is moving towards, not away from, electricity spot markets, price volatility and correspondingly poor visibility around the expected profitability of renewables generation.

By way of example, consider, very briefly, three countries that are absolutely pivotal to future trajectories of global greenhouse gas emissions insofar as they are highly populous and currently feature very low levels of electricity access and usage (which are anticipated to rise dramatically), or very carbon-intensive power generation sectors (which need to decarbonize dramatically), or both of those things – namely China, India and Nigeria.

Certainly, some commentators remain sceptical of the extent to which these countries will ultimately adopt market mechanisms of the kind examined in this chapter. Norman Waite, of the Institute for Energy Economics and Financial Analysis, for instance, believes that China, for its part, 'has no interest in having "wild west" power markets like what's seen in the West', and that, even if Chinese electricity prices eventually are 'market determined . . . the government's guiding hand will limit volatility'.[35]

Perhaps so. But all the accumulating evidence suggests otherwise, for both India and Nigeria as well as for China itself. 'China's central government', wrote Anders Hove in 2020, 'remains focused on promoting [energy] markets in the longer term', based among other things 'on market models that have worked in Europe and the US'.[36] Guangdong, which consumes more power than any other province in the country, was the first to experiment with the spot trading of electricity, in 2017, and began continuous operations in late 2021, by which time pilot spot markets had been trialled in a further thirteen provinces.

In mid-2022, an integrated regional power market was launched in China's south, covering five provinces (one of which was Guangdong) and incorporating both spot and futures transactions. This launch coincided with the government's announcement of its latest five-year plan for renewable energy, which hinges specifically on the intended shift from a 'policy-driven model to a market-driven one'.[37] Contra Waite, the policy traffic, in China, is all in one direction. 'The goal', Monica Sun and colleagues observed upon the release of the five-year plan, 'is to establish the initial phase of [a] national power market by 2025, and an improved national unified power market able to demonstrate its fitness for renewable power and enhanced competition among market participants by 2030.'[38]

Meanwhile, in India, where long-term bilateral contracts between generation and distribution companies have conventionally dominated the sector, the government is planning for the share of electricity traded

35    Cited in M. T. Lin, 'China's Energy Transition Hits a Bump in the Road amid Slow Power Market Reforms', 7 October 2021, cleanenergynews.ihsmarkit.com.

36    A. Hove, 'Trends and Contradictions in China's Renewable Energy Policy', August 2020, energypolicy.columbia.edu, p. 1.

37    C. Xuewan and D. Jia, 'China Curbs Renewable Energy Target through 2025', 2 June 2022, asia.nikkei.com.

38    M. Sun, J. Zhang, Y. Pei and L. Gao, 'The Energy Regulation and Markets Review: China', 1 June 2022, thelawreviews.co.uk.

through the country's nascent spot market to grow to around 25 per cent by as early as 2024. At the time of writing, the government is also reported to be considering the introduction of merit order dispatch.

Finally, in Nigeria, the government in 2013 launched a set of fundamental reforms of the electricity sector, initially comprising the privatization of the Nigerian Electric Power Authority and its unbundling into separate generation and distribution companies, but ultimately planned to culminate in a fully fledged spot market. A key waystation to that terminus occurred in 2020, when guidelines for merit order dispatch were announced by the Nigerian Electricity Regulatory Commission. This dispatch mechanism is now fully operational.

In sum, around the electricity world, markets remain the model of choice. The volatility that characterizes those markets can be expected to become much more common, not less. This volatility, as we have seen, has profoundly important implications for the ability of renewables developers and their financial backers to confidently predict future revenue and profit streams. The result, absent meaningful extrinsic mechanisms of stabilization, can be a dramatic chilling of investment – which, on a broad scale, would spell catastrophe.

# 7

# Eating Itself Alive

The oil and gas industry has attracted critics and opponents from all quarters as, in recent decades, it has continued broadly with business as usual, even as evidence of climate change and other deleterious consequences of its activities has steadily mounted. Among the more surprising has been the Roman Catholic Church. Since replacing his conservative predecessor, Benedict XVI, in 2013, current pope Francis has inveighed repeatedly against global foot-dragging on climate issues, drawing the ire of the fossil fuel sector in the process. Having got wind in early 2015 that the pope planned to deliver an encyclical dealing specifically with climate change, ExxonMobil, the West's largest oil company, even reportedly sent a representative to Italy to lobby the Vatican.[1] This proved to be in vain: the encyclical – subtitled 'on care for our common home' – was published on 24 May of that year.

Three days later, on the other side of the Atlantic, in Dallas, a new front in the skirmish between the church and the oil sector was opened. Exxon's annual shareholder meeting was on 27 May. Among eight proposals tabled by specific shareholders to be voted on by shareholders collectively was one sponsored by a community of friars based in Milwaukee called the Capuchin Franciscan Province of St Joseph, which owned Exxon shares worth around $2,000. Its proposal was for a climate

1    A. B. Lerner, 'ExxonMobil CEO Mocks Renewable Energy in Shareholder Speech', 27 May 2015, politico.com.

change expert to be added to the company's board. 'This company', Friar Michael Crosby told the meeting by way of explanation of the proposal, 'has to be making plans for the future.'[2]

Led by chairman and CEO Rex W. Tillerson, Exxon's board recommended its shareholders to vote against the proposal. No such expert was needed, it said. And it succeeded comfortably in swaying investors. Only around a fifth of shareholders voted in favour of the measure.

Meanwhile, by this point of the meeting, Tillerson was warming to his theme, and in responding directly to the Franciscan agitator he chose to address another, related question that had been asked, namely why did Exxon not invest more heavily in renewable energy? Tillerson's answer was withering. 'As to investment in renewables, quite frankly, Father Crosby,' the CEO said to loud applause, 'we choose not to lose money on purpose.'[3]


I


We saw in Chapter 6 that, in countries with liberalized electricity sectors featuring wholesale spot markets, a fundamental constraint on investment in renewables capacity is a lack of visibility and predictability with regard to expected profitability. Basically, nobody knows what is going to happen to electricity prices – which are highly volatile – or, therefore, to the revenues of generators that sell into spot markets.

In summarily rehearsing these findings here, one word needs particular emphasis – *expected* profitability. This book's argument is certainly not that operating wind or solar farms is never a profitable business in territories with liberalized electricity markets (still less around the world more generally). It often is; in fact, it can sometimes be highly lucrative. The point is that, in the case of a generating facility that will be substantially exposed to merchant risk, it is impossible to know anything reliably about profitability in advance. The facility *could* be hugely profitable, but, equally, it could make disastrous losses: price volatility is that extreme. This matters because, in a capitalist economy, expected

---

2   Cited in ibid.
3   Cited in C. Davis, 'ExxonMobil Chief Derides Renewables', 28 May 2015, naturalgasintel.com.

profitability is the measure according to which investment decisions are made.

If, in such liberalized energy markets, it is difficult to predict in advance whether a particular solar or wind farm will be profitable, then what, with the benefit of hindsight, are we able meaningfully to say about the circumstances in which renewables generators do in fact prove to be consistently profitable? The most notable and important fact is that the vast majority of such cases share a signal, common feature, whether the output is being sold mainly in wholesale spot markets or indeed under long-term contracts, as is principally the case in, say, India. That common feature is effective government support for renewables, of the kinds examined in earlier chapters. It is the one constant.

Proving that this is a matter more of causation than of mere correlation – that is, that government support, in fact, tends to play a crucial role in underpinning and sustaining the profitability of renewables generators – is not altogether straightforward. It is hard to imagine how one could isolate the impact of government support mechanisms on generator profits in an analytically robust fashion, given the overdetermined nature of the latter. Equally, governments tend to be loath to concede that private sector returns, in energy or indeed any other industry, are bolstered by taxpayers – although we shall shortly encounter exceptions to this rule.

Sometimes, however, and usually quietly, firms themselves acknowledge just how pivotal 'extra-market' forces are to the delivery of economic returns, and we shall begin our discussion here with an example of one such firm. That firm is NextEra Energy of the US. NextEra's history, which dates to the 1920s, is primarily as a classic US regulated 'power utility', which is to say, a vertically integrated entity with a regional monopoly – in its case in Florida – in the generation, transmission, distribution and sale of electricity. But, around the turn of the millennium, the firm began a period of aggressive expansion, principally into non-fossil-fuel generating assets in US states other than Florida, which included states such as Texas with deregulated electricity sectors. Previously called Florida Power & Light (FPL), it changed its corporate name to NextEra Energy in 2010, although the FPL brand has been retained specifically for the regulated Florida utility business.

Today, NextEra claims to be the largest generator of renewable energy from wind and sun in the world. Of a total of approximately 24.6 GW of total net generating capacity at the end of 2021 (of which only 2 per cent was located outside the US), over 80 per cent was renewable, comprising principally wind facilities, the latter scattered across twenty US states and amounting to 16.5 GW of net capacity. The firm's solar facilities were more dispersed – spread across twenty-nine states – but had a cumulative net capacity of only 3.4 GW.[4]

As a 2018 *Wall Street Journal* article with the unambiguous title of 'Green-Power King Thrives on Government Subsidies' observed, NextEra, in building its vast fleet of US wind and solar farms, has become the country's biggest generator not just of renewable electricity but also of the tax credits that the government awards when renewables facilities either are built (investment credits) or produce power (production credits), in NextEra's case 'selling some [of these credits] to other corporations interested in lowering their tax bills and using the rest to shrink its own'. Perhaps ungenerously, the *Journal* effectively depicted NextEra as a company sucking at the teat of the state, glossing its strategy as one of 'relentlessly capitalizing on government support'.[5]

What does NextEra itself have to say? It certainly revels in its profitability. But, as a paragraph secreted away in its 2021 annual filing to securities regulators admitted, it indeed 'depends heavily on government policies that support utility scale renewable energy'. Moreover, NextEra further admitted that the two – profit and policy – are intimately linked. Not only does government support, principally in the form of the aforementioned tax credits, serve to 'enhance the economic feasibility of developing and operating wind and solar energy projects in regions in which [NextEra] operates', but also, were such support to be reduced or eliminated, it could result in 'reduced project returns'. In fact, so detrimental would such a shift in policy likely be – another hypothetical consequence highlighted by NextEra was 'the lack of a satisfactory market for the development and/or financing of new renewable energy projects' – that, ultimately, it might see NextEra 'abandoning the development of renewable energy' altogether.[6]

---

4   NextEra Energy, 'Annual Report 2021', nexteraenergy.com, pp. 12–14.

5   R. Gold, 'Green-Power King Thrives on Government Subsidies', *Wall Street Journal*, 19 June 2018.

6   NextEra Energy, 'Annual Report 2021', p. 22.

Maybe, in this statement, there was a veiled threat to policymakers: *if you jettison tax credits, you risk us not investing further in green energy.* After all, this, when the report was published, was March 2022. President Joe Biden's hopes of renewing the US's renewables tax credits appeared to be hanging by a thread. NextEra would have been as keen as anyone to make the stakes as clear as possible.

But policymakers are not the audience for NextEra's securities filings. Investors are, and NextEra was unequivocally telling such investors that, for its renewables projects to be economically viable and deliver positive returns, government support is no less (and perhaps more) important – *heavily dependent*, were its words – than executive skill, healthy market demand, favourable weather conditions, efficient permitting and all the other things that go into making for a profitable solar farm or wind farm operator. Implicitly, even, NextEra was conceding that the *Wall Street Journal* had been broadly right in its characterization of the firm.

Nor was NextEra the first significant industry actor to tell investors that renewables profits in the US are utterly contingent on subsidy. Eight years earlier, the person to whom a generation of US investors has listened arguably more attentively than to any other, namely Warren Buffett, the 'Oracle of Omaha', divulged that his own firm, Berkshire Hathaway, had also been investing in US wind farms, and that it received tax credits when doing so. The latter, he emphasized, was no incidental detail. 'That's', Buffett said, 'the only reason to build [wind farms]. They don't make sense without the tax credit.'[7] The particular significance of NextEra's comparable admission about the necessity of government support to renewables profits is, of course, that it came after another near decade of reductions in turbine and generating costs.

In any event, it is little wonder that the months following the eventual passage in mid-2022 of Biden's climate legislation (the Inflation Reduction Act, IRA), with its flagship long-term extension of renewables tax credits, saw markets substantially mark up the shares of US clean power companies, NextEra among them.[8] More tax credits, Wall Street knew, should mean more profit, and more profit especially for

---

7   Cited in N. Pfotenhauer, 'Big Wind's Bogus Subsidies', 12 May 2014, usnews .com.
8   'RWE/ConEd: US Renewables Get a Fillip – Thanks to Biden', *Financial Times*, 3 October 2022.

NextEra. 'No company', Eric Lipton observed towards the end of that year, 'is better positioned to cash in on the subsidies than NextEra.'[9] As Lipton noted, the firm's response to the IRA was to swiftly and substantially expand its investment plans, with a view to building an additional 37 GW of renewable power over the next four years alone. This, of course, would take a vast amount of capital. But as Rebecca Kujawa, a president of the company, pointed out, the IRA more or less guaranteed a return on the capital that NextEra would now be putting to work. 'Now', she told Lipton, 'I have decades of visibility to being able to do that profitably.'[10]

One of the most significant things about the state's buttressing of the profits of renewables operators is that it can and does periodically generate windfall returns for those generators. It is always the case that certain expectations about future economic conditions – from interest rates to technology costs, land costs and electricity prices – are inscribed in the support mechanisms that governments implement; those mechanisms are necessarily designed with particular futures in mind. When future conditions turn out to be very different from what had been expected, as they so often do in the world of electricity, so also can the profitability of market actors.

In Chapter 10, we will be exploring in some depth what has surely been the most notable, broadly based example of such an outcome in recent times, and perhaps even ever – namely the windfalls seemingly achieved by selected renewables generators across large parts of Europe, including the UK, in 2021–2, when natural gas and electricity prices spiked. For now, we will focus on a more localized example, occurring around a decade earlier. It suffices to illustrate the key issues at stake.

In 2007, Spain introduced a revised suite of feed-in tariffs (FiTs) for producers of renewable energy. What turned out to be the most significant revision was a near doubling of the FiT rate for solar installations with a capacity of above 100 kW and below 10 MW, which was designed to stimulate what had hitherto been a sluggish solar sector.[11] Needless to say, in undertaking these revisions, the government assumed specific

9    E. Lipton, 'With Federal Aid on the Table, Utilities Shift to Embrace Climate Goals', *New York Times*, 29 November 2022.

10    Cited in ibid.

11    P. del Río and P. Mir-Artigues, 'A Cautionary Tale: Spain's Solar PV Investment Bubble', February 2014, iisd.org, p. 13.

future scenarios for technology costs, capacity investment, electricity prices and the like.

All the key assumptions turned out to be wildly wrong. The cost of procuring wind turbines and solar modules fell faster than expected. At the same time, and not unrelatedly, investment in new wind and solar capacity grew more strongly than anticipated, as developers and investors sought to exploit the government's support. Total annual installations of solar capacity leapt from around just 100 MW in 2006, to approximately 0.5 GW in 2007, and 2.7 GW in 2008.[12] In turn, between 2007 and 2013, the proportion of Spain's electricity supply generated by solar and wind increased from around 9 per cent to around 24 per cent – one of the highest shares in Europe at the time. Lastly, when the country entered recession following the global financial crisis of 2007–9, electricity demand slumped. Falling demand and burgeoning supply inevitably led to lower wholesale electricity prices than the government had reckoned with.

Because the market developed differently than had been assumed, so did the fortunes of key stakeholders. On the one hand, government finances came under increasing pressure. Monies owing to solar generators under the FiT scheme surged as a result of both the higher tariff and the rapid increase in solar capacity and output, but lower wholesale – and thus also retail – electricity prices meant that consumers funded only a relatively small portion of these monies. Government footed the bill for the lion's share: subsidies paid to solar generators increased more than thirteenfold in two years, from less than €200 million in 2007 to €2.6 billion in 2009.[13]

On the other hand, as technology costs fell, the profits earned by renewables generators holding the government's generous FiT contracts boomed. In designing the new solar tariff, policymakers had predicted – and thus allowed for – internal rates of return (IRRs) for generators of 5 to 9 per cent. In the event, actual rates of return were estimated typically to be between 10 and 15 per cent.[14]

Perhaps unsurprisingly, the Spanish government took the view that the one – 'excess' industry profits – was the answer to the other – strained

---

12   Ibid., p. 10.
13   Ibid., p. 11.
14   Ibid., p. 2.

government budgets. Between 2011 and 2014, it therefore took a series of measures aimed at reducing the pressure on the public purse by reining in the support it provided to renewables generators. The most significant legislation came into force in mid-2014, and included the imposition of a cap on profits from activities supported by FiTs. Two aspects of the government intervention particularly infuriated the industry. For one thing, it represented a reneging on promises: having been told they would be eligible for FiTs without time limits, early entrants into the sector were now informed that their subsidies would stop altogether. Moreover, the legislation was retroactive, being backdated to January 2013, meaning that producers had to repay a year and a half's worth of support.

What is especially important to take away from the Spanish case – and Spain's was far from alone among European governments in contesting the terms of legacy renewables contracts in that period, the Czech and Italian governments doing likewise – is that, ironically, the understandable attempt by governments to curb windfall profits can end up militating against the very objective behind the introduction of support mechanisms like FiTs in the first place: which is to say, to incentivize investment in new capacity.

'Europe's renewable energy investors', Brady Yauch, in discussing the Spanish case, observed in 2014, 'are facing a harsh reality – that the promises from politicians can be taken away at any moment.'[15] Developers and their financiers now felt disinclined to invest in new solar or wind farms in Spain because trust in government commitments had been eroded. Many investors actually ended up suing the Spanish government.[16]

The distrust lingered and festered. 'Investors are like elephants,' Christopher Jones would later remark, again in the context of Spain and the events of 2011–14; 'they do not forget.'[17] For several years, there was,

---

15    B. Yauch, 'Nations Rip Up Renewable Contracts', *National Post*, 19 March 2014.

16    Some of the ensuing legal battles, involving claims estimated at nearly $10 billion in total, rumble on, a decade later. Investors, including Infrastructure Services Luxembourg and Energi Termosolar, which had invested in solar facilities in Granada, have won compensatory arbitration awards worth more than €100 million against the Spanish government in cases brought under the international Energy Charter Treaty, an agreement dating from the 1990s that protects energy investors – but the government continues to fight enforcement of the arbitration rulings.

17    C. Jones, 'Spanish Electricity Windfall Tax Requires a Re-think', 8 October 2021, euractiv.com.

effectively, a moratorium on new investment, and thus, having reached around 24 per cent in 2013, the proportion of electricity generation supplied by solar and wind in Spain did not edge any higher than that level until as late as 2019. Six years, essentially, were lost, and when developers did eventually regain enthusiasm for the Spanish market, bankers – themselves still wary, being inherently risk-averse – charged an elevated cost of capital in view of their ongoing perception of elevated risk.

In short, government support mechanisms always exist in a complicated, multifaceted relationship with private sector profitability in the renewables industry. Often nothing less than essential to enabling profits insofar as they serve to mitigate revenue and development risk, such mechanisms themselves *represent* a risk of sorts to continued profitability, since what the government giveth it can also take away. Spain, among others, has seen that – and NextEra Energy, as we saw, likewise knows it.

## II

The global historical development of wind and solar power has in fact been a process replete with irony from the start. One such irony we have just discussed: that government policy pertaining to support for renewables can just as easily disincentivize as it can incentivize investment. Here is another irony, and one with a still broader and deeper import: when strong profits from the development and operation of renewables facilities are, or at least seem to be, attainable, the confidence to invest that is inspired by such (actual or apparent) attainability tends rapidly to set in motion actions and events that serve – with almost equal rapidity – precisely to render strong profits *un*attainable.

The basic dynamic can be simply expressed. High profit margins – or, more specifically, high expected margins – encourage new entrants, spurring investors to switch investment from sectors of the economy characterized by lower profitability. Competition from such new entrants then proceeds to depress the high profit margins that originally attracted them.

Of course, this is not by any means a phenomenon to do solely with renewable energy: it is a general characteristic of capitalist economies, or at least of those that allow the free movement of capital between competing investment alternatives. Indeed, the switching of investment between sectors of lower and higher profitability is a staple of classical economics, leading in theory – but only in theory – to the equalization of sectoral profit rates.

Even as this is a generalized phenomenon, however, it is especially pronounced in the case of renewable power. Why? The answer is that the one thing with the potential to arrest in meaningful fashion the inflow of capital into profitable sectors, and thus also to forestall the attendant increase in competition and decline in profitability, is conspicuous by its absence in the renewables sector. That thing is monopoly power.

If incumbents in profitable sectors have the capacity to resist increased competition, then above-average profitability can sometimes be maintained. But there exists precious little monopoly power in the business of developing and operating wind and solar farms, and almost no substantive entry barriers. 'The barriers to entry in the [renewables] sector', Nick Butler brusquely puts it, 'are low – anyone can become an electricity producer.'[18] This, of course, is to exaggerate: clearly, not just anyone can, in practice, or at least not at utility-scale production. But the basic observation is well taken. As we saw in Chapter 2, in parts of the world where aspiring new generators did once face significant entry obstacles, such as those relating, for instance, to ease of access to transmission and distribution networks, policymakers have widely removed such obstacles.

As a result, in places and periods in which renewable power is seen to be an economically attractive option, activity can be feverish. During the time of the writing of this book, in the early 2020s, the US has arguably been the primary such place. Competition in the US renewables sector, Camilla Naschert observed in 2021, was 'fierce'.[19] That, moreover, was before the passage the following year of the Inflation Reduction Act, which led, as we saw in NextEra Energy's case, to even greater private sector confidence in the profits theoretically on offer. Competition thus intensified further from late 2022, the *Financial Times*, for instance,

---

18   N. Butler, 'The Private Sector Alone Will Not Deliver the Energy Transition', *Financial Times*, 28 October 2019.

19   C. Naschert, 'Offshore Wind No Longer a Game with Big Returns, Says RWE', 16 March 2021, spglobal.com.

describing it simply as 'stiff', while the *Wall Street Journal* reported on 'rising competition among renewable-energy developers . . . seeking to supply power at the lowest cost'.[20] With the only significant economic obstacle to renewables investment – uncertain profit expectations – seemingly removed, developers were banging on the doors of the various authorities whose job it is to review permit and grid connection applications. Grid operators, for example, it was reported in early 2023, were 'overwhelmed by requests', with more than 8,000 proposed projects waiting in line.[21]

The key point here is that where, as in the renewables sector, entry barriers are low, the generalized swings in sectoral fortunes that are endemic to capitalism stand to be considerably exacerbated. There is no incumbent monopoly to slow the boom, hence competition mounts briskly and then forcefully drives down returns. Every time there has been talk of a renewables 'gold rush' – from Spain in around 2007 to China in around 2011 and India in around 2014, in the last of which enthusiasm rapidly escalated, in the words of one operator, into 'over-exuberance' – the days of capitalist bounty have been numbered more or less as soon as they have begun.[22] In short, even where they actually do exist in the first place, strong renewables profits rarely last for long. Informed economic historians of the sector will doubtless have looked at the latest round of gold rush talk – sparked by Biden's US climate legislation of 2022 – with a jaundiced eye. True to type, already by mid-2023 it was being reported in the US that the renewed burst of renewables competition sparked by the IRA was 'pushing margins lower . . . "When competition picks up, margins start to erode," said Guggenheim analyst Shahriar Pourreza'.[23]

And, for all the fact that various species of government intervention frequently do help to bolster profits, they generally do not stop the

20  'RWE/ConEd: US Renewables Get a Fillip'; K. Blunt and J. Hiller, 'Utility Companies Sell Wind, Solar Farms to Shore Up US Power Grid', *Wall Street Journal*, 3 July 2023.

21  J. Hiller, 'Investors Plow into Renewables, but Projects Aren't Getting Built', *Wall Street Journal*, 22 January 2023.

22  'Over-exuberance' was the term used by Bob Smith of Mytrah Energy. See V. Mallet, 'Consolidation Looms in Cut-Price Indian Solar Sector', *Financial Times*, 24 April 2016.

23  Blunt and Hiller, 'Utility Companies Sell Wind, Solar Farms'.

renewables industry from competing away those profits when it elects – or, after Marx, is compelled – to do so. Indeed, government 'support' mechanisms sometimes actively facilitate, even lubricate, the competition-led race to the bottom. The best example of this is the competitive auction processes that governments widely use in allocating renewables contracts. In 2021, for instance, when the UK government auctioned seabed leases for new offshore wind projects, 'fierce competition' among bidders resulted in 'sky-high prices' for seabed rights that will, commentators said, inevitably mean 'slimmer returns'.[24]

Of particular significance in expediting the erosion of industry profitability is the 'reverse auction' mechanism that is increasingly employed by governments specifically to award feed-in tariffs and comparable fixed-price output contracts. Under this model, rather than buyers bidding prices *up* (as per traditional auction formats, such as were used in the aforementioned UK auctioning of seabed lease rights), sellers – in this case, of electricity – bid prices *down*. By the mid-2010s, for example, aggressive bidding for contracts at India's reverse auctions, by both domestic and international firms, was driving prices to record low levels. One industry consultant described the spread of ultra-low bids across the country as being 'like a contagion'.[25]

Similarly, it was reported several years later that, across Europe, such auctions had become 'extremely competitive'.[26] Indeed, so competitive has bidding become on European auctions for offshore wind FiTs and the like, that, according to one study, the strike prices agreed by winning bidders have fallen faster than the costs of generation have.[27] Precisely the same price–cost dynamic has played out in India.[28]

At this point, then, it clearly pays to cast our minds back to Chapter 5. There, we ventured that lower costs – such as one repeatedly sees depicted in charts showing a declining LCOE for renewable energies – might not, in fact, mean higher profits for a capitalist firm if revenues

24   Naschert, 'Offshore Wind No Longer a Game with Big Returns'.

25   Mallet, 'Consolidation Looms in Cut-Price Indian Solar Sector'.

26   D. Frankel, N. Janecke, F. Kühn, I. Ritzenhofen and R. Winter, 'Rethinking the Renewable Strategy for an Age of Global Competition', 11 October 2019, mckinsey.com.

27   See O. K. Helgesen, M. Aanestad and M. Holter, 'World's Largest Offshore Wind Farm "Unprofitable" for Equinor, Say Government-Funded Researchers', 19 November 2021, upstreamonline.com.

28   Mallet, 'Consolidation Looms in Cut-Price Indian Solar Sector'.

fall by as much as costs do, or by more. We can now see that this is not merely a hypothetical conjecture: it is, in certain renewables contexts, the reality.


## III


After a short-lived boom, therefore, the typical outcome of the inrush of profit-seeking capital into the development and operation of new renewables facilities is oversupply, and a much longer bust. This was clearly evident, for example, in Spain after 2013. It was not just investment in wind and solar power that, as we saw earlier, collapsed; so also did generator profitability. The cause of the extended subsequent decline in both returns and investment was partly the government's decision to squeeze existing support mechanisms, of course, but partly also the massive overinvestment in generating capacity relative to consumption requirements that those very mechanisms had originally triggered.[29]

Something similar occurred in parts of the US in the late 2000s and early to mid-2010s. Precipitated partly by generous tax credits and partly by enforced industry restructuring and market liberalization in the regions in question, the late 1990s and early 2000s had seen a boom in investment in renewables undertaken not just by a new breed of independent generating companies but also by classic regulated utilities (such as the above-mentioned NextEra) seeking both geographic and product diversification beyond their remaining regulated, monopoly strongholds. But, with the capacity for transmission interconnection between regions remaining limited, investment hotspots such as west Texas soon fell prey to a long-lasting supply glut and falling power prices.[30]

In fact, NextEra was one of the few traditional utilities to stay the new course: most of its peers that had also invested in renewable generating assets in liberalized regional markets gave up, selling off these assets and retreating with their tails between their legs to the safe redoubt of

---

29    C. Bjork and S. Raice, 'German Power Utility E.ON to Sell Spanish Assets', *Wall Street Journal*, 28 November 2014.

30    R. McCracken and H. Carr, 'Wind Blows Ill for Natural Gas in Texas', *Platts Energy Economist*, 1 February 2016.

protected regional monopoly.[31] Writing in 2017, Raymond Gifford and colleagues described developments in the US renewables sector across the previous decade or so in terms of a 'vicious cycle': a gold rush mentality sparked vast (if regionally uneven) investment, precipitating local 'oversupplied conditions' that 'undermined the financial stability of merchant generators, and eroded their capacity to attract and deploy capital over the long term'.[32]

Baldly stated, the 'free market' in the generation of renewable energy evidently includes the freedom to overinvest and lose money. There is, in countries such as Spain and the US, no central planning authority to oversee and coordinate overall investment in new generating capacity, and to ensure that available operating capacity broadly matches demand both nationally and within particular regions. Moreover, the potential for the crystallization of profit-suppressing conditions of oversupply as a result of sporadic renewables booms is aggravated by the fact that, in such free-market contexts, conventional generating sources are not being systematically retired. Indeed, it is not altogether incorrect to say that often they *cannot* be retired. For one thing, renewables cannot be relied upon to generate at all times, and energy storage capabilities remain inadequate. Moreover, laws or treaties sometimes militate against such retirement. Perhaps most famously, the Energy Charter Treaty, which covers more than fifty countries, including across the European Union, allows owners of conventional generating assets to sue governments whose legislation or policy reforms threaten such assets.[33]

Crucially, however, we tend also to find comparable short-boom–longer-bust patterns even where pricing is more regulated and capacity investment to some extent *is* planned. China and India are striking examples. By the mid- to late 2010s, after several years of substantial build-out of renewables capacity driven in large part by government support programmes, both countries were plagued by significant

---

31   C. Harrison, 'Electricity Capital and Accumulation Strategies in the US Electricity System', *Environment and Planning E: Nature and Space* 5 (2022), pp. 1716–37.

32   R. Gifford, M. Larson and R. Lunt, 'The Breakdown of the Merchant Generation Business Model', June 2017, wbklaw.com, p. 2.

33   At the time of this writing, the Treaty appeared to be close to disintegration: countries including France, Germany and Spain have committed unilaterally to exiting, and the EU has mooted a collective exit.

oversupply in those regions where renewables facilities are concentrated. China, in particular, was 'suffering one of the worst overcapacity situations in history'.[34]

How could this be so, if governments were supposed to be coordinating matters? Several factors seem to have been pertinent. For one thing, one does not need to read Hayek to understand that central planners are not necessarily better at coordinating the economy than markets are. More pointedly, both countries are notable for having had a veritable hodgepodge of national and provincial rules and guidelines that often have not aligned with one another, from targets and quotas for renewable energy sourcing to the phased introduction of pilot market mechanisms of various kinds. In China, for example, provincial governments have generally enjoyed control over investment planning while the central government has retained primary price-setting authority.[35] Meanwhile, in India, there is now a synchronous national grid – the world's largest – formed out of five regional grids, yet much about energy policy is still decided provincially. In such circumstances, it is little wonder that, when investment conditions appear germane, supply can rapidly run ahead of demand and, as has occurred in China, 'price depression' and 'loss making' subsequently set in.[36]

A particularly striking symptom of boom-induced oversupply is the phenomenon of renewable power curtailment. This entails the enforced reduction of energy delivered to the grid by solar or wind farms, at times when local supply exceeds local demand and when it is not possible – for economic reasons, technological reasons, or a combination of the two – to export that surplus power to places where demand does exist.

In a world where the aim is to deliver as much electricity renewably as is possible, some degree of curtailment seems more or less inevitable. The sun and wind are unpredictable and variable, and it is better – the logic has it – to err on the side of overinvestment than of underinvestment.

---

34   M. R. Davidson, 'Creating Markets for Wind Electricity in China', unpublished PhD dissertation, Massachusetts Institute of Technology, 2018, mit.edu, p. 281.

35   For a particularly illuminating overview of the bewildering range of overlapping institutions, laws, regulations and guidelines that pertain to China's renewable energy sector, see R. Jiang, Y. He and L. Shi, 'China', in M. Hassan, ed., *The Renewable Energy Law Review*, 5th edn (London: Law Business Research, 2022).

36   Davidson, 'Creating Markets for Wind Electricity in China', p. 281.

Nevertheless, around the world, there have been various sustained periods of curtailment of renewable power occurring on a scale that is explicable only with reference to the logic of overoptimistic profit expectations (and subsequent bust), and not the logic of rational planning. Again, Texas in the late 2000s was one prime, and early, example. The UK in recent times has been another. In 2020, nearly 20 per cent of wind power generated by Scottish wind farms was discarded.[37] For comparison, the share of wind and solar power that was curtailed in Germany, Italy and the US between 2017 and 2020 ranged between only 1 and 3 per cent.[38]

The extent of renewables curtailment that occurs in any time and place is clearly influenced by local dispatch rules, which is to say, the criteria according to which the order of dispatch of different energy sources is determined; merit order dispatch, discussed in Chapter 6, is just one possible approach. But, if overinvestment in renewables (relative to the scope, at least in the short term, for such renewable power to be consumed) occurs on a sufficiently significant scale, then high rates of curtailment can in fact result even where renewables enjoy mandatory dispatch status.

Consider the crucial cases of China and India. Renewables have long enjoyed must-run status in both places, meaning that their curtailment is only permitted on grounds of grid security, with generators being instructed to lower output when transmission lines reach safe loading limits. But, in both countries, the past five to ten years have nonetheless seen curtailment rates reach unprecedented levels – of as high as 40 or even 50 per cent – in some regions, such as Xinjiang in north-western China and Tamil Nadu in southern India.[39]

What are policymakers' options when overinvestment occurs and curtailment rates climb? The most pressing imperative is invariably to build out interconnection capacity between regions. The lack of

---

37   Renewable Energy Foundation, 'Constraint Payments to Wind Power in 2020 and 2021', 17 February 2022, ref.org.uk.

38   IEA, 'Renewables Integration in India', June 2021, iea.org, p. 35.

39   W. Peng, Z. Mao and M. R. Davidson, 'Promoting Large-Scale Deployment and Integration of Renewable Electricity', in Lee et al., *Foundations for a Low-Carbon Energy System in China*, p. 40; K. Singh, 'Creating a National Electricity Market: India's Most Important Power Sector Reform', 19 August 2019, csis.org; IEA, 'Renewables Integration in India'.

sufficient such capacity is generally an important contributory factor in explaining why curtailment rises so high in the first place: as we have seen already, renewables generators tend to cluster in areas with cheap land, often far away from centres of demand, and most grid systems – dating to earlier eras of infrastructure investment – remain incapable of efficiently transporting large surpluses of renewable power from the former areas to the latter. Thus, when curtailment became a significant problem in Texas in the late 2000s, for example, policymakers soon set about improving connectivity between the west of the state, where most wind farms are located, and the main consumption areas in the state's east and south, and by early 2014, at a cost of some $6 billion, the state had built around 5,800 kilometres of new transmission lines capable of carrying 18 GW of power.[40]

Beyond the physical imperative of upgrading the grid, however, governments face some difficult economic policy choices. The choice they make necessarily shapes future private sector investment patterns and, indeed, the very phenomenon of curtailment itself.

One possibility is to ride things out, and accept the slump – and its temporary manifestation in the form of localized curtailment – for what it is. Generators are thus paid only for power that is accepted onto the grid, which means losses of significant proportions of the revenue that would have been earned had curtailment not been a factor. Some generators, perhaps many, will go out of business in such a scenario, unable to service their loan payments.

One country to have adopted this kind of Darwinian approach is India, where there is no remuneration for wind and solar curtailment. SunEdison of the US was a conspicuous casualty, its overly aggressive bids at India's reverse auctions for solar capacity – it set a record low price of 4.63 rupees per kWh when winning a 500 MW auction in Andhra Pradesh in 2015 – playing an important role in forcing the company into bankruptcy in 2016. Needless to say, such an uncompromising approach to curtailment and the corresponding difficulties encountered by generators – Canada-based SkyPower Global was another to endure a torrid time in India – can and does have a negative effect on confidence to invest in future generating capacity. The IEA reported that, by 2021, India's high curtailment and an apparent lack of

---

40   McCracken and Carr, 'Wind Blows Ill for Natural Gas in Texas'.

policy to address it had become a 'critical concern' for investors, and cited a study that found that investors' IRR on solar projects declines by 160 basis points for every 2.5 per cent production loss per annum.[41]

Vietnam is another country to have found itself in a comparable post-boom predicament. Massive growth in installations of solar capacity in 2019–20 in response to generous government incentives was succeeded in short order by the all-too-familiar bust in the form of 'oversupply', 'wasteful curtailment' – 'a big burden for projects' IRR' – and generators 'unable to pay bank debts on time'. A creaking transmission system with limited capacity that had not been upgraded in line with burgeoning generating potential was bad enough. The savaging of demand by the coronavirus pandemic temporarily made matters worse: in October 2021, daily electricity consumption only accounted for up to 40 per cent of installed generating capacity nationwide. This translated into epic curtailment rates.[42]

Meanwhile, a very different approach to curtailment has been taken in countries such as the UK, which have actively eschewed the Darwinianism of their Indian and Vietnamese counterparts. For all its reputation as a bastion of free market neoliberalism, the UK's renewables generators, mainly in Scotland, have historically been paid full compensation when they are not permitted to generate at their full capacity. One study calculated that the annual cost of this renewables curtailment to UK consumers reached over £500 million in 2021 alone.[43]

In other words, a subsidy, of a kind, has in this instance been used to resolve – or at least to help address – a problem rooted in another kind of subsidy, namely the government support mechanisms that stimulated investment in Scottish renewables capacity in the first place. The problem for the UK in the longer term is that rather than incentivizing investment in generating capacity in areas of the country closer to centres of demand, and thus potentially alleviating inflated curtailment levels, payment for curtailed generation does the very opposite.

41   IEA, 'Renewables Integration in India', pp. 37–8.

42   N. L. Dan, 'Vietnam's Renewable Energy Policies and Opportunities for the Private Sector', May 2022, nbr.org, pp. 1–2, 6.

43   LCP, 'Renewable Curtailment and the Role of Long Duration Storage', May 2022, drax.com.

## IV

And so we can now see that there are, in fact, not one but two considerable profitability-related obstacles to healthy ongoing investment in the build-out of renewable power worldwide. For not only is profitability becoming increasingly volatile and unpredictable as the marketization of electricity sectors around the world proceeds and deepens, but profitability is generally *low*, as well. Aside from temporally and geographically limited cases, the generation of electricity from the sun and wind, being a business protected by few entry barriers, is, even with state support, typically a low-profit-margin affair.

Awareness of this problem has been building for some time, even if many have been unprepared to acknowledge it. In 2017, Raymond Gifford and his co-authors encouraged policymakers, at the very least, to take 'pause', given the evident inability of many generators to even 'recover their fixed costs under current market conditions'.[44] This comment was directed specifically to the US context, but the problem was clearly wider. 'In today's competitive renewable energy environment, margins', the International Renewable Energy Agency (IRENA) observed the following year, 'are increasingly narrow.'

The question is, how narrow? The answer to that question obviously depends on where and when one looks. In certain places and periods, margins have been sufficiently narrow – to the point of being non-existent – to make even renewables' staunchest supporters squirm. A study published in 2023 of Swedish wind farms built in the years 2017–21, for example, found that the owners' average return on equity had been negative in every year of operation, notwithstanding the contribution of revenues from the country's renewable energy certificate scheme.[45]

But such localized examples clearly only provide a very partial picture. What of the profitability of renewables operators more generally, across both time and space? Publicly available estimates have in fact generally clustered within a relatively consistent and tight range. The

---

44   Gifford et al., 'The Breakdown of the Merchant Generation Business Model', p. 6.

45   C. Sandström, M. Staaf and C. Steinbeck, 'Vindkraft – en grön bubbla eller ett svart hål?', 23 May 2023, kvartal.se.

'ready availability of renewables', Nick Butler reported in 2019, 'means few projects can make returns of more than 5–8 per cent'.[46] The same year, in discussing the solar industry, Emma Merchant said that project returns 'usually range from 6 to 8 percent'.[47] Occasionally, estimates have dipped somewhat lower than this: returns of 4 to 6 per cent for solar operators (albeit specifically in France) were reported in 2020, for instance.[48] But generally, returns broadly in the range identified by Butler and Merchant, and almost never above 10 per cent (save exceptional, truncated cases such as FiT-turbocharged Spain in around 2008–10), are what appear to have become the norm, if we can speak of such a thing.[49]

In 2021, for example, Camilla Naschert said of offshore wind that returns on new projects were expected to land in the 5.5–8.5 per cent range. Naschert cited Markus Krebber, then the chief financial officer of Germany's RWE, one of the world's largest operators of offshore wind farms. The belief among some industry observers 'that you can earn excess returns significantly above your cost of capital for decades to come' is, Krebber claimed, 'totally unreasonable'.[50] Krebber, it seems, was right. By as early as the final months of 2022, with 'fierce competition' raging in the sector, 'baseline returns' in offshore wind had in fact settled at around an estimated 5 to 6 per cent.[51] A gold mine, renewable energy clearly is not.

Notably, all of the estimates cited in the previous two paragraphs concerned renewables operations located predominantly in the Global North. Indeed, generalized and intensifying pressure on the returns of renewables projects in wealthy countries is a substantial part of the explanation for one of the most significant trends in renewable energy investment during the second half of the 2010s, namely a geographical shift from Global North to South. The former region received the bulk of

---

46    Butler, 'The Private Sector Alone Will Not Deliver the Energy Transition'.
47    E. F. Merchant, 'Is the Utility-Scale Solar Industry in a Finance Bubble?', 23 January 2019, greentechmedia.com.
48    V. Mallet and D. Keohane, 'French Solar Investors Up in Arms over Threat to Renege on Contracts', *Financial Times*, 12 November 2020.
49    See for example, R. Bousso, 'Shell Pivots Back to Oil to Win Over Investors', 9 June 2023, reuters.com.
50    Naschert, 'Offshore Wind No Longer a Game with Big Returns'.
51    S. Flowers, 'Offshore Wind's Value Proposition', 20 October 2022, woodmac .com.

investment historically, but the balance shifted around 2015. 'Both then and in 2016,' a report published in 2018 noted, 'developing economies made up the majority of investment in renewable power and fuels – and in 2017, the gap grew sharply, so that the developing world accounted for 63% of the global total and developed countries just 37%.'[52]

It is true, as Sean Kennedy has observed, that there are other reasons why renewables investment in the Global South has grown markedly in recent years, including 'low electrification rates, increases in energy demand driven by rapid economic growth, [and] national and international greenhouse gas reduction commitments'. But, as Kennedy also explained, when profitability comes under pressure, as it evidently has done in more mature markets, the imperative to minimize costs becomes acute, and this is where the Global South has increasingly come into its own. The availability of, most notably, 'cheap land and labour have made many countries in the Global South . . . lucrative sites for the absorption [in renewable energy projects] of abundant finance capital'.[53] Two quick points about this geographic trend, both of which we shall return to in more detail, should be noted. First, renewables development in the Global South remains highly uneven, with many poorer countries continuing to receive almost no investment; second, if local land and labour often come cheap, the finance being 'absorbed' in renewables projects in the Global South typically does not.

Meanwhile, the fact is that returns from renewables projects are not just generally low in absolute terms, but also low in relative terms. Indeed, it actually makes little real sense to speak of returns from an absolutist perspective at all. The only reason that we are even in a position to describe returns of, say, below 10 per cent as 'low' is that we can readily imagine or point to returns that are higher than that. Much like costs, returns are always and everywhere ultimately a relative phenomenon. To argue, as I have done in earlier chapters, that it is misguided to use the relative costs of fossil-fuel-based and renewable power as our principal prism through which to evaluate renewables' prospects is definitively not to eschew relative measures and comparative analysis

---

52  Frankfurt School–UNEP Centre/BNEF, 'Global Trends in Renewable Energy Investment 2018', 5 April 2018, unep.org, p. 15.

53  S. Kennedy, 'Indonesia's Energy Transition And Its Contradictions: Emerging Geographies of Energy and Finance', *Energy Research and Social Science* 41 (2018), p. 232.

altogether. It is, rather, simply to insist that relative LCOEs do not represent the most relevant and meaningful comparator.

Our concern should instead be with relevant, relative profit expectations. There is always an opportunity cost associated with any investment insofar as directing capital towards one investment alternative means forgoing all others (and the returns they potentially will confer), including the option of investment in assets – cash and near-cash instruments – that are essentially risk-free.

Now, what the main option or options alternative to investment in solar or wind farms will in practice be varies enormously from firm to firm. As we saw in Chapter 3, all manner of different types of company are active in developing and then operating renewables power-generating facilities, and those different types of company will have a range of different alternatives in mind when weighing up whether to proceed with a particular wind or solar investment project. Very often, as Chapter 5 emphasized, renewables companies are renewables specialists whose choice is very straightforward indeed – to invest, or to not invest.

Here, two particular constituencies merit our specific consideration. First are traditional oil and gas companies such as Chevron and ExxonMobil in the US and BP, Shell and Total in Europe. These companies are repeatedly being encouraged to shift into renewables – by activist investors such as the Capuchin friars mentioned at the beginning of this chapter, for example. Expediting such an institutional shift is regarded by many experts as nothing less than a sine qua non of an effective and orderly energy transition.

But here is the problem: the returns ordinarily associated with wind and solar power are much lower than those to which fossil fuel companies are accustomed in their core businesses. As Butler observed in 2019, 'typical investments in oil and gas projects, where the barriers to entry are much higher [than in renewables], earn returns of 15 per cent or more'.[54] The big new hydrocarbon projects still being initiated by the international oil majors in the 2020s, in the face of widespread public fury and dismay, promise significantly higher rates of return – and, of course, on a significantly greater absolute scale – than renewables ever do.

---

54   Butler, 'The Private Sector Alone Will Not Deliver the Energy Transition'.

In a 2020 update for investors, for instance, France's Total highlighted three large recently greenlit projects in Uganda, Angola and Brazil, all of which would produce at least 150,000 barrels of oil equivalent per day. It assumed a relatively modest oil price in making its profit forecasts ($50 per barrel), but, even at that price, the first project was expected to generate an IRR of 15 per cent, while the second and third would generate IRRs in excess of 20 per cent.[55] What chance for renewables and their puny 5–8 per cent returns against such prodigious profits?

Consider, for instance, the recent experience of Equinor, the Norwegian state-controlled oil and gas giant. All the while Total was finalizing plans for its money-spinning hydrocarbon projects in Africa and South America, Equinor, alongside partners Eni and SSE, was itself finalizing plans for the development of the first phase of Dogger Bank in the North Sea, in which it owns a 40 per cent stake and which will be one of the world's largest offshore wind farms when operational. In June 2021, Equinor revised downwards its expected rate of return on offshore wind projects – from between 6 and 10 per cent to between just 4 and 8 per cent. But a study carried out by experts suggested that even this was too optimistic in the case specifically of the Dogger Bank project, calculating the expected IRR to be just 3.6 per cent, and equating to a payback period of a minimum of seventeen years.[56]

No wonder that when, the following year, Equinor approached BP – another European oil company that had said in the recent past that it would move into lower-emissions activities but which has found such ambition to be fundamentally incompatible with the profit motive – about joining it in competing for new wind power rights off the coast of California, the response was negative. BP, reported Jenny Strasburg in early 2023, had increasingly become 'disappointed in the returns from some of [its own] renewable investments', and was therefore planning to 'dial back elements of [its] high-profile push into renewable energy'. Offshore wind returns of 4 to 8 per cent? *No thank you.* When Equinor came calling, BP, in short, 'balked'.[57] The question, then, bears repeating:

55    Total, 'From Net Zero Ambition to Total Strategy', September 2020, totalenergies. com, p. 40.

56    Helgesen et al., 'World's Largest Offshore Wind Farm "Unprofitable" for Equinor'.

57    J. Strasburg, 'BP's CEO Plays Down Renewables Push as Returns Lag', *Wall Street Journal*, 1 February 2023.

in a world awash in hydrocarbon profits, what chance for renewables and their wafer-thin profit margins?

For a brief window of time during the early part of the COVID-19 pandemic, expected returns on oil and gas declined to the extent that they became comparable to expected returns on renewables. As environmentalists saw it, at least, it appeared to be one of the few silver linings to the spread of the virus. With oil prices languishing at under $25 per barrel in March 2020, the expected IRR on oil projects dipped to below 10 per cent, making wind and solar projects newly competitive with such projects on paper – which they would remain, analysts suggested, even at an oil price of $35 per barrel.[58] But, of course, hydrocarbon prices did not remain in the doldrums for long. As soon as they recovered, the window of opportunity for renewables seemingly slammed shut.

That the profitability of oil and gas has generally been far higher than that of renewables explains why, in the 1980s and 1990s, the oil and gas majors unceremoniously shuttered their first ventures in the renewables space – piecemeal, exploratory and never more than tentative – almost as soon as they had launched them: these were business decisions, first and foremost. The same comparative calculus equally explains why the same companies are shifting to clean energy at no more than a snail's pace today, and why such 'climate-friendly' investments as they are in fact making – BP, for its part, has mentioned hydrogen, biogas and electric vehicle charging networks, in each of which returns are expected to be above 10 per cent – increasingly are not in renewable power generation at all.

If anyone were still under the impression at this stage of the climate crisis that the oil majors would *ever* sacrifice profitability at the altar of climate, then the following recent statement by Shell's CEO Wael Sawan, in response to a question about whether he considered renewables' lower returns acceptable for his company, will have rudely disabused them of such a notion:

I think on low carbon, let me be, I think, categorical in this. We will drive for strong returns in any business we go into. We cannot justify

58   D. Snieckus, 'Investor Returns on Renewables Projects "Now Competitive with Oil and Gas" as Coronavirus Strikes', 25 March 2020, rechargenews.com.

going for a low return. Our shareholders deserve to see us going after strong returns. If we cannot achieve the double-digit returns in a business, we need to question very hard whether we should continue in that business. Absolutely, we want to continue to go for lower and lower and lower carbon, but it has to be profitable.[59]

Sawan's predecessor as CEO had staked his reputation on transforming Shell from an oil and gas company into a climate-friendlier power-generation company, all the while the US hydrocarbon majors stuck defiantly with hydrocarbons. Sawan was now responding to the market's unambiguous assessment of the two divergent strategies. 'Five years ago, when Shell embarked on a low-carbon push, its market capitalization was about $40 billion less than that of Exxon Mobil Corp. Now', noted one journalist, 'the different is more than $200 billion.'[60]

Electricity generation offers by some margin the lowest IRR of all of Shell's businesses.[61] Chastened by Wall Street's savage indictment of his company's erstwhile turn – effectively – away from profit, Sawan spent the first half of 2023 pivoting Shell back to oil and gas. Hence the horrific spectacle of a significant revival in upstream exploration activity on the part of the European majors, with Shell to the fore. In mid-2023, it was reported that daily rates for leasing drilling rigs had returned to their highest levels in nearly a decade.[62] At the same time, Shell and its peers were busily scrapping projects (including in wind) with 'projections of weak returns'.[63] Underperforming businesses such as renewables, one of Wael Sawan's key lieutenants confirmed, would have to 'earn back the right to grow.'[64]

Needless to say, the relatively higher returns historically available in oil and gas exploration and production are not 'natural' economic facts any more than the lower returns from renewables are. For one thing,

59  'Shell PLC (SHEL) Q4 2022 Earnings Call Transcript', 2 February 2023, seekingalpha.com.

60  K. Crowley, 'Shell Takes Hard Road to Wall Street Acceptance', 15 June 2023, bloomberg.com.

61  Shell, 'Delivering More Value, with Less Emissions', June 2023, shell.com, p. 43.

62  R. Bousso and N. Adomaitis, 'Oil Giants Drill Deep as Profits Trump Climate Concerns', 3 July 2023, reuters.com.

63  Bousso, 'Shell Pivots Back to Oil to Win Over Investors'.

64  Cited in Crowley, 'Shell Takes Hard Road to Wall Street Acceptance'.

government economic support has traditionally been a characteristic feature of the former business, too. This support has typically taken the form of subsidies to production (such as tax breaks or direct payments to producers), to consumption (principally reduced fuel prices for end users) or to both.[65] To make the point that the renewables business remains stuck on government support (Chapter 9) is certainly not to gainsay the continuing support simultaneously afforded to oil and gas production.

Moreover, there is a further significant respect in which the profitability of oil and gas in capitalism is 'externally' fashioned into existence much more than being in any way inherent or endogenous. Insofar as they are subject to relatively frequent supply and demand shocks, underlying fossil fuel prices are in fact highly volatile, even if not quite *as* volatile as electricity spot prices. There is therefore a long history of the industry, governments or a combination of the two – the line between them has always been blurred, and in many parts of the world they are the selfsame entities – actively assembling monopolistic or oligopolistic control specifically in order to subdue volatility, stabilize profits and encourage investment. OPEC (the Organization of the Petroleum Exporting Countries) is nothing if not a large-scale, long-standing and generally highly successful transnational exercise in such assembly. Indeed, arguably one of the most important political-economic distinctions between the renewables industry and the oil and gas industry is the absence in the former of the established institutional architectures of monopoly power that scaffold the latter.

Just because the higher profits in oil and gas are very much social and political artefacts rather than raw economic facts does not, however, make them any less real or consequential. It would, of course, be welcome, for the future of the planet and humanity, if it were not true that oil and gas are more profitable than solar and wind, but wishing it were not so does not make it not so. When the likes of Sawan and Exxon's Rex Tillerson remonstrate, as Tillerson himself did at the company's annual shareholder meeting in 2015, that renewables are not profitable enough (for them), theirs, unfortunately, is not necessarily a performance of disingenuity or ignorance.

---

65   J. Timperley, 'Why Fossil Fuel Subsidies Are So Hard to Kill', 20 October 2021, nature.com.

Meanwhile, if the returns associated with wind and solar power are ordinarily much lower than those to which fossil fuel companies are accustomed, then they are also much lower than those to which banks and other financiers are accustomed – and this, by some margin, is much the more significant comparator. Whoever it happens to be that develops and operates wind or solar farms, they need funds to do so, particularly at the outset of the project, when the bulk of its lifetime costs are incurred, and thus if financial institutions cannot see their way to providing funds at a cost that developers deem tolerable, a project will be dead in the water before a stone has been turned. As earlier chapters emphasized, financial firms, and especially the providers of debt, are in many ways the most important actors in the renewables drama: *they* are the ones who ultimately decide, or at least whose decisions make the difference between development and non-development.

Of course, the return on a renewables project, which has been our focus in the preceding paragraphs, is not the same thing as the return achieved by its funders. Even as both the owner of a wind farm and the provider of upfront loan capital share a central concern with project profitability (the lender knowing that its loan will be unlikely to be fully serviced if the project is loss making), it is quite possible for them to profit to widely varying degrees. If, for example, interest rates on a wind construction loan are fixed, as they usually are, the lender's return – assuming no default – is known and fixed in advance, whereas the owner's return will depend on lifetime revenues and costs.

The difference between the two sets of returns, and in particular the question of whose returns perspective one foregrounds in considering the profitability and viability of a renewables project, is in fact tremendously important. Clean power optimists invariably look at things from the developer/owner's perspective. Thus, from that perspective, reducing the developer's financing costs is deemed a strategic priority, and any indication of a fall in the average cost of capital is seen as cause for celebration insofar as this is taken to imply that projects will be more economically viable and thus more likely to materialize.

But every coin has two sides. One party's cost is another's revenue. A lower cost of capital for developers is, essentially, a lower return for the providers of capital. This lower return would not much matter, if it were on the developer's say-so, and the developer's alone, that renewables projects either go ahead or do not. But, as we have seen, it is not

developers who ultimately decide. If the key decision in the development process is the lender's decision to advance credit or not, and if,
accordingly, we should be looking at the matter of returns as much from
the lender's perspective as from the borrower's (if not more so), then
perhaps a lower cost of capital is not such a good thing after all. *Ceteris
paribus*, it would seem likely to lower, not raise, the likelihood of a
project proceeding.

And, in recent years, for two main reasons, investor returns from
financing renewable energy projects have indeed been under significant
pressure, and have generally been falling as a result. The first reason is
precisely the one we have been exploring at length throughout this
chapter – namely the weak underlying profitability of wind and solar
farms themselves. It would be wrongheaded to imagine that financiers
could make significant profits from financing an activity that is itself
usually only modestly profitable. Typically, they cannot and do not.

The second reason has to do with capital supply. The notion of
financial investing incorporating 'environmental, social and governance'
(ESG) criteria has become a source of much derision of late, on both
right and left. Whereas the right dismisses it as a woke-ist fad, the left
dismisses it as just so much greenwashing – that is, as rhetorical cover
for business as usual, which is to say decidedly dirty investment
behaviour.

Yet the reality, as is typically the case, is much more complicated than
either pole allows. Certainly, many investors continue to finance fossil
fuel companies and other environmentally (and socially) destructive
activities. Whether one labels it ESG or not, however, demand among
financial investors for genuinely clean investment opportunities *has*
surged in the past decade. That is simply a fact, even as it may well be the
case that such investors' primary interest is more in a low-carbon portfolio than in a low-carbon world as such.

Just as more competition in the generation of wind and solar power
depresses average generator profits, so also more competition in financing such generation activities depresses average financier profits. 'You
have all these investors that are like, "How do I get my hands on the
next solar project?"' Richard Matsui, a specialist in risk management
for solar investments, told Emma Merchant in 2019. 'The aggressive
guys win the deal right now,' Matsui continued, and as Merchant, in
turn, observed, 'aggressive' in the investor world means 'a willingness

to accept lower returns, which puts pressure on everyone else in the market to shift their standards as well'.[66] Such stories have increasingly become a commonplace. As the desire to finance renewable energy projects grows, the profits attainable from doing so are squeezed commensurately.

Thus it is no longer the case, if it ever was, that the financing of renewable power facilities delivers returns above those available in other asset classes on account – so the argument went concerning such ostensibly above-average returns – of the perceived riskiness of renewables. Such was long the received wisdom: that, in the words of Noël Amenc and Frédéric Blanc-Brude, there existed a 'persistent "green" risk factor premium from which investors in green infrastructure projects might benefit over the long term'.[67]

No. Renewables may indeed be risky; this book has, of course, argued precisely as much, at some length. But, as Amenc and Blanc-Brude discovered when crunching the numbers, financial investment in green infrastructure is in fact associated not with a green revenue premium but with a green cost premium. Specifically, there is 'a "green price premium" that investors have been willing to pay to increase their exposure to the asset class'. Just as renewables offer energy companies lower returns than oil and gas, in other words, they in fact also offer financial firms lower returns than other financial investment opportunities.

The existence of this 'price premium' really should give us pause. Banks and other financiers' willingness to support renewables projects is predicated in part, it appears, on their willingness to accept sub-par returns as the necessary price of going green. The key question, however, is how far such investor willingness to accept lower returns will stretch. Who knows? But if we have learnt anything from financial history, it is that banks, of all capitalist firms, are not charities. If we can be sure of anything, it is that their willingness to pay the premium in question will be limited, and at some point will be exhausted.

---

66   Merchant, 'Is the Utility-Scale Solar Industry in a Finance Bubble?'.

67   R. Lowe, 'Investors Now Paying "Green Premium" for Renewables', 23 September 2022, realassets.ipe.com.

## V

On 7 May 2016, something very striking and, at first blush, highly peculiar took place on Germany's EPEX wholesale electricity market. The hourly spot day-ahead price – specifically for the 2:00–3:00 p.m. time slot on Sunday 8 May – fell to a record low of minus €130.09 per MWh. It would be entirely understandable if reading this sentence were to cause a double take: surely there must have been a misprint here, one might imagine! But, perverse as it might sound, this is in fact no misprint: the electricity price indeed briefly fell to *minus* €130 that day. Generators were effectively paying wholesale buyers to take output off their hands. In turn, consumers lucky enough to be holding dynamic-pricing retail contracts, under which retail prices track hourly wholesale prices, were not only not paying to use electricity but were being paid – were *earning* money – for doing so. What on earth was going on?

Negative prices in wholesale electricity markets have occurred increasingly widely and commonly over the past decade or so. Germany represents the best-known example of the phenomenon: its number of hours with negative prices increased from 97 in 2016 to over 200 in 2019.[68] But it is not only in Germany that the phenomenon is visible. In the US, there have been instances of electricity prices turning negative in regions such as California and the Pacific Northwest for more than a decade. Meanwhile, the UK first experienced negative prices in 2019. The following year, negative prices in European wholesale markets at large were sufficiently common – occurring approximately 1 per cent of the time – for one report to envision such pricing as 'sweeping' across the continent.[69]

Generators of various kinds might periodically accept negative prices for a range of different reasons. Consider, for example, the case of large fossil fuel or nuclear power plants. Shutting down and then restarting these plants is, typically, very costly. If, at a particular point in time, the operator of such a plant expects wholesale prices to turn positive relatively shortly, it will often be willing to pay – rather than be paid – to generate power for a limited period of time to avoid those shut-down

---

68    'Negative Electricity Prices', 7 January 2020, smard.de.
69    A. Jones, 'Negative Energy Prices Sweep across Europe, Report Finds', 1 October 2020, industryeurope.com.

and restart expenses. That is, it will temporarily accept negative prices, while ramping down output to the plant's technical minimum. Some conventional plants also have contractual commitments – such as balancing energy, often under capacity agreements – to provide output to the grid operator when called upon, whatever the market price. And then there are combined heat and power plants: if such plants cannot readily separate heat from electricity generation, they may continue to generate electricity at negative prices if required to supply heat, or if profit from the latter offsets loss on the former.

Increasingly, however, negative electricity prices are a phenomenon associated principally with renewables. Let us return to the German case to see why. Under the country's revised Renewable Energy Sources Act of 2014, renewables generators selling into the spot market receive, on top of the hourly spot price, a sliding market premium that, similarly to under the UK's Contracts for Difference scheme (Chapter 6), represents the difference between a fixed strike price and the average monthly wholesale spot price. Prior to European natural gas and electricity prices beginning to rise in 2021, it was typically the case that the strike price in the contracts of renewables generators in Germany was higher than the spot price – in other words, such generators were usually in receipt of subsidy. In early 2020, for instance, the contractual strike price exceeded the average monthly spot price by an average of around €30 per MWh. That is, renewables generators were in receipt on average of a premium of approximately €30 per MWh.

Thus, if, around that time, the spot price for a specific hourly slot happened to be, say, €20 per MWh, the average renewables generator would earn around €50 per MWh for generating. But what if spot prices then turned negative? At minus €20 per MWh, it would still be profitable for the average solar or wind farm to generate, since the premium would outweigh the negative price. 'Only when a negative price cancels out the market premium completely,' as the Bundesnetzagentur has explained, 'will the operator have negative revenues and switch off the installation.'[70]

The precise form of the interplay between tariff mechanism and market price looks different in different countries. Nonetheless, wherever renewables generators are eligible for revenue subsidies of some

---

70  'Negative Electricity Prices'.

kind, it can sometimes be possible for those generators to produce and sell electricity profitably at negative wholesale prices, even if subsidy payments are not explicitly linked to those wholesale prices.

What, then, are we to make of this phenomenon? The practice of solar and wind farms generating and selling electricity into a negative-price market environment is best understood as the most extreme mani-festation of a broader dynamic. That dynamic can be expressed as follows. *The falling cost of generating renewable power has tendentially a depressive impact on the market price of electricity in general* – even, as we have just seen, to the point of market prices turning negative.

We have already encountered one significant lubricant of this tendency. That lubricant was competition. Insofar as they enjoy only limited monopoly power, operating, as they do, in a market environ-ment with limited barriers to entry, renewables generators struggle to capture incremental cost efficiencies themselves, instead seeing them competed away and passed downstream.

The example of negative pricing now points to a separate, if related, dimension of the tendency for lower renewables costs to feed through into lower market prices. That separate dimension concerns the degree of renewables penetration. The higher the penetration of renewables in the overall electricity generation mix, the more, generally speaking, the generation costs *of renewables* determine electricity pricing and reve-nues in the market as a whole. This, as the energy research and consult-ing firm Cornwall Insight explained in a 2018 report, is precisely why, in the second half of the 2010s, Germany became the home of negative pricing in Europe – because its renewable deployment was racing ahead of its peers'. As the proportion of renewables capacity on a network increases, so, broadly, does the frequency of low (even negative) whole-sale prices.[71]

The depressive impact of the roll-out of cheap-to-produce renewable energy on electricity prices has been particularly notable in countries, like Germany, that use merit order dispatch, which effectively institu-tionalizes the coupling of cost and revenue. As the Cornwall report put it, the growing penetration of renewables in such countries increasingly 'results in high-cost, inefficient thermal plant being squeezed to the

---

71   Cornwall Insight, 'Wholesale Power Price Cannibalization', 21 May 2018 – copy available from author.

margins, with cheaper more efficient thermal plant setting the price, or possibly all thermal plant being pushed out of merit. The result', Cornwall noted, 'is very low or even negative prices at times of high intermittent renewable generation.'[72]

But the depressive price effect is not only a phenomenon of the merit order. Why is it, after all, that the growing cheapness of renewables generation is more or less universally celebrated? In most cases, it is not because the celebrants spy an opportunity for generating companies to pocket the productivity gains. It is because they trust and assume that cheaper generation will ultimately mean cheaper wholesale and retail prices. As such, more or less all policymakers aim to one degree or another to ensure that cheapness in generation indeed is passed through to ratepayers as renewables' share of the generating mix grows.

What subsidies such as Germany's market premium tend to do is aggravate the depressive impact of renewables generating costs on market prices, inasmuch as they reward renewables generators for producing power without significant heed to conditions of demand. The UK government's support schemes, for example, like Germany's, enable renewables firms, under certain conditions, to generate profitably even at negative prices, and thus incentivize such generators, as the Cornwall report noted, 'to continue to produce when the market is otherwise oversupplied . . . [The schemes] provide generators with revenue based on volume of electricity produced, providing a simple prerogative to maximise output. No subsidy is paid when the generator is not producing, hence there is an opportunity cost for *not* generating.'[73]

Needless to say, if we assume that falling renewables costs do indeed depress wholesale electricity prices and that suppliers pass these lower wholesale prices on to users, then that, surely, is a good thing – at least from users' point of view. Yet, if lower power prices rooted in high renewables penetration is a boon for ratepayers, what about for the future of renewables investment? Here, the answer is: not so much. The more that the roll-out of renewables drives down wholesale prices over-all, the more that companies hoping to build the world's next generation of wind and solar farms are confronted with the prospect of a diminu-tion in the revenues that those future facilities can be expected to

---

72   Ibid.
73   Ibid. (emphasis added).

produce. To cite the Cornwall report one last time, the suppression of wholesale prices 'runs the risk of deterring investment' – just as happened at Fosen in Norway in 2015, readers will recall (from Chapter 5). It is, indeed, unimaginable that it would *not* elevate said risk. If the expected revenues available to prospective projects fall, 'how will these projects be financed?'[74]

And there is a closely related additional factor to consider here, too. What will also be remembered from Chapter 5 is the fact that, in view of wholesale price volatility, two electricity generators of different types, even if they have identical generating costs and produce and sell identical amounts of power over a given period, can earn markedly different revenues and profits if their respective output is traded at different times (of say a day or week). As various studies have found, the output of renewables facilities tends to be sold on wholesale markets disproportionately when electricity is cheap.[75] This stands to reason: sitting higher up the merit order stack, conventional generators, with pricier bids, are, by definition, not dispatched when prices are cheap – prices are cheap precisely *because* their dispatch is not required. The point now to be yoked to this foregoing insight, in any event, is that the more renewables production that occurs, and the more often that renewables set market clearing prices, the more broadly exposed renewables generators become to this phenomenon of price (and profit) suppression.

Readers will probably not be surprised to learn that there is a name for this paradoxical effect, whereby renewables potentially undermine the conditions of their own future viability and growth precisely by virtue of their own success in displacing more expensive, conventional generating technologies and thereby reducing the price of electricity. It is called, for obvious reasons, the cannibalization effect.

In other words, as if all the hurdles relating to price volatility and endemically low profitability enumerated to this point were not enough, there is a further problem to contend with: namely a tendency for renewables to eat themselves – or their progeny – alive as they increasingly become mass-market, price-setting propositions.

The result of all this is that, as they aim to accelerate the energy transition, policymakers have increasingly found themselves in the tricky

---

74   Ibid.
75   For example, Sandström, Staaf and Steinbeck, 'Vindkraft'.

position of trying to navigate between the Scylla and Charybdis of electricity prices that are too high or too low. Too high, and consumers suffer, and ask – reasonably enough – why they are not seeing the benefits of falling generation costs. Too low, and the furtherance of the transition is itself put in jeopardy because the economic incentive to build new zero-carbon capacity is diminished. The seriousness with which policymakers take the threat of cannibalization is evidenced by the fact that countries widely include the avoidance of such cannibalization among their explicit objectives in designing renewables support mechanisms.[76]

Sometimes, clearly, governments, and the electricity industries that their policies help to fashion, fail on the low side, which is to say that cannibalization does take place, as manifested most strikingly in the shape of negative prices. This cannibalization has happened historically, even if only ephemerally, but nevertheless with substantive effects – delayed or even cancelled installations of new renewables capacity, such as at Fosen in Norway in 2015 – across large parts of Europe and the US.

Meanwhile, sometimes, and even more clearly, the failure is on the high side. Indeed, sitting and writing the first draft of this section of the book in late 2022, when wholesale electricity prices across Europe, far from being negative, were as high as they had ever been, and when households across the continent were fearful of not being able to afford to heat their homes during winter . . . the very idea of negative power prices – still less the idea that such prices might be considered in any way problematic – felt almost cruelly comical. Why, exactly, the tendency for lower renewables generating costs to bring down market electricity prices evidently was not operative in Europe in 2022 is a question we will return to in Chapter 10.

To be sure, then, it can be hard sometimes, amid the cacophonic noise of the energy market, to discern the signal of the cannibalization effect. Negative – or even just low – prices? *We should be so lucky*, Europeans would doubtless have responded during the market turmoil of 2022. But the fact that the cannibalization effect was camouflaged – or, perhaps more accurately, smothered – by the turmoil does not

76  See, for example, P. del Río and C. J. Menzies, 'Auctions for the Support of Renewable Energy in Spain', D2.1-ES, September 2021, aures2project.eu, p. 6.

mean that this dynamic ceased to operate. In the background, it was still there, and its echoes occasionally still resonated, even against the tumult.

At that point in time, nobody imagined that negative prices would reoccur any time soon. But energy markets are wild, unpredictable phenomena, and, as ever, they would on this occasion rapidly make a mockery of even the most respected experts' prognostications. It turned out that by as early as May 2023 – which, in the context of the energy transition, is to say, within the mere blink of an eye – negative wholesale electricity prices had returned to large parts of Europe.


## VI


By the mid-2010s, the costs of producing wind and solar power had declined sufficiently far and fast that many governments around the world were pondering a significant adjustment of course. Having originally introduced subsidies and other support mechanisms in the light of the relative costliness of producing electricity renewably, now was the time, certain governments believed, to begin to withdraw or attenuate such mechanisms. The UK was one such government: as we saw in the previous chapter, it removed support for onshore wind projects in 2017. Within two years, multiple commentators had announced that the transition, more widely, to a subsidy-free era was indeed under way, and were actively discussing its potential implications.[77]

The move to reduce or eliminate state support for renewables raises all manner of questions. But one, of course, looms larger than all others. *Can* wind and solar power widely make do, even thrive, in the absence of substantive government support? To put the question another way: have the factors that made such support so valuable in the past lost some or all of their pertinence today? Or a third and final way: is it likely that renewable power will be developed as rapidly and expansively as the world needs, if it becomes more and more a

77   See, for example, A. Sankaran, 'Renewable Energy Is Taking Strides towards a Subsidy-Free Era, EY Report Reveals', 15 May 2019, ey.com; S. Dubos, 'Renewable Energy: Moving to a Subsidy-Free Environment', 4 June 2019, natixis.com; DLA Piper, 'Europe's Subsidy-Free Transition – The Road to Grid Parity', 19 December 2019, dlapiper.com.

political-economic constellation comprising strictly profit-seeking private actors and free market mechanisms?

The previous chapters and this one have identified already all manner of reasons to be doubtful in this regard. Further reasons will be identified later. But some influential commentators are nonetheless optimistic; the market *can* save the day, it is argued. We turn now in Chapter 8 to look at what, for many such optimists, is the supposed silver bullet.

# 8

# Market Failure

It is now time to go back to Norway. In earlier chapters, we considered the development of two different Norwegian onshore wind projects, one at Tellenes in the south and the other at Fosen in the west. Up to the point at which we left those respective stories, things had clearly gone much better and further at the former site than at the latter.

The key breakthrough at Tellenes came in 2016. Having been unable for several years to borrow money to finance construction, the project's developers – Zephyr and Norsk Vind Energi – finally found banks willing to loan them the necessary capital that year. This having been achieved, as we saw, the developers swiftly transferred ownership of the project to the giant US-based asset management firm BlackRock. Within around a year, the 168 MW wind farm was complete and generating power.

Meanwhile, up the coast at Fosen, development came to a standstill in mid-2015. Even as plans had seemingly been progressing smoothly until as late as autumn 2014, the lead developer of the project, the state-owned Statkraft, suddenly called a halt to proceedings. Wholesale electricity prices had plummeted to below €15 per MWh, casting doubt on whether the project would ever be able to turn a profit, and, in that bleak economic context, Statkraft and its development partners had been unable to achieve what they needed to achieve if construction were ever to go ahead – namely to secure additional equity financing from an external investor.

But 2016 turned out to be a breakthrough year for Fosen, too. Seemingly out of the blue, less than a year after the project had been shelved, Statkraft announced that it was back on. The project had been tweaked to improve projected profitability by planning for fewer and larger turbines at windier locations slightly further north. And, crucially, a new investor had successfully been found: Credit Suisse's energy asset management business, Energy Infrastructure Partners, invested an undisclosed sum in the project for a 40 per cent stake. Construction of what would become Europe's biggest onshore wind farm, with nearly 1 GW of installed capacity, began immediately, and by 2020 it was complete, though not without continuing protests by local Sámi communities.[1]

We have two different stories, then, from two different parts of Norway. Yet there is a vital dimension that evidently brings the two stories together. Both at Fosen and at Tellenes, the pivotal hold-up, we have seen, was raising funds, in the form of external equity in the former case and debt in the latter. It was the successful raising of such funds that ultimately broke the impasse in each case.

The parallels do not stop there, moreover. For what really unites Fosen and Tellenes – and makes their respective stories essentially a single story – is the question of precisely how this new funding was unlocked. To use the language we have been learning about in the preceding chapters of this book concerned with profitability and investment barriers, what exactly was it that in the final reckoning made Fosen and Tellenes 'bankable'? Why were projects that had been deemed uninvestible one day – or in Tellenes's case, for more than a decade – considered investible the next? In our prior discussion of Tellenes, we left this question hanging. In the case of Fosen, we did not even get to the point of the question being asked.

The answer turns out to be the same in both cases. Specifically, a major corporate electricity user entered the picture and signed a contract

---

1   Indeed, just a year later, Norway's Supreme Court judged that the facility was illegal, on the ground that it violated local reindeer herders' rights. At the time of this writing, however, the facility remains standing and continues to generate power, because the Norwegian government has not followed up on the court's decision – it appears to be hopeful that it can find mitigating measures, and thus an updated license that is not in breach of Sámi rights. See R. Milne, 'Greta Thunberg Accuses Norway of "Green Colonialism" over Wind Farm', *Financial Times*, 27 February 2023.

to purchase, for its own consumption, some or all of the electricity that would be generated by the proposed wind farm for many years to come – twelve years in the case of Tellenes, and fully twenty years in the case of Fosen. This proved decisive. At a press conference held to announce its equity investment in Fosen, for example, Credit Suisse's managing director, Dominik Bollier, emphasized that it was the long-term power purchase contract that 'finally provided' bankability.[2] Similarly at Tellenes. Once the agreement with the electricity buyer was in place, observed Zephyr director Olav Rommetveit, 'attracting investors to the project became easy'.[3]

Who were these all-important electricity buyers? At Fosen, it was the Norwegian aluminium company Norsk Hydro. To power its vast smelters, it contracted to take an annual supply of between 0.6 and 1 TWh for the period 2020–39, which on paper represented on average approximately one-third of the plant's total projected annual output. At Tellenes, Zephyr recruited a very different type of buyer. Contracting to purchase all of the electricity generated by the facility in order to help power its Northern European data centres, that buyer turned out to be none other than Google.

|

It will be remembered from Chapter 2 that, for unbundled electricity generation companies, bilateral power purchase agreements (PPAs) represent an alternative route to market than wholesale exchanges. That is to say, generating companies can sell power either on wholesale markets or via PPAs with specific off-takers. In many cases, they in fact do both: in other words, in any particular period, some output is delivered to off-takers under long-term contractual agreements while the remainder is sold on the spot market. Fosen in Norway is such a case – as we saw, Norsk Hydro contracted to take only a share of its vast output.

It will also be recalled from Chapter 2 that buyers of electricity under PPAs are of two main types. The first are electricity retailers (sometimes

2   J. Starn, 'Statkraft, Credit Suisse Fund to Invest \$1.2 Billion in Wind', 23 February 2016, bloomberg.com.

3   'Google Teams Up with Norway's Largest Wind Park', 30 June 2016, thelocal.no.

referred to alternatively as electricity suppliers or utilities). Instead of relying on wholesale markets to procure all the electricity that they resell to users, retailers can procure some of that electricity under so-called 'utility PPAs'.

The second main type of buyer is a large-scale institutional electricity user of some kind, which, unlike the aforementioned resellers, buys the electricity for its own consumption – thus allowing it precisely to disintermediate such resellers to one extent or another. Such a PPA is referred to as a 'corporate PPA', but it is important to recognize that, even though the buyer is indeed typically a private sector firm, it does not have to be; what matters is that the purchase is for their own use. In 2019, for example, twenty UK universities collectively signed a ten-year PPA to take (and use) electricity generated at a portfolio of Scottish and Welsh wind farms owned by Norway's Statkraft.[4] The following year, the City of London Corporation, the UK capital city's municipal governing body, entered into a fifteen-year off-take deal with a solar farm in Dorset owned by the French power producer Voltalia.[5]

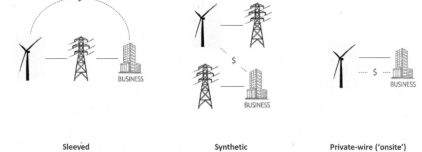

Figure 8.1 Types of corporate power purchase agreement
Source: Author

4   J. Ambrose, 'UK Universities in Landmark Deal to Buy Energy Direct from Windfarms', *Guardian*, 7 October 2019.
5   M. Lempriere, 'City of London Corporation Signs First of Its Kind £40m PPA for Dorset Solar Site', 18 November, solarpowerportal.co.uk. Note that, strictly speaking, there is also a third type of buyer under an electricity PPA. This is where a government uses a state-owned vehicle specifically to make contractual payments to renewables generating companies under support mechanisms such as feed-in tariffs or feed-in premiums. These instances are not included in our consideration of PPAs in this chapter, which restricts the PPA phenomenon to contracts undertaken between market actors and not explicitly involving government support measures.

While utility PPAs have existed for decades and are a feature of the worlds of both conventional and renewable power generation, corporate PPAs are of more recent vintage – dating to the late 2000s – and are largely a renewables phenomenon. They come in three main varieties in terms of financing structure and electricity delivery arrangements (Figure 8.1). The first is the 'sleeved' PPA, which is the most common variant in Europe. Under this arrangement, the generator and off-taker must be connected to the same transmission grid, through which the transmission operator (for a fee) 'sleeves' the electricity that the two parties have contracted to exchange. The second is a 'synthetic' PPA, more common in the US, and so-called because the off-taker does not actually purchase electricity from the generator; they do not even need to be connected to the same grid. Instead, they each buy or sell on the spot market, but separately enter into a private financial contract that serves to replicate the terms of a direct purchase through hedging against merchant prices. Third, finally, less commonly and typically on a much smaller scale, there are private-wire or 'onsite' PPAs. Here, generation occurs at or near the off-taker's premises, and the electricity is distributed directly from one party to the other rather than being routed through the grid.

In terms of bilateral contracts specifically with renewables generators, far and away the key trend of the past decade or so has been a relative shift from utility to corporate PPAs. This occurred first, and fastest, in solar and onshore wind. As a 2021 report on the global offshore wind industry by the US Department of Energy noted, 'conventional utility off-takers . . . dominated offshore wind procurements until 2018'.[6] But, even in offshore wind, where generating capacity is generally higher and, accordingly, off-take expectations are generally larger, the growing role of corporate PPAs is now also evident. Deals have been coming thick and fast in the past five years. In 2019, for instance, Northumbrian Water agreed the UK's first offshore wind corporate PPA, a ten-year deal for around 30 per cent of the electricity generated by Ørsted's 573 MW Race Bank Offshore Wind Farm. The next year, Amazon signed a carbon-copy deal for a share of the output – again around 30 per cent, and again for a decade – of the Borkum Riffgrund 3 offshore facility, also with Ørsted.

---

6   US Department of Energy, 'Offshore Wind Market Report: 2021', August 2021, energy.gov, p. 80.

Insofar as the output deals struck by the developers of Norway's Fosen and Tellenes onshore wind projects were also corporate rather than utility PPAs, they were, in other words, very much representative signs of changed times. Corporate PPAs have surged in importance since the early 2010s. Globally, the amount of wind and solar power procured annually under such agreements increased no less than a hundredfold between 2012 and 2021, from around 300 MW to more than 30 GW.[7]

A prime illustrative example of a place where the shift from utility to corporate renewables PPAs has played out is the US – or, at least, those parts of the US where the conventional electricity industry operating model of vertically integrated regional monopolies has been swept away. Take Texas. From the earliest days of liberalization of the state's electricity sector, utility PPAs were a cornerstone feature.[8] By the early 2010s, however, the landscape was clearly changing. On the one hand, there was, reported Michael Copley, a distinct, unprecedented dearth of such utility PPAs. On the other hand, however, corporate PPAs were appearing in their place, examples being Wal-Mart's deal to buy power from Pattern Energy's wind farm at Logan's Gap and Dow Chemical's contract with the Javelina Wind Energy Center, developed by Bordas Wind Energy.[9]

Across the US as a whole, the proportion of new renewables projects that were financed and built with corporate PPAs in place had increased to around 25 per cent already by the mid-2010s, despite the fact that such agreements did not feature at all in the relatively large number of states where utilities retained local vertical monopolies.[10] The flip side to this trend was the waning of utility PPAs: in the space of just two years, from 2012 to 2014, the share of new US wind capacity commissioned with utility PPAs in place slumped from 76 to 40 per cent.[11]

---

7   N. Bullard, 'Why Clean Energy's Corporate Patrons Are Buying Less This Year', 8 September 2022, bloomberg.com.

8   On the importance of utility PPAs to the early development of US wind power, not just in Texas but nationally, see M. J. Barradale, 'Impact of Public Policy Uncertainty on Renewable Energy Investment: Wind Power and the Production Tax Credit', *Energy Policy* 38 (2010), pp. 7702–3.

9   M. Copley, 'Questions Grow about the Appetite for More Hedged Wind in Texas', *SNL Power Daily*, 20 May 2015.

10   Two Lights Energy Consulting, 'A Virtuous Circle: Scaling Up Investment in Low Carbon Energy', November 2017, actalliance.org, p. 13.

11   H. K. Trabish, 'The Other Death Spiral Utilities Are Beginning to Deal With', 6 August 2015, utilitydive.com.

Companies like NextEra Energy have ridden this particular wave just as much as they have ridden the US's renewables tax credit wave (Chapter 7). Ever since it diversified into independent power generation, NextEra's strategy, in its own words, has been 'to enter into long-term bilateral contracts for the full output of its [renewables] generation facilities'.[12] In the 2000s and early 2010s, that principally meant utility PPAs. In fact, NextEra (then called Florida Power & Light) began developing wind assets explicitly backed by utility PPAs as early as the late 1990s, with examples including a plant at Vansycle Ridge in Oregon, which would sell its output to Portland General Electric, and one near Clear Lake in Iowa, which would generate for Interstate Power and Light. By the mid-2010s, however, such deals had taken a backseat; NextEra was, reported Russell Gold, 'expanding beyond its traditional utility customers to build wind farms and solar parks [supplying] large corporations such as Google'.[13] What remained consistent throughout was the strategic emphasis on long-term contracts, whoever the customer happened to be; at year-end 2020, more than 90 per cent of NextEra's net renewable generating capacity was committed under such contracts.[14]

## II

In much of all this, however, including with regard to the key generalized trend of a recent and ongoing shift from utility to corporate PPAs in the renewables space, there has been and still is significant variance from country to country.

First of all, power purchase agreements in general – which is to say, as a broad phenomenon, encompassing all different subtypes, whether renewable or non-renewable – are much more important in some countries than in others. Of course, it is only in countries where the electricity supply chain has been vertically unbundled (see Chapter 2) that PPAs play any role at all: they are, by definition, agreements entered into specifically *by generators*, which is to say companies that either have

---

12   NextEra Energy, 'Annual Report 2020', nexteraenergy.com, p. 17.
13   R. Gold, 'Green-Power King Thrives on Government Subsidies', *Wall Street Journal*, 19 June 2018.
14   NextEra Energy, 'Annual Report 2020', p. 17.

no local distribution assets or (under these agreements) are able to circumvent such assets. Yet, even as between countries that indeed have in large measure unbundled their electricity sectors, there is significant variance in PPA penetration.

Thus, at one extreme, there are countries such as India. To ensure the availability of sufficient generating capacity, regional DISCOMs, most of which are state-owned, run auctions at which generators bid to establish capacity. The successful bidders are awarded long-term PPAs – utility PPAs, to use our classification – with the relevant DISCOMs, lasting anywhere from seven to twenty-five years. Alongside these competitively awarded agreements there are also utility PPAs that have been awarded non-competitively, and which are held by state-owned generators. Of all electricity traded in India, 90 per cent or more is procured under such long-term utility PPAs of one sort or another.[15] The result is a quasi–merit order 'within' each of DISCOM's universe of contracted suppliers. 'To meet the majority of their daily power needs,' explains Kartikeya Singh, 'DISCOMs "self-schedule" generation from the portfolio of generators with whom they hold these long-term contracts.'[16]

As well as the vast array of such utility PPAs, India also has an emerging corporate PPA market. Large, so-called 'open-access' consumers can contract to buy power directly from any generator, at competitive rates, rather than through the local DISCOM, as for example ArcelorMittal Nippon Steel, to power one of its mills, did in 2022, signing a long-term deal with the Hyderabad-based Greenko Group for part of the output of its new 5 GW renewables mega-plant at Kurnool in Andhra Pradesh.

Meanwhile, much of the small amount of power that is traded on India's nascent spot market is itself in fact 'excess' power that has been contracted for under long-term utility PPAs, but which, in the event, proves surplus to local demand at the particular moment of its generation. The point, in short, is that the Indian electricity market into which generators sell *is*, essentially, the PPA market. Formal wholesale market exchanges play, for the time being at least, a peripheral role.

At the other extreme, one can point to a country such as Denmark. Its electricity sector represents more or less a mirror image of India's in

---

15   IEA, 'Renewables Integration in India', June 2021, iea.org, p. 76.
16   K. Singh, 'Creating a National Electricity Market: India's Most Important Power Sector Reform', 19 August 2019, csis.org.

terms of the relative significance of different transactional mechanisms. Whereas 90 per cent or more of electricity is sold under long-term PPAs in India, rendering spot markets marginal, the latter account for approximately 80 per cent of electricity trade in Denmark.[17] This renders PPAs marginal: not only is only a relatively small quantum of electricity traded via bilateral PPAs in Denmark, but also, partly as a result, the spot price strongly influences the prices stipulated by such PPAs as are signed. In India, the direction of influence tends to be the reverse.

In turn, corporate PPAs, more specifically, are also much more significant a phenomenon in some countries than in others. As intimated earlier, the US is one of the places where corporate PPAs have increasingly substituted for utility PPAs, and, looking at the global corporate PPA map as a whole, one sees that that map is, in fact, very much US-dominated. BloombergNEF estimates that, globally since 2010, the Americas have accounted for around two-thirds of all clean electricity purchased by corporations for their own consumption under long-term PPAs, with the US consistently contributing over 80 per cent of deal volumes in the Americas.[18]

Outside the US, corporate PPAs are largely a European phenomenon: deals agreed in territories other than Europe and the Americas, which means principally Asia, historically have represented less than 10 per cent of the global market. Though the shift from utility to corporate PPAs has occurred more slowly, and later, in Europe than in the US, the trend is nonetheless indisputable there too, and in 2021 corporate deals surpassed utility deals in Europe for the first time: across the continent, generators contracted for 6.5 GW of capacity under corporate PPAs, versus only 4.6 GW under utility PPAs.[19]

The picture within Europe is just as geographically variegated as the global one. Some large countries with large populations, economies and electricity sectors – the likes of France, Germany and Italy – have seen

---

17   P. E. Morthorst and T. Ackermann, 'Economic Aspects of Wind Power in Power Systems', in T. Ackermann, ed, *Wind Power in Wind Systems*, 2nd edn (Chichester: Wiley, 2012), p. 501.

18   BloombergNEF, 'Corporate Clean Energy Buying Tops 30 GW Mark in Record Year', 31 January 2022, bnef.com.

19   Pexapark, 'Market Volatility in 2021 Leads to Fundamental Changes for Renewable Energy PPAs', 10 February 2022, pexapark.com.

almost no significant corporate PPA activity. Most of the activity that has occurred, predominantly in wind power, has been concentrated in Northern Europe, namely in the Netherlands, Norway and Sweden.[20] In other words, the Fosen and Tellenes projects, at least in terms of their geographical and technological attributes, are very much exemplars of European corporate PPAs more widely. Meanwhile, since around 2018, a significant European market for solar corporate PPAs, led thus far by Spain, has also begun to develop.

Lastly, there is one important dimension on which we find much less variance from place to place. This concerns the main types of customers for corporate PPAs, and in this regard, Tellenes, of our two Norwegian case studies, is the more typical, for the biggest players on the buy side of the corporate PPA market, both specifically within Europe and also at the global level, are consistently ICT (information and communications technology) firms – that is, the likes of Google.

'The tech companies really do dominate the whole market from a size perspective,' Miranda Ballentine, head of the Renewable Energy Buyers Alliance, has observed of the corporate PPA space.[21] Alongside Google, the other major such buyers of renewable power under corporate PPAs, all in the position of needing to consume vast amounts of electricity to run and to keep cool their proliferating server farms, are Amazon, Apple, Facebook and Microsoft. The combined power consumption of these five now compares to that of whole countries such as Hungary, New Zealand, Peru or Portugal.

Of the five firms, the main driver of the market for corporate PPAs has increasingly been Amazon. In 2022, it was reported that, to date, Amazon globally had purchased under bilateral contracts some 19 GW of clean power – more than double the amount for which the next-largest corporate purchaser, Microsoft, had historically contracted, and indeed not far short of total historic corporate PPA volumes across the whole of Europe.[22]

---

20   G. Brindley, 'Financing and Investment Trends: The European Wind Industry in 2019', April 2020, windeurope.org, pp. 31–5.

21   Cited in L. Hook and D. Lee, 'How Tech Went Big on Green Energy', *Financial Times*, 10 February 2021.

22   Bullard, 'Why Clean Energy's Corporate Patrons Are Buying Less This Year'.

## III

To account for the shape of the PPA market – its commonalities, but even more so its variances, both historical and geographical – the best place to start is with the key parties to these contracts. What motivates off-takers of various types, on the one hand, and generators, on the other, to enter such contracts in the first place? And, when they do so, what are their respective priorities? If we understand what the main participants want out of the market, and how they have approached and sought to shape the market as a result, we can go a long way to explaining why the market has evolved in the way it has. Needless to say, our focus will be mainly on renewables.

Let us start with electricity retailers, and thus utility PPAs. The main reason utilities and other electricity resellers enter into bilateral purchase agreements with generating companies is to ensure security of power supply, where they do not possess (sufficient) generating capacity of their own. Needless to say, the incentive to use such agreements specifically to secure future supply is greater in countries, such as India, where wholesale spot markets are thin and illiquid. Insofar as security of supply is the principal motivating factor, utility PPAs tend to be baseload contracts, meaning that the off-taker buys a specified (and typically constant) volume of energy every hour of each month. 'Long term contracts', Jon Hinrichs and colleagues observed in the pre-corporate-PPA era, 'are based on providing base load energy.'[23] We will return shortly to why this is important.

As well as usually being baseload contracts, utility PPAs typically also feature variable pricing; that is to say, if the volume of power being traded is constant, the price at which it is traded is not. Again, this is readily explicable: resellers can generally pass price increases on to consumers, of whom only a minority are ever on fixed-price contracts of their own, and are therefore comfortable with supply-side price volatility. Hence, utility PPA prices are usually indexed to the spot market – so-called 'mark-to-market' contracts. Exceptions, to which we shall return, include countries where spot markets are peripheral, or retail prices are highly regulated, or (as in India) both.

23   J. Hinrichs, M. Hayes and B. Blankenhorn, 'Commercial Wind Farm Development', 26 September 2007, colorado.edu, p. 6.

This does not mean that electricity retailers in highly liberalized markets never sign PPAs that incorporate an element of price stabilization. But, where they do, this is usually in the form of floor rather than fixed prices, and they ordinarily only agree to such stabilization for the period over which the forward market contains sufficient liquidity to enable reliable hedging of the associated price risk. Thus, in the UK, for example, a reseller might sign a PPA with a generator for as long as, say, ten to twelve years, but historically only the first three years, at most, of such a contract would have been for a floor price or a fixed price.[24] Again, as we will see, this matters.

In terms of utility PPAs agreed specifically with renewables generators, off-takers' motivating factor in signing such agreements – in place of or in addition to the more general rationale of supply security – has principally been purchase obligations imposed by the government or regulators. The latter have in many countries required that a minimum proportion of the electricity that companies sell to consumers is cleanly sourced.

Certainly, in some such countries, ranging from India to the UK, renewable energy certificate schemes have allowed obligated entities to meet these requirements partly or fully without actually contracting directly with a renewable generator – the certificates are bought and sold separately from the power to which they pertain. Nevertheless, for suppliers lacking (whether by choice or by regulation) their own renewable generating assets, one or more PPAs with a wind or solar farm have been one principal way, and in some places the only way, to fulfil the obligations in question. 'Regional utilities facing state mandates often didn't have the know-how to build wind farms,' one observer has noted, for instance, of the US in the early 2000s, 'so many requested bids to buy the power from someone else.'[25]

Notably, the US is today experiencing something of a reprise of that phenomenon of twenty years earlier, albeit now in relation to offshore wind. Policymakers are keen to stimulate installations of the new technology, but they appreciate that utilities generally do not have the know-how or desire to develop offshore capacity themselves. Thus several

---

24   Solar Trade Association, 'Making Solar Pay: The Future of the Solar PPA Market in the UK', October 2016, resources.solarbusinesshub.com, p. 12.

25   Gold, 'Green-Power King Thrives on Government Subsidies'.

coastal states have in recent years found ways to encourage or compel local utilities to sign long-term contracts with offshore developers for new generating capacity. Such contracts in fact represent one of the few contexts today in the Global North in which electricity suppliers – sometimes, but not always – enter into PPAs with long-term fixed prices. Examples can be found among the offshore PPA contracts that, since 2016, the state of Massachusetts has required its utilities to sign. Some feature prices fixed for twenty-year terms.

Turning now to corporations such as Amazon, Google and Norsk Hydro, which sign (corporate) PPAs to procure electricity for their own consumption, there is, again, a range of motivations, of which two are paramount. The first of these, and probably the dominant one, pertains to public relations. As we have seen, such companies use vast quantities of electricity. Insofar as such electricity is generated from the burning of fossil fuels, the companies in question can be – and often have been – regarded as major contributors to the global warming phenomenon. By contrast, if they use electricity that has been generated renewably, it becomes possible for the likes of Amazon to depict themselves not only as not being part of the climate problem, but, more powerfully still, as being part of the solution.

For companies so often in the public spotlight (and usually not in a good way), this is an opportunity that has been far too good to pass up. 'We're one of the largest buyers of renewable energy in the world,' Facebook's Mark Zuckerberg proudly proclaimed in 2021, 'resulting in $8 billion invested in 63 wind and solar projects around the world, creating tens of thousands of jobs.'[26] Comparable feel-good proclamations accompany the announcement of essentially all substantial corporate PPAs for renewable electricity. The burnishing of green credentials, in short, is arguably the main rationale for off-takers to enter such agreements and helps explain why corporate PPAs *are* almost always renewables PPAs.

But there is a second significant rationale for large corporate users to sign PPAs. If electricity resellers are typically sanguine about electricity price volatility, corporate consumers typically are anything but. For the purposes of corporate planning, if nothing else, it can be enormously

---

26   Cited in D. Swinhoe, 'Amazon Announces Nine Renewable Energy Projects across Europe and North America', 21 April 2021, datacenterdynamics.com.

helpful for major consumers of power to know whether, in future, they will be paying closer to $10 or $100 per MWh consumed – unpredictability of significant items of expenditure intrinsically compromises meaningful planning capacity. Electricity retailers, for their part, will often allow for consumers (corporate or household) to fix prices for one year, perhaps two years, ahead, but never for longer than that – or at least, not at a non-prohibitive cost.

If it were the case, then, that, under corporate PPAs, users such as Facebook or Norsk Hydro could secure future electricity supply at fixed prices lasting five, ten years or more, it would clearly be an extremely valuable option. The fact that such an arrangement would also entail circumventing the electricity market middleman, mark-up and all, would merely represent the metaphorical icing on the cake.

Might renewables generators, in their turn, also have an incentive of their own to enter into such fixed-price long-term contracts? To find out, it is time to consider the motivations of the companies selling power under PPAs, as opposed to those purchasing and off-taking it.

## IV

It turns out that renewables generators indeed are widely willing to enter bilateral contracts to sell electricity at fixed prices for the long term. It is, of course, not difficult to understand that they should be so: such willingness goes to the very heart of the profitability and investment challenges inherent in today's renewables business, as we have described them in earlier chapters.

When considering the motivations of generators vis-à-vis PPAs, and especially generators seeking to develop greenfield wind or solar facilities (as opposed to selling the power of facilities already in operation), the overriding concern to consider is typically that of bankability: that is, do financial institutions regard the generator and its prospective or existing assets as a viable investment proposition, bearing an acceptable level of risk? Generators evaluate the opportunities occasioned by PPAs first and foremost in the bankability light. This is the case more or less everywhere. In India, for example, where utility PPAs dominate electricity trading and spot markets are peripheral, such PPAs, as the

IEA has observed, 'ensure the bankability of projects, which can then obtain financing'.[27] But it is especially the case in places where wholesale spot markets dominate electricity trade, such as Europe and large parts of the US.

In such places, as we have seen, the volatility of spot prices represents an existential threat to project bankability: for the most part, lenders simply will not support new solar or wind farms where their output will be sold wholly or largely into the spot market, at least absent a meaningful hedging instrument. The risk is considered too great. As such, and as we have also already seen, any mechanism that potentially provides long-term price and revenue stability harbours considerable value to renewables developers inasmuch as it can help to satisfy risk-averse bankers. If government feed-in tariffs and the like represent one such mechanism (and easily the most important historically), then fixed-price long-term corporate PPAs are clearly another, whereas utility PPAs – generally featuring variable, mark-to-market pricing, as noted above – conspicuously are not.

In other words, what we find with corporate PPAs in US and European renewables markets is a propitious alignment of interests around long-term fixed prices. It is in the interest of both the off-taker and the generator (or, more accurately and consequentially, the generator's lender) that the contracted electricity price should be fixed. This fixing – and the investment it crystallizes – is in fact the very kernel of the corporate PPA phenomenon.

Thus it is no coincidence that the prices agreed both by Norsk Hydro at Fosen and Google at Tellenes were fixed for the duration of the respective contracts, which were for twenty and twelve years respectively. Such fixing is the norm in the renewables corporate PPA space. The significance of this fixing lies precisely in the guarantee of stability and hence the mitigation of revenue risk. The PPA with Norsk Hydro, for example, enabled Statkraft to attract financing from Credit Suisse and thus revivify the stalled Fosen project specifically insofar, Credit Suisse acknowledged, as the contract offered 'the cash-flow stability needed'.[28] Similarly, at Tellenes, it was the success of the PPA with Google in

27   IEA, 'Renewables Integration in India', p. 76.
28   Starn, 'Statkraft, Credit Suisse Fund to Invest $1.2 Billion in Wind'.

effecting the 'removal of electricity pricing risk' that unlocked project financing.[29]

We see much the same thing in the few cases in liberalized electricity markets where utility PPAs likewise feature long-term fixed rather than variable prices. The primary rationale for PPAs in these circumstances is to fashion bankability, and where bankability is indeed achieved in practice, fixed prices are typically acknowledged to be the principal source of that bankability. Consider again the instructive case of offshore wind and the US state of Massachusetts. The 2016 legislation that requires Massachusetts utilities to enter long-term contracts with offshore developers does so 'to facilitate the financing of offshore wind energy generation'.[30] In turn, utilities that have signed such contracts and with fixed prices – as, for instance, the local utility units of National Grid USA, Eversource Energy, and Unitil Corporation did in 2018 and 2019 – did so, they said, 'solely in order to facilitate the financing of the [offshore] facility'.[31]

Of course, just because a PPA provides fixed prices and therefore mitigates the revenue risk faced by generators, it does not necessarily mitigate profit risk, any more than government-provided, fixed-price feed-in tariffs themselves do. Such fixed-price instruments certainly assure generator profitability if actual construction and financing costs (and to a much lesser degree of significance, operating costs) are broadly in line with, or lower than, those projected at the time of the project being scoped. But costs can change.

Certain developers that had entered into contracts with Massachusetts utilities to develop wind power off the coast of that state, for example, subsequently saw rapid inflation in raw material costs and interest rates before being able to actually raise the necessary finance and purchase turbines, let alone begin installation work. Now, the projects looked distinctly unprofitable, fixed prices or no, and one such developer, Avangrid, a subsidiary of the Spanish energy giant Iberdrola, filed a motion in late 2022 to have a signed contract annulled. Indeed, it did so

---

29    Two Lights Energy Consulting, 'A Virtuous Circle', p. 13.

30    General Court of the Commonwealth of Massachusetts, 'An Act to Promote Energy Diversity', Bill H.4568, 8 August 2016.

31    Commonwealth of Massachusetts, Department of Public Utilities, 'Joint Initial Brief on Behalf of Massachusetts Electric Company and Nantucket Electric Company d/b/a National Grid, NSTAR Electric Company d/b/a Eversource Energy, and Fitchburg Gas and Electric Light Company d/b/a Unitil', 14 August 2020, p. 52.

precisely on the ground that the state's legal threshold for such PPAs – that they should facilitate financing – was no longer met. The motion failed. That Avangrid was willing in mid-2023 to pay its utility counterparties nearly $50 million to exit that particular contract is a measure of just how unattractive its terms had become.

Essentially, such instances represent the inverse of what we saw happen in Spain in 2007–10 (Chapter 7), when, from Iberdrola's perspective, the shoe was on the other foot. Long-term fixed-price output deals – whether with government (as with the Spanish feed-in tariffs) or with market actors (as with the Massachusetts PPAs) – internalize assumptions about generators' likely costs. If those assumptions prove substantially erroneous on the high side, the result is likely to be windfall generator profits; if the assumptions are erroneous on the low side, the result is likely to be the opposite.

In any event, in incorporating fixed prices, the likes of the Massachusetts offshore contracts were, as we have seen, very much exceptions to the rule: fixed prices on renewables PPAs, at least in the Global North, are largely limited to the corporate off-take market. Meanwhile, if, from the generator's perspective, the superior bankability of such corporate PPAs versus their utility counterparts is indeed rooted principally in the phenomenon of fixed (versus variable) pricing, it also has an additional significant dimension. As we saw earlier, utility PPAs are generally baseload PPAs, whereby the off-taker contracts to purchase a specified volume of power. Corporate PPAs, by contrast, are usually 'pay-as-produced' contracts, meaning that the buyer takes all, or a fixed percentage, of the generator's power output, no matter what the production profile is. Again, Fosen and Tellenes are cases in point.[32]

The significance of this? Under pay-as-produced deals, the generating facility assumes no trading risk. But baseload deals are another matter: if the generator fails to meet the specified demand because, say, wind speeds are too low, it must acquire the shortfall on the spot market – where, of course, the price is unpredictable. 'While debt can be raised on the back of such baseload PPAs,' one investor has explained, 'it is

---

32 And here is another respect in which the offshore-wind PPAs signed by Massachusetts utilities such as Eversource and Unitil were in fact much more like corporate PPAs than standard utility PPAs: they, too, were for all the power delivered by the projects with which they contracted.

inherently risky for the bank since the seller needs to be able to show that he [*sic*] can properly trade the market and buy electricity when his project is not producing. This is not something all developers can do, so it makes project finance more challenging.'[33] *Not* usually being baseload deals is thus another reason why lenders prefer corporate PPAs, and why generators share that preference.

Essentially, then, in places where corporate PPAs have increasingly supplanted utility PPAs as a route to market for renewables generators, it is in large part because they are inherently the more bankable type of agreement. But it is worth noting, too, that the superiority of the former from the perspective of the generator has been further reinforced all the while by a gradual but unmistakeable deterioration in the quality and scope of the opportunity afforded by the latter, for all that exceptions such as in the US offshore landscape do exist.

For a variety of reasons, there simply are, for one thing, increasingly few utility PPA offers on the table. Already by the mid-2010s, the UK PPA market, for example, had reportedly seen the 'almost complete withdrawal of the large [utility off-takers]'.[34] Furthermore, those few utility offers that have remained on the table have themselves tended to become less attractive to generators. One reason for this twofold trend – not just in the UK but internationally, and especially in Global North territories – has been electricity retailers meeting the renewables targets set for them by governments: if new such targets are not set, a primary motivation for retail suppliers to enter into bilateral contracts with wind or solar farms disappears. Another reason has, as it so often does, to do with credit constraints. Credit-rating agencies have adopted more stringent treatments of the balance sheet liabilities that, for off-takers, long-term PPAs represent, and electricity resellers have adjusted terms, unfavourably for generators, accordingly.

In what specific way or ways have the (fewer) available utility PPAs become progressively less attractive to renewables generators, thereby further militating against the bankability of such contracts? There are two principal, linked answers to this. The first relates to pricing. As we have seen, utility-PPA off-takers have always been reluctant to offer generators

---

33    Email to author, 4 October 2021.
34    Baringa Partners, 'Power Purchase Agreements for Independent Renewable Generators – An Assessment of Existing and Future Market Liquidity', July 2013, gov.uk, p. 12.

price stability; where they have done so, it has usually been in the form of floor pricing. But, over the years, terms have become even more parsimonious, particularly on deals with anything other than very limited duration. One UK electricity supplier, for instance, acknowledged that 'whilst our short-term PPAs . . . remain competitive, the structures we can offer for long-term PPAs have become increasingly restricted'.[35]

The linked aspect of the deterioration of terms on utility PPAs concerns contract duration itself, which has widely shortened. In India, for example, in an environment of 'underutilised and unutilised generating capacities', a growing trend for DISCOMs to offer shorter PPA terms was reported as early as 2016.[36] The following year, in the US, it was likewise reported that utility off-takers that had previously offered solar developers 'generous long-term contracts' were now offering 'shorter-term fixed prices with a higher subsequent exposure to variable wholesale prices'.[37] Today, globally, utility PPAs are usually characterized by shorter contract periods than corporate PPAs.[38]

Of course, all of this is highly contingent on the local industry and regulatory context. Are corporate PPAs even allowed? Do Amazon, Google and the other big tech companies, which represent the main buy-side participants in the corporate PPA market, operate server farms in the countries in question? (In Europe, most such farms are located in colder, northern climes, fuelling the Scandinavian corporate PPA market while doing nothing to help the market in, say, Iberia.) And, more significantly perhaps than anything else, do *other* meaningful mechanisms exist to fashion the price and revenue stability that is so consequential to generators and their financial backers? From the perspective of the latter, there is much less need for a fixed-price PPA if, for instance, feed-in tariffs are readily available.

---

35   Ibid. More widely, beyond the UK, see B. Christophers, 'Taking Renewables to Market: Prospects for the After-Subsidy Energy Transition', *Antipode* 54 (2022), p. 1532.

36   S. Jog, 'Discoms Keen on Shorter Power Purchase Pacts Instead of 25-Year Contracts', 10 May 2016, business-standard.com.

37   'A World Turned Upside Down', *Economist*, 25 February 2017.

38   Baringa Partners, 'Corporate PPA Policy in Ireland: Final Report', December 2020, seai.ie, p. 39; 'Power Purchase Agreement', roedl.com (as of November 2022).

Thus it is exactly as one would expect that corporate PPAs have generally been less notable a phenomenon in places where government support schemes for renewables explicitly offer price stabilization than in either, first, places where little meaningful external support of any kind has been available, or, second, those where such support is available but does not actively stabilize output prices. We can briefly consider three example countries, one in each of these three categories, to help make the point.

The UK, with its long-standing, price-stabilizing feed-in tariff and then Contracts for Difference schemes (Chapter 6), is an example of a location where corporate PPAs were long relatively marginal, because largely unnecessary.[39] It is noteworthy, and readily explicable, that the UK's corporate PPA market only began to show significant signs of life, principally onshore, when, from 2018, solar and onshore wind were cut off from the main aforementioned government support schemes, which were then reoriented towards offshore wind.

Sweden, by contrast, has long been a significant market for corporate PPAs, partly by dint of a historically rather ineffectual government support scheme. Unlike much of the rest of Europe, Sweden has not provided support through feed-in tariffs or other such stability-oriented subsidies. Instead, such support as has been proffered to renewables generators has consisted principally of the incremental revenue that they are able to generate by selling clean energy certificates. In practice, however, this has amounted to decidedly thin gruel. Market prices for renewables certificates in Sweden have been low almost from the start, thus greatly augmenting the value to local wind and solar generators of instruments such as corporate PPAs, while also helping to explain the particular profitability challenges faced by the country's renewables sector (Chapter 7).

Lastly, the US is an example of the final country type. It has, of course, historically offered very generous tax subsidies, but, as we have seen, these, unlike feed-in tariffs, do not stabilize power prices. Hence, in part, the long-term buoyancy of its corporate PPA market. Indeed, corporate PPAs have frequently served to render bankable US renewables projects that are also supported by tax equity financing and investment

---

39   M. Grubb and P. Drummond, 'UK Industrial Electricity Prices: Competitiveness in a Low Carbon World', February 2018, ucl.ac.uk, p. 8.

or production credits, but which would likely not have proceeded without the PPA.[40]

In any event, in 2022, in the context of increasingly volatile domestic wholesale market prices and thus an augmented desire for mechanisms of price stabilization among both renewables generators and large corporate energy consumers, the corporate procurement of clean energy in the US under long-term PPAs reached a record high of 20 GW. The details of the deals that made up this 20 GW provide an illuminating and instructive snapshot of the basic complexion of the world's single largest and most important corporate PPA market at the time of this writing.[41]

Solar dominated the market, accounting for around 80 per cent of the newly contracted capacity. In terms of deal structure, synthetic (or 'virtual') PPAs were similarly dominant, representing some 85 per cent of deal activity. Meanwhile, just as overall contracted capacity was larger than ever before, so too, at 178 MW, was the average size of the newly announced PPAs, of which there were 112 in total. Finally, and emblematically, Amazon continued to tower over the rest of the sector: around fifty different off-takers signed corporate PPAs in the US in 2022, but Amazon alone, with deals in sixteen different states, was responsible for over 40 per cent of the new capacity.

## V

Notwithstanding the considerable variance from place to place enumerated thus far, the crux of the trend of the past decade or so is nonetheless crystal clear. Corporate PPAs have increasingly come to represent an integral component of the global landscape of renewable power, and especially its financing. Even China is now on board. In 2022, for example, in one of the first major deals of the kind in the country involving two foreign actors, Canada's Brookfield Renewable signed a twenty-five-year contract to supply electricity to the German multinational

---

40   See for example CohnReznick, 'US Renewable Energy Brief: The Tax Equity Investment Landscape', 1 September 2017, ourenergypolicy.org, p. 5; S. Golden, 'What Engie's Tax Equity Deal Tells Us about Financing Renewables', 1 May 2020, greenbiz.com.

41   BloombergNEF, 'Sustainable Energy in America 2023 Factbook', March 2023, bnef.com, p. 37.

chemicals producer BASF's Zhanjiang Verbund site in southern China, using that contract as the basis for the local development of a suite of new solar and wind farms.

In fact, already by the mid- to late 2010s, in places such as Norway, Sweden and large parts of the US where spot markets reign and other sources of price stabilization are absent, corporate PPAs had become nothing less than 'essential to make projects bankable', in the words of the professional services firm DLA Piper.[42] We have, of course, seen direct evidence of this essentialness ourselves: neither Fosen nor Tellenes would have gone ahead without their PPA agreements being in place.

Conversations held with numerous European-based bankers in 2021 amply confirmed this growing essentialness, and for a widening range of territories. The statement by one such banker, whose firm finances solar and wind projects continent-wide, that 'we are generally only funding projects that have corporate PPA contracts', was broadly representative.[43] 'Where there are no subsidies', conceded the executive of a firm that advises renewables developers on raising finance, 'developers and banks *have* to look to corporate PPAs.'[44]

This actually existing significance is certainly one reason for us having discussed PPAs, and especially corporate PPAs, at some length in this chapter. But it is not, in fact, the main reason. The primary reason why corporate PPAs are so significant to the argument developed in this book has to do less with the role that such agreements have played in electricity markets historically than with the role they increasingly are expected to play in future. This warrants elaboration.

For all that an energy transition led and steered by private capital and market mechanisms is, by any reasonable climate measure, failing, the powers that be continue to believe and maintain that markets and the private sector remain our best bet. Some such protagonists merely take this on faith. Others, however, do seek to provide substance to justify the belief in the transformative power of markets and capital, and, increasingly, corporate PPAs feature centrally in the arguments they make.

---

42   DLA Piper, 'Europe's Subsidy-Free Transition: The Road to Grid Parity', December 2019, dlapiper.com, p. 8.

43   Interview with author, 11 February 2021.

44   Interview with author, 10 February 2021.

This, ultimately, is why such PPAs matter for our purposes: in view, that is, of the way in which, and growing frequency with which, the corporate PPA phenomenon is invoked explicitly in support of a status quo approach to the management of the climate crisis, and more specifically to the fashioning and management of the energy transition that the crisis demands. Indeed, for many champions of the view that the energy transition – and especially the transition to renewable electricity – should remain capital- and market-led, corporate PPAs have come to represent something of a great white hope.

Of course, many 'experts' and policymakers see no need for such a quasi-messianic appeal. For them, government support has by and large done its job: historic subsidies to the solar and wind industries have catalysed vast investment in cell and turbine technologies, leading in turn to steep falls in technology costs and increasing cost-competitiveness with fossil-fuel-based electricity generation. The market, in short, by this way of thinking, can manage relatively comfortably without external support now that cost is no longer an obstacle; the only substantive obstacles that remain are, so the argument goes, 'extra-economic'. That so many powerful people and institutions subscribe to this view is not surprising, given the dominance of the cost-focused narrative (Chapter 4).

But not everyone has been blindsided. Other policymakers and experts possess a surer understanding of the economics of electricity generation and distribution. In particular, they know, while costs have indeed declined, that wholesale prices are volatile, that generator profits (or losses) are unpredictable, and that renewables investment is, as a result, uncertain. Such persons tend to be far less sanguine about the likely pace of the ongoing energy transition, even as they generally have a preference for the transition to remain in capital's and markets' hands.

It is among precisely such people and institutions that corporate PPAs have arrived on the industry scene as something of an apparent godsend. If, as appears to some extent at least to be the case, corporate PPAs can provide renewables developers with sufficient expectation of revenue stability to enable them to secure affordable financing, then might they be a silver bullet? Might they even enable policymakers to remove what government supports remain, or at least give such policymakers reason to believe that doing so will not unduly jeopardize ongoing investment in new renewables capacity?

Fervour around the potential ostensibly harboured by corporate PPAs in this regard has been building for a number of years. In 2020, for instance, the consultancy KPMG captured the zeitgeist in the following terms. 'While the recent growth of global corporate PPA volumes has been steep,' its consultants wrote, 'it is expected this is just the tip of the iceberg.'[45] Two considerations in particular stoked KPMG's optimism. On the off-take side, the firm anticipated 'increased demand for renewables by corporations driven by their renewable energy sourcing targets'. On the generator side, with 'a further decrease of government incentives with respect to renewable energy projects', it appeared inevitable to KPMG that 'risk-mitigated corporate PPAs will be required for developers to be able to attract competitive financing and realize new build of renewable generation assets'. 'This combination of elements', the report concluded, 'will likely further catalyze growth of global corporate PPA volumes in the coming decade.'

Corporate PPAs, by this increasingly common reckoning, represent the private sector at its entrepreneurial, creative best, 'fixing' the climate problem itself as the government progressively withdraws. Insofar as corporate PPAs effectively substitute for government support mechanisms as the principal source of investment bankability for renewables, such contractual instruments are, advocates infer, proof positive that a fundamental transformation of society's approach to infrastructure decarbonization – such as decommodification of the means of energy generation and distribution – is not needed. This, essentially, is the wider wager that market ideologues and other opponents of system change hang upon the struts of the corporate PPA phenomenon. In short, a renewables future free of government support is, in fact, viable.

Thus, 'while the energy transition towards renewables has been enabled by government through support mechanisms such as feed-in tariffs', DLA Piper declared in 2019, as if announcing the crossing of a Rubicon, 'the baton has now, for the most part, passed into the hands of the private sector'. And, with the market for corporate PPAs – 'the principal price hedging tool for both project sponsors and private off-takers' – roaring ahead in the shape of what was described as a 'deal

45   M. Hayes, R. Stegink and M. Santillana, 'Corporate PPAs – First Step in Corporate Decarbonization', April 2020, kpmg.com, p. 2.

flow boom', the private sector, DLA Piper surmised, was succeeding admirably.[46]

Perhaps predictably, the step from experts predicting that corporate PPAs could ensure renewables' continued bankability if governments withdrew support, to experts effectively advising governments to withdraw support on exactly such a premise, has been only a short one. In the same year as KPMG reported on the market, for example, the consultancy Baringa Partners produced a report on corporate PPAs for the Irish government.[47] The report positively brimmed with enthusiasm, specifically on the ground that this was indeed the market's own fix, obviating government financial backing to renewables. Corporate PPAs, Baringa explained, represent for renewables generators a 'market-led route-to-market which does not rely on state support'. More exactly, they represent 'the primary market instrument used in liberalised power markets to underpin project debt financing of subsidy-free renewables'.[48] If the Irish government needed any further encouragement in its avowed intention of making the facilitation of a thriving corporate PPA market one of its main policies for achieving a renewable share of electricity generation of 70 per cent by 2030, then this report, in no uncertain terms, provided it.

The following year, the rosy vision conjured by the likes of Baringa, DLA Piper and KPMG, namely of a market-led energy transition hinging substantially on corporate renewables PPAs, was effectively rubber-stamped by the world's leading prognosticator of global energy futures. 'An increasing proportion' of utility-scale renewables growth in most markets, the IEA confidently proclaimed, 'is expected to come from corporate PPAs.'[49] It was the clearest sign yet that the corporate PPA has been officially installed both as a substantive linchpin of the transition to a decarbonized power system and, accordingly, as a recursive validation of the market's ability to deliver that transition.

Little wonder, then, that the corporate PPA was never far from the conversation when, in 2022–3, commentators and policymakers were forced to reckon with the implications of one of the deepest and most

---

46   DLA Piper, 'Europe's Subsidy-Free Transition', pp. 2, 4–5.

47   Baringa Partners, 'Corporate PPA Policy in Ireland'.

48   Ibid., pp. 27, 35.

49   IEA, 'Renewables 2021: Analysis and Forecasts to 2026', December 2021, iea .org, p. 52.

broadly based energy crises for a very long time, and with the question of what the crisis meant for energy transition scenarios. The steep escalation in electricity prices experienced in 2022 in Europe, in particular, led to widespread calls for deep-seated reform of electricity markets (see Chapters 10 and 11). When it eventually came, however, the proposal of the European Commission (EC) for such 'reform' was, at best, limp.[50] No major redesign was needed after all, the EC evidently decided, either to protect consumers from the kind of price volatility seen in 2022, or indeed to maintain momentum in renewables growth. Why not? In large measure, because it was felt that the corporate PPA would enable Europe to pull through. Essentially, as the EC saw it, the problem the continent faced was not in fact poor market design, but rather that of member states not allowing markets – and especially corporate PPA markets – properly to flourish.

## VI

On numerous grounds, such positivity around the present and future role of corporate PPAs in electricity decarbonization seems deeply misplaced. Let us consider some of the main reasons for scepticism.

Partly, there is an obvious political concern. To many, relying on markets and the pricing mechanism to drive the transition away from fossil fuels – which, in terms of broad approach, is what the world widely and increasingly is doing – is itself problematic enough. Markets are not only impersonal and faceless; they are also unaccountable. Should not someone, or rather some democratically elected institutional collective of someones, be taking responsibility? One of the big problems, surely, with market-coordinated processes is that people cannot ask markets why they are doing things in a certain way. Nor can people ask markets why they messed up when things go awry. Market mechanisms preclude accountability.

But arguably, relying on a small coterie of big-tech companies, and their idiosyncratic energy-purchasing habits, to drive the transition

---

50   European Commission, 'Proposal for a Regulation of the European Parliament and of the Council Amending Regulations (EU) 2019/943 and (EU) 2019/942 as Well as Directives (EU) 2018/2001 and (EU) 2019/944 to Improve the Union's Electricity Market Design', March 2023, eur-lex.europa.eu.

away from fossil fuels seems, in political terms, even more problematic. One can quite imagine that, for many environmental and anti-monopoly activists, perhaps the only thing worse than nobody being responsible for driving and shepherding the energy transition would be Amazon, of all firms, being so responsible. Yet, to the degree that corporate PPAs are indeed being called upon to supplant government support mechanisms in catalysing renewables investment, this, effectively, is more or less the reality with which we increasingly are faced. It would be difficult to conceive of a more ironic statement on the warped political economy of contemporary green capitalism.

An especially bitter irony in this regard is the fact that those firms today enjoying the best publicity vis-à-vis their electricity purchasing habits happen to include some of the worst corporate offenders vis-à-vis carbon emissions. Take Amazon itself, the biggest of the procurers of clean electricity under corporate PPAs. On the one hand, buying such renewably generated power is certainly helping to reduce the relative carbon intensity of its operations, which it quantifies in terms of $CO_2$ emitted per dollar of sales. But, on the other hand, its business – and especially its energy-gorging cloud-computing Web services business – has been growing so quickly that its absolute overall carbon footprint, which is what ultimately matters, continues rapidly to grow.[51]

Another reason to be sceptical of the eager hubbub around corporate PPAs relates to the question of so-called additionality. On the generator side, corporate PPAs are signed not only by companies wanting to develop new generating facilities, and which regard such an agreement as a source of leverage with lenders in terms of unlocking construction financing; they can also be signed by companies with existing operational generating assets. In the latter case, the signing of a corporate PPA does not signify the accumulation of any new renewable generating capacity – there is, in the terminology of the sector, no additionality – and hence any claims to positive climate contribution on the part of the relevant off-taker ring rather hollow. Buying extant green power is simply not the same as helping to enable investment in new green power.

DLA Piper has noted that much of the early activity in, for example, the UK's corporate PPA market represented agreements to

---

51   See for example, A. Palmer, 'Amazon's Carbon Emissions Rose 19% in 2020 Even as Covid-19 Pushed Global Levels Down', 30 June 2021, cnbc.com.

purchase power from wind or solar facilities that had already been built – no fewer than eighteen of the twenty-six reported deals that had been signed by 2019, to be precise. It did also note that, by the late 2010s, the focus of UK corporate PPAs was finally shifting towards 'enabling new capacity to come online, for example facilitating the financing of a subsidy-free greenfield project that would otherwise not have been built'.[52] Moreover, many of the most active corporate PPA off-takers globally increasingly require evidence of additionality from generators before they will enter agreements. Nevertheless, concerns around additionality, or rather a paucity thereof, have not disappeared, and historically at least they have clearly had significant substance.

But far and away the most significant reasons for caution concerning corporate PPAs, and especially with regard to their putative potential to drive broadly based future growth in renewables investment, are economic. The key issue here, simply stated, is that there are few credible, bankable off-takers – far too few to enable corporate PPAs to power the renewables market at large.

The same issue, notably, has long plagued the parallel, longer-standing utility PPA sector. By their very nature, long-term bilateral PPAs of any kind entail massive counterparty risk – on both sides. The off-taker is essentially wagering that five, ten or fifteen years down the line, the generator will still be in business and able to deliver the contracted amount of power. The generator, for its part, is wagering that, equally deep into the future, the off-taker will still be in business and still willing and able to purchase the contracted amount of power at the contracted price.

How has this counterparty risk influenced the ability of companies developing new renewables plants to strike deals with electricity resellers (under utility PPAs) to the satisfaction of lenders? Naturally, it has constrained it. Typically, lenders have only been willing to finance projects backed by utility PPAs if the off-taker is very large, very established and perceived to be very creditworthy. 'Smaller [electricity] suppliers have, historically, been unable to play a significant role in providing long-term PPAs to new-build utility-scale renewable energy projects,' consultants wrote in a 2013

---

52   DLA Piper, 'Europe's Subsidy-Free Transition', p. 9.

report for the UK government. 'This', they went on, 'is because lenders tend to find it difficult to get comfortable with the credit risk given [those suppliers'] limited balance sheets and small retail positions.'[53]

Precisely the same constraints today encase the corporate PPA market. What do the banks that finance renewables projects look for in a potential corporate off-taker? A company willing to pay a decent electricity price, certainly. But not only that. Bankers operating in this space emphasize both 'the value of the revenue stream *and* the perceived security of the revenue stream.'[54] The latter, as Yannic Rack has observed, principally means a 'large and bankable balance sheet', and typically an investment-grade credit rating.[55]

Indeed, as one solar trade association has noted, 'a lower [electricity] price from a very secure creditor . . . may be worth more [to a lender] than a high price from a less creditworthy counterparty.'[56] Corporate off-takers that present (or are perceived to present) only limited credit risks in fact serially take advantage of this to negotiate for lower electricity prices in PPAs than their riskier peers are able to negotiate. More generally, to be deemed credible as a long-term PPA off-taker, a corporate consumer must have both sufficient power consumption requirements to be able to commit to acquiring all or a significant proportion of a project's electricity output, and sufficient commercial robustness to be likely to still be in business in the later years of a contract of a decade or longer duration.

The upshot, inevitably, is that the universe of corporate off-takers considered suitable by renewables generators and by those that finance them is inherently limited. 'It's not at all easy to find viable corporate PPA purchasers', one fund manager conceded in 2021.[57] In fact, in 2019, Aurora Energy Research estimated that companies covering only 14 per cent of industrial power demand in the EU would be able to absorb the long-term power price risk involved in a typical corporate PPA, while

53  Baringa Partners, 'Power Purchase Agreements for Independent Renewable Generators', p. 13.

54  Solar Trade Association, 'Making Solar Pay', p. 11 (emphasis added).

55  Y. Rack, 'European Renewable Developers Vie for Suitable Off-Takers as Subsidies Wind Down', *SNL Generation Markets Week*, 26 March 2019.

56  Solar Trade Association, 'Making Solar Pay', p. 11.

57  Interview with author, 12 February 2021.

also possessing the kind of credit rating required by lenders to PPA-backed renewables projects.[58]

This does not mean that lenders never back projects on the basis of PPAs signed with somewhat less credible corporate off-takers; they sometimes do – just, as we have seen, as they sometimes back projects exposed to a degree of merchant price risk (Chapter 6). But, as in the case of the financing of such merchant projects, when banks finance projects selling bilaterally to corporate consumers that are only semi-credible off-takers, they demand their pound of flesh. The risk, they say, is higher, and so, therefore, must be the cost of capital.[59]

The key issue in all this, needless to say, is that the dearth of robust, credible and (thus) bankable off-takers for corporate PPAs directly limits the potential size of the corporate PPA market, which is another way of saying that that dearth directly constrains the ability of the corporate PPA market to provide anything more than a marginal 'solution' to the wider problem of renewables bankability. If the answer to the interconnected problems facing the renewables sector of uncertain profits, volatile spot markets and jittery financiers is to agree to sell the power produced by future solar or wind farms to an Amazon or Google, it is difficult to get past the fact that there simply are not so many Amazons and Googles out there.

In fact, the obstacles are even greater than this discussion allows, because the shortage of credible off-takers also constrains the potential of the corporate PPA market to underwrite growth in renewables investment in a more indirect sense. As indicated earlier, the biggest, most sought-after corporate off-takers are able to drive down PPA prices because their perceived robustness is so highly valued by the counterparties to these agreements.[60] But they are also able to apply downwards pressure on prices on account of the very structure of the market. On the one side of the market there is an abundance of actual and aspiring generating companies seeking the bankability of a corporate PPA; on

---

58   Research cited in Rack, 'European Renewable Developers Vie for Suitable Off-Takers as Subsidies Wind Down'.

59   K. Ryszka, 'Renewable Project Finance: Can Corporate PPAs Replace Renewable Energy Subsidies?', 24 January 2020, economics.rabobank.com; Rack, 'European Renewable Developers Vie for Suitable Off-Takers as Subsidies Wind Down'.

60   See Solar Trade Association, 'Making Solar Pay', p. 21; Ryszka, 'Renewable Project Finance'.

the other, as we have seen, is a paucity of viable purchasers. The market, in short, is highly imbalanced, and from relative scarcity itself comes negotiating leverage.

In essence, the fact that there are so few potential electricity consumer-buyers of scale to whom aspiring developers realistically can turn for long-term, fixed-price contracts is good for the former but bad for the latter and their financial backers. The consultancy McKinsey was alive to this phenomenon of market imbalance in as early as 2018. 'The market pricing of individual projects already reveals the typical charac-teristics of a buyers' market', it noted, 'with discounts [on corporate PPAs] of 15 to 35 per cent compared with calendar-forward prices.'[61] That is, to secure the revenue stability demanded by their funders, devel-opers were having to accept PPA prices 15 to 35 per cent below prevail-ing wholesale market rates because there was insufficient competition on the buy side to push prices up.

In 2021, a European asset manager with a substantial portfolio of renewables generating assets had something similar to say. 'Corporate PPAs in the Nordics', the manager observed, 'are being priced at some-thing like €25 to €30 per MWh. But owners need €35 to €40 to make a decent return. So why are PPAs being sold at such a low price? It feels like buyers are getting a really good deal, and owners are getting poor terms. The obvious explanation', this individual concluded, 'is mismatch between demand and supply.'[62]

The companies benefiting most from the corporate PPA market being a buyers' market are, of course, the big tech companies mentioned above. As two industry experts explained to the *Financial Times*, the Amazons and Googles of the world are effectively able to bend the corporate PPA market to their own demands. 'The tech companies really do dominate the whole market from a size perspective', one said. 'Their influence is huge. These guys have a lot of market power', confirmed the second.[63]

Specifically, such companies uniquely have the power to make, and not passively take, price. 'Amazon and the like get really good deals', one banker to renewables developers gloomily observed.[64] Another industry

---

61    S. Heiligtag, F. Kühn, F. Küster and J. Schabram, 'Merchant Risk Management: The New Frontier in Renewables', 12 November 2018, mckinsey.com.

62    Interview with author, 12 February 2021.

63    Cited in Hook and Lee, 'How Tech Went Big on Green Energy'.

64    Interview with author, 11 February 2021.

expert described in the following terms how the tech titans wield and exploit their market power in practice, and how their actions then ripple through the rest of the value chain: 'The big tech companies are driving the whole sector. They run auctions to get the lowest [PPA] tariff that they can for ten to fifteen years. Developers jump on it, and then try to get the maximum amount of debt on the best terms, using the tech PPA as leverage.'[65] Whether, and at what cost, clean energy capacity gets built always depends on the terms on which its output will later be brought to market, and this statement represents an especially striking testament to that fact.

The threat that such aggressive pricing of corporate PPAs poses to growth in renewables development is, of course, that developers will not in fact build solar and wind farms and – ultimately amounting to the same thing – that banks and investors will not finance new such facilities, because the terms of corporate PPAs are simply not attractive enough: because, that is, the market power of Amazon, Google and the like squeezes developer and financier profitability too far. The asset manager who bemoaned corporate PPAs in the Nordic region being priced at €25 to €30 per MWh in 2021 implied that that point – the point at which developers, financiers or both perceive insufficient scope for profit to justify the risk of investment – was already close to being reached.

Thus, we are back again to the critical question of economic returns. 'Essentially,' the same asset manager put it, 'Google and co are profiting from investors' desperation to go green.'[66] But how desperate to 'go green' *are* asset managers and other financial investors? This is, surely, the pivotal question, to which we have already gestured at various points. If the price of going green specifically via PPA-backed renewables investments is indeed lower returns than are available from alternative investment opportunities, growth in the PPA market will perforce depend upon financial institutions' willingness to accept those lower returns. As we have said, however, such willingness is anything but unlimited.

All of which is to say that, for all the hype, corporate PPAs, as mechanisms of de-risking of investment, demonstrably represent a highly

---

65   Interview with author, 10 February 2021.
66   Interview with author, 12 February 2021.

imperfect substitute for effective government support instruments like feed-in tariffs. Asked to speculate about the extent of likely future growth in the corporate PPA market, one banker opted for a blunt, one-word answer: 'finite'.[67] Such caution is well warranted. If the corporate PPA is indeed the best solution to bankability that the private sector and 'the market' can come up with, then market failure is quite clearly what we are looking at.

## VII

Before moving on, let us briefly take stock of where we are at in our examination of the political economy of renewables investment, in terms of key learnings about how such investment is rationalized, financed and delivered. The previous few chapters, and this one, have taught us five main things.

First, we know that what ultimately determines whether solar and wind farms get built or not is not price – relative to that of other technologies of electricity generation – but profit, and, more particularly, expected profit. Is the investment expected to yield an economic return that the developer deems acceptable? That is what matters.

Second, we know that the relationship between price (of electricity generation) and profit is anything but straightforward. It would be easy to imagine that the cheaper it becomes to generate electricity, the more profit the generator will earn. But it would also be wrong. This was the lesson of Chapter 5: there *is* no straightforward such relationship, and thus even if solar and wind power are now 'cheap' it does not mean that profit-maximizing actors in the field of power generation will necessarily privilege them.

Third, from Chapter 6, we know that in the type of electricity sector that dominates the Global North, and towards which the rest of the world is indubitably shifting – which is to say, a sector in which electricity is predominantly traded in spot markets using merit order dispatch – renewable generators' expected profit is highly uncertain and unpredictable because wholesale prices are highly volatile. This, as we saw, represents a significant challenge to the bankability of proposed new

---

67    Interview with author, 18 February 2021.

capacity investments, at least in the absence of explicit mechanisms of price stabilization, of which government support schemes historically have represented the primary and most successful examples.

Fourth, we know that, for a variety of reasons, but in particular due to low barriers to entry and thus relatively high intensity of competition, profitability in renewables generation is not only often unpredictable but also, typically, very low. In the brief, infrequent periods during which strong returns are (or appear) achievable, capital floods in and swiftly pushes profit margins down. This was the thrust of Chapter 7, which also showed that there lurks in the background an arguably even more existential threat to renewables profits: price cannibalization.

Fifth, and finally, the current chapter has shown us that, as governments, convinced by the power of price in driving renewables investment, move to reduce or discard – or at least to pledge to reduce or discard – existing state-sponsored support mechanisms, the market has come up with one possible substitute, the much-feted corporate power purchase agreement. But the chapter has also shown that the potential for this 'substitute' to drive future renewables growth is, in reality, very limited.

Given all of this, then, the question we need to ask is: what is actually happening on the ground today? If profitability is not in fact propitious, and if PPAs are not in fact the silver bullet many imagine them to be, to what extent is new capacity investment taking place? And how successful *are* market-favouring governments proving to be in consigning subsidy schemes to history? These are the questions taken up in Chapter 9.

# 9

# Stuck on Support

The mid- to late 2010s marked a seemingly auspicious moment in the history of the political economy of renewable energy. Having long been considered too costly to be able to compete with fossil-fuel-based technologies of electricity generation on a level playing field, the costs of solar and wind power had by now declined to a point where this long-standing common sense began to be widely questioned. A new common sense thereby emerged. If not everywhere and under all conditions, *some* new solar and wind facilities, at least, could, it was argued, be developed without explicit mechanisms of support. It was time for renewables to try to stand on their own two feet.

And evidence soon emerged that seemed to suggest that indeed they could. Policymakers and renewables developers began to make announcements heralding pioneering support-free – or 'zero-support' – commercial, utility-scale wind or solar plants. Many of the first such declarations emanated from the United Kingdom. A number of firms publicized plans to develop support-free UK facilities from as early as 2016, among them Good Energy and Lightsource Renewable Energy. The first such purported facility to actually open for business was the 10 MW Clayhill solar farm in Bedfordshire, which was developed by Anesco and began generating power in September 2017. 'For the solar industry,' averred Anesco's chairman, 'Clayhill is a landmark development and paves the way for a sustainable future, where subsidies are no longer needed or relied upon.'[1]

The following year, another, much bigger, 'first' was hailed. The Swedish energy company Vattenfall announced that it was to develop the world's first 'subsidy-free' offshore wind farm, the vast Hollandse Kust Zuid (HKZ) scheme, around twenty to thirty kilometres off the Dutch coast between The Hague and Zandvoort. At the time of the announcement, HKZ was envisaged as a 750 MW facility, to be built by 2022; the schedule has subsequently slipped, while the scale has expanded (to a capacity of 1.5 GW) and new co-owners – Allianz Capital Partners and BASF – have been brought on board.

Numerous similar proclamations have followed over the ensuing half-decade. Situated predominantly, but not only, in Europe, these have ranged from Germany's first 'zero-support' solar farm (to be owned and developed by BayWa r.e.) to China's first 'zero-subsidy' wind farm (to be owned and developed by the renewables leg of the China National Nuclear Corporation), construction of each of which began in 2019.

Just one short decade earlier, Deutsche Bank's in-house environmental research and investment team had written a report that depicted an entirely different type of renewable energy world. The DB analysts calculated that the development of fully half of all installed solar and wind capacity in service worldwide as of 2008 – and as high as 75 per cent in the case of solar – had been supported by feed-in tariffs (FiTs): not government support mechanisms in general, note, but FiTs specifically, and this even before countries such as China had turned to FiTs as their subsidy mechanism of choice.[2]

Little wonder, then, that when they surveyed the brave new world of 'zero support' that seemed to be coming into being in the late 2010s, expert commentators often invoked awed, epochal terms. 'I think the word revolution is befitting,' maintained Mateusz Wronski of the energy research firm Aurora, 'because it is a marked departure from the old paradigm, where renewable deployment was driven by government intervention. This revolution brings a new paradigm, where decarbonisation can

---

1   Cited in E. Gosden and B. Webster, 'First Subsidy-Free Solar Farm Revives a Fading Industry', *The Times*, 26 September 2017.

2   DB Climate Change Advisors, 'Global Energy Transfer Feed-In Tariffs for Developing Countries', April 2010, Appendix II – copy available from author.

be brought about by sheer market force.'[3] The motive power of such 'sheer market force' is, of course, precisely what the protagonists of our relative-prices narrative – the argument that renewables ineluctably will win out, once the price is right – had long been insisting on, and indeed continue to insist on. In short, the price, it seemed, *was* now finally right. 'The demand for zero-support renewable electricity is booming,' the energy journalist Julian Wettengel wrote in 2021.[4]

But is this actually true? Given everything we have learned in the preceding several chapters about both the very real economic hurdles to renewables investment (not least those hurdles pertaining to profitability) that actually exist, and about the importance of various 'external' support mechanisms in helping these hurdles to be negotiated, 'booming' demand for zero-support renewables appears, on the face of things, to be surprising. So let us investigate.


I


The geographical pattern of recent global growth in solar and wind generating capacity is very easy to describe. Figure 9.1 depicts this pattern visually. The key feature is that the addition of new capacity remains geographically concentrated to a striking degree. In every year since 2016, three-quarters or more of all net new solar and wind capacity globally has been installed in Europe and just three other countries – China, India and the US. At the end of 2022, those regions held 81 per cent of the world's installed and connected solar and wind assets – some 1.59 out of 1.95 TW of total global capacity.

As the chart shows, China is utterly dominant. Not far short of half (specifically, 45 per cent) of all net new solar and wind capacity installed globally between 2017 and 2022 (inclusive) was installed in China. Remarkably, the proportion actually exceeded 50 per cent in 2020: the surge in new installation that occurred in China that year, after a dip in 2019, is something we will discuss later in the chapter.

---

3   Cited in S. Evans, 'Q&A: What Does "Subsidy-Free" Renewables Actually Mean?', 27 March 2018, carbonbrief.org.

4   J. Wettengel, 'EnBW to Supply Zero-Support Offshore Wind Power to Airport Operator Fraport', 13 December 2021, cleanenergywire.org.

The second most significant country in terms of recent capacity growth is the US. Though it lags a long way behind China, it is, equally, far ahead of any other individual country. Moreover, within the space of three short years, the amount of net new solar and wind capacity installed annually in the US more than doubled, from 15.1 GW in 2018 to 33.3 GW in 2021 – although, as we will see, new US installations fell sharply in 2022.

The final individual country for which data are provided in Figure 9.1 is India, and for the simple reason that during the period covered by the chart, it saw the third-largest absolute net growth in new capacity – although it did not necessarily rank third every single year within that period. Nor, it is worth pointing out, does India today hold the world's third-largest national stock of solar and wind capacity: it actually ranks fourth, behind Germany. But Germany's main growth in capacity occurred relatively earlier.

Meanwhile, within Europe, the countries that in recent years have been expanding their renewables asset portfolios most rapidly are generally those that one might intuitively expect to have been doing so, namely the larger Western European nations – the likes of Germany, Spain and the UK. But there are some important anomalies, or at least cases that someone with no knowledge of the often tortuous national political economy of energy provision might consider anomalous.

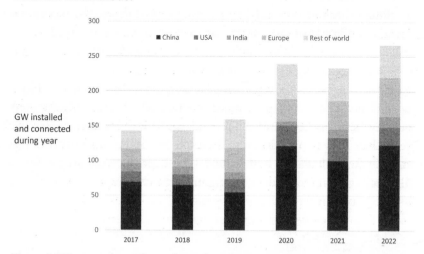

**Figure 9.1** Net annual growth in solar and wind capacity, selected regions, 2017–22
*Source*: IRENA

On the one hand, there are countries such as the Netherlands, which have been investing in solar and (especially) wind to a degree that far outstrips their relative size: more than 10 per cent of the overall new renewable capacity added in Europe between 2017 and 2022 was installed in the Netherlands, a country of fewer than 20 million people. On the other hand, there are countries such as France and Italy, in both of which renewables remain marginal – albeit for very different reasons, and with very different implications for the climate. As explained earlier in the book, France has essentially bet the metaphorical house on nuclear, thus mitigating much of the need for a domestic energy transition specifically on climate grounds. But, in Italy, fossil fuels in general, and natural gas in particular, remain dominant. It is far more reliant on gas for electricity generation than any other major European country – unless, that is, within Europe one includes Israel, where coal and (especially) gas continue to supply almost all electric power.

In any event, some of the countries that are clearly leading recent global investment in solar and wind power – China, Germany, the Netherlands and the UK – also appeared on the above list of countries that have reportedly been pioneering 'zero-support' renewables. We must, therefore, examine these particular national cases. But what of other major renewables investors? What, for example, of India? And what of the US? To what extent is the support-free phenomenon 'booming' there, too? We will begin our survey in Europe, the undisputed heartland of the phenomenon in question.

## II

Our first stop is Clayhill in Bedfordshire in the UK, which, as we have seen, was widely reported as being the country's first operational subsidy-free solar farm, and which started generating power in 2017. The facility even received a glowing mention for its apparent economic breakthrough in the government's annual 'State of the Energy Market' report.[5] It was, evidently, considered a genuine milestone.

---

5   Ofgem, 'State of the Energy Market: 2017 Report', October 2017, ofgem.gov.uk, p. 87.

Yet the reality belied the evangelism. Investigative reporting disclosed that part of – perhaps even the entire – reason why Anesco was able to develop Clayhill without using a formal government support mechanism such as a contract for difference (CfD) was that the facility was able to exploit (one commentator, Jamie Condliffe, said 'piggyback upon') infrastructure that had previously been built, and paid for by others.[6] One important component of this pre-existing infrastructure was a battery storage facility that Clayhill would be able to use to store power for subsequent sale during periods of high demand (and price). Anesco conceded that this storage facility was 'crucial' in making Clayhill viable as a 'subsidy-free' proposition.[7] Another important extant component was a grid connection. This existed because Clayhill was sited next to a solar plant of earlier vintage, which itself *had* benefited from a government subsidy.

Essentially, then, this much ballyhooed new renewables facility was, in fact, subsidized by the UK government, only the subsidy was implicit – invested historically, and sunk physically and economically in legacy infrastructure – rather than explicit. Condliffe's answer to the question he himself asked – 'How to Build a Solar Farm without Government Subsidies?' – spoke volumes: 'In a nutshell: find a site where you can lean on existing infrastructure.'

Vattenfall's answer, in the case not of solar but of offshore wind, and specifically the Hollandse Kust Zuid (HKZ) facility off the Dutch coast, was different, but nevertheless related. In HKZ, Vattenfall has indeed developed a new offshore wind facility without the support of a direct government subsidy: hence the labelling of the project as 'subsidy-free'. That is, HKZ is not part of a formal subsidy framework such as SDE+ (now SDE++), the principal scheme through which the Dutch government has in recent years supported renewable power development – a scheme aptly described by one report as a 'sliding feed-in premium structure, which takes away most, but not all, exposure to merchant price risk.'[8]

But, as at Clayhill, there nonetheless clearly is a significant state subsidy to HKZ, and, once again, it pertains to supporting

6    J. Condliffe, 'How to Build a Solar Farm without Government Subsidies', 26 September 2017, technologyreview.com.

7    N. Thomas, 'Solar Power Breakthrough as Subsidy-Free Farm Opens', *Financial Times*, 26 September 2017.

8    PwC, 'Financing Offshore Wind', August 2020, pwc.nl, p. 14.

infrastructure. Specifically, Vattenfall and its partners have not been required to pay the costs of grid connection, which in the Netherlands are socialized. 'It's a good way of de-risking the project,' Vattenfall's CEO, Magnus Hall, told Carbon Brief. 'But it also means that [the project] is not fully subsidy-free, if you want to say so.'[9] The Dutch government had also undertaken, and borne the costs of, all the site selection and other research that needed to be carried out before it could conduct the 'beauty contest' through which the HKZ tender was awarded.[10]

We should pause and expand at this point, because the socialization of the costs of grid connection is a form of subsidy with a wider applicability. One important reason why renewables developers such as Vattenfall do indeed regard such socialization as a form of subsidy – and why we in turn should do likewise – is that it is not universal government policy. While the governments of the Netherlands and certain other countries, including Germany, are willing to bear the costs of grid connection for certain categories of renewables developer, many other national governments are not, and hence, if development opportunities in the latter countries represent a baseline cost scenario, opportunities in the former clearly occasion a relative subsidy. Spain and the UK, for instance, are two significant examples of European countries in which the developer is itself required to fund the cost of grid connection (including in the case of offshore wind), on the so-called allocation-by-cause principle.

How significant a subsidy exactly is the state's selective shouldering of grid connection costs? It varies greatly and depends on the type of facility to be connected, and where. For onshore renewables plants, most studies suggest that grid connection accounts for in the region of 10 to 15 per cent of total capital expenditure – a not insignificant proportion. But, in the case of offshore wind farms, of which HKZ is of course one example, the proportion, unsurprisingly, swells. Anywhere between 15 and 30 per cent of the capital cost can go to grid connection.[11] And,

9   Cited in S. Evans, 'Q&A: What Does "Subsidy-Free" Renewables Actually Mean?'

10   PwC, 'Financing Offshore Wind', p. 6.

11   International Renewable Energy Agency Secretariat, 'Wind Power', *Renewable Energy Technologies: Cost Analysis Series, Volume 1: Power Sector*, Issue 5/5, June 2012, available irena.org, p. 19.

as we have seen, for renewables generators, unlike fossil-fuel-fired generating plants, upfront capital costs essentially constitute lifetime plant costs, or at least the lion's share. If, then, the government agrees through this mechanism to pay, say, a quarter of all your expected costs as an offshore wind farm developer, very clearly it is massively subsidizing you.

The socialization of grid connection costs represents, in fact, one of two main forms of implicit government subsidy that continue widely to support what are only nominally zero-support/zero-subsidy European renewables projects. The other main such form of subsidy consists of certain types of CfD scheme, operating under certain market conditions. But, inasmuch as CfDs are typically understood to provide an explicit subsidy, this 'implicitness' requires some explaining.

A key distinction to understand here is between zero-subsidy project *tenders* and zero-subsidy *bids*. The tender through which Vattenfall was awarded the HKZ contract was an example of the former. It explicitly precluded direct subsidy: all the developers that entered the beauty contest were aware that the Dutch government was not offering any mitigation of wholesale price risk, whether through a CfD or any other scheme.

Meanwhile, contrast such a tender mechanism with auctions for CfDs such as those which the Spanish and UK governments currently operate for specified renewables technologies. In these so-called reverse auctions (see Chapter 7), bidders bid prices down, and the winning bidder, offering the lowest bid, effectively receives a fixed price, as bid, for the duration of the contract period (typically twelve years in the Spanish case, for example).

Now, consider the crucial question of what the electricity spot price is at the time such a contract is awarded. If the spot price happens to be higher than or equal to the price bid and thus stipulated in the CfD (say, €50 versus €45 per MWh), then this is termed a zero-subsidy bid: at the time of the auction, and then for as long as the spot price remains equal to or higher than the contract strike price, the generator does not receive a direct subsidy. The auction mechanism made subsidy available (unlike in the case of zero-subsidy tenders), but *the bidders competed it away*. This is what happened, for example, when the Spanish government auctioned 1 GW of new wind capacity in January 2021. The winning bids ranged from €20.00 to €28.89 per MWh, hailed as 'the lowest ever prices for new wind energy in Europe.[12] That month's average electricity spot price in Spain was around €60 per MWh.

But, of course, if, during the period covered by the CfD, the spot price were subsequently to fall to below €45 in our hypothetical case (or below €20.00/28.89 in the Spanish case), then the generator *would* be in receipt of subsidy. This is why CfDs, FiTs and comparable mechanisms arguably should always be *understood as* subsidies even if they do not look like subsidies – and indeed are publicly posited as *not* being subsidies – at the time of their contractual agreement: that is, because they promise to provide subsidy as and when the market requires it. The subsidy is implicit, rather than explicit, since it may not ever kick in.

A widespread lack of understanding of these mechanisms leads to all manner of misinterpretations and misleading (and sometimes outright false) claims. 'Far from depending on subsidies,' the ubiquitous economics commentator Adam Tooze, for example, announced in early 2023, 'European wind power now operates on such a profitable basis that it returns revenue to European treasuries.'[13] Well, yes – and no. Yes, some operators in that period were earning windfall profits as a result of energy crisis–induced wholesale price spikes and were returning some of these profits as windfall taxes (Chapter 10). And, yes, spot prices were, at that time, higher than the fixed contractual strike prices that certain (largely other) European wind operators had agreed with governments at tenders for new capacity, meaning that in those cases, money – equivalent to the spot price minus the strike price – indeed was nominally being 'returned.'[14]

But also, no. For one thing, the latter operators in question would of course duly receive subsidy payments in the event that the spot price dipped below their respective contract prices. More importantly still, had the guarantee of such eventual subsidy not been part of the contractual agreement with the government, the banks to whom the developers holding such contracts turned to raise construction finance likely would have run the proverbial mile, in which case the generating facilities that

---

12   WindEurope, 'Onshore Wind Energy Scores Lowest Ever Price under New Spanish Auction Design', 27 January 2021, windeurope.org.

13   A. Tooze, 'Europe's Energy Crisis That Isn't', 5 April 2023, foreignpolicy.com.

14   The return was merely nominal in the sense that the element of revenue equating to the excess of spot price over strike price was only ever nominally the operator's in the first place.

the agreements in fact helped render bankable would not have been built in the first place. In other words, the types of operators to whom Tooze referred do in fact continue, absolutely and intimately, to depend on subsidy mechanisms, even, paradoxically, if no actual subsidy is ever received: in order to get their operations off the ground, they require confirmation that subsidy will be paid if and when needed.

Think of it this way. The Toozian argument that European wind power was operating without subsidy in early 2023 is analogous to saying that insurance schemes such as protection for bank depositors play no meaningful role in those periods during which no claims are filed and paid out. Both propositions are simply untrue. The mistake in each case is to presume that the support mechanism only applies ex post facto. But in reality, the role of deposit protection, as of CfDs, is not just to mitigate retroactively actual losses or revenue shortfalls incurred. It is as much, if not more, to provide, a priori, confidence in the existence of an eventual (strictly as necessary) safety net, this confidence being required to summon the relevant actors – depositors in the first hand, renewables generators in the latter – to even participate in the relevant market. Both depositor protection schemes and price-contingent renewables subsidy schemes (the latter themselves representing a form of insurance, if you like) perform a crucial market-making function, irrespective of whether they ever actually pay out a single penny.

Finally, for good measure, there was another awkward fact of which Tooze evidently was oblivious. The analysis to which he linked in support of his claim, and which showed (some) newer offshore wind farms not at the time being in receipt of effective subsidy, in fact assumed that all grid connection costs were socialized.[15] That is, there *was* assumed to be subsidy – it just was not categorized as such. And, when the authors of the study in question instead allocated the grid connection costs to the respective project developers, the finding that Tooze trumpeted no longer obtained: no money was 'returned'.

Interestingly, when governments attempt to minimize the likelihood that the contingent subsidy afforded by CfDs and FiTs ever will be required and paid, the attempt often backfires, and sometimes

---

15   M. Jansen, I. Staffell, L. Kitzing, S. Quoilin, E. Wiggelinkhuizen, B. Bulder, I. Riepin and F. Müsgens, 'Offshore Wind Competitiveness in Mature Markets without Subsidy', *Nature Energy* 5: 8 (2020), p. 617.

spectacularly so – a striking demonstration, in its own way, of the industry's ongoing need for support. The most common way in which governments do this is by imposing price caps at auctions. Consider what happened, for example, when the Spanish government auctioned up to 3.3 GW of wind and solar capacity in late 2022, soliciting project proposals for CfDs subject to a price ceiling of €47 per MWh. With developers' raw material and financing costs – not to mention electricity spot prices – having increased dramatically since the same government's wind auction in early 2021 attracted winning bids of below €30 per MWh, the new auction was an utter failure: Forestalia and Elewan Energy were the only developers awarded allocations, these totalling just 45 MW, or around only 1.5 per cent of cumulative tendered capacity.[16] A year later, the UK government managed to go one better, when its auction of contracts to deliver up to 5 GW of new offshore wind capacity, which likewise capped contract prices, attracted precisely zero bids.

It is also, of course, the case that a CfD such as those awarded by the Spanish and UK governments represents a significant external support mechanism – and one that crucially enables developers to raise finance – quite aside from any subsidy element that it vouchsafes but may or may not occasion. This is because it actively stabilizes (if not ever subsidizing) revenues – such an important support factor, as we have seen, in liberalized electricity markets, like Europe's, with volatile wholesale prices. Not for nothing does the 2020 Spanish regulation setting out the country's current CfD framework focus specifically on this aspect rather than on that of subsidy. The main aim, the regulation explains, is to 'favour [revenue] predictability and certainty, to encourage new investments in new renewable energy capacity'.[17]

And then there are power purchase agreements (PPAs), another important potential source of revenue stabilization which can help fashion project bankability (Chapter 8). Germany's first 'zero-support' solar farm, the 8.8 MW BayWa r.e. facility mentioned above, was, for instance, not, in fact, a zero-support facility: its financing and development were enabled by a long-term PPA with unnamed industrial customers that

16   D. F. Christensen, 'Spanish Wind and Solar Auction Ends in Big Disappointment', 25 November 2022, energywatch.com.

17   Cited in P. del Rio and C. J. Menzies, 'Auctions for the Support of Renewable Energy in Spain', September 2021, aures2project.eu, p. 6.

was announced at the same time as the construction plans.[18] Furthermore, as if the Dutch government's waiving of grid connection costs were not enough, Vattenfall proceeded to reinforce the viability and bankability of HKZ over the course of 2021 and 2022 by signing fixed-price, long-term corporate PPAs with the industrial consumers Air Liquide and BASF – thus adding stability to implicit subsidy.

None of this is to say, however, that, at the outset of new projects, eventual project profitability is ever wholly certain in today's European renewables industry, for all that the industry indeed remains solidly buttressed by robust mechanisms of economic support. As we saw in Chapter 8 when we discussed recent wind power development offshore from the US state of Massachusetts, the various types of advance off-take contract that developers commonly sign to mitigate revenue risk and enable capital-raising can themselves rapidly become millstones rather than manna if conditions in equipment or financial markets move against the developer after such a contract has been signed but before equipment and capital costs have been finalized, however attractive the terms of the off-take contract (for instance, long-term fixed prices at rates above prevailing spot market prices) may initially appear.

This is seemingly what happened, for example, in the government-supported UK offshore wind market during 2022–3. Companies that perhaps thought they had struck gold when they signed CfDs for new projects with the UK government in 2022 were, by early the following year, warning the government that the projects would be difficult to deliver at the strike prices agreed, such had been the rapid inflation in the costs of both finance and turbines. Overall projected project delivery costs had risen by an estimated 20 to 40 per cent in most cases, in less than twelve months. Ørsted and Vattenfall were among those reported to have lobbied government for eleventh-hour investment allowances and other tax breaks to help revalorize schemes that now threatened to be loss making.[19]

As in Massachusetts, however, such appeals fell on deaf ears. The upshot? Some projects came to a standstill. In mid-2023, for example,

18   B. Wehrmann, 'Energy Company BayWa Re to Build Germany's First Zero-Support Solar Farm', 10 May 2019, cleanenergywire.org.

19   N. Thomas, 'Wind Farm Developers Demand UK Tax Breaks to Offset Rising Costs', *Financial Times*, 26 February 2023.

Vattenfall downed tools on the 1.4 GW Norfolk Boreas scheme, for which, twelve months earlier, it had signed a fifteen-year, inflation-linked CfD with a starting strike price of £37.35 per MWh at 2012 prices. 'It's important to invest only when our return requirements are met,' insisted Anna Borg, Vattenfall's chief executive, while booking an impairment charge of over $500 million. Meanwhile, Ørsted's own boss threw his support behind his competitor, describing Borg's decision to halt the development as 'courageous', imploring governments such as the UK's to 'realise that offshore wind ambitions will only happen with sane auction frameworks and realistic prices', and hinting that Ørsted might itself have to pursue similar measures.[20]

The more general point is that where it is specifically revenue that in one way or another is 'controlled' (by being delinked from market spot prices), renewables profits always remain uncertain until such time as the costs of construction and its financing have been locked in.

To begin to sum up, therefore, we can say that the support on which Europe's renewables power sector remains demonstrably stuck comprises a complex and variegated mix of both subsidy (sometimes explicit, sometimes implicit) and stabilization. Some projects enjoy one, for example subsidy; some enjoy the other; and some enjoy both.

There are, it follows, two common fallacies that need to be dispelled. One is that there is no subsidy unless such subsidy is explicit – the cases of socialized grid connection costs and zero-subsidy-bid CfDs both give the lie to this notion. The second fallacy is that which conflates support *with* subsidy; this fallacy elides the significance of price stabilization. As Simon Peltenburg of the UK's RES Group has put it, 'Subsidy-free renewables does not mean "support-free"' – or at least, it 'does not have to'.[21] The evolving landscape of European renewables development is ample testament to this fact.

Last but not least, across Europe it is clear that, having selectively experimented with attenuation of their packages of renewables support, governments – still far and away the main source of support for European renewables, whether that support incorporates subsidy or not – have increasingly

20   R. Millard, A. Williams and L. Patel, 'Soaring costs threaten offshore wind farm projects', *Financial Times*, 8 August 2023.

21   Cited in 'Subsidy-Free Renewables Does Not Mean "Support-Free", Says RES Chief', n.d., scottishenergynews.com (website no longer active) – copy available from author.

come to appreciate the economic obstacles to effecting such attenuation without simultaneously subduing renewables investment, and are therefore typically now renewing and bolstering support packages rather than doing the opposite. Germany is perhaps the most notable and significant example of this, with its new Renewable Energy Act of 2023 serving to extend support through to 2026, in the form principally of feed-in premiums for larger generators and feed-in tariffs for smaller ones.

## III

That the US landscape of renewable power generation also remains stuck on support is considerably plainer to see. For one thing, one searches in vain for evidence of (or even mere allusions to) US 'support-free' or 'zero-support' renewables: not a whiff of such a phenomenon can be detected. Furthermore, and as we shall shortly see, the long-term extension of direct government support for renewable electricity generation – successfully accomplished in 2022 – has in recent years been an issue with very high political and public visibility. It would have been hard to miss.

As we saw earlier in the book, US government support for renewable energy generation has long been predicated predominantly on a system of tax credits, which work through subsidization rather than stabilization. For stabilization, developers must turn instead to fixed-price PPAs or financial hedging instruments such as swaps, which they often do in conjunction with tax credits: it is rarely a question of either/or (see Chapter 8).

Ordinarily monetized through deals with third-party financial investors (in the form of so-called 'tax equity'), the US's renewables credits subsidize either construction – the Investment Tax Credit (ITC) – or generation – the Production Tax Credit (PTC). The former has historically been utilized principally by solar developers and the latter principally in the wind sector, a product of the fact that the rules applying to the two types of credit have conventionally been different for different technologies.

In the US, unlike in Europe, the essential nature of the main mechanism of government support for renewables generation has, to date, been notably consistent. Certainly, as we will see, rules and rates have periodically been tweaked. Moreover, to bolster the efficacy of tax credits, both federal and state governments have at times used various tributary instruments. But, in terms of the principal policy, there has been no flip-flopping between reliance on, say, renewables obligations and FiTs. The core mechanism was tax credits twenty years ago and it remains tax credits today. As such, subsidy remains explicit rather than implicit.

Nevertheless, the inclination that, with declining technology costs, solar and wind power *should* be able to do without subsidy – or, at the very least, with substantially less of it – has long been evident in the US no less than it has in Europe. Such an inclination is writ large in the fact that US policymakers have repeatedly legislated that renewables tax credits will be time-limited (that is, scheduled to terminate at a particular, agreed juncture), or will be reduced in scale over time, or indeed both these things. In repeatedly so legislating, policymakers have signalled (and sometimes stated) their conviction that the need for support is declining and will continue to decline.

Indeed, when, in 2022, US policymakers agreed on the most significant renewal and fortification of the country's renewables tax credits in a generation, in the shape of the Inflation Reduction Act (IRA), the same question continued to hang in the air, haunting the legislators' actions. As Eric Lipton posed the matter in the *New York Times*, were the revised credits in fact 'constructed in ways that reward companies for taking actions that market forces would lead them to take anyway'? After all, Lipton said, 'renewables even without federal subsidies are now cheaper than coal, meaning that the market was already giving [private sector actors] plenty of incentive to change how they produced power'.[22] There was definitely a sense – a lingering inclination, if you like – that tax credits were and are a policy that *should* not still be necessary, but which somehow still are.

Because, for all the aspiration, expectation and indeed legislation of subsidy attenuation, it has plainly not worked out as planned. In repeatedly hazarding withdrawal, the US, like the perennial junkie, has repeatedly failed, the IRA representing the latest and most dramatic failure. Exactly why the US has failed to wean its renewables sector off support remains an open question. One relevant factor, to be sure, has been

---

22   E. Lipton, 'With Federal Aid on the Table, Utilities Shift to Embrace Climate Goals', *New York Times*, 29 November 2022.

industry lobbying for support *not* to be withdrawn. As Lipton himself observed, for example, the successful passage of the IRA in 2022 was greased by significantly increased spending on lobbying and campaign contributions by the renewables sector, not least NextEra Energy, which by itself had around fifty registered lobbyists at the time. That those benefiting from the tax credit system include not just renewables companies themselves but, through tax equity financing, also big Wall Street banks – with all their famed lobbying clout – should not be underplayed, either.

An attempt at an explicit answer to this 'why' question is beyond this book's purview. But it is certainly within the book's purview to make a pertinent observation. Price volatility, low underlying profitability, and boom–bust dynamics are, in the US renewables sector, long-standing historic facts (Chapters 6 and 7). Whatever the influence of industry lobbyists, policy concerning economic support for the industry has been made and remade in this particular factual context. And given such a context, the direction that policymaking has taken is, to say the least, hardly surprising. Ongoing maintenance of healthy support for renewables operators – encouraged by growing recognition of the significance of that support to sustaining investment appetites – is, actually, exactly what one would have expected.

In fact, notwithstanding the relevance of lobbying, it should not go unmentioned that 2022 actually saw a significant decline in utility-scale wind and solar installations in the US. The 32 GW of new renewables capacity added to the grid was nearly 20 per cent lower than in 2021.[23] Why? There appeared to be several possible contributory factors, but, as Jennifer Hiller observed, 'a significant factor slowing installations' was the 'uncertainty over the details of federal tax policy' that pervaded the country until the IRA was finally sealed in August.[24] Other commentators concurred with Hiller's explanatory assessment.[25]

---

23   BloombergNEF, 'Sustainable Energy in America 2023 Factbook', March 2023, bnef.com, p. 7. Note that these figures differ from those (reported by IRENA) charted above in Figure 9.1; they are for gross rather than net additions, and include all renewables, not just solar and wind. But the IRENA data, too, showed a significant year-on-year decline in new capacity installation – of around 25 per cent.

24   J. Hiller, 'Investors Plow into Renewables, but Projects Aren't Getting Built', *Wall Street Journal*, 22 January 2023.

25   BloombergNEF, 'Sustainable Energy in America 2023 Factbook', p. 7; 'US Onshore Wind Came to a Screeching Halt in 2022', 28 March 2023, energywatch.com.

Whatever else it represented, this episode of significant disinvestment throws cold water on the oft-heard theory, alluded to by Lipton, that the US's renewables tax credits reward developers for doing things that, in view of renewables' cheapness, they would now be doing without such support, by dint of pure market logic. In the first half of 2022, when nobody knew what the support framework was going to look like twelve months – still less two years or more – ahead of time, developers evidently *did not do* those things, at least not on anything like the scale of 2021. Had the fulsome subsidy support available historically in fact by this juncture become more or less immaterial, essentially rewarding developers unnecessarily, one would have expected investment to remain robust, regardless of what was or was not happening vis-à-vis tax credit policy.

In any event, a potted history of the past two decades of the ITC vividly illustrates the dependency-like pattern of repeated failed attempts at withdrawal from the support 'drug'. (The details would be slightly different, but a history of the PTC would show the same basic dynamic.) Although it had existed in one form or another since the late 1970s, the ITC only came to prominence (and fiscal significance) in 2005 when the Energy Policy Act increased the subsidy to solar installations from 10 to 30 per cent. This higher rate was originally slated to expire at the end of 2007, but no fewer than three times during the following decade it was extended: first in 2006, again in 2008 and then once again – through to 2019 – in 2016.

This last extension of the three was effected by the Consolidated Appropriations Act, which also legislated that the higher rate of 30 per cent would then be phased out, with a 26 per cent credit applying to facilities beginning construction in 2020, 22 per cent to those entering construction in 2021, and 10 per cent to those starting in 2022 or thereafter. Even this more moderate plan for attenuation – that is, gradually weaning the sector off subsidy rather than requiring it to go 'cold turkey' – did not hold, however. In December 2020, Congress passed a two-year deferment of the phasedown, meaning that the 26 per cent rate was extended to the end of 2022 and the 22 per cent rate to the end of 2023.

As we saw in this book's introduction, many advocates of clean energy were deeply concerned during 2021–2 that this deferred phasedown *would* hold, and that solar developers would indeed have to make do with a 22 per cent credit in 2023 and a 10 per cent credit from 2024. For while President Biden was in favour of another, long-term extension, the Republicans, and the Democrat Joe Manchin, stood in his way in the Senate. But, at the eleventh hour, the impasse was broken. The Inflation Reduction Act of August 2022 legislated a major renewal of all of the country's renewables tax credits, the ITC included.

A brief overview of the new framework is worth rehearsing. Essentially, all credits were extended to 2033, with the value of the PTC being maintained (at 1.5 cents per kWh) and the ITC being restored to the full 30 per cent subsidy. Moreover, three notable new provisions were introduced. First, utility-scale projects must satisfy apprenticeship and prevailing wage requirements to receive full credit value. Second, both the PTC and the ITC will be technology-neutral from 2024: in other words, the rates and rules applying to each, which historically have differed as between different technologies, will be standardized. And, third, there is a 'direct pay' provision. Historically, only entities with tax liabilities could claim the credits, which is why developers often have only been able to access the subsidy by transferring it to an entity with such a liability – typically a bank, in return for tax equity financing. But direct pay allows entities without tax liabilities, including non-taxable bodies such as public agencies, to benefit from the credits.

Most experts expect that the 2022 strengthening and extension of the US's principal mechanism of state support for renewables will have a substantial impact on the country's ability to achieve its climate goals. Researchers at Princeton's REPEAT Project, for instance, estimated that, all told, the Inflation Reduction Act would see the US cut its emissions by 42 per cent on 2005 levels by 2030 (versus anywhere from 24 to 35 per cent under pre-Act policies), with electricity generation playing the leading role, and this 'in large part' due to the new tax credit framework.[26]

Our own immediate interest, of course, is less in what this support framework will in practice achieve, than in what its materialization suggests about the contemporary political economy of renewable power. Certainly, the IRA makes a mockery of the argument – which, bafflingly, some high-profile commentators continued to make even after its legislative passage – that clean energy in the US 'no longer . . . requires

---

26   Z. Hirji, 'How the Senate's Big Climate Bill Eliminates 4 Billion Tons of Emissions', 4 August 2022, bloomberg.com.

political interventions for survival'.[27] This is an adulteration of the truth. That external economic support for the development of solar and wind power, despite the historic cheapness today of such power, remains utterly fundamental to the renewables landscape is, ironically, perhaps clearer and more explicit in the US – the putative home of 'free markets' – than anywhere else in the world.

## IV

In many significant respects, India's electricity sector looks very, very different from the US's. Where the latter is dominated – depending on the region – either by territorially delimited, vertically integrated monopoly suppliers or by wholesale spot markets featuring unbundled power producers and distributors, the former is dominated by bilateral, long-term power purchase agreements (PPAs) between producers and distributors, through which the vast bulk of electricity is transacted.

In other respects, however, there are important similarities, not least with regard to renewables. Most notably, the idea of 'zero-support' renewable power is conspicuous by its absence in both: in India, as in the US, state support for renewables remains integral, and continues to be understood as such. This, pointedly, is despite India already enjoying the world's lowest weighted-average total installed costs for renewables projects – some \$618 per kW in 2019.[28] In fact, as we will see, this is part of the problem. So much, in short, for the nostrum that cheapness somehow obviates economic support.

What form or forms does such support take in India? Much discussion of Indian solar and wind power makes mention of the country's Renewable Purchase Obligation (RPO) scheme, which is designed to compel distribution companies to procure a minimum share of their power requirement from renewables generators. Attention to this scheme is understandable. Even as enforcement historically has been

---

27 D. Wallace-Wells, 'Even in Texas, You Can't Stop the Green Revolution', *New York Times*, 14 June 2023.

28 A. Kumar Shukla, D. V. Thangzason Sonna and V. Kumar Srivastava, 'Renewable Energy – The Silent Revolution', *RBI Bulletin*, October 2021, rbi.org.in, p. 221.

lax, the RPO certainly plays an important role.[29] Moreover, in recent years, the government has reaffirmed the importance of this mechanism, lifted targets – rising from 25 per cent in 2023 to over 40 per cent by the end of the decade – and, perhaps most significantly, created an RPO Compliance cell, indicating newfound emphasis on adherence. Experts regard all this as being likely to provide 'further impetus' to renewables' development.[30]

Nevertheless, the main form of support offered to renewables in India is long-term price stability. As mentioned, PPAs between generators and distributors (DISCOMs), most of the latter being state-owned, provide the core scaffolding of the electricity market. In the case of PPAs specifically with solar or wind plants, these contracts historically used feed-in tariffs, priced on a cost-plus basis. In the 2010s (2010 for solar, 2017 for wind), the country transitioned to reverse auctions for renewables contracts, much like across Europe. It is at these auctions that companies bid to establish new capacity, with the winning bidder being awarded the PPA. But, even if the method of price setting has changed, the contractual price *form* remains the same in terms of its essential characteristics: the price is fixed, and for the long term.

While this framework supports and occasions investment in new renewables capacity, it is not without its difficulties. On the one side, rising equipment costs beginning in early 2021 are, as the IEA has noted, 'putting additional stress on developers who bid aggressively in auctions, betting on further continuation of earlier cost reductions'.[31] There are echoes here of, for example, Avangrid, and the impact of similarly rising costs on the profitability of its own recently signed PPAs in the US offshore sector (Chapter 8). On the other side of the market, the financial health of India's DISCOMs has been parlous for a decade or more, and this has had increasingly deleterious knock-on effects in recent times for renewables investment.

For one thing, as the *Economist* has observed, the DISCOMs' lack of financial sturdiness unnerves banks seeking to finance generating

29   S. Ahluwalia, 'National Electricity Policy 2021: Making India's Power Sector Future-Ready', June 2021, orfonline.org, p. 14.

30   R. Agarwal, S. Gulati and S. Thangzason, 'Renewable Energy and Electricity Price Dynamics in India', *RBI Bulletin*, May 2019, rbi.org.in, p. 27.

31   IEA, 'Renewables 2021: Analysis and forecast to 2026', December 2021, iea.org, pp. 43–4.

companies, since such DISCOMs 'do not look like the safest of [PPA] counterparties'.[32] Furthermore, in view of their indebtedness, DISCOMs have been serially delaying signing PPAs with auction winners, thereby risking project postponement and even cancellation.

Nor is the phenomenon of delays in PPA consummation just a matter of the DISCOMs' particular financial straits. More significantly, perhaps, it reflects developments in the sector's economic fundamentals. Specifically, DISCOMs also delay signing new contracts because the medium-term trend in auction prices – in line with generator costs – has been solidly downwards, raising, as the DISCOMs see it, the possibility, or at least the hope, that delay might allow for market-aligned price renegotiation.[33] Indeed, some DISCOMs have also been attempting to renegotiate the prices of contracts already signed.

For all these reasons, policymakers, along with commentators both in and outside India, have been insistent on the need for continuing, even bolstered, sector support. That renewables' very cheapness has been a material factor in necessitating such renewed support is eminently paradoxical, but nonetheless true.

What we have seen is effectively a variant on the phenomenon of price cannibalization (Chapter 7). The Indian government has been required to reinforce its role in supporting the renewables sector because falling generator costs and thus auction prices raise expectations of more of the same, exerting a chilling effect on the willingness of off-takers to lock in prices that may in due course appear uncompetitive. Generators, too, have themselves been up in arms, urging the government to instead use closed bids when tendering for new renewables capacity. The reverse auctions currently used, the generators maintain, depress prices and hence their own profits, thereby constraining their appetite for further investment.[34]

Though certainly not appeasing all parties, the government's response to these recent challenges has been relatively robust, taking two main forms.[35] First, it has provided support to the struggling DISCOMs – and by extension, one can add, to their generator counterparties – by

32    'Will India Become a Green Superpower?', *Economist*, 20 October 2022.
33    R. Baruah, 'No Takers for Green Power Worth 5 GW', 28 October 2022, livemint. com.
34    Ibid.
35    'Will India Become a Green Superpower?'

effectively underwriting new long-term renewables PPAs. Second, it has provided increasingly valuable indirect subsidies to renewables generators by facilitating processes of land procurement, most strikingly through the establishment of clean energy 'parks' complete with grid connections.

Devleena Ghosh and colleagues have recently written about a particularly notable example of the latter policy. At Pavagada, in the southern state of Karnataka, the years 2015 to 2019 saw the development of one of India's – and the world's – largest solar parks, comprising a cluster of generating facilities under heterogeneous ownership and with a cumulative capacity of around 2 GW spread across some 12,000 acres. Key to making the opportunity bankable for private sector developers, Ghosh and her co-authors explained, was the method of land aggregation employed. The state – in the shape of a joint venture between provincial and central government bodies – did all the work, and shouldered all the expense, of arranging twenty-eight-year leases with over 1,400 local landowners, then subleasing this land affordably to the various generating companies that were successful in securing long-term PPAs at auction.[36]

For now, at least, the combination of fiscal guarantees to DISCOMs and indirect, land-based subsidies to generators seems to be doing the job. Indeed, as economists from the Reserve Bank of India have pointed out, if renewable power in India today can indeed be generated as cheaply as fossil-fuel-based power, it is in significant measure *because* of the state's latter-day twofold role in the renewables sector as both financial backstop and land agent.[37]

## V

For all the opprobrium frequently heaped on China in view of its continued substantial investment in fossil-fuel-based power, it is unarguable that China, historically and today, has also been the world's leader in

36   D. Ghosh, G. Bryant and P. Pillai, 'Who Wins and Who Loses from Renewable Energy Transition? Large-Scale Solar, Land, and Livelihood in Karnataka, India', *Globalizations* (2022).

37   Kumar Shukla, Thangzason Sonna and Kumar Srivastava, 'Renewable Energy – The Silent Revolution', p. 227.

driving investment in solar and wind power – in terms both of wind and solar plants generating electricity renewably, and of the turbine and cell technologies used not just by generating plants in China itself, but around the globe. Such, indeed, are the contradictions of the contemporary political economy–ecology of the world's largest nation. At any rate, across the five years beginning in 2017, China added more net solar and wind capacity than all of Europe has installed in its entire history.

Given the sheer scale and rapidity of this historical investment, and given also the degree of power over economic life that remains vested in Chinese state institutions, it would be naive to imagine that the investment has occurred purely by dint of market forces. It plainly has not. Ever since growth in Chinese solar and wind capacity entered overdrive a little more than a decade ago – it took about twenty years, from the beginning of the 1990s to the beginning of the 2010s, for the share of solar and wind in national electricity output to go from 0 to 1 per cent, but only around another ten years to go from 1 to 10 per cent – government support mechanisms have been nothing less than pivotal.

The key intervention came with the introduction of feed-in tariffs designed specifically for renewables operators, and initially modelled on Germany's version of this popular policy instrument. FiTs for onshore wind were introduced in 2009, and for solar PV in 2011; offshore wind came later, in 2014.

Two aspects of China's renewables FiTs immediately warrant comment. First, subsidy was explicit, inasmuch as the tariffs received by the wind or solar generator were higher than the tariffs received by fossil-fuel-based generating plants. In China, there is a so-called 'benchmark' tariff, established by regulators and varying from region to region, which is that which is paid to coal-fired plants, which still dominate overall generation. We will have more to say about this benchmark tariff, and its importance, in due course. The point to make here is simply that renewables FiTs were set higher than this tariff. The increment (that is, the subsidy) was to be paid by central government, out of a central fund of renewables energy surcharges on electricity consumption.[38]

Second, the expectation and aim from the outset was that the subsidy

38  M. Davidson, 'Policymaking and Energy Supply and Demand in China's Domestic Economy', 17 March 2022, china.ucsd.edu, p. 2.

element incorporated in renewables FiTs would be temporary. As investment in the underlying technologies expanded and their costs duly fell, the renewables sector, it was thought, could gradually be weaned off subsidy through progressive reductions of that subsidy. This approach, of course, has not been unique to China. What *has* been unique to China, however, is the extent of domestic influence over the relevant economic dynamics: it has been principally investment and innovation by Chinese manufacturers that have driven down solar and wind technology (and thus also power generation) costs worldwide in recent times.

Since China introduced its renewables FiTs, investment has occurred in waves rather than evenly, featuring a series of investment peaks and troughs. These oscillating investment rhythms can be traced in large measure to a series of policy-related factors. One such responsible factor has replicated that which drove a sharp uptick in Spanish renewables investment in the years from 2008 to 2010. As we saw in Chapter 7, Spain, in 2007, introduced FiTs that soon turned out to be extremely generous insofar as technology costs fell much faster and further than policymakers had anticipated. Comparable advantageous conditions have been evident in China, in particular in the early 2010s: materializing, that is, in Anders Hove's words, due to 'declines in wind and solar capital costs that outpaced adjustments to administratively set feed-in tariffs'.[39] Essentially, renewables developers exploited an opportunity for arbitrage represented by the growing gap between cost price and tariff price, which was opened up by administrative sluggishness.

Something else that we discussed in Chapter 7 was the high levels of curtailment of renewable power that historically have plagued a number of countries, China included. By the mid-2010s, renewables curtailment rates nationwide in China had climbed to above 10 per cent, rising to multiples of that figure in those regions where renewable capacity was concentrated. Government policy vis-à-vis remuneration for curtailment lacked clarity, but the basic position to that point had been that renewables generators whose production was curtailed

---

39   A. Hove, 'Trends and Contradictions in China's Renewable Energy Policy', August 2020, energypolicy.columbia.edu, p. 2.

were generally not compensated.[40] Clearly, however, high levels of curtailment were a problem for the government's objective of phasing out renewables subsidies. From the perspective of developers, a high probability that a substantial share of output would be curtailed and not remunerated was reason enough not to invest in new capacity; the government reducing or withdrawing subsidies would only compound matters.

So the government took action. Most importantly, in 2016, it mandated that renewables generators henceforth must be compensated for curtailment, principally by grid operators, which remain state-owned. Meanwhile, additional measures were introduced to back this principal strategy up. Inspection teams were sent around the country to check that grid operators and local governments were indeed prioritizing renewables integration, and provinces not effectively tackling curtailment were banned ('red-lit') from approving new renewables projects, with Gansu, Xinjiang and Tibet all suffering this ignominy at one point or another.[41]

Together, all this worked. By 2019, China had largely solved its curtailment problem, with wind curtailment having fallen to 4 per cent (from a high of 17 per cent just three years earlier) and solar to just 2 per cent (from a 2015 high of 11 per cent).[42] If an initial surge in renewables investment in the early 2010s in response to the introduction of FiTs (and their maintenance at generous levels) had contributed to causing the elevated curtailment rates of the mid-2010s, then the successful tackling of curtailment from 2016 onwards served, in turn, as a spur – though not the only one – for a noteworthy later investment surge: in 2020, China's net additions of solar and wind capacity more than doubled year-on-year, to an all-time high of approximately 120 GW.

Finally, there has been a third, more readily explicable policy-related driver of swings in renewables investment in China over the past decade or so. This concerns the extent and timing of reductions in the country's central FiT subsidies, which the government eventually felt confident enough to begin to implement. Historical investment

40    Ibid., p. 4.
41    'China Pushes Regions to Maximize Renewable Energy Usage', 30 August 2019, reuters.com.
42    Hove, 'Trends and Contradictions in China's Renewable Energy Policy', p. 5.

data for China – but also for many other countries – show that when deadlines for subsidized renewables investment have been approaching, which is to say when investment must occur by a particular point in time in order to benefit from a rate of subsidy that will subsequently be reduced, money has often poured in, in order to take advantage while the opportunity lasts. Such last-minute 'binges' represent among the clearest evidence there is of the economic significance that renewables subsidies indeed bear. Unsurprisingly, perturbations of more regular rhythms of investment have tended to be particularly pronounced when policy changes have been substantial and have not been signalled well in advance.

Take China's experience with solar as an example. The first half of the 2010s saw a FiT-inspired boom in Chinese solar investment that many commentators expected to last for much longer than it actually did. During the course of 2016, however, the government began making noises to the effect that the bonanza was soon to end, with subsidies to be cut, and perhaps dramatically so.[43] As a result, developers swiftly ramped up capacity investment to avail themselves of the extant subsidies while they still could. In 2017, China, remarkably, accounted for over 55 per cent of global net solar capacity growth.

In the event, the government not only did subsequently reduce solar subsidies, but did so in a fashion that sharply limited companies' ability to plan accordingly. In mid-2017, it announced an accelerated attenuation of subsidies, to take immediate effect.[44] No wonder that, having jumped in 2017, the annual amount of newly installed solar capacity then fell back in both 2018 and 2019.

Already by 2017, then, the proverbial writing was on the wall for renewables developers in China: the government was indeed determined to phase out explicit subsidies, and it was now beginning the process of doing so. This process was hastened by financial difficulties at the fund that channelled renewables surcharges on electricity consumers into the hands of subsidy recipients. With more renewable capacity having been built than officials had originally expected, and with the

43  'China Looking to Dramatically Cut Solar PV FiT', 29 September 2016, pv-magazine.com.

44  L. Bin, 'China's Solar Industry Is at a Crossroads', 13 August 2018, chinadialogue .net.

same officials having been unwilling to raise the consumer surcharge, the fund had accrued what one observer described as a 'yawning deficit', leading to payment of the subsidies increasingly often being 'extremely delayed'. This, the same observer said, was a 'major factor' in the eventual closure of the central subsidy programme.[45]

By 2019, it was clear to all concerned that perhaps two or three more years of such subsidies was probably the most they could hope for. Thus, while the significant increase in investment in new wind and solar capacity that occurred in 2020 – and which was sustained to an impressive extent in 2021, despite a material hit from COVID-19 – was spurred in part by the government's successful easing of the country's curtailment problem (and of the associated obstacles to new investment), it was spurred principally by developers' eagerness to squeeze the final remaining juice out of China's renewables FiTs. Such eagerness proved justified. In mid-2021, Beijing terminated explicit central government subsidies for newly installed, utility-scale solar and onshore wind; offshore wind had its subsidy abolished at the beginning of 2022.

It is, needless to say, too early to tell what the impact of such subsidy withdrawal will be on the scale and pace of Chinese renewables investment in the medium term. Plenty of observers have worried that investment will now enter a period in the doldrums. But all the evidence suggests that the impact is in fact unlikely to be dramatic; solar and wind net capacity additions actually reached an all-time high of around 123 GW (slightly above 2020's total) in 2022. There are several reasons for supposing that investment will remain robust.

For one thing, although the central government revenue subsidy has been removed, support in the form of revenue stabilization has not. Companies developing new renewables facilities in China today typically have a choice between selling power into China's embryonic wholesale markets, or taking a twenty-year contract that, in place of the specific renewables tariff previously available, pays a fixed price pegged to the regulated provincial benchmark (that is, coal) tariff.[46] 'In most provinces,' the IEA remarked in late 2021, 'utility-scale onshore wind

---

45   Davidson, 'Policymaking and Energy Supply and Demand in China's Domestic Economy', p. 3.

46   They might also sign a bilateral PPA with a corporate consumer or local electricity retailer, but such contracts remain relatively few and far between.

and solar PV projects can achieve reasonable returns with a twenty-year fixed price contract at provincial coal prices.' As such, the IEA fully expected that most developers would continue to choose this less risky option rather than braving wholesale markets 'nascent with high price volatility', and that renewables installations in China would remain buoyant despite the termination of the central revenue subsidy scheme.[47] The aforementioned data for capacity installations in 2022 appeared to bear this optimism out.

Then there is the matter of support from the central bank, the People's Bank of China (PBOC). It is surely significant that just as the government was eliminating its central feed-in tariffs, the PBOC – an arm of the self-same government – was introducing the Carbon Emission Reduction Facility (CERF), which, it will be remembered from Chapter 4, helps lower the cost of borrowing for renewables developers. The CERF was launched in November 2021, exactly in time to provide a soft landing for developers newly cut off from central FiTs. Whether one calls this a 'subsidy' or not, it quite clearly bolsters the economic viability of new solar and wind projects. Notably, in early 2023, the PBOC announced it would keep the CERF in place until at least the end of 2024.

Moreover, the reality is that subsidies per se – namely of the type that have stimulated China's solar and wind sectors historically – have not disappeared so much as been decentralized. In terminating central subsidies, the government has made it clear that it expects provincial and local authorities to take up the baton instead. To what degree this expectation effectively represents an order is, of course, difficult to tell: one commentator describes the onus that Beijing is now placing on regional state actors vis-à-vis renewables development in terms of 'active encouragement'; others have written simply of increased 'pressure' being applied.[48] At any rate, subsidies do still exist, even if, in view of their devolved nature, they are now considerably harder for external analysts to scrutinize, summarize and sometimes even see.

Monica Sun and colleagues, for example, have noted that local

---

47   IEA, 'Renewables 2021: Analysis and Forecast to 2026', p. 36.

48   A. Wantenaar, 'China's Green Subsidies Shift to Provinces and Specific Initiatives', 28 April 2022, rethinkresearch.biz; C. Xuewan and D. Jia, 'China Curbs Renewable Energy Target through 2025', 2 June 2022, asia.nikkei.com.

renewables subsidies in China can and do take a range of forms.[49] One, notably, is a FiT designed more or less exactly along the same lines as that which was previously offered by the central government, only now granted locally – such a subsidy is expected to be widely available for offshore wind projects in particular. In April 2022, for instance, the province of Zhejiang, one of the country's most important for offshore wind, announced a subsidy of precisely this type. For projects approved and connected to the grid in 2022 or 2023, the province said it would pay a ten-year subsidy of $0.0042 per kWh (for those 2022-connected, and up to a maximum of 600 MW) or $0.0021 per kWh (2023-connected, up to 1.5 GW) above the provincial coal tariff.[50]

Other leading offshore wind provinces, interestingly, have opted for one-off subsidies to directly support upfront investment, as opposed to such ongoing revenue subsidies. Guangdong, for example, agreed to meet the cost of $236 per kW of offshore capacity installed in 2022, $157 per kW installed in 2023, and $79 per kW in 2024. Shandong's comparable per-kW subsidies were set at $126, $79 and $47 for the same three years respectively, and it said that it would pay such subsidies up to maximum cumulative capacity installations of 2 GW in 2022, 3.4 GW in 2023 and 1.6 GW in 2024.[51]

Given all of this, then, what are we to make of China's 'zero-subsidy' renewables plants, such as the one referred to at the beginning of this chapter, which was the 50 MW Heiyazi wind farm that the China National Nuclear Corporation built at Yumeng in Gansu province in 2019? Two observations seem particularly important to make.

First, such plants are often not in fact zero-subsidy – still less zero-support – enterprises. The label 'zero-subsidy' typically means zero-*central*-subsidy: that is, national feed-in tariff subsidy. What has or has not been subsidized locally – or, since 2021, by the central bank – is another matter, and in any event long-term fixed output prices, often a prerequisite of bankability, remain available.

Second, and maybe just as importantly, the phenomenon of 'zero-subsidy' renewables, to the extent that it actually exists, remains strictly

49    M. Sun, J. Zhang, Y. Pei and L. Gao, 'The Energy Regulation and Markets Review: China', 1 June 2022, thelawreviews.co.uk.

50    B. Lepic, 'Chinese Offshore Wind Capacity Boom Driven by State Subsidies', 23 November 2022, rigzone.com.

51    Ibid.

at the demonstration or pilot stage of development in China – hence the relatively small scale of all such facilities, Heiyazi included. The central government clearly hopes that zero-subsidy proves viable. But the evidence suggests that it is not by any means yet certain that this will indeed be the case. What the Chinese state is doing with subsidy-free renewables is what it almost always does in areas of fast-moving policy evolution, not just in the climate or energy space but more generally, which is to experiment with different policy models locally to see what works, before only then rolling out best-practice models nationwide.[52]

And, for all the recent shift in renewables subsidies of a conventional form from the centre to the provinces, the willingness – and staggering ability – of Beijing to itself plan and produce major developmental outcomes as it sees fit remains abundantly clear to see. The most noteworthy and significant recent example concerns the gargantuan 'clean energy bases' announced by President Xi Jinping in 2021. To be built mainly in the Gobi and other desert areas, the first batch of these new bases will have a combined capacity of around 100 GW; a second batch, announced the following year, will have a combined capacity of around 450 GW – broadly equivalent to Europe's total solar and wind capacity at the time of this writing. Both batches are scheduled to be completed by 2030.

The point to be emphasized here is that these new megaprojects are about as far from being market-led developments as is imaginable. This is not a case of the private sector identifying investment opportunities, weighing profitability prospects and deciding – invest or not? – accordingly. This is the state, in its most centralized and authoritative form, taking the proverbial bull by the horns, and mustering whatever resources it needs at its disposal to ensure that it delivers what it has said it will deliver.

Not only does this inevitably mean the involvement principally of state-owned enterprises. More importantly, it means that the very notion of subsidy-free or support-free renewables would, in this instance, be more or less absurd. As one of BloombergNEF's experts on the Chinese power sector observed, 'the GW-level bases that will be under construction on massive deserts will require multiple channels of

---

52   See for example, Edelman Global Advisory, 'Developments in China's Climate Finance Journey', 1 November 2022, edelmanglobaladvisory.com.

financing and policy support, which China excels at'.[53] Nothing if not explicit exercises in central planning, these bases seemingly are, in significant measure, the future of renewables expansion in China.

## VI

With the termination of the central government's core framework of solar and wind feed-in tariffs and the concomitant shift in support for private renewables development to the provincial level, there is certainly some evidence in China of increased anxiety among private sector renewables developers. Indeed, one well-informed commentator went so far as to suggest, in early 2022, that having 'played an important role in the growth of [China's] renewable energy', the private sector was showing signs of 'retreating from generation due to policy uncertainty and other barriers to competition'.[54]

Yet any such 'retreat' in contemporary China is, as yet at least, as nothing compared with what the private sector does when support really is meaningfully removed from a political-economic context in which it is patently still needed. For illustrative purposes, let us briefly consider what appears to be the best recent example of that happening.

A particularly good question for a future energy market trivia quiz would be the following: Which country installed the third most new renewable energy capacity worldwide in 2020? It turns out that the answer is not the US, or India, or one of the leading European nations. In third place that year on the list of renewables investors was a country that only just sneaks inside the world's top twenty on population, and which is outside the top twenty on economic output – Vietnam. In 2020, Vietnam added 11.8 GW of net new renewables capacity, of which 99 per cent was solar.

Why so much? The explanation is straightforward. Having introduced a subsidy for solar projects in 2017 in the form of a special feed-in tariff, the Vietnamese government announced that the subsidy would be withdrawn for any projects commencing after the end of

53   Z. Xin, 'China Furthers Efforts in Wind, Solar Power', *China Daily*, 7 June 2022.
54   Davidson, 'Policymaking and Energy Supply and Demand in China's Domestic Economy', p. 6.

2020. It was this policy deadline, explained the IEA, among others, that precipitated the 'unprecedented boom in renewable capacity additions in 2020'.[55]

The following year's investment outcome was equally striking. Solar installations collapsed – literally, to zero, if the data that the International Renewable Energy Agency was able to get its hands on are to be believed. Meanwhile, however, wind installations jumped – from around 140 MW of net new capacity in 2020 to 3.6 GW in 2021. Again, the explanation was the same. Vietnam's wind FiTs – introduced in 2018 – were slated to expire at the end of October 2021, spurring, in Daniel Kemp's words, a last-minute 'flurry of development'.[56]

In 2022, Vietnam's renewables sector found itself saturated with uncertainty. One contributory factor was the fact that a long-trailed pilot programme for corporate power purchase agreements – a potential mechanism for giving developers and their financial backers confidence about long-term revenue prospects – continued to be delayed. But the main cause of the uncertainty was clearly the absence of the government's historic explicit subsidies. What principal subsidy or support regime, if any, would follow the FiTs? Would it perhaps be auctions, as in most of Europe? Nobody appeared to know. As recently as early 2023, the issue, the IEA reported, had still not been resolved.[57]

Unsurprisingly, this uncertain environment proved discomfiting for market actors. Solar and wind developers in Vietnam told the reporter Pei-Hua Yu that they had been left 'in limbo, unclear about the future of the country's electricity procurement schemes and whether they should even stay in business'. What seemed to make especially little sense was that, in the very month – November 2021 – in which Vietnam had moved into the post-subsidy era, Prime Minister Pham Minh Chinh had pledged at COP26 to achieve net zero carbon emissions by 2050. 'All eyes are now on how this pledge to adopt a more extensive use of clean energy will materialise,' Yu wrote in May 2022. 'Five years since Hanoi rolled out incentives for solar and wind energy generation – which led

---

55    IEA, 'Renewable Energy Market Update: Outlook for 2021 and 2022', May 2021, iea.org, p. 6.

56    D. Kemp, 'Vietnam's Bid to Become a Wind Powerhouse', *Infrastructure Investor*, 14 March 2022.

57    IEA, 'Electricity Market Report 2023', p. 59.

to both sources combined contributing about one-tenth of total electricity generation by the end of last year – the industry is now at a standstill.'[58]

Across 2022 as a whole, net solar and wind capacity additions totalled 2.3 GW, representing a 35 per cent decline on 2021, and the lowest level of installations since 2018. The decline would have been considerably steeper had development finance institutions (DFIs) not stepped into the breach to provide at least some new projects with the bankability that the withdrawal of Vietnam's FiTs had summarily eliminated. To take one prominent example: an 88 MW wind farm in Ninh Thuan province developed by BIM Wind was principally facilitated by some $50 million of loans at below market rates from two DFIs (the Asian Development Bank and the Japan International Cooperation Agency) and by a $5 million grant from the Climate Innovation and Development Fund (backed by Goldman Sachs and Bloomberg Philanthropies).[59]

That investment plummets when meaningful support for renewables investment is substantially or wholly removed demonstrates precisely how significant that support in fact is, and also just how marginal – or even downright unappealing – revenue and profitability prospects, in the absence of such support, actually are. Vietnam's recent experience clearly testifies to this; but so also, if in less dramatic ways, does the recent experience of the rest of the world as surveyed in this chapter.

## VII

Let us make one final brief stopover on our whistle-stop tour of the world of 'zero-subsidy' renewables. We are heading to sub-Saharan Africa, and Zambia. Partly we are heading there because Africa has been notably absent from the chapter thus far, and indeed from much of the book more generally: as we have seen, progress in the development of solar and wind power has been slow there, these two

---

58   P-H. Yu, 'After COP26 Pledge, Can Vietnam Revive Flagging Wind, Solar Industries to Transition to Clean Energy?', 8 May 2022, scmp.com.

59   'ADM, BIM Wind Sign $107 Million Financing Package to Support Wind Energy in Viet Nam', 21 December 2022, adb.org.

generating sources still accounting for only around one-twentieth of overall electricity generation across the continent. Considering African examples is of course important in itself to the building of a balanced picture. But we are also heading to Africa because it turns out the Zambian case we shall consider provides a crucial lesson of much wider significance: namely that the notion of 'zero-subsidy' renewables not only typically is misleading, but can be positively damaging to the very prospects of renewables development.

Entering into operation in 2019, the two Zambian solar facilities we are interested in were commissioned in 2016 under the 'Scaling Solar' initiative launched the previous year by the International Finance Corporation (IFC), which is part of the World Bank. The IFC intended Scaling Solar to facilitate the rapid development of privately owned, utility-scale solar projects in lower-income countries. It would do so, the IFC said, by assisting governments in procuring new solar-generating capacity transparently and at the lowest possible cost, including by helping them to organize competitive auctions for the commissioning of such capacity. The target for the initiative was 1 GW of new capacity to be developed by 2019.[60]

The Zambian plants were the inaugural fruits of Scaling Solar. Two international developers won bids in 2016 to develop, respectively, a 54 MW and 34 MW plant. They would each sell their output under twenty-five-year fixed-price PPAs signed with ZESCO, the country's state-owned, vertically integrated electricity company, and the only buyer of power from independent producers.

In hailing this outcome, protagonists, including the World Bank itself, emphasized two principal features. The first was the strikingly low power prices that Zambia had been able to negotiate – 7.84 cents and 6.02 cents per kWh.[61] Gevorg Sargsyan, the Bank's then global lead for clean energy, further remarked that, insofar as these prices were fixed for a quarter-century, they were actually even lower than they appeared. 'This', he said of the 6-cent contract (and making an unspecified guess-timate of future inflation), 'makes the average price in real terms an even

60   A. Lee, 'Zambia Teuder Delivers Africa-Record Six-Cent Solar Under IFC Scheme', 14 June 2016, rechargenews.com.

61   T. Emery, 'Solar Can't Scale in the Dark: Why Lessons about Subsidies and Transparency from IFC's Scaling Solar Zambia Can Reignite Progress toward Deploying Clean Energy', May 2023, energyforgrowth.org, p. 9.

more astonishing 4.7 cents per kWh.'[62] Equally astonishing, secondly, were the circumstances under which this rock-bottom price had evidently been achieved, with Sargsyan, among others, assuring interested observers that 'there aren't any implicit or explicit subsidies involved in the deal'.

If the Zambia developments represented an auspicious start for Scaling Solar, however, subsequent years would profoundly disappoint. Certainly, other developments in other countries did follow: specifically, a 60 MW dual-plant facility in Senegal (Chapter 4) and a 100 MW facility in Uzbekistan, both of which began producing power in 2021, two years after the Zambia plants began generating. But that, at the time of this writing in mid-2023, has been all. Representing around only a quarter of the new capacity that the IFC had been targeting for Scaling Solar by as early as 2019, the cumulative capacity successfully commissioned under the initiative is, as the energy analyst Teal Emery has caustically observed, 'modestly larger than rooftop solar in the IFC's hometown of Washington, DC'.[63] Zooming in on the region of specific interest to us here, Emery went on to say that 'despite plentiful equatorial sunshine, falling equipment prices, and massive additions to solar capacity globally, Sub-Saharan Africa continues to lag as a global outlier in solar development'.

Why is that? Why has Scaling Solar made barely a dent in the massive stock of latent solar capacity in Africa that could, in principle, be developed? Needless to say, there are numerous contributory factors, but a key one, Emery has convincingly argued, is the fact that the Zambia breakthrough was *not* in reality subsidy-free.

Emery has documented at least three different sources of support for the Zambian solar developments that it would be disingenuous to understand as being anything other than subsidies. The first was a subsidy to the cost of the capital that the developers raised to develop the facilities – as in our abovementioned Vietnamese example. As Emery noted, this subsidy was almost certainly the most financially significant of the three, while also being the hardest to quantify. Multilateral and bilateral DFIs, including the IFC itself, provided all of the approximately $80 million of debt financing to the Zambia plants, yet they did so at

62    G. Sargsyan, 'Why Zambia's 6 cents is more significant than Dubai's 3 cents', 7 June 2016, blogs.worldbank.org.
63    Emery, 'Solar Can't Scale in the Dark', p. 5.

undisclosed rates. How can Emery – and we – be so sure that the actual lending rates were at a discount to market rates? For one thing, the rates offered by institutions of that type invariably are so discounted – that is part of their raison d'être and operating model. More importantly, and as a BloombergNEF analyst concluded in examining the case, the developers simply could not have made the numbers work *unless* there was significant subsidization of capital costs: market interest rates would have been prohibitive.[64] Hence Emery's (and others') judgement that the debt was likely 'heavily subsidized'.[65]

Second, the Zambian government provided 'infrastructural' subsidies of a type that will be familiar to readers from earlier in this chapter. Located to the south of Lusaka, the Zambian capital, the two plants were both built on land provided by the government, within an industrial park that already had a reliable grid connection via a substantial local electricity substation.[66]

Third and lastly, a study of the Zambian case carried out in 2018 found that, subsequent to the commissioning of the plants, the government also furnished incremental subsidies via tax renegotiations with both developers.[67]

And, of course, as we have seen, economic support for renewables projects does not necessarily take the form only of subsidy (explicit or otherwise), and in Zambia the relevant non-subsidy forms of support were several. Most obviously, there were the fixed-price contracts themselves, which provided the promise of revenue stability widely sought by renewables developers and their lenders. On top of that, World Bank bodies provided additional forms of risk mitigation. To offset the perceived risk of signing a long-term off-take agreement with an entity – ZESCO – with a history of well-publicized financial difficulties, the International Development Association, a sister organization to the IFC, provided payment guarantees worth around $6 million. And because the loan financing of the facilities incorporated an element of interest-rate risk, the IFC provided rate swaps to mitigate that risk.[68]

---

64    J. Chase, 'Scaling Solar for Africa: Zambia's 6-Cent PV', 1 June 2016, scalingsolar
.org.

65    Emery, 'Solar Can't Scale in the Dark', p. 10.

66    Ibid., pp. 9, 14.

67    Ibid., pp. 12–13.

68    Ibid., p. 9.

More valuable still than Emery's documentation of the various forms of support afforded the 2016 Zambian solar developments was his analysis of how the case was presented to the wider world, not least by the World Bank. As we saw, the Bank's Gevorg Sargsyan insisted there were no subsidies; 'other official messaging', Emery found, then 'parroted this zero-subsidy narrative'.[69] Such concordant messaging included, most notably, a TED talk praising the inaugural Scaling Solar project by the former World Bank president Jim Yong Kim, which has been viewed more than 100,000 times.

If we want to understand why Scaling Solar subsequently stalled, Emery has maintained, it is essential to recognize the counterproductive impact of this messaging. The flatly untrue zero-subsidy claim damaged the prospects for further development of the solar market in low-income countries and thus undermined the basic goals of the Scaling Solar initiative itself because, said Emery, it 'skewed market expectations' and thereby generated misalignments between governments, developers and lenders.[70]

'If six-cent solar can be achieved in Sub-Saharan Africa without explicit or implicit subsidies, why', DFIs, for their part, now wondered, 'should [we] lend scarce concessional dollars to these projects?' It was a reasonable question to ask. The World Bank's messaging intimated that subsidized capital was not needed because cheap solar could be developed at market-based financing rates, thus perpetuating what Emery has described as the myth 'that with some good advice and a little guarantee, small amounts of DFI capital can catalyze large sums of private investment'.[71]

Meanwhile, the governments of other low-income countries now expected developers to offer bargain-basement electricity prices without subsidies being provided to them – this, after all, was what they were told had happened in Zambia. But of course, when not offered subsidies on the same scale as the developers had *actually* received in Zambia, it proved impossible for developers elsewhere to offer such competitive bids, or at least to do so with any expectation of turning a profit. With developers 'unable to match Scaling Solar [Zambia]'s purportedly

---

69   Ibid., p. 14.
70   Ibid., p. 15.
71   Ibid.

unsubsidized low tariff rates', the upshot, unsurprisingly, was 'disappointment and consternation amongst African governments'.[72]

Put out not to be receiving the same attractive terms seemingly available in Zambia, some governments even backed out of signed deals. Emery cited Nigeria as an example. In 2016, to accelerate the process of speeding renewables development towards its target of 40 per cent penetration by 2030, the Nigerian government announced it would be awarding a new set of PPAs to solar producers through competitive tender. In the event, contracts were given to 14 producers at a reported tariff of 11.5 cents per kWh. But in October 2018, the government reneged. It considered the price too high, and was insisting on a price – 7.5 cents – that the developers rejected. In support of its objection, the government cited competitive solar procurements elsewhere in Africa with prices below 7 cents. Foremost among them was Zambia's.[73]

Emery's account of the fate of Scaling Solar in Africa and beyond is a salutary one. That governments around the world should today laud the alleged economic competitiveness of renewable power is, on the one hand, entirely understandable. It will be recalled from earlier chapters – and will perhaps be recognizable to readers from ongoing daily news reports – that, in many places, opposition to faster renewables deployment remains forceful and fierce. The claim that renewables no longer need economic support can perhaps help quell such opposition, much of which is based on economic arguments, many of these being specious.

Yet at the same time, to maintain that renewables are 'subsidy-free' in cases when in fact they are not is to play with fire. It is – if the mixing of metaphors can be excused – to create a rod for the back of the renewables cause. *Why won't developers do what we want in the absence of subsidies?*, governments are liable to ask. Seen in this light, dubious 'no subsidy' claims are, at the very least, unhelpful, and if they lead to governments digging in heels and thus abandoning or scaling down potential renewables developments, such claims are positively detrimental.

---

72  Ibid.

73  B. Bungane, 'Nigerian gov continues to battle tariff structure with solar IPPs', 5 October 2018, esi-africa.com.

## VIII

How should we sum all this up? Not only, it is evident, has renewables investment worldwide been growing much more slowly than all credible commentators agree that it needs to be doing. And not only, moreover, is demand more specifically for zero-support renewables definitively not 'booming' (to use the word employed by the journalist Julian Wettengel in 2021, and cited at the beginning of this chapter). But there is in fact a serious question mark as to whether a single example of a substantive and truly zero-support facility even actually exists, anywhere in the world.

In other words, despite the remarkable progress that has undoubtedly been made in the past decade in bringing down the costs of solar and wind technologies, the remaining obstacles to generator profitability and attendant investment concerns mean that the renewables sector is still utterly dependent on government support for continuing growth.

Or, to express things differently, let us put it this way. If, notwithstanding renewables' relative cheapness, support remains essential, and remains so everywhere, then the inescapable lesson is that however significant an economic impediment to the growth of renewables their cost has been in the past, cost has not been – and today clearly is not – the only such significant impediment.

The world in which we currently find ourselves, at any rate, represents a textbook example of what Antonio Gramsci famously called an interregnum, when the old – fossil-fuelled power – is dying, though not dead, and the new – clean power – cannot be fully born. That such a scenario is neither one thing (the old) nor another (the new), but rather an awkward and dysfunctional hybrid of the two, is, as Gramsci said, the crux of its crisis tendencies. A 'great variety of morbid symptoms' tend to proliferate in this interregnum, Gramsci remarked. It is these morbid symptoms – not electric dreams so much as electric nightmares – that we will look at now.

# 10

# Electric Nightmares

In the summer of 2022, much of the Indian subcontinent was roiled by a deepening electricity crisis. The crux of the crisis was insufficient power generation. In parts of Bangladesh, where the government battled to dampen demand through measures such as controls on the use of air conditioning, rolling power blackouts of five, nine or even twelve hours a day were reported. It was a similarly bleak picture across India and Pakistan. In the former, schools were forced to close ahead of schedule for the summer break. In the latter, the official working week was cut from six days to five. Everywhere, discontent, dissent and, on occasion, demonstration were fuelled by the toxic mix of unstable and deficient electricity supply on the one hand, and, on the other, disruptive state interventions in working and domestic life designed to mitigate the crisis.

The proximate causes of the crisis were easy to identify. Most obviously, there was the heat. India, for instance, recorded its warmest weather in over a century, causing peak electricity demand – driven by tens of millions of air conditioning units being switched to full capacity – to surge to all-time highs of above 200 GW. Neither in India, nor in Bangladesh or Pakistan, in the latter of which the situation was exacerbated by severe summer flooding, could generators cope. Partly the problem was a simple shortfall of generating capacity, and, in particular, of capacity located close to where demand was concentrated, and hence not separated from it by strained transmission networks. But more than that, the problem was fuel shortages. All three countries still rely predominantly on fossil fuels to produce power – especially Bangladesh (mainly gas) and India (mainly coal) – and all three were faced with acute fuel deficits.

For those sweltering in the sun, it truly was a nightmare. Not only did blackouts cut off the one source of relief for those households fortunate enough to own air conditioners. But, as Premsagar Tasgaonkar of the climate-resilience group WOTR observed, those power cuts that occurred – as they often did – during evening hours disturbed sleep cycles and left people increasingly fatigued.[1] As resistance to environmental stress was sapped, hospitalizations and deaths from heatstroke soared.

Not least among the nightmarish implications were environmental ones, as political commitments to cut emissions paled in the fire of the energy emergency. Insofar as gas supplies were the most pressured, the region engaged in a collective dash for coal. In Bangladesh, for example, the authorities hurried to ready new coal-fired power plants at Payra and Rampal. Pakistan expanded domestic production of lignite, among the dirtiest of coals from a climate pollution perspective. Meanwhile India doubled down on its own existing coal dependency: in the six months from March to September, the country's coal-fired power output was fully 10 per cent higher than in the equivalent period in 2021.[2]

Interestingly, there was only one region of the world where coal-fired power output grew at a faster rate than in India over that time frame. The region in question? The European Union.

|

We will come to Europe in due course. Oddly, though, the best place to begin in attempting to come to grips with what was happening on the Indian subcontinent is somewhere even further away, indeed more or less on the other side of the world. In February 2021, around a year

---

1   S. Debroy, '25 Heat Stroke Deaths in Maharashtra, Most in 6 Years', 2 May 2022, timesofindia.indiatimes.com.

2   S. Varadhan, 'India Power Binges on Coal, Outpaces Asia', 18 November 2022, reuters.com.

before the emergency situation in South Asia began to develop, the US state of Texas endured its own – albeit considerably shorter – electricity crisis. Untangling the threads of that crisis can help us to frame our understanding of how such crises are both shaped by, and also often reshape in their turn, the political economy of electricity that we have been exploring in this book: that is, a political economy in which the private sector and markets increasingly take pride of place and are expected to do the work of decarbonization that, ultimately, they are ill-equipped to perform.

As on the Indian subcontinent, the trigger of the Texas crisis was the weather, though in this case it was cold rather than heat. And whereas in Bangladesh, India and Pakistan the nub of the problem would be surging demand, in Texas the core problem was constrained supply: while demand, for heating, did surge, the challenge of meeting that increased demand became a crisis principally because the state's generation infrastructure failed it. At one point, almost half the state's generating capacity was offline, literally frozen. Rolling blackouts became, for millions of homes and businesses, outages lasting multiple days, leading directly and indirectly to the loss of life and livelihoods.

Initially, in what is a largely politically conservative state, the finger was pointed at its vast network of wind farms. It was these, it was said, that had failed, as turbines lacking the heating kits that come with plants installed in colder climes iced up; for climate naysayers, this was yet more evidence of the folly of (alleged) excessively hasty decarbonization.

But the reality was different. Certainly, many wind farms seized up. But so also, on no less a scale, did plants of other kinds. 'All types of generation technologies failed', as the authoritative scientific report on the crisis simply put it.[3] Moreover, natural gas failed doubly. Not only did gas-fired electricity plants themselves widely shut down, but gas production, storage and distribution facilities also failed to provide those generating plants with sufficient fuel. 'Failures within the natural gas system', in short, 'exacerbated electricity problems.'[4] So also, notably, did failures within the state's system of forecasting for energy

---

3   The University of Texas at Austin Energy Institute, 'The Timeline and Events of the February 2021 Texas Electric Grid Blackouts', July 2021, puc.texas.gov, p. 8.

4   Ibid., p. 9.

preparedness. The electricity demand projection contained in the most extreme weather scenario modelled by the Electric Reliability Council of Texas (ERCOT), the state's grid operator, turned out to be short by almost 15 per cent.[5]

In the official response to the crisis, one feature stood out more than any other. This was the insistence that pricing and markets – the alchemy of supply and demand – should be allowed to do their job. Not only was the crisis not taken to be evidence of the failings of markets, or even a reason to question their role as the pre-eminent mechanism of coordination of the state's electricity sector; the market was regarded as the very means to *manage* the crisis. Demand was far higher than available supply, the logic went, so it was only right and proper that wholesale prices rise.

They quickly did – from around $50 per MWh to the maximum allowable $9,000. This, reasoned the Public Utility Commission of Texas (PUCT), was rational and beneficial because it would suitably incentivize the reduction of consumption among price-sensitive – not to mention freezing – users whose retail tariffs followed wholesale rates. As Bill Stetson of the Atlantic Council's Global Energy Center noted at the time, this was hardly a new regulatory standpoint where Texas was concerned. The state, he reminded people, had 'a history of generator failure during cold weather events', and the primary regulatory response had indeed long been 'to rely on the market to increase prices during a crisis'.[6] So it was once again.

In fact, so sacrosanct were the market and the price mechanism that PUCT felt obliged to intervene in the market when it judged that the market had been prevented by ERCOT from operating in an unobstructed fashion. To be precise, it temporarily suspended and overrode market norms, specifically – if paradoxically – to reinforce the market's integrity.

The stimulus for this action was ERCOT's imposition of blackouts to maintain system balance across the grid. This, PUCT conceded, was technically necessary, but it was economically undesirable. Why? Because the result of demand being artificially reduced in this manner

5   Ibid., p. 8.
6   Atlantic Council, 'Rapid Response: SPP/ERCOT Winter Freeze Energy Crisis', 17 February 2021, atlanticcouncil.org.

was a fall in the spot price of electricity from \$9,000 to around \$1,200 per MWh. One might think that such a fall would have been welcomed, not least given the implied relief for consumers. But one would be wrong for imagining so. The fall was *unwelcome* because it effectively represented mispricing: an artificial fall in demand had led to an artificial fall in the price.

As PUCT explained in the extraordinary letter that it released on 15 February, 'energy prices should reflect scarcity of the supply', and now they did not: supply was just as scarce relative to actual, underlying demand as it had been before ERCOT intervened, but prices had – wrongly – fallen.[7] As such, it was time for price controls, of a sort. That day, PUCT directed ERCOT to modify its pricing models in such a way that the wholesale price would be restored without delay to \$9,000 per MWh. Deemed a more accurate reflection of actual scarcity, this is where prices remained, on PUCT's orders, for five days.

PUCT's specific argumentation for this intervention was incredibly revealing. Partly, of course, this was about price signals being allowed to perform their magic. Insofar as the \$1,200 price level was wrong, PUCT said, 'pricing mechanisms were not generating an optimal response to the challenge'.[8] In other words, market actors were not responding to the challenge in an optimal way. Electricity users were not cutting consumption as much as they should, and electricity generators (those still operating, at any rate) were not boosting production as much as they should – 'as if a generator [accustomed to prices of \$50 per MWh but now] being paid \$1,200', Stetson witheringly remarked, 'was insufficient to incent generator performance'.[9] In any event, by setting prices 'to more accurately reflect the scarcity conditions in the market', PUCT figured that responses on both the supply and demand sides would be optimized.[10]

But there was a deeper, more fundamental rationale for PUCT's price directive. As well as being erroneous as a measure of the actual relationship between supply and demand, the lower price that cleared after ERCOT imposed blackouts was also considered institutionally

---

7   'PUC Issues Emergency Order on Electricity Pricing', 15 February 2021, puc .texas.gov.

8   Ibid.

9   'Rapid Response: SPP/ERCOT Winter Freeze Energy Crisis'.

10   'PUC Issues Emergency Order on Electricity Pricing'.

disruptive, even threatening. Specifically, it contravened convention. 'When notified,' their letter opined, 'the Commissioners agreed that energy prices across the system clearing as low as approximately $1,200 during the first day of the weather crisis was *inconsistent with the fundamental design of the [spot] market*.'[11] This was quite the consensus: seemingly, a very way of ordering economic life was ostensibly at stake. And, so, while Stetson was undoubtedly correct to say that PUCT's intervention demonstrated 'a fundamental flaw in the over-reliance on markets to provide adequate service to customers' (for in no conceivable way did the price increase to $9,000 help consumers), this was not the most important thing the intervention demonstrated.[12] It demonstrated, at its core, a commitment to protecting a particular institutional arrangement – the market as political-economic shibboleth.

Turning specifically to the fate of renewables operators during the Texas crisis of February 2021, we find certain equally revealing outcomes. To be sure, some wind farms profited handsomely. If they continued to be able to operate more or less as normal, and if they were selling all or most of their output into the spot market, wholesale prices of $9,000 meant vast (albeit relatively brief) windfalls for some generators, used as they were to rates of less than $100 per MWh.

Yet not all emerged financially in the black. For one thing, even those that were able to continue to generate power did not necessarily benefit from the rocketing of wholesale prices. As we saw in earlier chapters, many of the renewables generators that have sprung up in the US in the past two decades, and especially in Texas, have chosen to mitigate the volatility of spot market prices by entering into either financial hedging contracts such as swaps, or bilateral fixed-price power purchase agreements (PPAs) with corporate electricity users. In fact, doing so has generally not been a *choice* – it has been necessary, to enable the raising of construction finance. For such generators, there were no windfalls to be had, either because they were actually selling at fixed prices (in the case of corporate PPAs), or because financial hedging effectively replicated fixed prices.

Moreover, for the owners of some of the many wind farms that were physically compromised by the weather, the financial impact was

---

11    Ibid. (emphasis added).
12    'Rapid Response: SPP/ERCOT Winter Freeze Energy Crisis'.

nothing less than catastrophic. This was because they were legally contracted to deliver a certain amount of power. Unable to generate that power themselves, they were required to purchase the shortfall on the spot market – at what were now, as we have seen, exorbitant rates. This occurred under two different scenarios. One was where the generator held a utility PPA, which, as we saw in Chapter 8, is typically a baseload contract, in which the amount of power to be traded is determined in advance. The other was where the generator had entered into a financial hedge incorporating a similar commitment to supply a specified quantum of power at specified dates and times.

The latter scenario proved especially ruinous in Texas, the very home of wind hedging (Chapter 6). Numerous renewables generators failed to produce enough power to satisfy the terms of their hedges, thus having to turn to the spot market, at $9,000 per MWh, to comply with their delivery obligations. RWE, the German company with wind facilities in the north and west of the state, alone reported a staggering €400 million hit.[13] At least one wind farm owner, in a financial hole to the tune of $71 million for the ten days during which its turbines iced over, went to court to try to extricate itself from its contractual obligations to the counterparty to its hedging contract, arguing that the storm was an unforeseeable act of God.[14]

It was notable who the counterparty was in this particular case: JPMorgan Chase, the investment bank. Most counterparties to the financial hedges entered into by US renewables generators are indeed financial institutions, and many enjoyed a very good Texas crisis. Where RWE lost hundreds of millions of dollars, for example, Bank of America gained hundreds of millions. 'Bank of America takes part in the Texas energy market by trading power and gas and selling products that enable generators and other asset owners to hedge against fluctuating prices,' explained the *Financial Times*. 'That activity left Bank of America with an inventory of power contracts that surged in value during the blackouts.'[15] As so often, mayhem for Main Street translated into windfalls for Wall Street.

---

13   C. Naschert, 'Offshore Wind no Longer a Game with Big Returns, Says RWE', 16 March 2021, spglobal.com.

14   T. Cochran, 'Lawsuit Claims TX Panhandle Wind Farm Not Financially Responsible after Winter Storm Causes Frozen Turbines', 11 March 2021, kltv.com.

15   G. Meyer and L. Noonan, 'Bank of America Reaps Trading Windfall during Texas Blackouts', *Financial Times*, 5 March 2021.

The irony here is extraordinary, and difficult to miss. More than any other deregulated electricity sector, the US's lacks the state-sponsored mechanisms for providing price and revenue stability that renewables generators and their financial backers value so highly: hence the popularity there of corporate PPAs and, going even further back in time, financial hedging. Nowhere has this been more evident than in Texas. Such arrangements constitute market solutions to a problem – price volatility – *created by* marketization. It was one such market solution, namely financial hedging, that floored renewables generators like RWE, effectively hoist on the petard of the misplaced faith that 'free' markets are an appropriate framework for electricity generation in general and for renewable electricity development and operation in particular.

Before we leave Texas, there is one final crucial dimension of the crisis to mention. Why, one might ask, when local electricity generation widely failed, did Texas not simply import power from elsewhere in the US? The simple answer is that by and large it *could* not – physically. For a whole range of historical reasons, not the least of which has been a desire to limit the extent of federal jurisdiction, Texas's electricity grid is almost entirely isolated, enjoying only limited interconnection to the country's other two main grids.

While the exact outcomes would be different, the brief Texas electricity crisis of February 2021, in surfacing this complex but crucial interplay between the respective dynamics of price, profit, power and place, proved a potent harbinger of what was to come.


## II


By early 2021, of course, the world was already one year into dealing with COVID-19. Whereas the Texas crisis was precipitated in part by a local surge in energy demand, the pandemic itself was notable for the opposite. As societies and economies went into varying degrees of lockdown, energy demand was widely, though not evenly, suppressed. Globally, primary energy consumption fell by as much as 4 per cent in 2020 – the largest fall in decades.

If this represented an energy crisis, it was generally not one for electricity generators, still less for renewables generators more specifically, except perhaps to the extent that lockdowns impinged on the ability of contractors to start, progress or complete new renewable energy developments. No: the COVID-19 energy crisis, such as it was, was a crisis, or so it appeared, for fossil fuels. As demand for oil and gas plunged, in particular in the transport sector, so also did oil and gas prices. From around $70 per barrel at the beginning of 2020, the oil price had collapsed to less than $30 by March, and it would remain below $50 for the rest of the year.

'Broken and in survival mode', then, was how the *Guardian,* for instance, described the state of the global fossil fuel industry in April 2020, as a result of 'plunging demand for oil wrought by the coronavirus pandemic combined with a savage price war'.[16] Citing industry experts, the newspaper said that the industry faced 'the gravest challenge in its 100-year history' and confidently predicted that it would emerge from the crisis permanently altered. If anything, all of this was expected to be a boon for renewables. At oil prices of $30 per barrel, few new hydrocarbon projects would be considered viable, thus ostensibly redoubling the impetus to rapidly develop wind and solar resources.

But, as we now know, the COVID-induced suppression of global energy demand – and the fossil fuel industry's putatively grave challenge – turned out to be relatively short-lived. During the course of 2021, overall energy demand bounced back strongly and rapidly, indeed to a level higher than in 2019. And when, and partly because, it did so, what ultimately transpired was a more or less global energy crisis that very much was about electricity, although certainly not only that.

While the vast bulk of commentary on the global energy crisis that began in 2021 has focused, somewhat understandably, on Europe, the crisis extended far beyond Europe's borders – as we saw at the outset of this chapter – and, arguably, did not begin there. Michael Davidson, writing in late 2021, made a convincing case that it actually began in a country which very few Western commentators have even considered to be a meaningful part of the crisis phenomenon.[17] That country was China.

The crisis in China began around the same time as Texas experienced its own (only temporary) local seizure, which is to say in early 2021.

---

16   D. Carrington, J. Ambrose and M. Taylor, 'Will the Coronavirus Kill the Oil Industry and Help Save the Climate?', *Guardian*, 1 April 2020.

17   M. Davidson, 'China's Power Outage', *Foreign Policy*, 18 November 2021.

Throughout 2021 and extending into 2022, it took the form, as electricity crises typically do, of an underlying imbalance between supply and demand. On the supply side, the key issue was a secular decline in the ability of China's coal-fired power plants – which continue to dominate domestic power generation – to respond to abrupt changes in demand. This, Davidson explained, was partly because Beijing had cut coal production capacity since 2016 in response to historically low profitability in the mining sector, and partly because of a near total ban on Australian coal imports imposed in October 2020.

On the demand side, the most significant factor was 2021's resurgence in global economic activity as countries – though not, ironically, China itself, or at least not its non-factory workers – emerged from lockdown. In light of China's role as the twenty-first century's workshop to the world, the uptick in global activity from the beginning of 2021 'created soaring demand for electricity in China's coastal provinces, which are home to many of the country's largest factories'. In May 2021, various cities in Guangdong implemented industrial power rationing. By September, power restrictions had already spread to more than twenty provinces, as unseasonal weather – cold in the north, warm in the south – inflated electricity demand further and pushed grids 'to the brink'. Shortages were especially severe in the north-east, where whole communities endured rolling blackouts.[18]

In a number of important respects, China's experience foreshadowed much of what we would see in the emerging energy crisis elsewhere in the world. One was the particular significance of interactions between fuel markets and electricity markets in the shaping of the crisis. In Europe, as we shall see, the fuel in question would mainly be natural gas, but in China it was coal. It was difficult for China's coal plants to respond to surging electricity demand not only in simple physical terms (that is, in terms of available fuel supply), but also economically.

On the one hand, such plants faced rapidly rising coal prices, resulting from the aforementioned supply shortages. But crucially, they were substantially unable to pass these increased costs on to electricity distribution companies and ultimately consumers because they were required to sell their output at regulated provincial tariffs that had been formally

18   Ibid.

delinked from coal prices in 2019.[19] Beijing's decision to permit plants' sale prices to depart modestly from these benchmark rates helped somewhat, but only somewhat. Essentially, as Yan Qin observed, coal-fired plants found themselves 'squeezed between "market coal prices" and "regulated electricity prices"'.[20]

This squeeze persisted into 2022, and intensified in the summer months, when the central and eastern parts of the country suffered the most serious heatwave in decades, renewing upwards pressure on both electricity demand and the price of thermal coal. Reporting in late 2022, China's electricity regulator said that the power supply situation in the aforementioned parts of the country was 'severe' and that across the first nine months of the year, the fuel costs of China's coal-fired plants were around $40 billion higher than 2021's already inflated levels.[21]

Another important way in which China foreshadowed subsequent experiences elsewhere in the world was in how the profit motive, and generators' understandable compulsion to prioritize it, tended to worsen matters. One research organization estimated that, in September 2021, on account of the dynamics identified in the previous paragraphs, Chinese coal-fired plants were on average operating at a loss of around $0.02 per kWh of output.[22] Indeed, the authorities themselves later conceded that making a loss had become more or less endemic in the sector: as of October 2022, more than half of the country's state-owned coal power companies, by Beijing's own admission, remained in the red.[23]

Unsurprisingly, many generators, and especially those in the private sector, were highly reluctant to continue to generate if doing so meant continuing to incur losses. The rational response in this (irrational?) situation was not to ramp generation up, as grids and users urgently required given rampant demand, but down. Which, to avoid generating

---

19   L. Han, Y. Hu, T. Zhang, J. Zhang, Z. Tu and Y. Chen, 'Review of Benchmark On-Grid Power Tariffs in China', *E3S Web of Conferences* 228 (2021), 01013, p. 3.

20   M. T. Lin, 'China's Energy Transition Hits a Bump in the Road amid Slow Power Market Reforms', 7 October 2021, cleanenergynews.ihsmarkit.com.

21   China Electricity Council, 'Analysis and Forecast Report on the National Power Supply and Demand Situation in the Third Quarter of 2022', 25 October 2022, cec.org.cn.

22   Lin, 'China's Energy Transition'.

23   China Electricity Council, 'Analysis and Forecast Report'.

at a loss, is what many plants did, specifically 'by drawing down inventories or faking outages'.[24] Perhaps it was indeed the self-interest of the butcher, brewer and baker that kept people fed in Adam Smith's eighteenth-century Scotland, but the self-interest of the coal-fired power generator did not serve to keep lights on in China in 2021–2.

Australia, interestingly, being part of the same broad regional trade bloc, experienced in mid-2022 a similar squeeze, eliciting a similar response from its conventional power plants. High demand for power generation combined with shortages of both coal and gas to produce rising fuel prices and – Australia's electricity market being based, like Europe's, on the merit order – rising wholesale and retail power prices. The response of the regulator, AEMO, was to cap the spot market power price, which in some states had been allowed to rise to above AU\$15,000 per MWh, at just AU\$300. Naturally, given fuel prices, many conventional generators – as in China – were faced with huge losses if they continued to generate. So they did not continue to generate. The amount of generating capacity online collapsed and AEMO was forced to suspend wholesale trading. Briefly, Australia had an electricity sector with no recognized transaction mechanism – a 'market without a market', as one observer put it.[25]

Meanwhile, where China not only gave a strong foretaste of subsequent developments elsewhere, but also closely replicated developments in Texas, was in the striking hegemony of market ideology among sundry leading 'experts'. The consensus among such experts was that China was enduring an energy crisis not *because* of the marketization that had been undertaken over the previous decade or so, but because the country's embrace of energy marketization had been half-hearted, partial and incomplete: the invisible hand was still unduly fettered, in short.

Thus the answer – including, notably, to the still-burning question of how best to hasten decarbonization – was not backtracking, but, instead, further market-led reforms. 'It takes effective market mechanisms to ensure that each power generating and related technology, in particular clean technologies, is compensated sufficiently to operate and invest in

---

24   Davidson, 'China's Power Outage'.

25   N. Bullard, 'Why Australia's Power-Grid Debacle Matters for Global Energy', 23 June 2022, bloomberg.com.

a sustainable manner,' argued Lara Dong. 'I wouldn't call it a failure of the electricity market,' Dong's own – entirely representative – assessment of the turmoil in China's energy sector in 2021 therefore ran, 'but rather say that China has not yet been able to set up a functional power market.'[26]

Of course, for evidence of the dangers of Dong's supposition, one needed only to look at what was concurrently happening in the region of the world that has long been the very poster child for electricity in its most marketized imaginable form – namely Europe.

## III

It started later in the year, but when energy crisis hit Europe in 2021 it bore considerable resemblance to the crisis that was already in full bloom in China. For, more than anything else, the crisis was rooted in a surge in energy demand for which the relevant infrastructure and institutions were not prepared. In Europe, that post-COVID surge came in the autumn. And much like in China, part of the reason why Europe's electricity system failed to respond as hoped was that it could not lay its hands quickly enough and cheaply enough on sufficient fuels to fire its power plants.

There were, however, three major differences between what transpired in Europe and what had been going on for months already in China. They are crucial to understand. First, it was a different pivotal fuel that was suddenly in short supply. Whereas China scrambled for coal, Europe was now scrambling for natural gas. Gas was (and is) the single largest source of electricity generation in Europe – accounting for around a quarter of all output in 2020, the year before the crisis developed – and, crucially, the cold winter of 2020–1 had left stocks relatively depleted. In autumn 2021, these stocks could not be replenished fast enough.

Second, gas shortages had a material impact on the finances of electricity retailers and consumers in Europe in a way that coal shortages did not in China. In the latter, as we have seen, electricity tariffs are heavily regulated: in 2021, Chinese coal-fired plants were largely unable

---

26   Cited in Lin, 'China's Energy Transition'.

to pass on increases in fuel costs – indeed, that was part of the problem, at least for generators. In Europe, however, increased natural gas costs in autumn 2021 – a result of the sudden paucity of supply relative to surging demand – could be, and were, passed on to electricity retailers and consumers.

Indeed, for reasons we established earlier in this book (Chapter 6), wholesale and retail electricity prices in Europe are in fact disproportionately influenced by gas prices. The proportion of the time when gas provides the all-important market-clearing and price-setting 'last unit' of supply in Europe's merit-order-based electricity sector substantially outstrips the proportion of electricity that gas actually physically serves to help generate. Thus, if Europe's gas prices increase, so, in turn, do its electricity prices – not for every hour, every day, since there will be periods when gas plants are not required to fire and thus when other sources will set the spot price; and not in the same degree in every country, since some countries (such as the UK) are more reliant on gas for electricity generation than others (such as Sweden); but, averaged out, the relationship holds. And that is exactly what happened in Europe in late 2021. As gas prices climbed, the prices paid by electricity retailers and users also climbed.

Notably, in Europe, the combination of rising natural gas prices with dispatch based on merit order had deleterious – indeed morbid – environmental implications as well as deleterious economic ones. By 2020, coal had seemed destined for the scrapheap of history as a major source of European electricity: its LCOE had been progressively deteriorating (that is, increasing) relative to renewables and gas, meaning it had increasingly dropped out of merit – between 2012 and 2020, the share of Europe's electricity generated using coal declined every year, nearly halving from 24.4 per cent in the former year to 12.8 per cent in the latter. But as gas prices spiked in 2021, coal, in many European countries, was suddenly back *in* merit. Coal-fired generation in Europe leapt by more than 10 per cent in 2021, therefore.[27]

Third and finally, if, in Europe, the evolving energy crisis in 2021 had an impact on the costs incurred by electricity users more than in China, there was much less of an impact in terms of service. As we saw earlier, China experienced relatively widespread rationing and blackouts.

---

27   IEA, 'Electricity Market Report: January 2022', iea.org, p. 25.

Europe did not. In fact, not only did service continue broadly as usual across the continent, but in 2021, at any rate, even the possibility of rationing, still less blackouts, was barely whispered.

This would change, however, in 2022. If Europe was definitively experiencing an electricity crisis of sorts by the winter of 2021, the crisis deepened, and took on an entirely new hue, in February 2022, when Vladimir Putin's Russia invaded Ukraine. When the rest of Europe threw its support behind Ukraine and behind a battery of international sanctions aimed at kneecapping the Russian economy, Putin responded with the only meaningful geo-economic weapon at his disposal – energy. Much of the imported coal, oil and gas upon which Europe in around 2021 was heavily reliant was imported from Russia; during the course of 2022, Putin therefore increasingly cut off those supplies, presumably in an attempt to drain Europe's enthusiasm for support for Ukraine.

Where gas specifically was concerned, Europe's imports from Russia fell by more than half year-on-year in 2022.[28] Needless to say, the effect was to intensify the principal dynamics familiar from late 2021. Thus gas prices soared ever higher as Europe, already experiencing significant supply constraints, was increasingly required to turn elsewhere than Russia for its imports, and electricity prices continued to follow gas prices vertiginously upwards. By late summer, with Putin turning the screw ever tighter, a perfect storm appeared to be approaching, as the continent's hydro and nuclear generating capacity also wobbled. The *Economist* glossed the evolving European electricity nightmare thus:

In recent weeks, forward prices for daytime electricity for the fourth quarter of the year briefly spiked above €1,200 ($1,200) per megawatt hour in Germany and above a surreal €2,500 in France. The usual price is around €50. The reason for this is simple: scarcity. The loss of [nuclear and hydro] generating capacity to maintenance (in France), closure (in Germany) and drought (across the continent) brought more and more gas plants into action, and their fuel has become extremely expensive since Russia wielded its energy weapon.[29]

---

28   G. Zachmann, G. Sgaravatti and B. McWilliams, 'European Natural Gas Imports', 8 February 2023, bruegel.org.

29   'Europe's Energy Market Was Not Built for This Crisis', *Economist*, 8 September 2022.

Sky-high prices were one thing: indeed, across 2022 as a whole, European gas prices were more than five times higher than their 2016–21 average, and the demand-weighted average wholesale electricity price for France, Germany, Spain and the UK in the second half of the year was almost four times as high as the 2019–21 average for those six months.[30] But now, as the summer of 2022 turned to autumn, rationing and even blackouts seemingly also loomed. Experts prognosticated about which European countries and regions were the most likely to face winter power cuts.

## IV

What did Europe's policymakers do in the face of this crunch? Their main priority on the electricity front was to shield users, to a certain extent, from rising costs. They did this in an assortment of different ways, comprising various combinations in different countries of tax deductions, price controls and transfers to vulnerable groups.[31] The overall tapestry of interventions was, and indeed remains, highly complex and constantly evolving. The details need not detain us, but, in the context of the key themes of this book, five brief points about these measures are particularly important to highlight.

First, policies were discussed and enacted at a range of different geopolitical scales. Some were EU policies, which individual countries were expected – albeit with a certain degree of freedom – then to implement at the national level, and to which they were required to adapt their own chosen national measures. Alongside these transnational and national policies, some of the bigger European countries also featured significant sub-national interventions.

Second, policymakers attempted to varying degrees to avoid generating moral hazard. The worry was that, if electricity users were fully

---

30    IEA, 'Electricity Market Report 2023', February 2023, iea.org, pp. 28, 35. As the same IEA report shows (p. 37), the extent to which wholesale electricity prices in 2022 rose above the average levels of the pre-crisis years varied significantly between different European countries. There were a whole range of reasons for this variance, a significant one being different degrees of dependence on gas for electricity generation.

31    See G. Sgaravatti, S.Tagliapietra, S. Trasi and G. Zachmann, 'National Fiscal Policy Responses to the Energy Crisis', 13 February 2023, bruegel.org.

shielded from the risk of high energy prices, they would have no incentive to reduce their exposure to that risk. In short, the policy objective – easily articulated, fiendishly difficult to realize in practice – was to protect users from savage cost increases without further fuelling consumption, and thus making the underlying imbalance between supply and demand even worse. One way in which policymakers sought to do this, at least in some countries, such as Germany, was by introducing measures to curb electricity demand, alongside measures relating to the cost of its supply.

Third, this wariness of moral hazard was part and parcel of a deeper, long-standing commitment to the sanctity of markets and price signals. The fundamental concern with measures such as price controls, from this standpoint, was that they would interfere with markets, muffle price signals and – as in the case of ERCOT and Texas discussed earlier – prevent actors from responding 'optimally'. The International Monetary Fund was just one of the bastions of market orthodoxy to encourage EU policymakers to keep the faith, permit markets to continue to function 'normally' and thus pass the full increase in costs on to users.[32]

No European government did this, in reality, but some would brazenly claim to have in fact remained strictly true to market discipline. Germany's finance minister Christian Lindner was perhaps the most brazen of all, describing his government's electricity 'price brake' – which literally and overtly reduced the price paid by consumers – as an instrument that functioned 'without any intervention in markets or prices . . . In contrast to instruments used in other countries,' Lindner crowed, 'our new arrangements will not affect the price formation process driven by supply and demand.'[33]

Fourth, we should nonetheless remember – from Chapter 2 – that, for all the talk of 'normal' market functioning, the European electricity sector never actually had been quite the unblemished market mecca

---

32   V. Romei, 'IMF Urges Europe to Pass On Energy Costs to Consumers', *Financial Times*, 3 August 2022.

33   C. Lindner, 'A Resilient Germany Is Weathering the Energy Crunch', *Financial Times*, 2 January 2023. The reasoning behind the claim not to be distorting markets or prices was presumably the fact that the price brake would be calculated on the basis of a user's consumption in the prior, rather than the current, year. But it is a disingenuous argument: however it is calculated, a pledged consumption subsidy influences demand and price outcomes.

that, during the crisis, many, on both left and right, imagined that it had. Even before the beginning of the energy crisis in Europe (specifically, as of 2020), the state was actively involved in intervention in price setting for household electricity customers in more than half of EU countries. The point, to which we shall return in Chapter 11, is that the closer one looks at electricity 'profits' and 'markets', even in the most 'normal' of times, the more chimerical – and less 'free' – they appear.

Finally, and most importantly of all from our perspective, the (extra) support that European governments did elect to provide to electricity users during the crisis that began in 2021 and intensified in 2022 was to be funded partly by taxes on suspected windfall profits at generating firms. Insofar as the main motor of the upwards pressure on wholesale electricity prices was rising gas prices and their channelling into power prices through Europe's merit order electricity pricing model, generators of some types, it was widely concluded, must now have been swimming in profits, not least the operators of solar and wind farms, which therefore found themselves directly in the crosshairs of European policymakers looking both to fund user subsidies and to crack down on perceived 'profiteering'.

The logic underlying the conviction that renewables firms operating in Europe were now enjoying inflated levels of profitability is not difficult to grasp, and indeed makes perfect intuitive sense.[34] Wholesale prices had increased substantially. But, for renewables firms – unlike for gas-fired plants, which were now contending with soaring gas prices – operating costs had not similarly increased: such costs, as we have seen, are minimal, and do not comprise fuel costs (Chapter 3). It was, or rather seemed, as simple as that. *Quod erat demonstrandum*: costs flat, revenues up, profits also up.

The flaw in this logic, of course, is that even in Europe, with its deep and wide electricity spot markets, not all renewables power output is actually valorized at spot market prices. Some such output circumvents the spot market altogether and is commonly sold at fixed prices, either via government feed-in tariffs or under long-term bilateral commercial contracts. And much of that which is in fact sold in the spot market is not monetized by the generator at the spot price because the generator

---

34   The argument was applied to nuclear and hydro generators, too, but our focus, for obvious reasons, will be on solar and wind.

has hedged its exposure to price volatility either through the use of market-based financial instruments like forward contracts or, more often, through government mechanisms of revenue stabilization such as feed-in premiums (see Chapters 6–9).

So, when policymakers across Europe, initially convinced by the aforementioned straightforward logic, began drawing up plans for windfall taxes on generators, they quickly discovered the issue to involve enormous conceptual and informational headaches. As the *Economist* abruptly pointed out: only some renewables capacity was 'really rak[ing] it in'.[35] In fact, some facilities, having hedged too aggressively, were now, almost perversely, losing money, among them French and German wind and solar farms owned by Norway's Statkraft.[36]

Warming to its theme, the *Economist* made the important additional observation that because many of the contracts that determine generators' ultimate revenues are private and confidential, even just identifying winners and losers – never mind taxing the former – would be challenging, and perhaps even impossible. The 'true recipients of the windfall profits', it warned governments, 'may prove hard to find'. Moreover, as had been the case with Texas and Bank of America, such recipients, the *Economist* further cautioned, 'may in fact sit outside the energy market'.[37]

Flummoxed by the complexity, some European countries briefly shelved their plans to impose such windfall taxes. Having announced in May 2022 that he would introduce such a tax, for example, Rishi Sunak, then the UK Chancellor, indicated just a month later that he had cooled on the idea, his officials signalling that it 'was proving to be too complicated to instigate'.[38] Others, however, pushed ahead, Germany among them.

Country-specific taxes within the EU, such as Germany's, were to some extent superseded in September 2022 when the bloc's energy ministers agreed an EU-wide windfall tax on non-gas power producers (including, but not limited to, renewables operators), taking the form of

35  'Britain's Government Wants to Reform Power Markets', *Economist*, 25 August 2022.

36  Statkraft, 'Interim Report Q3 2022', 11 November 2022, statkraft.com, p. 19.

37  'Europe's Energy Market Was Not Built for This Crisis'.

38  J. Pickard, G. Parker and N. Thomas, 'Rishi Sunak Cooling on Windfall Tax on UK Electricity Generators', *Financial Times*, 28 June 2022.

a revenue cap set at a maximum of €180 per MWh.[39] To apply in the period from 1 December 2022 to 30 June 2023, revenues earned above that threshold were to be redistributed to electricity users. Notably, upon announcing the tax, the EU's ministers highlighted what to them was a pivotal feature of the tax's design. It was one with which we are, by now, very familiar. A primary consideration, it was explained, had been 'to avoid distorting the wholesale electricity market'.[40] The market is dead, long live the market!

Meanwhile, the UK, now with a new Chancellor at the helm, soon followed suit. Its own windfall levy was different – a temporary 45 per cent tax on the 'extraordinary profits' of renewables and nuclear generators, namely those made on electricity sold above £75 per MWh – but it had the same premises and purpose.

Shortly after the UK's version of the tax was announced, the research firm BloombergNEF reported the results of its preliminary analysis of the policy. Perhaps the most interesting part of the analysis concerned its estimate for how much of the UK's renewables capacity would potentially be subject (or not) to the tax, given the extent of utilization of the types of direct and indirect mechanisms of price stabilization mentioned above. BloombergNEF reckoned that, in the event, only a minority share of such capacity would actually be liable. More than half of UK onshore wind, almost half of offshore wind and 'almost all' solar would likely be exempt.[41]

For observers of the political economy of energy, the crisis that engulfed Europe beginning in 2021, and governments' various attempts to respond to that crisis, summoned all manner of different powerful images – price charts exhibiting exponential growth rates, diagrammatic explanations of the hitherto mysterious but suddenly all-important merit order, and so forth. But none, maybe, would be more abiding, or more important to thinking about our energy futures, than the image

---

39   The words 'to some extent' are important: national governments were allowed to deviate from the single EU-wide cap, and indeed set different caps for different technologies. Among the governments that set the market revenue cap below the maximum level were those of Belgium, France and the Netherlands.

40   European Council, 'Three EU-Coordinated Measures to Cut Down Bills' (December 2022), consilium.europa.eu.

41   N. Bullard, 'UK Windfall Tax on Renewables Could Hurt Decarbonization Efforts', 1 December 2022, bloomberg.com.

of *themselves* that policymakers collectively, if unwittingly, presented to the world. This revealed, in short, an institutional community that, in its efforts of the past three decades first to liberalize, and then to decarbonize, the continent's power sector, has fashioned a creature whose complex and contradictory nature they barely even understand, let alone can begin effectively to manage. This image was never clearer than during all the confused political deductions, deliberations and decision making with regard to power sector windfall taxes.

## V

When the winter of 2022–3 finally arrived in Europe, commentators increasingly began to notice and discuss an interesting phenomenon. For all the widely voiced fears about absolute energy shortages, electricity blackouts and crippling knock-on effects on households and industry alike – the Federation of German Industries had predicted a 'massive recession', for instance – the reality, it appeared, was that none of this was in fact coming to pass.

Two comment pieces in the *Financial Times*, by two of the newspaper's highest-profile writers, captured the shifting mood. 'The end of Europe's energy crisis is in sight', enthused Chris Giles, as early as October 2022.[42] Two months later, noting that there had been zero impact on output levels in European manufacturing, Martin Sandbu was even minded to ask, 'What Energy Crisis?'[43] Writing in the same newspaper, the German finance minister, Christian Lindner – whose spurious claims about his country subsidizing power consumption without distorting price signals we encountered earlier – argued something similar in the first week of 2023. 'Horror scenarios of a dangerous energy rationing or a massive slump in our economy have often been bandied about', Lindner wrote. 'But we are nowhere near that.'[44]

For our purposes, commentaries such as these are important less for the degree of accuracy with which they represented the actual extent of 'crisis'

---

42   C. Giles, 'The End of Europe's Energy Crisis Is in Sight', *Financial Times*, 27 October 2022.

43   M. Sandbu, 'What Energy Crisis? European Industry Is Showing Its Adaptability', *Financial Times*, 1 December 2022.

44   Lindner, 'A Resilient Germany Is Weathering the Energy Crunch'.

(a non-crisis for some actors can of course still be a very severe crisis for others), than for how they chose to explain Europe's apparent robustness in the face of its manifold energy challenges. And, on this point, Giles, Sandbu and, indeed, Lindner were evidently in full agreement with one another. What had saved Europe, they argued, was the market.

More exactly, Europe (unlike, say, China) had, the argument ran, remained committed enough to market processes to enable the price mechanism to promote relatively optimal responses. Thus, when the price of gas surged, by this argument, both the 'intermediate' consumption of gas for electricity generation, and the final consumption of gas by households and businesses, declined, partly through switching to cheaper substitutes – precisely as, in a landscape of rational economic actors, they would be expected to do.

All three writers, then, interpreted Europe's 'non' energy crisis as a story of the triumph of the market specifically in the sense of successful behavioural adaptation. As Giles, for instance, cheerily put it, 'the price signal has done its job. It has forced Europe to adapt. Advanced capitalist economies', he went on, as if to drive his point home, 'are remarkably successful in this regard.'[45] Lindner made the same case, but with a focus just on his homeland. 'German industry and society', he proudly proclaimed, 'are once again proving much more resilient and adaptable than certain people feared.'[46]

What are we to make of these assertions? The appalling, unmentioned environmental implications of Europe's 'successful' adaptation are certainly one thing to reckon with. 'Adapting' entailed another significant annual increase (of 6 per cent) in coal-fired power generation, coming on the back of 2021's own disastrous such increase.[47] This increase was the main explanation for 2022 seeing the highest growth in $CO_2$ emissions from EU power generation for half a century; the $CO_2$ intensity of all-source generation rose by 7 per cent.[48]

Among the notable national contributors to this increase was Spain, which, alongside Portugal, received an exemption from the European

---

45   Giles, 'The End of Europe's Energy Crisis Is in Sight'. 'Liberal democratic capitalist economies are remarkably adaptive', was how Sandbu, in his turn, expressed the position ('What Energy Crisis?').

46   Lindner, 'A Resilient Germany Is Weathering the Energy Crunch'.

47   IEA, 'Electricity Market Report 2023', p. 28.

48   Ibid., pp. 8, 75.

Commission allowing it to cap the price of coal and gas used by its electricity generators, leading to an annual increase in its coal-fired power generation of around 50 per cent, albeit from a low base.[49] But, in absolute terms, the biggest contributor to 2022's increase in coal-fired generation in Europe was, ironically, Lindner's 'resilient and adaptable' Germany, where, for the second year running, such generation increased by more than 10 per cent.[50]

Leaving aside the environmental impact, however, the narrative rehearsed by Giles, Sandbu and Lindner was wrongheaded and misleading even as a reading of how Europe managed to avoid greater turmoil among energy users. Certainly, some actors adapted in 2022 to changed price signals, at least somewhat. But, in reality, despite gas prices reaching all-time highs, the intermediate consumption of gas – that is, its use for electricity generation – in the EU actually increased year-on-year, by 2 per cent.[51] At the same time, 'adaptation' to sky-high electricity prices took the form of an annual reduction of power consumption of only 3.5 per cent EU-wide, even with the considerable benefit of one of the warmest winters on record.[52]

More importantly, the role of the adaptation lauded by those writing in the *Financial Times* in steering Europe through choppy waters and keeping lights on across the continent was trivial in relative terms. To read Europe's fortune in avoiding the traumas of, say, China or Texas as evidence of the wonders of price signals in nudging market actors to adapt is to ignore the role of other, considerably more consequential, forces. To wit: what has been narrated as a parable about the productive powers of markets is in fact principally a story about two other things.

The first is government support. Europe's households and industry came through the energy crisis relatively unscathed thanks mainly to the fact that European governments came to their aid. Marshalling their unrivalled financial wherewithal, rich-country governments, in particular, supported homes and firms on a prodigious scale. Researchers for the economic policy think tank Bruegel calculated that, between September 2021 and the end of 2022, European governments stumped

---

49   Ibid., p. 88.
50   Ibid., p. 85.
51   Ibid., p. 75.
52   Ibid., p. 6.

up not far short of €1 trillion to protect residents from rising energy costs.[53] The beneficial effect of any behavioural 'adaptation' in response to price signals was utterly dwarfed by the cushioning effect of this largesse.

Which government was the most lavish in its support? In irony of ironies, it was Christian Lindner's ostensibly non-market-distorting German government. In terms of both absolute expenditure (€268 billion) and the proportion of gross domestic product that that expenditure represented (more than 7 per cent), the German state's largesse outstripped that of all its European peers.[54]

The second thing that enabled Europe to ride out the energy storm much more than did price-motivated behavioural adaptation was a strategic shift in gas procurement – and here we come to an altogether less laudatory aspect of market mechanisms, but arguably their nub. To survive the crunch precipitated by Putin's invasion of Ukraine in 2022, Europe, in reality, did not cut back on gas consumption so much as change where it is imported from. That is, to compensate for the huge decline in imports from Russia mentioned above, it rapidly ramped up imports of natural gas from other world regions. This was, by a huge margin, *the* most important measure in enabling Europe to maintain its electricity generation capabilities in a functional state. In 2021, European imports of natural gas from regions other than Russia totalled 220 billion cubic metres; in 2022, they leapt to 292 billion.[55]

European nations pulled this trick off because they could. In other words, they could afford it. The fact is, however, that the gas supplies that Europe successfully hoovered up from elsewhere in the world were ones on which other, poorer world regions – now priced out – were themselves substantially relying in order not to be pitched into their very own gas and electricity nightmare. And what facilitated this trick was, of course, the market. Europe got its supplies because it had money, or, at least, more of it than other places; and money, in markets, talks.

Who lost out? More than anywhere else, the Indian subcontinent did – and hence we are back to where we started at the beginning of this chapter. As we saw, when the electricity sectors of Bangladesh, India and

53   Sgaravatti et al., 'National Fiscal Policy Responses to the Energy Crisis'.
54   Ibid.; IEA, 'Electricity Market Report 2023', p. 83.
55   Zachmann et al., 'European Natural Gas Imports'.

Pakistan widely stuttered in the summer of 2022, the crux of the problem was insufficient fuel to fire power plants challenged by unprecedented weather-driven demand. Gas was the fuel in shortest supply, and Europe's new import strategy, it turned out, played an increasingly significant role in exacerbating the shortages in question. All three countries, together with Sri Lanka, saw imports dry up as trade was effectively diverted to wealthier, European-based customers. 'The European gas crisis is sucking the world dry of liquid natural gas,' Valery Chow of the energy research firm Wood Mackenzie observed in July 2022. 'Emerging markets in Asia have borne the brunt of this and there is no end in sight.'[56]

Alongside Bangladesh, Pakistan was seemingly the worst affected. In 2017, Pakistan had handed long-term contracts for the supply of gas to Italy's Eni SpA and the Cypriot-domiciled trading house Gunvor Group. In 2021–2, however, as gas prices in Europe, and in turn globally, climbed, both of these suppliers cancelled numerous shipments to Pakistan while continuing to supply within Europe. Industry insiders told Bloomberg reporters Stephen Stapczynski and Faseeh Mangi they 'couldn't remember the last time so many cargoes were scrapped without being directly related to a major outage at an export facility.'[57]

There was, seemingly, a brutally rational economic logic to this. Whereas energy contracts with Western customers typically incorporate 'failure-to-deliver' penalties of up to 100 per cent – recall the owners of frozen Texan wind farms being required to buy power at sky-high prices on the spot market to meet the delivery terms of hedges – Pakistan's contracts evidently contained a cancellation penalty of only 30 per cent – 'most likely', Stapczynski and Mangi conjectured, 'in exchange for lower prices'. The reporters estimated that in the summer of 2022, the price at which natural gas could be sold in Europe was more than 150 per cent higher than the price stipulated in Pakistan's contracts with Eni and Gunvor.[58] A 30 per cent penalty for cancellation would presumably have seemed a price very much worth paying for such a premium.

---

56  Cited in S. Shah and A. Hirtenstein, 'Poorer Countries Struggle to Secure Supplies of LNG', *Wall Street Journal*, 8 July 2022.

57  S. Stapczynski and F. Mangi, 'Europe's Plan to Quit Russian Fuel Plunges Pakistan into Darkness', 14 June 2022, bloomberg.com.

58  Ibid.

In any event, Ananya Bhattacharya spoke for many when, months later, she raged at Pakistan's market impotence relative to 'richer countries that are able to pay higher prices. All this', she reminded readers, 'while millions of citizens continue to live without electricity for more than 12 hours a day.'[59] At one point, as much as around a quarter of Pakistan's operational power generation capacity of 28 GW was shuttered, due principally to fuel shortages, and with most of the forced outages occurring at gas-fired plants.[60]

If, then, as both the German finance minister Christian Lindner and the *Financial Times*'s Chris Giles insisted, energy markets and price signals indeed saved the day during the 2021–2 crisis, then they did so only – but also *by their very nature* – for those countries that happened to be relatively rich in the particular currency that serves as the medium of exchange in such markets, which is, of course, money. It was ever thus. Europe's answer to the gas crisis that Vladimir Putin dramatically escalated in early 2022 was, in large measure, effectively to export that crisis to the Indian subcontinent. That it did so indirectly and, one imagines, unwittingly does not diminish the fact that it happened.

Thus Martin Sandbu's rhetorical 'What Energy Crisis?' was the conceit of someone who only failed to see crisis because it had been successfully displaced elsewhere. While it is capitalist markets that facilitate such displacements, it is the fetishism that haunts market capitalism that perennially makes it difficult for us to see the displacements in question. Sandbu, after all, was scarcely alone. Markets are the supreme vehicles of desocialization. What we see being traded in markets is a thing – a trinket, a laptop, liquid natural gas. We systematically reify this thingness, thereby treating it, rather than the social and geographical worlds in which it is embedded, as what really matters.

---

59   A. Bhattacharya, 'Power-Hungry Europe Is Leaving Developing Countries Starving for Electricity', 6 October 2022, qz.com.

60   H. Zamir and E. Yep, 'Fuel Shortages Hit Nearly a Quarter of Pakistan's Operational Power Plants', 20 July 2022, spglobal.com.

## VI

What, meanwhile, did Europe's electricity crisis, such as it was, mean for renewables, beyond the windfall taxes levied on (some) solar and wind generators? Data suggest that the crisis provided something of a fillip to the sector. Europe, as a whole, added 56 GW of net new solar and wind capacity in 2022, which represented a gain of around a third on net capacity growth achieved in 2021. The counterfactual – how much, all other things being equal, would have been added in 2022 were it not for the crisis? – is, of course, something that can only be guessed at. What is nonetheless clear is that this was both the strongest growth in years, and considerably stronger than forecasters had expected. It is, to be sure, possible that the crisis was not, in fact, a significant boon for the renewables sector, and that growth would have been strong regardless; but it definitely was not a bust. We know that much.

Predictably, commentators were quick to thank markets and the hallowed signals contained in market prices for the apparent hastening of the shift into renewables. This was the main line taken, for example, by the IEA, when, in late 2022, it revised its renewables projections upwards in the light of recent developments. As gas was becoming more expensive as a source of energy generation, so the IEA's argument went, the cheaper sources to which European countries were increasingly turning included not just dirty coal (back in merit, as discussed earlier) but also, in terms of new capacity investment, clean renewables. Chris Giles at the *Financial Times* said much the same. So did Adam Tooze. 'This investment is happening', Tooze confidently asserted, 'because solar and wind offer power at unbeatably low cost.'[61]

Again, however, it is far from clear that the uptick in renewables investment in Europe in 2022 actually had much at all to do with price. If one paid attention to the statements of the various European policy-makers who, in 2022, urged and facilitated (through, for example, new contract awards) expanded investment in renewables capacity, one discovered that something else was powerfully motivating them. That something was concerns around energy security.

If 2022 taught European policymakers anything, it was that relying on foreign nations for energy provision was a greater risk than had

---

61   A. Tooze, 'Europe's Energy Crisis That Isn't', 5 April 2023, foreignpolicy.com.

widely been presumed. The more a country can generate its own power, the lesson seemed to be, the better. And one of the ways in which renewables plants are unique, of course, is that, unlike nuclear or fossil-fuel-fired plants, they are self-sufficient once built. There is no fuel, and hence no potential dependency on unpredictable fuel suppliers. 'In the past, the big driver for renewables was decarbonisation,' Edurne Zoco, executive director for clean energy technology at the financial analysis firm S&P Global, remarked in early 2023. 'What has changed since 2022 is that energy security has also become a big driver of policy for renewables – especially solar.'[62]

Thus when, for example, in November 2022, Prime Minister Rishi Sunak pledged to accelerate the UK's switch to renewable energy, he did so explicitly on the ground of energy security and environmental benefits – *not* cost benefits. Energy security, similarly, explicitly inspired renewed vigour in renewables investment in 2022 in countries ranging from Greece to Denmark, and from Switzerland to the Baltics.

More than anywhere else, perhaps, it was Germany that epitomized this overt political insistence on a newly augmented synergy between renewables investment and energy security.[63] Its reliance on Russian coal and gas, now perceived as reckless and misguided, had got Germany into the predicament in which it found itself in 2022 as energy ties with Putin were severed; doubling down on renewables, whose capacity growth had in fact markedly slowed in Germany since around 2018, was now posited as the way out of that predicament.

If the new spring in renewables' step in Europe in 2022 was not principally about price, neither, it should be emphasized, was it about profit. From the perspective of renewables developers and the banks that lend to them, Europe had not suddenly become a significantly improved investment proposition. Certainly, wholesale electricity prices had increased dramatically, meaning that wind and solar farms selling predominantly at merchant rates could expect to generate much higher revenues if those higher prices persisted. But, as we have seen (and as

---

62   Cited in M. McCormick, 'Solar Set to Overtake Other Energy Sources by 2027', *Financial Times*, 27 February 2023.

63   As Stephen Gross has recently noted, the centrality of concerns around energy security to Germany's push for renewables investment has a long history. See Gross, *Energy and Power*, pp. 284–5.

policymakers discovered), many generators did not and do not sell predominantly at merchant rates. Furthermore, if wholesale electricity prices had increased, so too, of course, had raw material, construction and financing costs.

No less importantly, the question that developers contemplating new investments had to reckon with was: for how long would spot market rates remain inflated? Would they come back down to earth once Europe had fashioned and adjusted to a new, post-Ukraine gas supply regime? Nobody with any substantive experience of Europe's capricious energy markets, least of all risk-averse debt financiers, would have been willing to wager that inflated electricity prices represented some sort of new European norm, and thus would remain in place after the several years needed to plan, develop, finance and build new generating facilities. Moreover, whatever their absolute level, wholesale electricity prices in Europe remained as volatile as they had ever been.

Of particular significance to the all-important yardstick of expected profitability were the windfall taxes on low-carbon electricity generators that European governments introduced in 2022. The risk that governments always face in imposing such levies is that of disincentivizing future investment. It will be remembered, for example, from Chapter 7 that this was exactly the outcome of Spain's effective windfall tax on 'excess' renewables profits in the early 2010s: money withdrew en masse from the market.

European legislators were very much alive to this risk in 2022, and they made it clear that, in crafting their windfall taxes, they were determined to protect underlying profitability – 'not to jeopardise and compromise the profitability of existing plants and future investments' were the EU's exact words – as well as market integrity.[64] But, for all that policymakers remained alert to the dangers of exerting a chilling effect on future investment, and though they designed their taxes accordingly, they could not wholly mitigate that risk. Sure enough, within months of the taxes being announced, renewables developers were warning about project cancellations. Calling the UK's levy 'unfairly disproportionate, discriminatory and adverse to the government's [2050] net zero [emissions] strategy', one such

---

64   European Council, 'Three EU-Coordinated Measures to Cut Down Bills'.

developer even threatened the UK government with legal action unless it amended the tax.[65]

Furthermore, as BloombergNEF's Nathaniel Bullard, among others, pointed out, windfall taxes not only suppress profits in the short term but exacerbate uncertainty around profit expectations in the longer term. 'Even if projects remain profitable,' Bullard observed, 'the tax injects uncertainty that could impede further renewable development.'[66] When, and how, might the state cap revenues or profits next time? Developers surveying the European renewables landscape in around 2022 could not but ask themselves this question. Indeed, some did so very publicly, Ignacio Galán, executive chair of Spain's Iberdrola, asking – equal parts rhetorically and indignantly – in an interview with the *Financial Times* conducted shortly after the EU announced its €180 revenue cap, 'If you intervene at €180 … And why not tomorrow €120?'[67]

Bullard made another important observation in this regard. He reminded his readers that many renewables developers operate internationally and inevitably weigh investment opportunities in different countries against one another. Thus he proceeded to compare the renewables windfall taxes introduced in the EU and in the UK with one another, and to ponder which might be the more likely to deter future investment, and which territory – seen from the other side – might henceforth be the more attractive investment option.

But the more relevant comparison actually would have been between Europe (including the UK) and the US. That any boost to the European renewables sector associated with the energy crisis of 2021–2 was definitively not about enhanced profitability prospects in the region was confirmed by developers' own statements concerning the relative attractiveness of investment opportunities on either side of the Atlantic. A matter of months before the EU and the UK introduced their windfall taxes on renewables generators – denying investors the 'certainty, stability, predictability' they needed, as Iberdrola's Galán saw it – the US, of course, had passed the Inflation Reduction Act, granting renewables

---

65   See N. Thomas and J. Pickard, 'UK Faces Legal Action over Windfall Tax on Energy Companies', *Financial Times*, 28 December 2022.
66   Bullard, 'UK Windfall Tax on Renewables Could Hurt Decarbonization Efforts'.
67   Cited in B. Jopson, 'US Beats EU as Magnet for Green Investment, Says Iberdrola', *Financial Times*, 9 November 2022.

developers another ten years of generous tax credits (see Chapter 9). If anywhere in the Global North now looked decidedly better from the perspective of expected profits than it previously had done, then it was the US, *not* Europe.

Galán said precisely as much to the *Financial Times*. Although Europe, in his view, had been ahead of the US in driving decarbonization to that historical point, the balance had shifted in 2022, with Europe's interventions being likely, he argued, to stunt renewables investment while the US's own legislation had made it, by contrast, a 'very much' more attractive place to invest. Iberdrola, Galán said, would be revising its investment priorities accordingly. 'The US government took longer to take the climate change theme seriously,' he maintained. 'But now they are committed to it they are putting in all the necessary support.'[68] Indeed, in early 2023, it was reported that US economic officials were 'stepp[ing] up efforts to lure European clean energy businesses across the Atlantic', touring Europe in delegations and 'armed with details of subsidies offered by the Inflation Reduction Act'.[69]

And in any event, it is quite clear that in 2022, as, of course, had been true historically, not remotely as much capital was going into renewables investment in Europe as could (and should) have been the case – and, doubtless, *would* have been the case, if profit prospects had in fact been positive. To demonstrate this, one need only consider briefly the example of the European oil and gas majors, led by the UK's BP and Shell.

In 2020, as national governments around the world increasingly made pledges to transition national economies to 'net zero' within the coming decades, both companies similarly pledged to substantially reduce the emissions for which they are directly or indirectly responsible. The principal way they would do so, they said, was by scaling up renewable energy production while scaling back fossil fuel production, thus giving themselves a new raison d'être for the post-carbon economy.[70]

Fast forward to 2022, and the opportunity to begin to make good on this pledge was, on the face of things, perfect. Soaring oil and gas prices

---

68   In ibid.

69   A. Chu, D. Bower and A. Williams, 'US Touts Biden Green Subsidies to Lure Clean Tech from Europe', *Financial Times*, 23 January 2023.

70   See B. Christophers, 'Fossilised Capital: Price and Profit in the Energy Transition', *New Political Economy* 27 (2022), pp. 153–6.

meant that BP and Shell were generating unprecedented profits. They were also under increasing pressure from activists, governments and even formerly indulgent bodies such as the IEA not to reinvest these profits in their core hydrocarbon business – pressure that, in the case of governments in the UK and the EU, materialized partly in the shape of windfall fossil fuel taxes.

In short, the time could not have been better for BP and Shell to make the strategic pivot they had promised – to start walking the renewables walk as well as talking the talk, and, in the process, to secure a viable business model for the long term. If profit opportunities in renewable energy generation had indeed looked strong to their analysts, we can be as sure as night follows day that the two firms would have grasped the nettle then and there.

But they did not. They failed dismally, effectively turning their noses up at the strategic opportunity that their hydrocarbon windfalls had, fortuitously, conferred upon them. Both chose, instead, principally to use the vast surplus capital freshly at their disposal to return money to share-holders via dividends or share buybacks, with BP, one research group calculated, spending more than fourteen times as much on such payouts in 2022 as on 'low-carbon' capital expenditure.[71] The same research group found that the ratio was nominally lower at Shell – 'just' 7.5 times. But another research organization alleged that much of the spending by Shell's Renewables and Energy Solutions division in fact had nothing to do with renewables at all.[72] Globally, just 1 per cent of the oil and gas industry's cash spending in the pivotal, crisis-wracked year that was 2022 went on investment in low-carbon technologies.[73] Even the *Financial Times*, normally reluctant to pass judgement of any kind on capital allo-cation, editorialized that the European oil majors' puny investment in renewables represented a clear case of 'underspending'.[74]

In the energy world, estimating underlying rates of profitability is always a difficult business. What appears to be a relatively profitable

---

71   Common Wealth, 'BP's Q4 Results', 7 February 2023, common-wealth.co.uk.

72   See O. Milman, 'Shell's Actual Spending on Renewables Is Fraction of What It Claims, Group Alleges', *Guardian*, 1 February 2023.

73   'Spending on Oil and Gas Dividends Hits 15-year High', *Financial Times*, 4 June 2023.

74   'Renewables: Big Oil Is Missing the Opportunity High Profits Create', *Financial Times*, 27 October 2022.

sector may, in reality, be a sector which is perennially dogged by intense competition and low profits, but in which government intervention such as subsidies of various kinds serves broadly to maintain returns at levels that secure ongoing investment, thereby muddying underlying economic dynamics. Renewable electricity generation, this book has claimed, approximates relatively closely to such a hypothetical sector. But, based on the data alone, it is difficult to be completely sure.

The investment behaviour of the European oil and gas majors in 2022, however, arguably provides about as much certainty on this matter as we can have or would likely ever need. Definitive proof of poor underlying returns in renewables is probably impossible, given the ubiquity of external support. Yet, if anyone were looking for such definitive proof, the majors' categorical snubbing of renewables when drowning in free cash flow in 2022 was surely it. *Saving the planet*, they were telling the world, *is just not profitable enough for us*. Among others, the *Financial Times* was paying attention, and it understood the significance. This, it soberly remarked, 'does not bode well'.[75]


## VII

Periods of crisis are typically times of ferment in ideas as well as practice. New questions get raised as new issues arise and new challenges are posed. Meanwhile, old questions tend to resurface, as the realization dawns that old answers – and the institutional and organizational orthodoxies they seeded – no longer appear to be adequate: if, indeed, they ever were.

From Texas to China and from Pakistan to Portugal, the rolling electricity crises of 2021–3 have been no different in this regard. Commentators, policymakers and industry participants have grappled with all manner of vexing questions. Some of these have, of course, been of the here-and-now variety. Where can we buy the necessary fuel to keep our power plants running this winter? Can surging wholesale and retail electricity prices be moderated – and, indeed, should they be? Why are we exporting electricity to other countries when demand can barely be satisfied at home?

75   Ibid.

Alongside such urgent questions, however, we have seen questions of a more fundamental nature increasingly being asked. These have been concerned less with dealing with the present crisis than with averting the likelihood of more crises further down the road, or indeed with addressing long-standing crisis tendencies that short-term emergencies may have led the world to neglect. Should we continue the process of unbundling, privatizing, de-monopolizing and marketizing our electricity sectors? Is a method of pricing in which the price of natural gas ordinarily determines system-wide electricity prices the right one for a decarbonizing world? How can decarbonization and energy security best be reconciled in the long term?

Whatever the territorial scope, the 'meta-questions' effectively being asked in all such instances are, in essence, the following: Is our electricity system fit for purpose? Is it actually going to get us where we need to go? If not, can it be modified to make it shipshape? Or is a more radical overhaul required? It is to these critical questions, of a more fundamental nature, that we turn now, in the book's final chapter.

# 11

# Roads to Nowhere

Established in 2005 as a wholly owned, pure energy-trading business by the global financial institution Bear Stearns, Bear Energy gained effective control of its first power generation assets the following year. It did so by entering so-called tolling agreements for approximately 6 GW of fossil-fuel-based generating capacity in the western and north-eastern US owned by the New York–based LS Power Group. Under a tolling agreement, a firm – Bear Energy in this case – pays a rent (the 'demand payment') to the owner of a generating plant, in return for which it secures the right to purchase fuel for the plant and sell its electricity output. In 2007, Bear Energy took control of substantial further generating capacity when, for around $500 million, it acquired several tolling contracts from the Oklahoma-based energy company Williams. Among these was an agreement covering the output of certain gas-fired plants in California owned by another US energy firm, the AES Corporation. These plants could collectively produce about 4,000 MW of electricity, and were thus known as the 'AES 4000' units.

In 2008, at the height of the global financial crisis, Bear Stearns famously collapsed. Much better known for its securities brokerage and investment-banking operations, Bear Stearns's energy business has barely merited a footnote in the vast commentary that the financial crisis, and Bear's role in it, subsequently elicited. Nevertheless, Bear Energy's assets, its tolling agreements included, passed into the hands of a new owner when Bear Stearns was sold in May 2008 in an emergency deal brokered by the Federal Reserve Bank of New York. Bear's new owner was JPMorgan Chase, another global financial institution. What had been Bear Energy was folded into JPMorgan Chase's own energy subsidiary, namely JPMorgan Ventures Energy Corporation (JPMVEC), itself originally founded, like Bear Energy, to trade energy commodities.

The tolling agreements for the AES gas-fired plants that JPMVEC inherited in 2008 extended through 2018 and required it to pay AES a total annual rent of $170 million. In the event, however, JPMVEC did not actually get to sell the electricity generated by the AES 4000 units until several years later. The reason was that, shortly prior to its parent company failing, Bear Energy had 're-tolled' (subleased) its rights to those plants to one of California's primary electricity supply companies, Southern California Edison (SCE). SCE would hand back responsibility for the plants to JPMVEC on a rolling basis, beginning with four plants at the start of 2011, followed by six more at the start of 2012.

Partly to develop experience with the business of electricity generation – to which it was new – before retaking control of the AES 4000 units, JPMVEC acquired short-term rights to two other California plants (Huntington Beach 3 and 4, or HB3 and 4) from January 2010. For eight months, these two plants then ran at a consistent loss, with large demand payments on the one hand and only infrequent dispatch, and hence little revenue, on the other. But JPMVEC was evidently quick to learn. In October of that year, it began to use a new bid strategy for HB3 and 4, which proved 'highly profitable'.[1] The team that developed this strategy, JPMVEC's Principal Investments unit, calculated that were the same bid strategy to be implemented at all the AES plants in California as and when they returned to the firm's control, those plants would earn JPMVEC estimated profits of $1.5 billion to $2 billion through 2018.[2] Principal Investments, it seemed, had managed to turn dirt into gold.

JPMVEC did not get to see this plan all the way through, however. In 2011, the operator of the Californian wholesale electricity market referred JPMVEC to the Federal Energy Regulatory Commission

---

1   Federal Energy Regulatory Commission, 'Order Approving Stipulation and Consent Agreement', Docket #s IN11-8-000 and IN13-5-000, 30 July 2013, ferc.gov, p. 6.
2   Ibid., p. 6.

(FERC) on suspicion of improper bidding practices. Focusing mainly on the AES plants newly controlled by JPMVEC, FERC conducted investigations both that year and in 2012. In 2013 it delivered its ruling. JPMVEC, it concluded, had indeed gamed the market: specifically, it had violated the commission's Anti-Manipulation Rule. And it had clearly done so highly profitably. In addition to a civil penalty of $285 million, JPMVEC agreed to 'disgorge' (repay) alleged unjust profits of $125 million.[3]

And that, in short, was basically that for JPMorgan Chase and the business of electricity generation. FERC handed JPMVEC a six-month suspension of its market-based rate authority. Meanwhile, the bank announced it would be exiting physical wholesale power selling altogether; it started by handing the tolling agreements for AES's California plants back to SCE, this time through a sale – estimated to be worth around $750 million – rather than a sublease. To paraphrase Bryan Burrough and John Helyar, the financial 'barbarians' had been shown to the energy market's exit gate.[4]


I


While it is vital for any number of reasons not to be excessively pessi-mistic about humanity's prospects of keeping global warming to a broadly tolerable level, it is also vital to be realistic and to face facts. For all the impressive-sounding rhetoric at the twenty-sixth United Nations Climate Change Conference (COP 26) in 2021, for example, it is strik-ing that what the UN Environment Programme (UNEP) labels the 'emissions gap' – the gap between greenhouse gas emissions reductions *promised* and the emissions reductions *needed* to achieve the 1.5 °C temperature goal of the Paris Agreement – remains essentially as large as ever: 'immense', was the adjective used by UNEP in its October 2022 update. Specifically, UNEP estimated that this gap would amount to 23 gigatons of $CO_2$ equivalent ($GtCO_2e$) annually as of 2030.[5] What was

3   Ibid., p. 1.

4   B. Burrough and J. Helyar, *Barbarians at the Gate: The Fall of RJR Nabisco* (New York: Harper & Row, 1990).

5   UNEP, 'The Closing Window: Climate Crisis Calls for Rapid Transformation of Societies', Emissions Gap Report 2022, October 2022, unep.org.

particularly depressing was that, fully a year on from COP 26, revisions to countries' emissions pledges – their so-called nationally determined contributions (NDCs) – had served to reduce the estimated emissions gap for 2030 by only a paltry 0.5 $GtCO_2e$. As things stand, these pledges have set the world on track for estimated warming of approximately 2.8 °C by 2100.[6]

And all this is before even raising the question of whether countries will actually make good on their pledges – which, UNEP observed, they presently are not remotely on course to do. Thus, in addition to the aforementioned emissions gap, UNEP also estimates an 'implementation gap', representing the difference between projected emissions under *current* policies and projected emissions under full implementation of countries' NDCs. This gap, too, is yawningly large, likewise measuring in gigatons of $CO_2$ equivalent. In a sobering article published upon the release of the UNEP update, the *Economist* noted comparable findings from Systems Change Lab, a conglomerate of environmental organizations and think tanks.[7] The latter's State of Climate Action 2022 report identified forty key emissions indicators – for example, the amount of $CO_2$ generated per unit of steel produced – and a 2030 target for each that must be met if the Paris pathway is to be achieved. The *Economist* was interested in the question of how many of these forty were on track for 1.5 °C. The answer? 'Not a single one of them.' Indeed, five, it learned, were 'heading in the wrong direction entirely'.

In other words, there are essentially two connected problems. One is that we, collectively at the global level, are not being ambitious enough in our objectives for cutting emissions. The other is that we are not currently doing enough to make the achievement even of these inadequate objectives credible. We are, in other words, utterly failing.

Of course, not all of this, by any means, has to do with electricity and our failure to decarbonize its generation as rapidly and comprehensively as is required. In fact, the *Economist* argued in the article referred to above that if there was 'a glimmer of hope', it was that the burning of fossil fuels – responsible for around three-quarters of global

---

6  A. Mooney and C. Hodgson, 'Global Warming Set to Reach 1.5C in the Near-Term, UN Reports', *Financial Times*, 20 March 2023.

7  'Few Governments Have Done Much about the Climate this Year', *Economist*, 27 October 2022.

anthropogenic emissions of $CO_2$, which in turn represent around three-quarters of all global anthropogenic greenhouse gas emissions – had risen only marginally in 2022, thanks, in no small part, to growth in solar and wind power.

And the IEA, in its turn, was positively bullish when updating its forecasts for renewables in December 2022.[8] Its new report heralded the 'largest ever upward revision' of the IEA's renewables numbers: projected global renewables capacity growth of 2,400 GW between 2022 and 2027, almost entirely concentrated in wind and solar, was some 30 per cent higher than it had forecast just a year earlier. Renewables, the IEA said, were now the only electricity generation source whose share was expected to grow.

Nonetheless, electricity generation demonstrably remains the nub of the climate change problem. It is, as we saw in Chapter 1, the single largest source of global anthropogenic $CO_2$ emissions. Moreover, to ensure that the brutal truth is not obscured, we can and should when assessing the scope of the problem essentially set aside positive data and estimates concerning solar and wind power. This is not to say that such positive data and estimates are not relevant and promising: they clearly are. But solar and wind power do not produce $CO_2$.

The burning of fossil fuels to generate electricity produces $CO_2$, and it is entirely possible for solar and wind capacity and generation to grow at hitherto unprecedented rates, while harmful emissions from fossil-fuel-based electricity production themselves also still continue to escalate. The fact that solar- and wind-based electricity is growing in absolute terms does not mean that dirty electricity generation is not also doing so. Indeed, even if renewables are the only source to grow their proportional share of overall generation – as the IEA says will likely be the case in future – it is still possible for other sources to grow in absolute terms, if overall global demand for electricity is itself growing fast enough.

The all-important metric, then, is not renewable electricity capacity or generation, but fossil-fuel-based electricity generation. We should not let apparent good-news stories about the former blind us to facts about the latter. It is fossil-fuel-based electricity generation that, one way or another, has to end. And, if the volume of such generation grows,

8   IEA, 'Renewables 2022: Analysis and Forecast to 2027', December 2022, iea .org.

the problem we face – the thing that must be eradicated – is getting *bigger*, not smaller, however 'well' we seem to be doing on the renewables front.

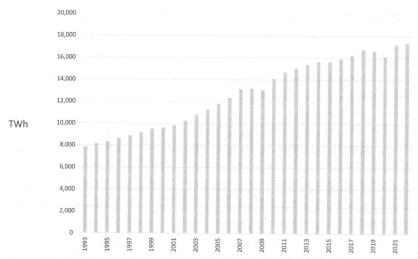

**Figure 11.1** Global electricity generation from fossil fuels, 1993–2022
*Source*: Our World in Data

And this is exactly what is still happening. The stark reality, as Figure 11.1 shows, is that, during the past two decades (the period of what many call the 'renewables revolution'), electricity generation from fossil fuels has consistently been increasing, interrupted by only short periods of substantive decline associated with the global financial crisis (in 2009) and the COVID-19 pandemic (in 2020). Even in 2022, the latest year for which we have data, in which the *Economist* saw its 'glimmer of hope' and during which Europe was forced to contend largely without Russian gas, our key metric registered yet another increase. That year, global electricity generation from fossil fuels totalled around 17,400 TWh, which was nearly double what it had been two decades earlier; such generation was also on average more carbon-intensive than in 2021, due to a relative substitution of coal for gas in Asia and Europe. Not only are we failing in the pivotal domain that is electricity production, then, but the scale of our failure – captured in the lengthening bars in Figure 11.1 – continues, seemingly inexorably, to grow.

As we saw in Chapter 1, and should remind ourselves here, the geography of this global predicament is enormously significant. The main reason why global emissions from electricity generation continue to grow as much as they do is that the countries in which growth in electricity demand has latterly been concentrated rely overwhelmingly on fossil fuels to produce power.

In large part, this is a story about China and India. These two have in recent years typically accounted between them for around four-fifths of global annual growth in electricity consumption. It is true, as we have repeatedly seen in this book, that both, and especially China, have made great progress in installing solar and wind capacity. But there remain significant headwinds to such progress. Having said in early 2021 that renewables would provide for two-thirds of the country's increase in electricity consumption through 2025, for example, China, as recently as mid-2022, substantively moderated this target, lowering it to 50 per cent. Around the same time, amid the country's continuing energy crisis (Chapter 10), China's government laid out a plan to add 300 million tons of new coal production capacity.[9] The reality is that, in both China and India, notwithstanding all the progress on renewables that has indeed been made, electricity generation remains extremely dirty, with fossil fuels (mainly coal) presently supplying around two-thirds of electricity in China and around three-quarters in India.

Moreover, with only a handful of exceptions – China and India themselves being prominent among them – the countries that continue to add most new renewables capacity are Western countries, in which future growth in electricity demand is expected to be relatively modest by global standards. To be sure, Europe and the US will need more electricity as they proceed with the electrification of transport, buildings, heating and so on. But these increases, while material, nevertheless will be almost as nothing compared with those predicted for many countries in Africa and Asia, in which the electrification of currently non-electric sectors such as transport will widely go hand in hand with ongoing developments that – as the twentieth-century experiences of Europe and the US can themselves attest – will also drive significant growth in

---

9   X. Chen and D. Jia, 'China Curbs Renewable Energy Target through 2025', 2 June 2022, asia.nikkei.com.

electricity consumption. Foremost among such developments are population growth, industrialization, urbanization and, last but not least, the introduction of electricity to significant numbers of households that historically have not had access to it.

Policymakers and grid operators in countries such as the US often become exercised when contemplating the fact that national electricity demand will potentially double or treble by mid-century – which is a reasonable enough standpoint. But try to consider things for a moment from the perspective of their counterparts in countries such as Bangladesh, Egypt, Indonesia, Nigeria and South Africa. Bangladesh's population, for example, is expected to grow by another 20 per cent or so, to around 200 million, by 2050. Meanwhile, a recent study projected that per capita electricity demand in Bangladesh will be some *twenty-two times* higher in 2050 than it was in 2014.[10] Now that, one might say, is what a real challenge looks like.

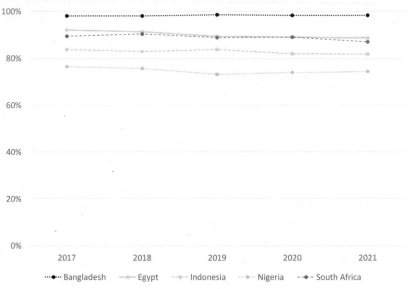

**Figure 11.2** Share of electricity production from fossil fuels, selected countries, 2017–21
*Source*: Our World in Data

10   K. B. Debnath and M. Mourshed, 'Why Is Bangladesh's Electricity Generation Heading towards a GHG Emissions-Intensive Future?', *Carbon Management* 13: 1 (2022), p. 216.

Almost without exception, these expected territorial focal points of future global growth in electricity consumption are both heavily reliant on fossil fuels for existing power generation and are decarbonizing such generation at an extremely slow pace – if at all. It is a toxic combination, illustrated with striking clarity in Figure 11.2.

Needless to say, none of this is about finger pointing. As is well recognized, the countries in question have made only trivial contributions to the vast amounts of greenhouse gases currently lodged in the atmosphere, for which Europe and the US are overwhelmingly responsible. Neither should we forget that such countries' efforts to decarbonize – efforts that, as this book has shown, are always and everywhere as much about financial wherewithal as about political ambition and technical capability – are being pursued within the context of political economies that are 'post'-colonial only partly in reality, and, at least as much, merely in name. Chronic debt burdens and fiscal incapacity have been the trademark colonial legacy.

When the cost of finance for new renewables projects is around 9 to 10 per cent, as it is in, say, India (compared with around 2 to 5 per cent in Europe and the US), political ambition and technical capability can only get you so far.[11] The stark, incontestable reality is that, as things stand, in countries such as those referenced in Figure 11.2, it is not just difficult but more or less impossible for new renewables projects to turn a profit *unless* their financing is heavily subsidized. 'Utility-scale solar', confirms Teal Emery, 'is unviable at market interest rates in lower-income countries and is not being built.'[12] That less than 1 per cent of the $434 billion invested globally in clean power projects in 2021 went to Africa is explicable only with direct reference to punitive capital costs and their rooting in historically overdetermined political-economic inequalities within and between nations.[13] It is little wonder that Derek Brower, outgoing US energy editor at the *Financial Times*, recently expressed astonishment that anyone still questions the idea

---

11   IEA, 'The Cost of Capital in Clean Energy Transitions', 17 December 2021, iea .org.

12   T. Emery, 'Solar Can't Scale in the Dark: Why lessons about Subsidies and Transparency from IFC's Scaling Solar Zambia Can Reignite Progress toward Deploying Clean Energy', May 2023, energyforgrowth.org, p. 6.

13   BloombergNEF and Bloomberg Philanthropies, 'Scaling-Up Renewable Energy in Africa', 9 November 2022, bnef.com, p. 1.

that the 'western nations that did so much of the damage [to the global climate] will have to finance the [energy] transition in the developing world'.[14]

So, no, this is not finger pointing – at least, not in the direction of poor countries seemingly lumbered with fossil fuels. The point, rather, is that organizations such as the IEA can celebrate all they like Western policy breakthroughs such as the US's Inflation Reduction Act of 2022, and the expected positive impact of such breakthroughs on domestic renewables growth. But, increasingly, the developments that really matter to global electricity sector emissions will be ones occurring elsewhere in the world, and as the IEA's own executive director, Fatih Birol, himself has conceded, it more and more looks to be the case that poor countries with fossil-fuel-heavy electricity sectors – in which, the IEA says, investment in clean energy must rise a staggering sevenfold within seven years if climate goals and energy demand are to be met – are in fact 'being left behind' in the 'global' energy transition.[15]

## II

From China to India, Nigeria and beyond, one common trend that we have observed at various points in this book is that, in different ways, at different speeds and with varying degrees of success, policymakers in such non-Western countries are attempting to move their electricity sectors in broadly the same direction that Western countries, especially in Europe, have previously taken. We examined the core components of this prototypically Western sectoral model in Chapter 2. It necessitates unbundling of vertically integrated operations. It entails, where possible, but especially in generation, the introduction of competition. It means more private ownership of operating assets. And, perhaps most challengingly of all, it means markets, in both electricity wholesale and retail.

The reasons for pursuing this model are as varied as the routes to its achievement, but one key rationale looms large in most places. That is,

---

14   D. Brower, 'The Energy Transition Will Be Volatile', *Financial Times*, 29 June 2023.

15   R. Millard, 'Developing Countries "Left Behind" in Clean Energy Shift', *Financial Times*, 20 June 2023.

governments regard privatization and marketization, in particular, as a means to the putatively desirable end of reducing both state funding and involvement in the electricity sector. Of course, such views have hardly materialized out of thin air. Neoliberal ideologues – purveyors of the so-called Washington Consensus – at institutions such as the International Monetary Fund have long told non-Western policymakers that this is exactly how they *should* regard electricity privatization and marketization. Furthermore, fiscal constraints, often fashioned by the very same ideologues, have widely given impetus to attempts to restructure electricity sectors along such privatized and marketized lines. The sharp increase in sovereign financing costs worldwide since late 2021 has only added to such impetus.

Yet it should be abundantly clear to readers, by this point in the book, that there is a considerable irony about all this, not least, though not only, in terms specifically of renewables. For as we have repeatedly seen, the reality of the electricity industry in places where the sector *has* been substantially restructured along the lines being pursued today in many non-Western territories is actually very different from the model that is rhetorically presented as being the objective and the end point of such reform.

Government financial support and active involvement in the electricity sector are in fact arguably no less integral in substantially restructured and 'liberalized' contexts than they are elsewhere. Even before the energy crisis of 2021–2, for example, more than half of the countries in the EU – the very home, materially and symbolically, of marketized electricity – had some form of retail price control. And, everywhere, the development of renewables remains propped up by government support. It surely cannot have escaped the notice of policy-makers elsewhere in the world that in 2022, the US, of all places, extended explicit and substantial government financial support for the private sector development of solar and wind power for another entire decade.

The ubiquity of such government support should be a crucial consid-eration when thinking through arguments about how electricity sectors around the world might best be reconfigured to accelerate processes of decarbonization while keeping – or making – power affordable to users. The fact that governments have generally been unable safely to remove mechanisms of support for renewables, even with the costs of the underlying technologies having fallen as far as they have, does not necessarily tell us what roads *should* be taken. But it does help provide clarity on what roads probably should not.

Clearly, the answer is not for governments to do what they long presumed they *would* be able to do once the cost of generating electricity renewably had fallen to levels comparable with the cost of fossil-fuel-based power – which is to say, to remove support. This, naturally, has been the approach advocated by free-marketeers all along. Philip Booth of the UK's Institute of Economic Affairs, for instance, articulated this position several years ago, and the position has not changed. What he called 'green groups' support renewables subsidies, Booth wrote, because such subsidies 'increase demand for renewables compared with carbon-intensive energy production. However,' he maintained, 'this approach is mistaken.'[16]

Why? 'Renewables', Booth claimed, 'do not have a "negative social cost" (or positive social benefit) that would justify a subsidy. At best, they have a zero social benefit or cost. The neutral position is not to tax or subsidise them any more than any other product or service is taxed or subsidised.' But what about the pesky matter of carbon and climate? 'Some', but presumably not Booth himself, would, he admitted, 'argue that renewables may have lower social costs than carbon-intensive energy forms.' But that, he insisted, 'is an argument for taxing carbon intensive energy forms and not for subsidising renewables'.

Interestingly, parts of the left have, in recent years, formulated arguments about government support for the private sector development of renewables that appear to come to the same conclusion about the merits of such support, even as they operate from very different principles and postulates, and even as they possess very different views on what roads to future energy infrastructure provision the world should in fact be taking. Such left critics, too, are hostile to the feed-in tariffs, tax credits and the like that governments serially extend to renewables developers. If, however, for Booth and others on the free market right the objection to subsidies is that they obscure price signals and generate 'inefficient' outcomes, the left's objection, by contrast, is that, by de-risking private sector investment, the state socializes risk

16    P. Booth, 'UK Energy Policy – When the Left Hand Doesn't Know What the Far Left Hand Is Doing', 12 November 2014, iea.org.uk.

– financial and non-financial – while guaranteeing and inflating private gain.[17]

Yet such left objections to de-risking are not particularly helpful. If the problem as it is is indeed de-risking, the answer, we are told, either explicitly or implicitly, is for the state not to de-risk – just as Booth at the Institute of Economic Affairs would have it. But what then? Unless the state were successfully to arrogate to itself the job of developing, financing, owning and operating renewable energy infrastructure, or were willing and able widely to compel private-sector actors to invest in the development of such infrastructure against their own volition, it is hard to see what good would come of a refusal to de-risk.

The unspoken assumption in the left critique of de-risking seems to be that such de-risking is unnecessary. Remove the government support mechanisms, the logic evidently runs, and the private sector will continue to invest regardless, even if the available profits might be lower than they would otherwise be. If that is not in fact the assumption, then the question surely arises of what such critics would make of the inevitable decline in renewables investment that would occur were (necessary) mechanisms of de-risking cut short.

If this book has shown us anything, however, it is that government support to renewables development is not unnecessary. At least where markets for the commercialization of renewably generated electricity output are structured in the ways they currently are, both in the Global South *and* across the Global North, de-risking is more or less essential inasmuch as the revenue risks are otherwise too substantial to enable affordable private financing. To suggest otherwise is to dismiss what we actually know about the economics of the electricity business. If anyone tells you that de-risking is not necessary – the greatest trick the private sector ever pulled, even – then refer them to the experience of the UK's onshore wind sector in 2018 (Chapter 6) or Vietnam's solar sector in 2021 (Chapter 9).

Of course, this is not to suggest that de-risking in practice is unproblematic. On the contrary. From the perspective of concerns such as those around justice, equity and public sector institutional capacity

---

17   See especially D. Gabor, 'The Wall Street Consensus', *Development and Change* 52: 3 (2021), 429–59.

building, external support to private sector renewables development clearly can be less or more problematic – and to widely varying degrees – in terms, for example, of what types of bodies shoulder the de-risking burden and how risk and reward are actually apportioned. To say that de-risking of renewables remains broadly necessary within the global business of electric power as currently constituted is not to say that it is always effected in desirable ways.

Nevertheless, it is probably worth posing the matter in the stark terms demanded by the climate crisis. What is the greater risk we face? Is it states continuing financially to support private sector renewables development, and thereby continuing to pad investor returns? Or is it states not deigning to de-risk, and potentially seeing renewables development – for as long as it is something expected principally of private sector actors – wither on the vine?

## III

An end to government support was not necessarily their recommended solution, but even before the global energy crisis of 2021–2 put some of the problems associated with liberalized, capital-centric Western electricity systems under the spotlight (Europe, after all, was a focal point of the crisis), many mainstream organizations and commentators were already arguing that such systems were no longer fit for purpose – if, indeed, they ever had been.

Both the growing significance, in practice, of renewable sources of electricity generation, and the growing importance in policy of optimizing conditions for further renewables development, have long been pivotal to such concerns about inherited, liberalized systems. The central point that has been made is that electricity systems as they exist today in places such as Europe and the US were designed and built in and for a fossil fuel world. As such, the argument runs, the systems in question are optimal neither to encouraging the development of renewable power nor to enabling its production and consumption once installed.

This critique has always been partly about engineering issues – about the fact that, bluntly stated, our transmission and distribution networks were, in Gill Plimmer's words, generally engineered physically 'to serve large coal-powered plants . . . [and not] dispersed renewables developments such as solar and wind farms'.[18] But, more than that, the critique has been about economic issues. That is to say, our complex institutional arrangements for translating the physical generation and delivery of electric power into a series of interconnected revenues and costs earned and borne respectively by different actors, have, the critics maintain, also always been, and remain, intrinsically fossil-fuel-based systems.

Energy economists were the first to make this case. Thus, as early as a decade ago, Malcolm Keay, John Rhys and David Robinson, emblematically, had this to say about the electricity business: 'Existing markets are designed around the characteristics of fossil generation but are not so well adapted to the newer [renewables] entrants.' Such markets, they went on to observe, 'themselves remain in essence unreformed' – an observation that is as true today as it was when they made it. 'The problem', as they therefore saw it, 'is that markets as they exist were not designed to, and do not, reflect the cost structures and operating characteristics of the growing new energy sources.'[19]

In time, this would become more or less orthodoxy within the mainstream of energy economics opinion. By 2017, for example, the *Economist*, picking up on important developments within the scholarly literature, was also convinced of the case for 'changing the way the world buys, sells, values and regulates electricity to take account of the new means by which it generates it'.[20] By early 2021, even the IEA – scarcely a revolutionary organization – was willing to accept that the existing rules for electricity commercialization in liberalized markets probably did need ripping up. 'If the share of renewables in the electricity generation mix is to rise as envisioned in the Net-Zero Emissions by 2050 Scenario, it would', the IEA maintained, 'be highly desirable to effect significant changes in the design of electricity markets so as to provide signals for investment.'[21]

---

18   G. Plimmer, 'Renewables Projects Face 10-Year Wait to Connect to Electricity Grid', *Financial Times*, 8 May 2022.

19   M. Keay, J. Rhys and D. Robinson, 'Electricity Markets and Pricing for the Distributed Generation Era', in F. Sioshansi, ed., *Distributed Generation and Its Implications for the Utility Industry* (Oxford: Academic Press, 2014), pp. 172, 175.

20   'A World Turned Upside Down', *Economist*, 25 February 2017.

21   IEA, 'Net Zero by 2050: A Roadmap for the Global Energy Sector', May 2021, iea.org, p. 164.

That economists and those institutions substantially guided by economists should come to these views about the deficiencies of existing forms of market organization is unsurprising. Much of this book, after all, has been about highlighting outcomes of the maladaptive contemporary political economy of electricity that, in many cases, it would be a stretch even for those who are relatively invested in the existing scheme of things to consider beneficial or satisfactory.

Perhaps the most obvious of these deleterious outcomes is the simple fact that, as and where governments have sought to reduce or remove support for renewables, developers and, in particular, their financiers have shown almost no inclination to take on merchant price risk. If this implies that 'the market', under its existing constitution, will always be stuck on support, then no wonder there have been growing calls to reform it. As we saw in Chapter 6, the volatility of liberalized electricity spot markets is generally anathema to the banks that finance wind and solar plants.

It is true, as one equity investor has observed, that 'certain debt funds are starting to offer pretty flexible debt instruments based on a long-term merchant production profile'.[22] But what that investor failed to mention was the onerous terms that such 'flexibility' always entails. As José Donoso of the Spanish solar association UNEF has noted of the Spanish renewables landscape, for example, when lenders do finance merchant projects, they require around twice the share of equity financing compared to subsidized projects.[23] Providers of funding on terms that developers are actually comfortable with accommodating are, as the aforementioned investor conceded, 'still struggling with full merchant exposure' – and the struggle looks set to continue.[24]

And so we remain in a paradoxical world that seems, at least, ripe for reform. The economists and economic commentators mentioned above do not quite put it in these terms, but the reality today in liberalized electricity systems such as Europe's is that, to secure financing, renewables developers ordinarily do everything they can – whether it be through feed-in tariffs, corporate power purchase agreements or

22   Email to author, 4 October 2021.
23   Y. Rack, 'European Renewable Developers Vie for Suitable Off-Takers as Subsidies Wind Down', *SNL Generation Markets Week*, 26 March 2019.
24   Email to author, 4 October 2021.

financial hedges – to avoid selling their output at the market price. This, in fact, is arguably the market's signal feature – a form, if you like, of categorical negation: we have a market that perversely requires certain increasingly significant participants to systematically evade its own price signals.

Thus a head of steam for reform was certainly already building momentum well in advance of the global energy crisis. In the UK, for instance, to take just one example, influential mainstream experts were calling for sweeping market reform from as early as the mid-2010s. Particularly vocal on this front was the Oxford energy economist Dieter Helm, whose 2017 Cost of Energy review, commissioned by the government, laid out a whole series of reform recommendations.

What the crisis of 2021–2 did was redouble the momentum, particularly in Europe.[25] If, prior to 2022, European policymakers – at least those who actually listened to the likes of Helm – had been dimly aware of problems with the existing ways in which electricity was bought and sold, they had also been able collectively to bury their heads in the sand inasmuch as the system of provision continued broadly to function, even if idiosyncratically and clearly far from optimally, and inasmuch also as renewables penetration continued broadly to rise. Burying their heads, then, is what such policymakers had been doing, to the exasperation of Helm and legion other economic advisers.

But, in 2022, denial was no longer an option. That it was specifically in the spring of 2022, as electricity prices soared across Europe in the wake of Russia's invasion of Ukraine, that the UK, for example, finally launched its long-awaited Review of Electricity Market Arrangements, was hardly coincidental. As the *Economist* had presciently said in 2017, 'although voters give little thought to electricity markets when they are working, they can get angry when prices rise . . . and they scream blue murder when the lights go out'.[26]

Prices were indeed now rising, and sharply, and attention became focused on precisely why (Chapter 10). The answer, as we have seen, had

---

25   But not only there: in the US, too, influential voices have been prompted by the events of 2021–2 to actively reconsider existing electricity market designs. See, especially, the intervention in 2023 of Mark C. Christie, 'It's Time to Reconsider Single-Clearing Price Mechanisms in US Energy Markets', *Energy Law Journal* 44: 1 (2023), pp. 1–30.

26   'A World Turned Upside Down'.

much to do with the disproportionate impact of gas prices – themselves spiking – on electricity prices in Europe's wholesale markets. All of a sudden, the merit order was a topic of everyday conversation rather than an esoteric nugget of energy economics. As rising gas prices pushed up the price of electricity produced by *all* generators, whether gas-fired or not, the gap between the average cost of electricity generation to its producer and the average price of that electricity to wholesale market purchasers, and ultimately to users, widened.

Short-term fixes to high electricity prices – those discussed in Chapter 10 – could not do much about these underlying market mechanisms. But more fundamental, longer-term reforms potentially could and, policy-makers now promised, eventually would. 'Decoupling' gas and electricity prices thence became a political clarion call – nothing less than a *s*ine qua non, European publics were told, of market restructuring.

Unsurprisingly, the most vocal advocates of such decoupling came from those European countries in which gas contributes only a rela-tively small share of electricity, and thus in which the disproportionate impact of gas prices on electricity prices seems particularly incongru-ous, and even unfair. France, where nuclear dominates, was one; Spain, where renewables (including hydro) supply nearly half of all electricity, was another.

All manner of proposals for such reform have been and continue to be circulated. One is to split the market, and to price renewable electric-ity differently from fossil-fuel-based electricity. Another suggestion is to use an average cost of generation – a sort of throwback to pricing models prior to the liberalization of the 1990s – or to pay generators the average bid. A third is to pay each generator what it bids, rather than (as at present) the single market-clearing price. And in countries, like the UK, where geographically differentiated pricing is not currently used, introducing such locational pricing is regarded by some as a potentially propitious alternative, although the fact that countries that do price in this manner, such as Sweden, did not escape the electricity market carnage of 2021–2, should clearly give pause.

To some eyes, no doubt, such proposals – these have been the most commonly and widely propounded – would likely appear positively transformative. But, before proceeding further, we should be clear about one thing. All these proposals are firmly couched within a framework that a priori assumes that electricity continues to be something bought and sold in markets, and predominantly by private sector actors. The aim shared by such proposals, in short, is to make markets work better – to extend and fine-tune existing processes of marketization – and not anything more radical than that.[27]

## IV

What to make of these various proposals for market reform?[28] All, it is clear, have likely drawbacks. 'Costly generators would make losses under average pricing, yet are sometimes needed to keep the lights on,' the *Economist* noted. 'Paying what is bid could give generators an incentive to inflate their bids. Localised pricing', meanwhile, 'might skew generators' decisions on where to build capacity.' And the 'radical' option of splitting the market into two, one for renewable power and one for fossil-fuel-based power? Insofar as most renewables generators avail themselves of mechanisms of price stabilization, and insofar as the price of much renewable power is therefore already effectively fixed, the option of splitting the market, according to experts such as Rahmat Poudineh of the Oxford Institute for Energy Studies, 'doesn't make sense.'[29] The *Economist* seemingly shared this scepticism.

In fact, the more that commentators at the leading mainstream chronicles of Western capitalism such as the *Economist* and the *Financial Times* contemplated the disarray in European and global electricity markets during 2021–2, the more sceptical they evidently became about the prospect of root-and-branch electricity market reform in general.

---

27 More radical proposals have been made, but have tended not to receive comparable airtime. Foremost among these have been proposals arguing for substantively greater public sector involvement in funding, developing, building, owning and operating renewable generation capacity – a possibility to which we shall return at the end of the chapter. See, for instance, J. Bozuwa, S. Knuth, G. Flood, P. Robbins and O. O. Táíwò, 'Building Public Renewables in the United States', March 2023, climateandcommunity.org; D. Brown, C. Hayes, M. Lawrence and A. Buller, 'A Wholesale Transformation: Evaluating Proposals for Electricity Market Reform', March 2023, common-wealth.co.uk.

28 Angwin, *Shorting the Grid*, pp. 94–6, has a useful discussion of the pros and cons of some of the main alternative market designs – especially price-as-bid models – that have been mooted in recent years.

29 'Britain's Government Wants to Reform Power Markets', *Economist*, 25 August 2022.

It is true, such commentators conceded, that high electricity prices – the source of so much consternation during the period in question – are clearly in many respects a problem. But low electricity prices, they sought to remind readers, are actually not unproblematic themselves, and especially not, it was argued, when it comes to the crucial matter of incentivizing the further development of renewable power.[30] Doubtless mindful of the ever-present spectre of price cannibalization (Chapter 7) – the *Economist*, citing the energy scholar Francis O'Sullivan, had noted in as early as 2017 the inherent tendency for solar power under merit order dispatch to 'eat its own tail' or 'cannibalise its own competitiveness away' – commentators now actively highlighted the spur that relatively high electricity prices, underpinned by the existing market designs, could theoretically provide to decarbonization.[31]

Writing in August 2022, for example, Sam Fleming and Valentina Pop of the *Financial Times* observed that Europe's existing system of electricity pricing 'provides the basis for future investments in renewables and other power infrastructure'.[32] Shortly afterwards, writing this time with Alice Hancock and Tom Wilson, Fleming expanded on this argument, adding that herein lay some of the traditional reluctance among European policymakers to rip up the institutional status quo. 'Historically', the three reporters wrote, 'there was little desire to overhaul the system, even as the proportion of clean power in the energy mix increased. It was hoped that higher wholesale electricity prices would incentivise the development of green energy by increasing the profit margin for lower-cost renewables projects.'[33]

Amid the growing calls for fundamental reform of European electricity markets that reverberated around the continent in 2022, therefore, the *Economist* and the *Financial Times* – such important weathervanes of informed mainstream political-economic orthodoxy – increasingly sounded notes of caution. *Don't throw the baby out with*

---

30  A. Hancock, S. Fleming and T. Wilson, 'What Are the EU's Plans to Curb Electricity Prices?', *Financial Times*, 1 September 2022.

31  The 2017 piece was 'A World Turned Upside Down'.

32  S. Fleming and V. Pop, 'EU to Unveil Emergency Measures to Curb Soaring Energy Prices', *Financial Times*, 29 August 2022.

33  Hancock et al., 'What Are the EU's Plans to Curb Electricity Prices?'.

*the bathwater,* was effectively their message. *We might end up with something worse.*

Needless to say, these publications were not alone in urging policymakers to retain faith in the existing system design, or at least to think extremely long and hard before jettisoning it. Energy companies that benefit handsomely from that system understandably were also keen to emphasize the putative positive role of its design in encouraging ongoing renewables growth. 'Talking about reworking the electricity market', said Ørsted's Ulrik Stridbæk, 'is the wrong thinking at a very critical moment.'[34] When, a few months later, the government of Denmark, Ørsted's home territory, floated the idea of the state taking stakes in future offshore wind farms, opposition parties retorted with the same objection as had Stridbæk. Why fix what is not broken? 'We don't understand what problem you want to solve with public ownership,' said Samira Nawa of the Social Liberal Party, 'given the market works satisfactorily.'[35]

Meanwhile, regulatory bodies charged with administering Europe's energy markets, and which in many cases have long been prone to capture by the very companies they are meant to regulate, have also – equally predictably – proven to be conservative voices, similarly preaching prudence and caution. Nowhere was this clearer than in the case of the EU Agency for the Cooperation of Energy Regulators (ACER). In April 2022, as momentum for reform was building, ACER swiftly issued a report warning against tearing up existing market structures.[36] It repeated its warning in January 2023, again invoking opportunistically the inviolability of 'the right investment signals for all the new build necessary to carry our very accelerated and ambitious energy transition'.[37] Little wonder, then, that when the European Commission did eventually deliver a firm proposal for electricity market 'reform' in March 2023, it was a damp squib, containing nothing by way of fundamental redesign, and certainly not the modification of spot market price formation (enabling the decoupling of gas and electricity prices) that had been widely promised.

---

34   Cited in A. Hancock and R. Milne, 'Brussels Plans Energy Market Overhaul to Curb Cost of Renewables', *Financial Times*, 2 January 2023.

35   Cited in L. W. Jensen, 'Opposition kritiserer statslig ejerskab af havvind', 21 April 2023, energiwatch.dk.

36   See Hancock et al., 'What Are the EU's Plans to Curb Electricity Prices?'.

37   Cited in Hancock and Milne, 'Brussels Plans Energy Market Overhaul'.

If the likes of the *Economist* and the *Financial Times* were not the only members of the chorus to voice warnings about market reform, they were the most noteworthy. They are, after all, independent – of industry interests, if not necessarily of political-economic dogma. More importantly, perhaps, they had themselves, at least in the case of the former publication, been among those who only a few years previously had seemingly been convinced that fundamental reform *was* required. As we saw earlier, the *Economist* had explicitly called for 'changing the way the world buys, sells, values and regulates electricity'.

What is particularly notable about the back-and-forth in thinking about electricity market design exhibited in recent times by magazines and newspapers such as the *Economist* and the *Financial Times* – fully in favour of an overhaul one year, reluctant to countenance such reform just a few years later – is not so much the specificities of the various recommendations that happen to have been made at one point or another. Rather, what stands out is the principal wider 'meta-conclusion' about electricity markets that the commentators themselves have drawn from their own analytical vacillation.

The *Economist*'s writers appear already to have had a hazy sense of this meta-conclusion well in advance of the ructions of 2021–2. 'Getting renewables to today's relatively modest level of penetration was hard and very expensive work,' they wrote in 2017 in an article devoted to the question of market design. 'To get to systems where renewables supply 80% or more of customers' electricity needs', they reckoned, at a time when very few others would have agreed, 'will bring challenges that may be far greater' – 'even though', they added, in a throwaway remark whose actual significance this book has endeavoured to bring home to us, 'renewables are becoming comparatively cheap'.[38]

Over the following years, and especially once the crisis that began in 2021 was in motion, it became clearer still what the upshot of all this was. Evidently, the main, overarching conclusion to be drawn was, simply stated, the following: *none of this is easy*. If, for instance, low electricity prices are a problem, but high prices are too, and if the apparent logic of wholesale market reform can strike analysts as compelling at one juncture but strike the same analysts as anything but certain at a later point in time, then there can, it was intuited, be only one reasonable

---

38   'A World Turned Upside Down'.

deduction. 'The problem', in short, the *Economist* had concluded by September 2022, 'is that designing an electricity market is hard.'[39]

## V

The *Economist* identified a number of reasons for this difficulty in designing an electricity market. Among them were the following:

> The juice cannot yet be stored at scale, and has to be delivered at the exact moment it is needed. Producers need to spend a lot of money upfront to build a windmill or power plant, and need to be able to recover it and make a profit over decades. Climate-change policies dictate that more and more renewable electricity is fed into the system, despite being mostly at the whim of wind and sunshine.[40]

There is, it should be said, nothing substantive to quibble with in this: everything in that paragraph is true, at least if one takes as read the necessity of profit making. And, yet, reading this text and others like it concerning the legion difficulties involved in fashioning a functioning market in electricity, it is difficult to avoid the sense of commentators not seeing the forest for the trees. Or, to use a different metaphor, the sense is of commentators identifying the mice in the room, but failing to spot the elephant.

Such accounts steadfastly refuse to countenance what is, actually, a much more obvious explanation for the difficulty of designing an electricity market featuring producers consistently able to make a profit. What is that explanation? That electricity essentially was and is not a suitable object for marketization and profit generation in the first place. To the extent that this alternative explanation holds, it is not only more obvious than the various explanations proffered by the *Economist* and the like, but also more fundamental – it is the meta-explanation, as it were, that underlies all others.

Let us briefly consider such an explanation conceptually. A helpful touchstone in this regard is the work of the economic anthropologist

39   'Europe's Energy Market Was Not Built for This Crisis'.
40   Ibid.

Karl Polanyi. Writing in the 1940s, Polanyi argued that in capitalism there are real commodities and what he called 'fictitious commodities'.[41] A 'real' commodity, he said, was something that was originally brought into being explicitly for sale on the market: commoditization, in other words, was intrinsic to it. Commodities were 'fictitious', by contrast, if they were treated by society *as* commodities by being bought and sold in markets, but had not been created with such commoditization in mind. Rather, the market had subsequently been imposed upon them.

Fictitious commodities, Polanyi pointed out, are typically awkward, unruly things from a capitalist market perspective. Not being originated *for* markets, marketization does not come naturally to them. When society goes about treating such things as commodities by buying and selling them, therefore, they seem to resist such efforts, and all manner of difficulties tend to arise which one typically does not encounter in the case of 'real' commodities.

The result, Polanyi observed, is that in order for markets in fictitious commodities ever to cohere and function (even imperfectly), various props, rules, regulations and norms must be fashioned and applied. These serve to make it *appear* like what exists is a real market, featuring real prices and actors earning real profits. But this is always a fiction – a kind of pretence. Prices and profits in such cases are always as much a matter of external institutional intervention (essentially, social construction) as of supply and demand, and all market actors are party to the collective fiction, participating in it with varying degrees of awareness.

Polanyi claimed that there were three such fictional commodities: land, labour and money. But, on his terms, electricity absolutely is one too. Never mind the fact that electrical energy occurs naturally, as in lightning. Scholars who have undertaken research into the historical origins of the industry that ultimately developed around humanly produced electricity have shown that commoditization occurred only haltingly and contingently. Here is obviously not the place to go into that history in any detail, but a particularly salient fact is that, for many years, it was far from clear that electricity itself – that is, the producible energy form that is bought and sold as kilowatt-hours today – would eventually

---

41   K. Polanyi, *The Great Transformation: The Political and Economic Origins of Our Time* (Boston: Beacon Press, 1944).

emerge as the principal locus of commoditization.[42] More generally, as Simon Pirani has observed, in most times and places around the world since its invention, humanly produced electricity has been regarded 'more as essential infrastructure, or a means of social provision, than as a business.'[43] A commodity *by its nature*, electricity is not.

The point of relevance for us is that, as we have seen in this book, there is ample evidence of various props, rules, regulations and norms being required to render electricity buyable and sellable at profit – that is, to tame its unruliness and render it commodity-like – and to sustain the fiction that all of this somehow represents 'real' profit in a 'real' market. Yet it plainly does not represent such. Few have made this point more powerfully than Meredith Angwin, who had the following to say about the electricity 'markets' that have been created in those parts of the US where vertical unbundling and de-monopolization have occurred:

> They are not markets as we know markets. They are complex systems, with new regulations constantly tweaking and trying to improve existing regulations. They are a bureaucratic thicket, not a market. It's Orwellian. [Electricity is] 'deregulated' only if 'deregulated' actually means 'lots more regulation'. 'War is peace.' 'Deregulation' is 'lots more regulation'. Orwell would be amused.[44]

Consider, for instance, the profits of renewables generators. Nothing could be more un-'natural', as Polanyi would have seen it. Certainly, the profits are 'real' in the sense that they represent revenues less costs. But more than anything else perhaps, they are the product of continual, ongoing and, ultimately, rather haphazard efforts by policymakers to keep that magical financial output – revenues less costs – within what is best conceived as a zone of reasonableness. If profits are too low, developers will not invest; too high, and critics will cry foul. Thus

---

42   See especially M. Granovetter and P. McGuire, 'The Making of an Industry: Electricity in the United States', *Sociological Review* 46: 1, suppl. (1998), pp. 147–73.

43   S. Pirani, *Burning Up: A Global History of Fossil Fuel Consumption* (London: Pluto Press, 2018), p. 143.

44   Angwin, *Shorting the Grid*, p. 82. Here, Angwin was explicitly drawing on T. Kavulla, 'There Is No Free Market for Electricity: Can There Ever Be?', May 2017, americanaffairsjournal.org.

policymakers are forever in the position of needing to pull one (or even both) of two levers: subsidies and other support mechanisms to enable profits when they are scarce, windfall taxes to cap them when they become abundant.

As for the market, the fact that state intervention and support – not least, though not only, with regard to renewables – are endemic is the very least of the reasons to view electricity through a Polanyian lens. After all, this market's signal feature in the age of climate crisis is, as we saw earlier, that the hallowed market price, which theoretically congeals all relevant information and sends signals to actors as to how to respond, is the one price that renewables operators endeavour *not* to sell at. It would be hard to imagine stronger refutation of ACER's risible claim, at the height of Europe's energy crisis, that, under 'normal' conditions, the continent's electricity markets work well.[45]

Perhaps Polanyi's sharpest insight of all, however, was that maintenance of the fiction that a thing such as land or labour is genuinely amenable to commoditization ultimately depends on major market actors abiding by norms and conventions that are fragile even under relatively benign conditions. In other words, it is crucial that actors with the power to make or break brittle markets contribute to the collective fiction of commoditization by behaving in a conventional manner. The market edifice – or artifice – depends upon such observance of the formal and informal codes that scaffold markets in fictitious commodities.

The risk, of course, is that someone comes along who is not party to these codes, or who simply does not care about maintaining the pretence, and who proceeds to blow the fiction apart. And this, it turns out, is exactly what happened when JPMorgan Chase entered the business of electricity generation in 2010.

## VI

It will be recalled from the beginning of the chapter that, in 2013, Chase's energy arm JPMVEC was found to have earned over $100 million in 'unjust' profits from its control of various power plants

---

45   On which see Hancock et al., 'What Are the EU's Plans to Curb Electricity Prices?'.

including the AES 4000 units in California inherited from Bear Stearns. It had amassed these profits in a short space of time. To do so, it transpired, it used various strategies for bidding the output of the plants into California's wholesale electricity market, adopting different such strategies for different plants at different times. Though the strategies certainly varied, we can illuminate the basic principle animating each of them by exploring the simplest – labelled 'Strategy B' in FERC's analysis of the case.[46]

To understand Strategy B, there are some important contextual considerations, beginning with the nature of the plants where JPMVEC used it. These – Alamitos 3 and 4 (AL3 and 4), two of the AES 4000 units – were hugely inefficient gas-fired facilities built in the post-war era. Their inefficiency manifested in two main ways. One was an operating cost that was 'typically higher' than the spot market price, which itself averaged about $30 to $35 per MWh during the period in question.[47] The other was a slow 'ramp rate', meaning that the plants could only gradually increase ('ramp up') or decrease ('ramp down') their output. Crucially, wholesale market operators such as California's (CAISO) endeavour to respect such physical limitations in giving contract awards to power plants.

Strategy B expertly exploited these factors. For every third hour, JPMVEC submitted a so-called 'self-schedule' for AL3 and 4. This is a price-taker bid, meaning the generator accepts whatever price is set by the market – say $30 per MWh in our example. For the two hours in between, however, JPMVEC submitted bids with much higher prices – between $73 and $98 per MWh. Needless to say, for the hours when the plants were price-takers, their bids were accepted. But what of the intervening hours? One might assume that with market prices being $30 to $35 per MWh and the bids being above $70, the bids would be rejected, being well out of merit (or 'out of the money'). But no. FERC explained why not:

> CAISO's software needed to take into account . . . the fact that just as cars can only accelerate or brake at a certain rate, a power plant can only

---

46   Federal Energy Regulatory Commission, 'Order Approving Stipulation and Consent Agreement'.

47   Ibid., p. 7.

increase or decrease its output . . . at a certain speed . . . [The software therefore also accepted the bids] in the intervening hours to respect the units' ramp rates that JPMVEC had registered with CAISO.[48]

In short, JPMVEC was paid the market price for every third hour, while being paid as bid, which is to say at between $73 and $98 per MWh, for the intervening hours.

And this was how the strategy generated vast profits. The electricity that the AL3 and 4 plants generated and sold every third hour was unprofitable, because the market price was below the plants' operating costs. But the electricity the plants generated and sold in the hours in between was highly profitable, because the bid price – $73 to $98 per MWh – was significantly *above* operating cost.

Of course, stories such as this are usually narrated as morality tales about malevolent financiers engaging in manipulation, deceit, fraud or all three. And this was certainly how FERC sought to present the matter publicly.

But the story is much better read as an allegory about fictitious commodities. To render a commodity out of the unruly object that is electricity, market makers and regulators such as CAISO and FERC have had to fashion all manner of guidelines, norms and conventions. In turn, to enable the production and reproduction of markets in said commodity, the same institutions have serially depended on market actors respectfully observing those guidelines, norms and conventions. JPMorgan Chase, however, signally did not respectfully observe.

Chief among the core conventions in a spot market such as CAISO's is the principle that conventional generators bid at the marginal cost of production, which is to say the cost of generating an extra unit of power. Indeed, the idea of marginal cost pricing is so engrained in the episteme and regulation of merit-order-based markets that the theory – that this is how conventional generators rationally *should* bid – is frequently mistaken for the reality. Even the *Economist*, usually so informed, gets this wrong. 'Suppliers bid', it recently explained to readers, 'according to how much it would cost to provide an extra unit of power, known as its marginal cost.'[49]

---

48   Ibid., p. 9.
49   'Europe's Energy Market Was Not Built for This Crisis'.

But it is simply not true. Regulators and economists certainly assume that this is in fact how conventional generators bid. More importantly still, the integrity of markets such as CAISO's substantially *depends upon* such generators bidding in this way. Had JPMVEC done so at all times, of course, its bids ordinarily would not have been accepted. 'Based on their costs', FERC lamented, as if in mitigation of being gamed, 'the [AES] units were typically out of the money.'[50]

Yet the theory is not the reality. As FERC quietly conceded, the prices that generators submit 'are not required to be at marginal cost'.[51] They are not required to be – and yet it is essentially taken on faith that they will be. JPMorgan Chase, though, effectively laughed in the face of such faith. *To hell with that*, it essentially said. *We are allowed to bid however we like, and so we will. Isn't this supposed to be capitalism?*

This perhaps is the nub of the matter. What the bankers broke was convention rather than rules. As Matt Levine wrote, in a typically astute commentary, 'there was no lying, or need for lying, about what happened. This is not like Libor, where you had to affirmatively lie. Here JPMorgan just followed the rules, simply and literally, but they followed them to places they were not meant to go.'[52]

The reason why JPMorgan's actions were so threatening to FERC and the rest of the industry establishment is that they rattled the market façade – the notion that a functional market in electricity is indeed possible because electricity is indeed a reasonable thing to be bought and sold in markets. FERC and the US's grid operators had built what Levine witheringly described as 'a dumb system that rewarded a modicum of perfectly transparent gamesmanship'. To be sure, JPMorgan Chase did not play the game according to established norms, but it did play by the rules, just as all the generators briefly earning $9,000 per MWh in Texas in February 2021 did (Chapter 10).

To treat this case as being about bankers' ethics, therefore, would be to overlook the much more important and interesting lesson it delivered about the marketization of electricity: namely that the market per se is a

50   FERC, 'Order Approving Stipulation and Consent Agreement', p. 4.

51   Ibid., p. 4. If bids were indeed required to be at marginal cost, of course, renewables generators would rapidly go out of business as their marginal costs are close to zero.

52   M. Levine, 'Electricity Market Rules Did Not Provide a Worthy Opponent for JPMorgan's Brainpower', 30 July 2013, dealbreaker.com.

'dumb', ill-equipped system for electricity provision, reliant for its successful operation upon, inter alia, strictly conformist behaviour from participants.

One might protest that the case was a one-off, and an extreme one at that. But it was not; nothing could be further from the truth. By 2013, the designers and custodians of electricity markets in the US and worldwide had had decades of experience in building and operating such markets, punctuated by numerous previous cases of market manipulation – Enron, anyone? – from which to learn about design faults, and thus ample opportunity to perfect market mechanisms – were it the case that such mechanisms were indeed perfectible.[53]

Furthermore, it is not like JPMVEC unearthed just one minor loophole in an otherwise watertight system. FERC found that JPMVEC had 'manipulated' the market – a market essentially the same in its constitution as those found in restructured electricity sectors elsewhere in the world – using no fewer than twelve different bidding strategies.[54] FERC's analysis of the case almost made it sound like it was harder for market participants to successfully observe market conventions than not to.

Did the case lead to the world's experts patching remaining holes and finally getting electricity market design 'right', at least in terms of immunity from manipulation? Of course not. Polanyi's teaching is that an infallible market in a fictitious commodity is a contradiction in terms.

Just three years later, for example, on the other side of the Atlantic, the UK power generator InterGen successfully 'misled [the] National Grid system operator into paying millions more than it needed to for electricity generated by the company'. Suffice to say, on the reading of the UK's industry regulator, Ofgem, the breach in question demonstrated not the inherent incongruity of a market in electricity, but rather idiosyncratic 'weaknesses in InterGen's procedures, management systems and internal controls'.[55]

Then, in 2023, reporters for Bloomberg unearthed an even bigger and wider case of apparent manipulation of Britain's wholesale electricity

---

53   On the long history of generators' gaming of US electricity markets specifically, see Angwin, *Shorting the Grid*, pp. 78–9.

54   FERC, 'Order Approving Stipulation and Consent Agreement', p. 2.

55   Ofgem, 'Ofgem Requires InterGen to Pay £37m over Energy Market Abuse', 15 April 2020, ofgem.gov.uk.

market.[56] Several conventional generators had been achieving huge profits by engaging in so-called 'off–on' supply gaming: essentially, claiming an inability to deliver in the day-ahead market, which serves to push wholesale prices up, only then to actually deliver – and thereby exploit those inflated prices – in the real-time balancing market (see Chapter 2). As in the case of JPMVEC and California, such gaming did not contravene existing market rules. It was considered, rather, ungentlemanly. Meanwhile, Ofgem added to the picture of absurdity by sending letters to the responsible companies asking them kindly to stop.[57] Polanyi, one imagines, would be wearing a wry smile at the thought. Notably, these latest UK revelations were published the very same month as the European Commission, similarly fighting a long-standing losing battle, published a proposal for improving the protection against manipulation of its own wholesale electricity markets.[58]

Needless to say, the startling thing about all this is that policymakers evidently still believe – or at least pretend still to believe – that they actually can consummate the market. They cannot. As long as electricity continues to be bought and sold in markets, such cases will perforce remain endemic, because a better example than electricity of an awkward fictitious commodity – stubbornly confounding efforts to construct a sound market around it – it would, we can perhaps agree, be hard to find.

The particular value of the JPMorgan story, then, is as a cautionary tale, precisely at a time when the mainstream consensus in places such as Europe is that the answer to deficiencies with electricity markets – the grievance of the hour happening to be the deleterious coupling of electricity prices to gas prices – is not something *other* than markets, but rather markets of a slightly different and better hue than we presently have. To imagine that this is indeed the answer is to ignore all the accumulated evidence around us about what kind of 'commodity' electricity is, and about the myriad contortions perennially required to effect a

---

56    G. Finch, J. Grotto and T. Gillespie, 'Consumers Foot the Bill for Traders "Manipulating" UK Power Market', 23 March 2023, bloomberg.com.

57    That was in March 2023. In August, as this book was going to press, Ofgem announced new rules, to come into effect in October, designed to prevent off–on supply gaming.

58    European Commission, 'Proposal for a Regulation of the European Parliament and of the Council Amending Regulations (EU) No 1227/2011 and (EU) 2019/942 to Improve the Union's Protection against Market Manipulation in the Wholesale Energy Market', March 2023, eur-lex.europa.eu.

market for its delivery and to stabilize at a reasonable level that mysterious thing we call 'profit'.

Markets never will cohere 'naturally' and unproblematically in this setting. Doing the same thing over and over again and expecting different results may not always amount to insanity, but nonetheless, attempts to 'reform' and 'improve' the electricity market are doomed, and, as the climate crisis escalates, such attempts summon a mishmash of fearful metaphorical imagery. 'Roads to nowhere' is certainly one such image. 'Fiddling while Rome burns' might be more apposite yet.

## VII

Not everyone, of course, believes that capital and the market – in either its existing shape or suitably reformed – are going to get us where we need to go in terms of electricity decarbonization. Throughout the past few decades of increasing awareness that electricity generation must be rid of fossil fuels, there have been those who insist that sticking with (or continuing to move towards) a model that a priori prioritizes markets and the private sector is the wrong approach. Their voices have been growing in number, volume and pitch in recent years.

They have also, notably, been growing in range. If the proposition that markets and the private sector will not themselves successfully decarbonize global electricity within a reasonable time frame was once the preserve of political-economic radicals, that is clearly no longer the case. Said proposition has, for example, been appearing with increasing frequency in the pages of the *Financial Times*, no less. 'The private sector alone will not deliver the energy transition,' wrote Nick Butler – who had worked at BP for the best part of three decades – in 2019.[59] 'Capitalism won't deliver the energy transition fast enough,' Derek Brower has more recently concurred. 'There's too much to do, and given the urgency and the need to get the solution right, this isn't a task for your favourite ESG-focused portfolio manager or the tech bros. The sheer scale of the physical

59   N. Butler, 'The Private Sector Alone Will Not Deliver the Energy Transition', *Financial Times*, 28 October 2019.

infrastructure that must be revamped, demolished or replaced is almost beyond comprehension.'[60]

For such disputants, a massively expanded role for the state is typically the answer. 'Governments, not BlackRock, will have to lead this new Marshall Plan. And keep doing it,' insisted Brower.[61] Not only, critics of status-quo approaches say, should the state invest heavily in new renewable energy capacity, but, many (though not all, and certainly not Butler) argue, it should also nationalize existing privately owned electricity generation assets, whether green *or* brown, thereby giving it considerable power to control output and prices rather than leaving production and pricing to the fate of private and market forces.

Part of the logic of this standpoint is that, as we have seen at length in this book, the state is in fact already deeply implicated in the project of electricity decarbonization. Through renewables capacity auctions and feed-in tariffs and the like, it plays a fundamental role not just in shaping the pace and form of decarbonization, but also in funding it. Only it typically does not own and control the assets and income streams that eventuate; it takes the risks – actively removing them from the shoulders of reluctant developers and financiers – yet seldom gets any of the pecuniary rewards. If the state is already doing so much, and paying so much, to drive electricity decarbonization, does it not make sense, critics of electricity's current political-economic configuration have long asked, that the financial and operational ledger should be evened up?

There is, of course, an obvious potential third way of sorts, somewhere between decentralized markets and capital holding sway at one end of the political-economic spectrum, and, at the other end, control and ownership by the centralized state. Instead of through the proprietary development, ownership and operation of power generation assets, governments could in theory substantially hasten and scale up the shift to renewable energy by *compelling* capitalists to invest more and faster in renewables, even as – in view of profitability concerns – they choose not to. Like the public-ownership approach, this, too, would be very much a state-led transition, but the state would effect the transition by ordering rather than doing.

60   Brower, 'The Energy Transition Will Be Volatile'.
61   Ibid.

In one sense, this third way could be seen as a mere variation on what already happens: to get capital to invest, the state would simply be wielding sticks rather than offering carrots, would it not? But there is no 'simply' about it. To oblige private sector actors to do what they do not want to do, which would amount to taking the existing capital-and-markets orthodoxy and jettisoning the markets component, would surely be a bridge too far for any major national government of the contemporary era, right or left. The industrial policy of 'picking winners' – firmly back in fashion since the coronavirus pandemic – is one thing; forced investment is another thing entirely. To pursue it on a massive scale would be tantamount to publicly asserting that there is in fact nothing 'free' about 'free markets'.

If, therefore, the state is ever to step up to the plate in driving rapid power decarbonization in more substantive and meaningful fashion than it is presently doing, extensive public ownership of renewable energy assets appears the most viable model. Indeed, it is more or less inevitable that, among the various constituencies that could potentially take ownership – figuratively *and* literally – of our collective energy future, the state *is* ordinarily regarded as the best alternative to the default existing combination of markets and private firms. If not markets and the private sector, then who, *other* than the state, could possibly undertake the necessary transformative project? Local community or 'distributed' development, ownership and control of renewable resources is all well and good, but it is fanciful to imagine that it can ever be the main answer to the challenge, especially given the speed and scale at which electricity decarbonization is required.

Beyond capital (indeed, arguably even if one includes capital), only the state, by which I mean national governments considered collectively, potentially has both the financial wherewithal and the logistical and administrative capacity rapidly to lift annual global investment in solar and wind capacity from a few hundreds of billions of dollars to substantially in excess of one trillion – and then keep it there; which, of course, is not to say that this would be anything other than a monumental political and economic task even for state institutions to achieve. Moreover, as numerous scholars have pointed out, the state taking a leading role in owning and controlling renewables energy infrastructure does not necessarily mean other actors – from the private sector to community groups – taking no role: instead of crowding out such alternative investment, public direct investment can just as easily crowd it in.[62]

The exemplar of this vision of state leadership and ownership of renewable electricity generation is the so-called Green New Deal (GND). Though it comes in various recommended guises, all of them frame the GND as a modern, green successor programme to the original New Deal, which entailed a vast programme of national infrastructure renewal in the US in the mid-1930s designed to drag the country out of the depths of the Great Depression, and in which almost all the new infrastructure was funded and owned publicly. Notably, public ownership specifically of renewable energy has been the kernel of all significant contemporary GND proposals, including both that on which the UK Labour Party campaigned in the 2019 general election, and that on which Bernie Sanders campaigned for the US Democrats' presidential nomination the following year.

Generally, the main argument that GND-type proposals have marshalled in favour of state ownership and control of relevant infrastructure – and, no less explicitly, against a capital-centric model hinging on markets and private actors – has been an essentially Keynesian one. Given the scope and ambition of these proposals, this makes perfect sense. Though renewable electricity generation certainly is at their substantive core, such proposals are per se concerned with 'system transformation' on a much broader, society-wide level, and hence the sheer scale and complexity of the transformational challenge tends to be the overriding consideration. Keynes's thought is particularly enlightening in this regard.

If, after Polanyi, a profit- and market-centred model is inappropriate to the relatively simple proposition of delivering a single fictitious commodity such as electricity, it is manifestly more inappropriate still when society is faced with the prospect of transforming – quickly, seamlessly and comprehensively – a whole complex system of social and economic life. As Keynes argued, market signals fail when it is the case that numerous different actors need to make coordinated changes and yet none can take all others' choices as given. Only a central decision

62   For example, M. Deleidi, M. Mazzucato and G. Semieniuk, 'Neither Crowding In Nor Out: Public Direct Investment Mobilising Private Investment into Renewable Electricity Projects', *Energy Policy* 140 (2020), p. 111195.

maker, Keynes's successors insist, can hope to bring about such coordinated, collective transformation in a timely and effective manner. The interlocking matrix of changes required of innumerable stakeholders by the climate crisis is a quintessential example of a transformation of this type.[63]

In other words, the arguments underpinning GND and similar 'macro' proposals for state ownership and control of climate-relevant infrastructure (including, but not only, renewable electricity infrastructure) generally are not the argument that this book has made about capital's difficulty with electricity decarbonization – an argument that is fundamentally about profit. This does not mean that I disagree with those arguments (I do not), nor that they are incompatible with the thesis that uncertain or unappetizing profitability prospects widely militate against the faster private sector build-out of renewables (I do not think they are incompatible). It simply means that this book has made a different – if complementary – case.

Now, critical interventions that *are* focused specifically and more narrowly on renewable energy generation, and which argue in favour of public ownership of this particular activity (and only this activity), do sometimes touch on the question of profitability. But here is the curious thing. They usually, though not always, argue the case back to front. The state should build, own and control wind and solar farms, purveyors of this argument propose, precisely because this *is* putatively a highly profitable activity – and not because, in fact, it is not.

To take a recent instructive example, consider the proposal by the UK Labour Party – the leadership of which has passed from Jeremy Corbyn to the more centrist Keir Starmer since the GND-inspired 2019 election campaign – to launch a publicly owned renewable energy generation company, called Great British Energy (GBE), if it were to win power. GBE, Labour has said, would enable the UK government to reduce household electricity bills because the profits presently being siphoned off by private renewables generators would be socialized instead.

Indeed, in support of its proposal, Labour invoked a 2022 report by the Trades Union Congress that attacked the 'excess profits taken by privatised electricity generators', not least in renewables sectors such as

---

63    See, for example, J. W. Mason, 'Climate Policy from a Keynesian Point of View', May 2021, jwmason.org.

fixed offshore wind with, in the TUC's words, 'known profitability'.[64] The TUC had estimated that the excess profits that a 'public energy champion' such as Labour's proposed GBE would be able to capture were equivalent to some £2,250–4,400 per UK household.

Such claims, this book suggests, betray a deep and perilous misunderstanding of the economics of renewable energy, and of the weak and uncertain profitability that actually plagues the sector.

## VIII

If, therefore, the case is going to be made for the state substantially arrogating renewable energy generation to itself in order to drive electricity decarbonization, and if that case is going to draw on arguments about industry profitability, then it will need to be very different from the one propounded by the UK Labour Party. Its core logic would presumably be that the state needs to drive electricity decarbonization more actively, directly and proprietorially than it currently does because the anticipated profits available from renewable energy generation are in fact *not* sufficiently attractive to incentivize the private sector to pursue decarbonization quickly and comprehensively.

It was, therefore, a particularly noteworthy political development that took place in the US state of New York in 2021. That year, a small coalition of lawmakers introduced a bill designed to transform the state's existing institutional landscape of electricity generation. The bill was called the Build Public Renewables Act (BPRA). Its aim was to precipitate rapid decarbonization of the state's power generation infrastructure by enabling and requiring the public sector itself to build out solar and wind power in the state at scale.

The impetus was the state's ambitious 2019 Climate Leadership and Community Protection Act, which set targets for 70 per cent of the state's electricity to be renewably generated by 2030, and for generation to be wholly carbon-free by 2040. The state is home to the largest publicly owned utility in the country, the New York Power Authority (NYPA). Yet, as of 2021, the NYPA was restricted by its charter from owning or

---

64  TUC, 'Public Ownership of Clean Power: Lower Bills, Climate Action, Decent Jobs', 24 September 2022, tuc.org.uk.

building new utility-scale renewable generation projects. The BPRA sought to strike down this restriction and compel the NYPA to develop its own solar and wind farms.

Not only was the introduction of the BPRA arguably the boldest substantive legislative proposal for publicly owned solar and wind power in the US's history. But the logic underlying it happened to be the exact inverse of the flawed logic underlying UK Labour's GBE proposal the following year. To wit: the bill's sponsors worried not that private firms were swimming in renewables profits, but that they were not.

Assembly member Bobby Carroll, for example, one of the bill's co-sponsors, made this particular point in the following terms when interviewed in 2022 by Kate Aronoff.[65] 'If we're going to meet our climate goals,' Carroll began, 'we need the state to play a large role.' The reason? 'We're not just going to hope the market decides a certain project is bond-able and profitable and thus will go forward.' For that way, reckoned Carroll, lay only failure: the targets set in 2019 would inevitably be missed.

The same view was held by the environmental campaigners who, in 2021, enthusiastically took up the cudgels and, for two years, fought doggedly for the BPRA to be passed. If profit expectations were the sole determinant of whether, where and when solar and wind farms were to be built, New York state's climate ambitions would be thwarted. The campaigners' conviction, in Grace Ashford's words, was that 'in order to meet the electricity needs of the state, projects will need to be undertaken in locations that are unattractive or unprofitable for private industry.'[66] Carroll had come to the same conclusion, his summation being one that in fact could very well serve as a reasonable synopsis for the book you have been reading. 'There are a lot of projects,' Carroll said, 'that I don't think will ever get built if we rely solely on a profit-driven model.'[67] Indeed not: not in the US, and not elsewhere in the world either.

Riffing on Carroll, a slightly fuller and more precise synopsis of this book might read as follows: if private capital, circulating in markets, is still failing to decarbonize global electricity generation sufficiently

65    Cited in K. Aronoff, 'If Democrats Can't Pass Climate Legislation in New York, We're All Doomed', *New Republic*, 2 June 2022.

66    G. Ashford, 'In Rare Show of Force, House Democrats Pressure Hochul on Climate Bill', *New York Times*, 30 March 2023.

67    In Aronoff, 'If Democrats Can't Pass Climate Legislation in New York, We're All Doomed'.

rapidly *even with* all the support it has gotten and is getting from governments, and *even with* technology costs having fallen as far and as fast as they have, it is surely as clear a sign as possible that capital is not designed to do the job.

And so, in the shape both of the thesis of this book, and evidently also the thinking of those behind the BPRA, we have what is in fact a relatively atypical rationale for public infrastructure ownership. From this standpoint, the reason for favouring public ownership would not be – as it so often is – objection to rampant private sector profiteering. It would be the opposite. Our position would be that the private sector needs to be stripped of responsibility for renewable energy generation because renewable energy generation is not – or is not typically expected to be – consistently profitable *enough* for the private sector to develop it as urgently and massively as we need.

Furthermore, the BPRA holds up a mirror to our wider story in another important way. The bill failed to pass in legislative session both in 2021 and in 2022. Hopes were especially high in the latter year, when it sailed through the State Senate. But Carl Heastie, speaker of the state assembly, stonewalled it by refusing to bring it to a vote.

This difficulty should not surprise us. The death of the neoliberal faith in capital and markets has been pronounced too many times to remember in recent years, but the faith remains strong where it counts. In the face of all the evidence to the contrary, Germany's finance minister, Christian Lindner, for instance, was shameless enough to write in the *Financial Times* in early 2023 that the European and global energy crisis had served to 'confirm the effectiveness of a market-based approach' to energy supply – and served, for good measure, to 'show that we should also rely on price signals when it comes to reducing $CO_2$ emissions'.[68] In New York state, the BPRA was up against not only relatively robust such faith in markets and the profit motive, but also determined organizational lobbying.[69]

This decisive combination of factors had, of course, been enough already in the US to see off the prospect nationally of a meaningful

68   C. Lindner, 'A Resilient Germany Is Weathering the Energy Crunch', *Financial Times*, 2 January 2023.

69   G. Brown, 'New York's Fight to Put Renewable Energy in Public Hands', 7 November 2022, tribunemag.co.uk.

Green New Deal. President Biden's climate-focused Inflation Reduction Act of August 2022 was, in reality, a pale imitation of the vision on which Sanders had campaigned two years previously – a 'dwarf GND', as one commentator has felicitously put it.[70]

Meanwhile, across the world, renewables continue to substitute for conventional generating sources far, far too slowly. Given everything we have learned, the fact that China continues to be easily the main driver of such renewables growth as is occurring should be no more surprising to us than the political resistance in the US to the BPRA. One does not in any way have to be an admirer of China's political economy to acknowledge that, as Michael Davidson has pointed out, while Western policymakers – including those holding the reins of power in New York State – remain broadly convinced that they really do possess only one trick, namely deference to capital and the price mechanism, 'markets represent just one tool among many available to Beijing'.[71]

Even as the BPRA's difficulties should not surprise us, however, they should certainly worry us. This, after all, was not a red state like Kentucky, West Virginia or Wyoming. This was New York, and as Aronoff emphasized, Heastie was not a Republican firebrand: he is a Democrat, and the fight over the BPRA that raged for two years from 2021 was a battle among Democrats. In short, in New York, the political stars were arguably as propitiously aligned as they ever will be for BPRA-type legislation that is designed to shift renewable energy provision in the Western world away from its current capital-centric configuration.

And then, in May 2023, a breakthrough of sorts. The campaigning had finally borne fruit. New York legislators passed a state budget that incorporated what was, essentially, a watered-down, compromise version of the original BPRA's core demand. It will require the NYPA to build, own and operate new renewable generation capacity, but only if (and to the extent that) the private sector indeed fails – as Carroll predicted it will – to keep the state on track to achieve the targets for renewables penetration laid out in the 2019 legislation.

---

70  T. Meaney, 'Fortunes of the Green New Deal', *New Left Review* 138 (2022), p. 81. See also B. Christophers, 'Why Are We Allowing the Private Sector to Take Over Our Public Works?', *New York Times*, 8 May 2023.

71  Davidson, 'China's Power Outage'.

How this 2023 New York budget item might be read by those in the wider world who are convinced of the need for substantially greater public ownership of renewable power will likely depend largely on whether they incline to seeing the proverbial glass as half-empty or half-full. Those of the former tendency would probably point to what happened in New York and say that if it took so much hard work, in such ideal conditions, to achieve a relatively modest victory for publicly owned renewable power, what realistic chance is there further afield, on a bigger scale, for an energy transition that is not capital- and market-led and hence not perennially hamstrung by the profit imperative and the developmental limitations it imposes?

Those accustomed to taking a more optimistic view would likely scoff at this. Look at New York, they would say, and feast your eyes on a world of newfound political, economic and environmental possibility.

Time will tell which camp has it right.

# Acknowledgements

Thanks to Andreas Malm for encouraging me to write this book, which would be much poorer were it not for the individuals working in renewables development and energy finance who kindly gave of their time to help me understand the workings of their worlds. I am extremely grateful to them.

Thanks, too, to all the people at Verso who continue in one way or another to support and enable my work with them: Michelle Betters, Sebastian Budgen, Cian McCourt, Colby Groves, Mark Martin, Maya Osborne, Anne Rumberger, Michal Schatz and Catherine Smiles.

Gabe Eckhouse, Dan Hirschman and Mat Paterson kindly read in draft various chapters or, in Gabe's case, the whole manuscript, and I thank them wholeheartedly for their feedback, while absolving them of any responsibility for any remaining errors of fact or interpretation. For diligent and sharp copy-editing, I thank John Gaunt.

Last but also, of course, first, thanks to my family – Agneta, Elliot, Oliver and Emilia – for being such a constant source of inspiration and indescribable happiness in my life, and for tolerating the fact that dealing with copy-edits impinged on this year's summer in Dalstuga.

*August 2023*

# Index

Page numbers in **bold** refer to figures.